D1191551

COOPERATIVES:
TODAY AND TOMORROW

COOPERATIVES:

EWELL PAUL ROY, Ph.D.

Associate Professor of
Agricultural Economics and Agribusiness
Louisiana State University

TODAY AND TOMORROW

THE INTERSTATE
PRINTERS & PUBLISHERS, INC.

Danville, Illinois

Library of Congress
Catalog Card Number 64-11484

Printed and Published by
THE INTERSTATE PRINTERS & PUBLISHERS, INC.
Danville, Illinois

Printed in U.S.A.

DEDICATION —

This book is dedicated to two professors emeritus of agricultural economics at Louisiana State University who first inspired this author to pursue studies in cooperatives. The professor who provided stimulation primarily in the "business" side of cooperatives was Dr. B. M. Gile. The professor whose influence was in the "philosophic and social" aspects of cooperatives was Mr. J. M. Baker. To these two, this book is dedicated.

PREFACE—

The primary purpose of this book is to provide a suitable college text for teaching about cooperatives during a 3-hour semester course. The text is so organized that approximately 40 to 45 lecture hours may be utilized. Adjustments can be made for a shorter course taught on the "quarter" system.

For teachers of vocational agriculture in high schools and for seminar and workshop purposes, certain chapters may be used, such as those on organizing, capitalizing and managing a cooperative.

The author believes that many differences between cooperatives are more superficial than real. For this reason, the text is intended to cover all types of cooperatives, both farm and nonfarm. More emphasis is given to basic co-op principles and issues than to daily operating practices in cooperatives.

EWELL PAUL ROY

Baton Rouge, La.

ACKNOWLEDGMENTS —

Acknowledgment is extended to the many students enrolled in the course on cooperatives at Louisiana State University during the spring semesters of 1961, 1962 and 1963. They contributed immensely toward finalizing the present manuscript.

Acknowledgment is also extended to the following for their help:

Michael Armand, Undergraduate Assistant, Louisiana State University, Baton Rouge, La.

Nellis Briscoe, Department of Agricultural Economics, Oklahoma State University, Stillwater, Okla.

M. J. Danner, Department of Agricultural Economics, Auburn University, Auburn, Ala.

Mary Louise King, Typist, Louisiana State University, Baton Rouge, La.

Raymond J. Mischler, Office of the General Counsel, USDA, Washington, D.C.

Paul O. Mohn, Federal Extension Service, USDA, Washington, D.C.

J. K. Stern, American Institute of Cooperation, Washington, D.C.

Walter C. Verlander, Bank for Cooperatives, New Orleans, La.

Fred H. Wiegmann, Head, Department of Agricultural Economics, Louisiana State University, Baton Rouge, La.

CONTENTS—

COOPERATIVES: TODAY AND TOMORROW

INDICES

CHAPTER 1 –

Cooperatives and
Economic Systems

The last end of the State is not to dominate men, nor to restrain them by fear; rather it is so to free each man from fear, that he may live and act with full security and without injury to himself or his neighbor. The end of the State, I repeat, is not to make rational beings into brute beasts and machines. It is to enable their bodies and their minds to function safely. It is to lead men to live by, and to exercise a free reason, that they may not waste their strength in hatred, anger and guile, nor act unfairly toward one another. Thus the end of the State is really liberty.

—17th century philosopher

DEFINITION OF A TRUE COOPERATIVE

A TRUE COOPERATIVE is defined as "a business organized, capitalized and managed by, of and for its member-patrons, furnishing and/or marketing, at cost, goods and/or services to patrons."

Member-patrons need not consist only of individuals. Partnerships and profit-type corporations, as well as cooperatives themselves, may also organize and operate cooperatives. In addition, households or consumers often organize cooperatives. Municipal, state and federal governments may also cooperate and form co-op business institutions (Figure 1-1).

ROLE OF COOPERATIVES IN ECONOMIC SYSTEMS

It is necessary to determine if cooperatives are an economic system themselves or if they are a species belonging to capitalism, socialism, communism, fascism or mixed systems.

Foundations of Economic Systems

An *economic system* is defined as a "set of customs, laws, rules and

1

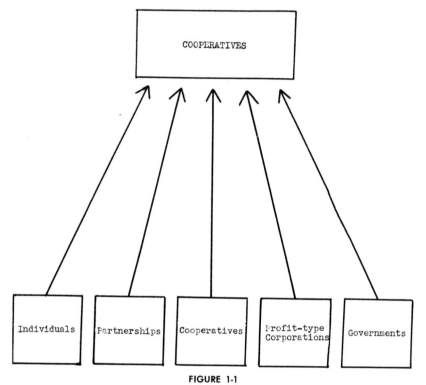

FIGURE 1-1

Cooperatives may be organized by individuals, partnerships, profit-type corporations, cooperatives themselves or governments.

regulations dealing with the production, exchange and consumption of goods and services." Due states, in somewhat different terms, that an economic system consists of a set of controls which determines the manner in which the various resources available are utilized in the satisfaction of wants.[1]

Economic systems vary greatly in the manner in which resources are controlled by individuals, business organizations and governments. Capitalism, or the free enterprise system, permits maximum individual freedom. On the other hand, communism, or state socialism, permits the least amount of any system. Between these two extremes are found socialism, fascism and mixed systems. Mixed systems are those which

---

[1]Due, John F., *Intermediate Economic Analysis*, R. D. Irwin, Inc., Homewood, Ill. 1950. p. 2.

FIGURE 1-2

This family is part of an economic system. They own property, initiate enterprise, have incentives, sell on the open market and compete with others. In this case they are part of the free enterprise system. (Courtesy, Mo. Agr. Ext. Serv., Columbia, Mo.)

contain elements of two or more systems operating simultaneously within an economy.

Regardless of the type of economic system, there are at least five basic features which characterize any system. These are: (1) ownership of property, (2) initiation of enterprise, (3) economic incentives, (4) pricing mechanism and (5) market competition. Interwoven in these characteristics is the role of government.[2]

Ownership of Property

Someone must own such property as land, houses, factories, cars, clothing, etc. Ownership might be left entirely to individual citizens, be left to the government or, in some cases, ownership of certain property is private while other ownership is by government.

---

[2]Butz, D. E., Mauch, A. and D. B. Varner, *Capitalism-Socialism-Communism*, Mich. Agr. Ext. Serv. Cir. 13, East Lansing, Mich. 1951.

Initiation of Enterprise

Under any economic system, someone must bring together land, labor, capital and management to initiate and operate business enterprises. Initiating enterprises may be left entirely to individuals, to governments, or to both.

Economic Incentives

Under any economic system, there must exist some incentives so that people will work and apply themselves up to their full capacity. Economic incentives may consist of higher pay, promotion, bonuses of various kinds, fringe benefits and other types of economic rewards. No economic system can exist very long without a set of incentives. In addition to economic incentives, other types of awards and commendations may be used to spur individuals to produce more.

Pricing Mechanism

Under any economic system, there must be a pricing mechanism so that consumers can decide how and on what to spend their money. At the same time, enterprise operators can get some idea of what is and what is not desired by consumers and make plans accordingly. In some economic systems, the matter of pricing is left entirely in the hands of private citizens; in others, a central government makes most of the pricing decisions. In still other systems, both methods are used.

Market Competition

Under any economic system, there must exist some degree of market competition to prevent economic stagnation. In some economic systems, market competition is effected by individuals and companies competing among themselves with the government as a watchdog to see that all parties are competing fairly. In other systems, market competition is between and among government enterprises, each one trying to out-compete the other. In still other systems, both individual-corporate enterprise and government enterprise compete or co-exist.

COMPARISONS OF ECONOMIC SYSTEMS

There are at least five types of economic systems in the world today: (1) capitalism, (2) fascism, (3) socialism, (4) communism

FIGURE 1-3

This cattleman is part of the free enterprise system, or capitalism. He values his individual freedom. (Courtesy, National Live Stock Producer, Chicago, Ill.)

and (5) mixed systems. Each economic system is analyzed in terms of the five basic foundations just discussed.

Capitalism

Capitalism, or the free enterprise system, permits the widest scope of individual action of any system. In so doing, it also provides abundant religious, civil and economic liberties because the role of government is held to a minimum. It is an economic system which respects and allows private ownership and the use for private profit of man-made and nature-made capital. The government recognizes the rights of private property, freedom of enterprise, initiative, competition, entrepreneurial energy and political and economic freedom. The desirable goal of a capitalistic system is to improve the standard of living and general economic welfare of the individual citizens. The United States is a prime example of a capitalistic system or free enterprise economy.

Under capitalism, the individual is entitled to use and control the economic goods which he acquires, to prevent other people from using them and, in general, to decide how they shall be disposed of after his death. The individual may abuse as well as use his wealth if his activities do not interfere with the rights of other people. Since property rights are granted by society as a whole, these rights can be limited by social action. However, except for such regulations, a capitalistic economic system wholeheartedly attempts to protect the possessions of the individual.

All wealth in a capitalistic system is not totally owned and controlled by private individuals. There is some public property within most capitalistic systems. However, government ownership and control of productive resources are held to a minimum.

Under capitalism, each individual has a general right to engage in any line of economic activity which appears desirable to him. This is based on the theory that when the individual chooses the field of activity which he likes best, he will also be making his most productive and most useful contribution to society. Freedom of enterprise means only the right to choose an occupation. It does not guarantee the individual the necessary resources or assure success in his chosen field of work. Capitalistic societies have never been willing to extend complete freedom of enterprise to individuals or to groups. There is always the possibility that some people might choose antisocial professions. In such cases, governmental units under capitalism have not hesitated to step in with prohibitions or restrictions. Thus, individuals are forbidden to steal, organize murder for profit or otherwise engage in antisocial activities. Zoning regulations, for example, are designed to restrict individual usage for the good of society. However, the individual can appeal from zoning regulations if he considers them too harsh.

Individuals under capitalism usually orient their activities on a desire for profit. However, many other factors besides the desire for more money influence individuals, even under capitalism. Desire for power, prestige or self-satisfaction may also serve as a motivating factor responsible for economic activity. Economic motivation is much broader than the "profit motive." But under capitalism, profits and monetary gain are the most important factors prompting economic activity. The desire for economic gain is supposed to make individuals behave economically and thus make the scarce agents of production go as far as possible toward increasing production, satisfying wants and bettering social welfare. When the desire for private gain leads individuals to antisocial activities, society as a whole generally steps in with governmental regulations.

Individuals under capitalism are supposed to make most types of economic decisions on the basis of prices, price relationships or price changes. Price relationships are considered in deciding what and how much of a product to produce and how existing supplies of land, labor and capital are to be used among the various industries and enterprises. Similarly, how much of the national money income is used for current operation and how much is set aside for saving and investment are determined on the basis of relative prices and expected future price relationships. Price movements are supposed to keep the supply of goods in line with what the buyers are willing to purchase. Customers' desires are expressed in the market place through the prices they are willing to pay for the various products. The changes in price reflected in this process automatically adjust production.

Competition is usually considered to be the driving force behind any capitalistic system. In industry and business, competition brings about efficient operations and thus cuts costs to secure a larger share of the market. This same desire of businessmen leads to new inventions, new or changed products and other changes in technology. In the development of capitalism, large corporations may become very important. In many cases, competition has been reduced or not allowed to operate freely because of these concentrations of economic power. In other cases the government has seen fit to limit competition where such activity would appear wasteful as in the case of public utilities, such as telephones, electric companies, street railways and railroads. Generally speaking, however, in the capitalistic system competition is a more powerful force and is allowed to operate more freely than in any of the other economic systems.

Fascism

Fascism is an economic system, basically capitalistic, which forces entrepreneurs and consumers to follow the will of the state. Like communism, it also combines a political doctrine with its economic planning. Fascism mobilizes all physical, economic, social and spiritual resources into a regimented whole. Primary emphasis is placed on central power. The Hitler and Mussolini regimes were examples of fascism.

Under fascism, ownership of property remains in private hands as long as property owners fulfill the wishes of the state. If property and the use of such property do not conform to the national or state objectives, either political and/or economic, such property is confiscated in the name of the state.

Enterprise may be initiated by private citizens under fascism subject to certain limitations. The state itself may initiate enterprises or direct that certain enterprises be started for the national good. However, the principal fascistic influence on enterprise is its reliance on the corporative system. Corporate boards can control production, fix wages and prices and perform many other functions under surveillance of the state.

FIGURE 1-4

From left to right: Chamberlain of England, Daladier of France, Hitler of Germany and Mussolini and Ciano of Italy at the Munich Conference of 1938. At this conference, Hitler and Mussolini consolidated their Fascist power. Fascists tolerate cooperatives if they obey the state. (Courtesy, Wide World Photos)

Economic incentives of a private nature are retained under fascism. Management and workers in industries, closely allied with the state and its nationalistic program, are well compensated. In addition to economic benefits, many incentives other than money are distributed in order to enhance the fascistic doctrine and to spur output. Those who abide by the state fare exceptionally well. Those who refuse to conform to the state's objectives fare exceptionally badly.

The pricing mechanism is allowed to remain free under fascism as long as the goals of the state are met. If the free market cannot function in a manner acceptable to the state, autocratic or dictatorial controls over prices and wages are substituted in many areas of the economy. To prevent private companies and workers from producing products considered undesirable by the state, price controls, direct allocations of productive resources and strict investment controls are instituted.

Competition in the market under fascism is severely restrained because firms are not free to buy inputs or produce and sell what they desire. Although private property remains, a fascistic government sponsors cartels or industry-groups, such as a steel group, an oil group, etc. These groups, acting as committees in consultation with fascist officials, decide what and how much to produce. Ample profits are guaranteed firms in each group although the further use of these profits becomes subject to state control. Thus, private monopoly and public power become merged. The primary purpose of this merger, however, is to enhance fascism.

For example, the fascistic agricultural cartel or group tells the farmer how to utilize his land, when to market his crops and also fixes his prices. State bureaus control cooperatives, telling them what to do. If marketing cooperatives interfere, for example, they are abolished by edict.[3]

Socialism

Socialism is an economic system which desires to vest in society as a whole, rather than in individuals, the ownership and management of all nature-made and man-made producer goods, especially in large-scale productions. Socialism refers to the social ownership and control of industry, substituting the principle of public service or social usefulness for the principle of private profit. Great Britain under Labor Party leadership after World War II serves as an example of socialism.

---

[3]*Fascism in Action,* Government Printing Office, House Document 401, Washington, D.C. 1947. p. 97.

Under socialism, government ownership of the means of production is limited to the land and capital used in large-scale production—only the larger industries are owned and controlled by the state. Many small businesses and most of the land are still owned by private individuals.

The individual in a socialistic state is able to own and control more property than under communism but much less than under capitalism.

Since under socialism many industries are owned and operated by the state, freedom of enterprise would apply only to those lines of work still privately operated. While workers are still free to choose occupations, the opportunities to become businessmen and receive profits as private owners of large industries are slight as compared with a capitalistic system.

Private enterprises under socialism really do not have freedom of enterprise in the usual sense of the term. Their activities are rigidly controlled by means of prices, taxes, interest rates, rentals and other forces which are directly under governmental control. Freedom of enterprise really exists only for society as a whole. The governing body is able to choose which industries or lines of work shall be started, expanded or discarded since much of the productive wealth is owned and controlled by the state.

A socialistic economy relies on economic incentives to some extent, but their importance is much less than under capitalism. The profit motive is almost entirely eliminated, since private individuals are not allowed to own or operate large-scale enterprises for private gain. Socialism permits moderate differences between wages for different jobs. Such differences would be large when compared to perfect equality but small when compared to the wide range of income under capitalism. A socialistic society attempts to emphasize other types of motivation such as working for the good of society, security, prestige, or to obtain positions of power in the economic system. Public honors are given for unusual accomplishments.

A socialistic system does not do away with the money and pricing system. However, it does not rely on price movements and price relationships in making important economic decisions nearly so much as the capitalistic economy. Important decisions are made by governmental agencies or other groups on the basis of economic planning. Price relationships are relied upon, however, to distribute workers among industries and occupations and to bring market demands and supplies of the various economic goods into balance. The amount and type of goods and services to be produced are decided by the central authority. Once the goods are produced, the pricing system is allowed to allocate or ration them among the customers or users. Thus the pricing and profit mechanism is crippled in that relative prices no longer serve to regulate the kind and amount of goods produced. The central authority might take these prices into consideration in making its decision, but many other things might also affect this choice.

Individual workers compete to get into better jobs and more pleasant occupations of the socialistic system. Consumers compete for the limited supplies of consumer goods and services since the socialists' intention is to give consumers considerable freedom of choice in spending their money incomes. In other respects, the governing influence of competition is replaced by the decisions of economic planners.

Communism

Communism is a radical socialistic economic system which is also a political doctrine based on the teachings of Karl Marx. The government, made up of a minority of the people with a dictator as head, exterminates all opposition and tends to collectivize the whole economy including consumer goods. All land and capital, nature-made and man-made, are completely in the hands of the state. The government proposes to emancipate the common people who do not own property from dependence on those who do own property. The people are to receive income according to their needs, not according to their abilities.

Under communism, consumer goods, as well as land and capital, are owned by society as a whole. Of course, various goods, such as groceries and clothes, have to pass into private possession to be used, but the basic title to such things still belongs to the entire society. Production is carried out by agencies of the state. Industries are organized chiefly on the individual plant basis. Agricultural production is organized and supervised on a so-called collective basis. Trade is conducted by store units or large merchandising groups. The managers of these various agencies are employees of the state and are subject to the rules and regulations laid down by the government. Such corporations as are allowed to develop are entirely state owned and controlled. Experience of Soviet Russia indicates that the complete destruction of private property usually results in a decline in production. In several cases the Russians have been forced to reinstate limited property rights in order to revive or maintain production. Small plots of land alloted to Russian peasants and worked by and for themselves have produced abundantly. In some degree, Russian Communism deviates from Marxian doctrine.

Under communism, freedom of enterprise is completely eliminated. The deciding factors at the time the individual is making his occupational choice are the needs of the state as determined by the government. The individual is expected to choose that occupation in which he would be of the greatest benefit to society or to the welfare of the state. Individuals are completely prohibited from starting any business for profit. All such business organizations are undertaken by the state.

Under a free enterprise system, potential profits and fear of losses help to increase the efficiency of a business. Since there are no profits under communism, such a system must depend upon loss of position and prestige or upon reprisals to bring about efficiency.

Another facet of communistic enterprise is that the state may appropriate the children in a family, educate and train them in the interest of the state.

Under communism, the ordinary individual is not allowed to promote or develop new products, new industries or new methods for private gain. Such changes must come from the small groups that make up the central authority or from individuals selected by the state to do the job. In a communistic society, economic incentive is severely limited. In Marxian theory, everyone gets paid according to his needs. Since the needs of people differ, incomes are not exactly equal for all. Any difference in income is not based upon the worker's productivity or occupation. Thus everyone is about equal from the standpoint of economic advantage.

The Russian economy deviates from Marxism and follows more closely the socialistic ideals with respect to economic motivation. There are wage differentials in Russia. Competition between workers for the better jobs and, in addition, enthusiasm for socialism and economic planning under the various five-year plans are relied upon as motivating factors.

In a purely communistic state there is no place for a pricing system. All important economic decisions are made by the governing body and not on the basis of price movements and price relationships. If enough goods were available in the public storehouse so that each individual could satisfy his needs, no pricing system would be necessary. In actual practice, however, human needs are so great that it is almost impossible for any type of government to produce enough goods and services to satisfy them. Therefore, a rationing system is usually adopted by the governing authority. Since the quantities of the various types of goods received under the rationing system rarely are the same as the demand for these goods, considerable trade or bartering takes place among the people.

The competitive situation in Russia is very similar to the outline just presented for socialism. Russia also has a type of socialistic competition in which the emphasis is on prestige, power and medals or awards for outstanding achievements under the socialistic state. Competition also takes the form of having one brigade, platoon or squad compete against other such groups on the same farm or in the same factory. There appears also to be some unauthorized competition of enterprises and industries to secure supplies of materials, fixed capital goods and labor. This results from the fact that the heads of the various branches of the governmentally owned and operated industries try to outdo one another in the eyes of their superiors. There would be no competition under the ideal or purely communistic system. There would be few if any wage differences, and consumer goods and services would be so plentiful that each person could have all he wanted. In actual practice, it has been pointed out that wage differentials do exist under communism and that consumers do not have everything they desire. Therefore, there is a form of competition even in communistic countries. Under most systems of this type which have been set up, the major competition has been for survival. Living standards have been so low and poverty and hunger so widespread that there has been rather strong competition for enough food, clothing and shelter to permit a bare existence. The managers produce what they are authorized to produce, and the individual workers take the jobs assigned to them by the authoritarian government. In short, the individual under practical communism serves as ordered and consumes as permitted.

Mixed Systems

It is a truism that there are perhaps no *pure* economic systems. In highly developed capitalistic systems one may find instances of socialistic enterprise, although these are at a minimum. In highly developed socialistic and communistic systems one may observe many instances where capitalistic devices are employed. For example, in Communist Yugoslavia, workers in some state enterprises share in the profits made by these enterprises. In Communist Russia, peasants have been allowed to cultivate and own produce from small garden plots, as well as to own some animals, such as chickens, hogs and sheep. In Communist Poland, about 87 percent of the land in use is privately owned by small farmers.

In some of the newly established countries in Africa and the Middle East, a mixture of free enterprise and socialism is attempted. A government may nationalize the railroads, heavy industry and electric power. It may leave private ownership in agriculture intact, or it may buy up large estates and sell the land to small farmers under private ownership on a long-term loan basis.

Under a mixed economy, ownership of property may range from absolute individual ownership to complete state ownership. The ratio of one to the other may change as the mixed economy matures and develops. It is usually more difficult to return to private ownership than it is to move toward complete state ownership.

Initiation of enterprise also has a wide range. Small-scale enterprises may be left to individuals, while larger ones may be state owned and operated.

Various techniques may be employed in a mixed economy to furnish economic incentives in addition to those furnished by a free market. Subsidies and grants are examples of such techniques. Mixed economic systems resemble socialism in its elementary form.

ROLE OF COOPERATIVES IN ECONOMIC SYSTEMS

Cooperatives and Capitalism

The word *capitalism* means profit seeking. Through the cooperation of individuals, cooperatives are formed. These individuals produce and consume goods. The goods are bought or sold through the cooperatives, and net savings obtained. Cooperatives in a capitalistic economy could not properly service members if they did not produce profit in behalf of their members.

Cooperation is strongly in favor of privately owned property. The members produce on their own property, sell goods which they own and buy goods through the cooperatives. The cooperatives own land, buildings and produce. Cooperatives believe in freedom of initiative. The members, by producing more, receive more profit, which enables

TABLE 1-1

Comparisons of the Five Economic Systems

Item	Capitalism	Fascism	Socialism	Communism	Mixed
			Economic Systems		
Ownership of property.	Individual.	Individual, but with state direction.	State owns basic industries; balance owned by individuals.	State owns everything.	Individuals and government.
Initiation of enterprise.	Individual, partnership and corporate, including co-ops.	Corporate structure emphasized.	State owns basic industries; free enterprise permitted elsewhere.	Only the state initiates enterprise.	Individuals and government.
Economic incentives.	Profit motive predominates; nonprofit motives supplement.	Profit motive and state power are interrelated.	Limited economic incentives are provided; emphasis is on incentives other than profit.	Economic incentive is severely limited.	Mixed. Some economic; some political.
Pricing mechanism.	Free market prices guide individuals and businesses in producing, exchanging and consuming.	Free market prices guide the economy if they fulfill the state's goals.	Free market prices do not predominate; state administered prices prevail.	State planners and technicians set prices at their will.	Mixed. More like socialism.

(Continued)

TABLE 1-1 *(Continued)*

Item	Economic Systems				
	Capitalism	*Fascism*	*Socialism*	*Communism*	*Mixed*
Market competition.	Various types of enterprises compete, with the government as watchdog.	The state fosters corporate monopoly as a means of political control.	The state has no competition if it does not want it.	No one competes with the state.	None in heavy industry; competition otherwise; situations vary.
Can true cooperatives exist?[1]	Yes. Cooperatives are truly consistent within capitalism.	Yes. However, cooperatives are often rendered ineffective when they oppose the state.	Yes, in the consumer goods sector. No, in the producer goods sector.	No. Cooperatives cannot exist because of the economic and political control of the state.	Yes. But much depends on the influence and control of the government.

[1] A true cooperative is defined as a "business organized, financed and managed by, of and for its patrons, furnishing and/or marketing at cost, goods and/or services to patrons."

them to obtain more private property. Cooperation welcomes freedom of enterprise and competition. Since the bulwark of capitalism is competition, cooperatives are actually competitors with private and corporate business establishments.

FIGURE 1-5

This cooperative operates within the free enterprise system. It must compete alongside other types of business organizations. (Courtesy, G.L.F., Ithaca, N.Y.)

Cooperatives may render at least four valuable services to the capitalistic system of which they are a part: (1) enhance private property, (2) preserve market competition, (3) retain the profit motive and (4) maintain and strengthen the individual consumer and entrepreneur.

Cooperatives and Socialism

Under socialism, cooperatives cannot exist in those areas where government ownership prevails, such as in heavy industry. In the consumer goods sector, such as retailing, and in agriculture where land is not nationalized, cooperatives may exist. Cooperatives often travel a precarious road under socialism. Especially is this true when a socialistic economy moves toward a more centralized power structure which may ultimately end in communism.

Cooperatives and Communism

Under communism, many state or government enterprises are

designated as "cooperatives." For example, a group of farm families
may be located together in a communal village and work several
thousand acres together under a chairman or manager who is a member
of the Communist Party. This Communist official receives his production quotas from Moscow headquarters and attempts to organize and
direct the farm workers to achieve these quotas. All land, equipment
and facilities belong to the state. That which is produced also belongs
to the state. But whatever is left over-and-above the quota delivered
to the government at extremely low prices remains with the collective
group. Each member of the farm group is paid according to his or
her skill and the number of days worked. The Communist manager
is an arm of the state.

The Communists often call these government enterprises "cooperatives" in order to capitalize on the good name of cooperatives earned
in the free enterprise system. It must be remembered that capitalistic
cooperatives had already earned the respect and admiration of the
whole world before the Communist revolution in Russia in 1917. Therefore, it is to the advantage of Communists to try to capitalize on the
reputation of *cooperatives* and use this term to characterize their
collective efforts, which are not truly cooperative but rather state
controlled and directed.

More recent Communist policy in Russia points to the abolition of
even "collective" farms and the expansion of full-fledged "state" farms,
which is another step away from true cooperation.

An unfortunate development concerning cooperatives is that too
often socialist and communist propaganda has hidden behind the shield
of the cooperative. A respectable capitalistic business organization,
such as a cooperative, is often prostituted with socialist and communist
subversion. The Cooperative League in 1948 adopted a resolution
against such propaganda which said, in part:

> Believers in communism and fascism consequently cannot
> desire the success of any cooperative. Their purpose in at-
> tempting to join a cooperative, if they do so, would be to use
> it for their own propaganda purposes for a temporary period
> and then destroy it as inevitably constituting a barrier against
> the achievement of communist or fascist goals.[4]

---

[4]Parker, Florence, *The First 125 Years*, Cooperative League, Chicago, Ill. 1956.
p. 124.

FIGURE 1-6

*This collective farm is part of the communist system. Communist collectives are not coopera-
tives because the government owns everything; it has a complete monopoly over all enterprises, provides little or no economic incentives, fixes all prices and orders its people to work
as the government may prescribe. (Courtesy, USDA, Washington, D.C.)*

If the socialist and communist proponents were to gain control, one
of the first economic institutions they would destroy would be the
capitalistic cooperative. The Communists regard the typical American
cooperative with as much hatred as they generate for capitalism itself.
It is perhaps wrong to say that cooperatives directly combat communism. But cooperatives strengthen capitalism and make it more democratic which in turn acts as a bulwark against communism.

Aizsilnieks, an exiled Russian, pin-points in specific terms what the
Russians mean by their use of the term *cooperative:*

> In the USSR, cooperation has been used by the Soviet
> states from the very first year of power as a lever and as a
> driving belt for a socialist transformation of the USSR's eco-
> nomic life. In order to serve this role, a radical conversion
> of its activity, which originally received its impetus from
> capitalism, was necessary in both form and content.[5]

---

[5]Aizsilnieks, A. P., *Cooperation Behind the Iron Curtain,* Mimir Publishers, Madison, Wisc. 1952. p. 7.

Aizsilnieks points out further that Communists have an entirely different concept of what cooperatives are as compared to the western world. They see their so-called cooperatives as being tools for the furtherance of communism. They have the utmost contempt for capitalistic cooperatives. He warns us that any collaboration between capitalistic cooperatives and communistic cooperatives will result in the latter subjugating the former.[6]

According to Bogardus, the International Cooperative Alliance concluded that whenever governments liquidate, change, coerce or compel cooperatives to act in a manner other than self-determination by their own membership, they cannot be counted among the real cooperatives of the world.[7]

Under such a policy one would, by necessity, conclude that all communistic cooperatives are fictitious.

Cooperatives and Fascism

True cooperatives may exist under fascism as long as the dictatorship does not interfere with them. Whenever they are compelled to serve the will of the state, they cease to be true cooperatives and become an arm of the state. Often, managers of cooperatives in a fascist economy will be appointed by the government.

Cooperatives in Mixed Systems

Cooperatives in a mixed economy usually receive much attention since they can be used to bolster the free market and, at the same time, serve as an arm of the state. Usually, the government will decide the goals or objectives of these cooperatives and then lend money and provide technical assistance for the people to organize cooperatives. The operation of the cooperatives comes under close scrutiny of the government and usually cannot deviate from government policies. In many cases, the co-op members are promised that government control will be withdrawn in time, but often these promises are not fulfilled. It is open to serious question whether cooperatives of this kind are truly cooperative or a concealed arm of the state. The excuse usually given for this situation is that "we are in a transitional period." If

---

[6]*Ibid.* p. 8.
[7]Bogardus, Emory, *Principles of Cooperation*, Cooperative League, Chicago, Ill. 1958. pp. 36-37.

governments in mixed economies are sincere in relinquishing control over the cooperatives they have initiated, then true cooperation may eventually exist.

ARE COOPERATIVES AN ECONOMIC SYSTEM?

There is some controversy as to whether cooperatives are an economic system of their own or are a part of other economic systems. Various scholars have differed concerning this question over the years.

Those who argue that cooperatives represent an economic system by themselves allege that the profit motive is eliminated and thus cooperatives become different from capitalism. This is a serious error. Cooperatives do not eliminate the profit motive; they extend it to more people, thus strengthening capitalism and broadening its base of operation.

Co-op Schools of Thought

Casselman classifies three schools of co-op thought: (1) Socialist Cooperative school, (2) Cooperative Commonwealth school and (3) Competitive Yardstick school.[8]

The Socialist Cooperative school promotes cooperatives with socialism as the final goal. In other words, cooperatives are a transitory medium on the way to state socialism. This school of thought predominates in socialistic and communistic economies. It is totally rejected by cooperators in capitalistic countries.

The Cooperative Commonwealth school visualizes a capitalistic economy in which cooperatives are the dominant type of business organization, with sole proprietorships, partnerships and profit-type corporations occupying a secondary role.

Loucks has made a thoughtful analysis of this co-op philosophy which is held by a minority of cooperators in the free enterprise economies. He expresses concern over the naive assumption that consumers' cooperation can evolve as a substitute for capitalism without either using the force of government or encountering a government hostile to this goal. Another point is his disbelief that the cooperative common-

---

[8]Casselman, Paul, *The Cooperative Movement and Some of Its Problems*, Philosophical Library, New York, N.Y. 1952. p. 9.

wealth possesses real merit when viewed as an alternative to capitalism. Loucks sees a fusion of consumer-interest and owner-interest in which consumers would have all the power they previously had plus all the power the owners previously possessed. Such a concentration of economic decision-making power would not necessarily lead to more optimum decision-making.

In his final analysis, Loucks aligns himself with the Competitive Yardstick school of co-op thought: "In all of these ways, the consumer cooperative movement may advantageously supplement private capitalist trade and industry."[9]

The Competitive Yardstick school views cooperatives only as a means of checking the evils of the capitalistic system and correcting these defects within the system, thereby making the capitalistic system stronger and more nearly perfect. A majority of the cooperators in the free enterprise system belong to this school of thought. This book accepts the Competitive Yardstick school and none other. Each type of business organization (proprietorship, partnership, profit-type corpora-

FIGURE 1-7

Cooperatives are viewed in harmony with other types of business organizations, such as single proprietorships, partnerships and profit-type corporations. (Courtesy, American Institute of Cooperation, Washington, D.C.)

---

[9]Loucks, W. N. and J. W. Hoot, *Comparative Economic Systems*, Harper & Bros., New York, N.Y. 1948. p. 758.

tion and cooperative) is viewed in harmony. Whichever survives must do so within a competitive economy. A discussion of these four types of business organizations is found in the next chapter.

SUMMARY OF COOPERATIVES AND ECONOMIC SYSTEMS

From all evidences, it must be concluded that cooperatives do not constitute an economic system of their own. Under capitalism, cooperatives are a form of business organization within the system. Under socialism, cooperatives can exist only with respect to consumer goods because the government does not directly control or interfere in this area. Under communism, true cooperatives do not exist at all because government enterprise prevails both in producer and consumer goods industries. Under fascism, true cooperatives may exist if there is no control or direction from the state. In mixed systems, true cooperatives may exist provided the influence of government and subsequent political considerations are held to a minimum.

WHAT'S AHEAD?

We shall discuss cooperatives operating throughout the economic system, particularly those in a free enterprise system. These will include *farmers' cooperatives* in marketing, purchasing, servicing, bargaining and credit. Also treated will be *consumers' cooperatives* in purchasing, servicing, housing, education and credit, among others. *Businessmen's cooperatives,* such as retailer-owned co-op wholesale, business and industrial sales and service cooperatives, also will be included. In addition, *workers' productive cooperatives* in which workers own their own plants will be covered. Finally, *quasi cooperatives,* or those which use at least some co-op techniques, will be discussed.

TOPICS FOR DISCUSSION

1. Define a true cooperative.
2. Name the five basic characteristics of any economic system. Discuss each one.
3. Name the five economic systems in the world today. Discuss each one.
4. Discuss the role of cooperatives in each of the five economic systems.
5. Name and discuss the three schools of co-op thought. Are cooperatives an economic system themselves?

SELECTED REFERENCES

1. Bell, Richard, "How Soviet Agriculture Compares with Ours," *Foreign Agriculture*, Washington, D.C. Sept. 1961.
2. Belov, Fedor, *History of a Soviet Collective Farm*, Praeger Publishers, New York, N.Y. 1955.
3. Cole, G. D. H., *The British Co-op Movement in a Socialist Economy*, Allen & Unwin, London, England. 1951.
4. Cotta, F., *Agricultural Cooperation in Fascist Italy*, King & Son Ltd., London, England. 1935.
5. Daniels, John, *Cooperation—An American Way*, Covici-Friede Publishers, New York, N.Y. 1938.
6. Fairless, B. F., *The Great Mistake of Karl Marx*, U.S. Steel Corp., New York, N.Y. Oct. 22, 1952.
7. Koller, Fred, "Cooperatives in Our Capitalistic Economy," *Farm Policy Forum*. Apr. 1948.
8. Kress, A. J., *Capitalism, Cooperation, Communism*, Ransdell, Inc., Washington, D.C. 1932.
9. Pasto, J. K. and Jan Prybyla, "Russia's Farm Problem," *Farm Economics*, Pa. Agr. Ext. Serv., University Park, Pa. Aug. 1, 1962.
10. Schumpeter, Joseph A., *Capitalism, Socialism and Democracy*, Harper & Bros., New York, N.Y. 1942.
11. Smith, L. P. F., *Evolution of Agricultural Cooperation*, Blackwell, Oxford, England. 1961.
12. Staff, *Communism in Action*, Government Printing Office, House Document 754, Washington, D.C. 1946.
13. Sullivan, Lawrence, "The Collapse of Communist Economic Theory," *The Freeman*, Irvington-on-Hudson, N.Y. Apr. 1961. pp. 17-22.
14. Suranyiunger, Theo., *Comparative Economic Systems*, McGraw-Hill, New York, N.Y. 1952. pp. 390-399.
15. Tawney, R. H., *Religion and the Rise of Capitalism*, Harcourt, Brace and Co., New York, N.Y. 1926.
16. Volin, L., *The Agricultural Picture in U.S.S.R. and U.S.A.*, ERS Rept. 27, Washington, D.C. Apr. 1963.

CHAPTER 2 –

Cooperatives and Other Types
of Business Organizations

TYPES OF BUSINESS ORGANIZATIONS

THERE ARE basically four types of business organizations in a free enterprise economy: (1) single proprietorships, (2) partnerships, (3) profit-type corporations and (4) cooperatives.

Single Proprietorship

Doing business as an individual is the oldest and most numerous of all forms of business enterprise. Despite the growth of other forms of business organization, the individual enterprise remains very popular. It is still the most common. The farmer and the general storeowner serving a small community are typical examples of persons engaged in this form of business.

As in any other type of business, the individual enterprise has its merits and demerits: (1) It is a very flexible method which may be employed in almost any field of human activity. (2) It offers great opportunities for personal initiative and ingenuity. (3) No special

FIGURE 2-1

This farmer is a single proprietor. He owns, directs and controls his own enterprise. Single proprietorships are still the most numerous type of business organizations in the United States. (Courtesy, Farm Equipment Institute, Chicago, Ill.)

legal formalities are usually required to form an individual enterprise. If the law requires some formalities in certain fields of business, these usually consist of the procurement of a business permit and payment of local license fees.

Partnership

The essence of doing business on a partnership basis lies in joint contributions of labor or property, or both, by the partners, joint control of the operations and a division of resulting profits or losses. The partners enter a business in order to make a profit for themselves.

Partnership is an advantageous method of doing business when partners have insufficient capital or skill to operate individually and labor is performed largely by the partners themselves. Also, it is more cheaply and speedily set up than a corporation, and it is a suitable method in those fields of business in which corporate organization is not authorized, such as in medicine and law.

On the other hand, if there are too many partners, a partnership may turn into a rather unwieldy enterprise. A partnership requires good teamwork, and it must be reorganized when one partner withdraws or dies. Also, it may hardly serve the purpose when great concentration of capital is required.

FIGURE 2-2

These two farmers are partners in an agricultural operation. However, partnerships are used more in the legal, medical and engineering professions where personal services are important. (Courtesy, Calif. Agr. Ext. Serv., Berkeley, Calif.)

Profit-Type Corporation

A unique feature of the corporation is that it is treated by the law as a "legal person" distinct from its constituent human members. Another characteristic is that it may exist continually, notwithstanding the death or withdrawal of its owners. The primary purpose of a profit-type corporation is to make a profit for its investor-owners.

Cooperative

The primary purpose of a cooperative is to make a profit for its patrons or users of the cooperative, not for its investors. The members of a cooperative serve themselves. They are both the owners and users

FIGURE 2-3

Profit-type corporations comprise the most important type of business organizations in the United States from the standpoint of business volume conducted. They are important in practically every phase of business. Some of them form co-op corporations to improve their economic positions. (Courtesy, Chamber of Commerce, Baton Rouge, La.)

of the service. A contractual arrangement between the cooperative and the member-patrons requires that all margins above the cost of operation be returned to the member-patrons in proportion to their business with the cooperative. In effect, the cooperative is a hybrid institution containing some features of a proprietorship, partnership and corporation. A cooperative is usually organized by single proprietorships; it is taxed as if it were a partnership but is legally constituted as a corporation.

COMPARISONS OF BUSINESS ORGANIZATIONS

The economic and legal differences among single proprietorships, partnerships, profit-type corporations and cooperatives are discussed in subsequent sections. This discussion is then summarized in Table 2-1.

Purpose of Operation

All four types of business organizations are operated for the purpose of buying, selling or producing goods and services. They may do all three.

Recipients of Goods and Services

The single proprietorship, partnership and profit-type corporation render their goods and services to, and trade them with, the general public. Profit-type corporations may incidentally trade with their owners. For example, a Standard Oil shareholder might buy his gasoline regularly from a Standard Oil station, but no special consideration is given him just because he is a Standard Oil stockholder. On the other hand, co-op corporations trade primarily with their own members or stockholders. Incidentally, they may also trade with the general public or with nonmembers. If cooperatives were to make it a practice to deal with nonmembers or the general public, they would resemble closely profit-type corporations.

FIGURE 2-4

Cooperatives are an important type of business organization. They help to strengthen single proprietorships, partnerships and profit-type corporations by group buying, selling and servicing. Cooperatives are often referred to as the "balance wheel" in a free economy. (Courtesy, Bank for Cooperatives, Columbia, S.C.)

Starting the Business

The single proprietor may decide to go into business at his own will and discretion. A partnership depends on an understanding between two or more partners. A profit-type corporation begins by meeting the requirements of state law and by investor-owned stock subscriptions. A co-op corporation begins by meeting the requirements of state law (in some cases, federal law) and by patron-owned capital subscriptions. Borrowed capital is also used in all types of businesses.

Legalizing and Chartering

A single proprietor needs no charter but usually must be age 21 or over to control the business legally. A partnership requires no charter. Usually, the partnership agreement or contract is recorded in the county recorder's office so that official note is taken of the partnership. A profit-type corporation must charter under state law; there are no federal provisions for chartering a profit-type corporation. State restrictions on profit-type corporations are very few, which allows considerable latitude in their operations. Co-op corporations, for the most part, charter under state law. Federal chartering of cooperatives is possible for credit unions, federal land bank associations, production credit associations and banks for cooperatives, for example. Both state and federal charters are very restrictive on co-op corporations, and the businesses must abide closely by these restrictions. Co-op corporations have less freedom of operation as compared with profit-type corporations.

Joining the Business

The single proprietor starts a business himself or may buy one already in operation. A new partner entering a partnership forces the creation of a new partnership agreement and the dissolution of the prior one.

In a profit-type corporation, one joins by purchasing one or more shares of stock on the national stock exchanges, on state stock exchanges, through brokers or through private purchases. In a co-op corporation, joining is not so easy. First, one must meet the qualifications specified for membership; second, he must be approved by the board of directors; and third, he must be active in the affairs of the association.

In an ordinary corporation, the number of shares of common stock an individual may hold is not limited. Each share of stock entitles the owner to one vote. The earnings or profits of the corporation are distributed as dividends to its common stockholders on the basis of the number of shares each owns. Common stockholders are not necessarily interested in doing any business with the ordinary corporation.

In cooperatives, common stock is the means of acquiring membership in those associations which are organized on a stock basis. It is also a means of providing part of the necessary capital to finance a cooperative. Stock in a cooperative does not attract profit dividends as such; it technically draws interest because of its "loan" characteristics.

Control of the Business

The single proprietor controls his business, and the partners control the partnership. In the profit-type corporation, the stockholder-investors elect a board of directors which in turn elects its officers and appoints top management. Proxy voting is permitted. Voting is done according to shares of stock, usually one share, one vote. In a co-op corporation, member-patrons elect a board of directors which in turn elects its officers and appoints top management. Voting is done according to persons, usually one man, one vote. Proxy voting is sometimes permitted. Sale or transfer of stock is not permitted unless the board approves. Stock is redeemable at par value.

Ownership of the Business

The single proprietor invests his money, personal efforts and sometimes borrowed money into his business of which he is the sole owner. In a partnership, the partners may make various contributions—some may put in money only; another may put in personal effort only, while others may put in both. In a profit-type corporation, stockholder-investors put in money, seeking returns on this money. They may or may not be active in the business. 'In a co-op corporation, the patrons are the owners and usually subscribe funds. As they do business with themselves, they may choose to leave the net savings as further contribution to their capital investment.[1]

In a profit-type corporation the stock capital itself is entrepreneurial or acquisitive for profit. The firm seeks to acquire profit from anyone

---

[1] *Net savings* refers to the excess of receipts over costs.

and any transaction. Its capital is impersonal and may move freely.

In a cooperative, the capital subscribed is neither entrepreneurial nor acquisitive. In fact, it is a loan from a member to his cooperative with either a stipulated interest rate or a specified maximum. The cooperative seeks to acquire profit for its member entrepreneurs, not for itself. Its capital is personal and does not move freely because it is a loan contracted between the member and the cooperative.

Sliger has summarized this difference between profit and nonprofit corporations very well by stating that "in profit-type corporations the patron is a means *to* an end (profit) while in the cooperative the patron is both the means *and* the end."[2]

Return on Investment

There are no limits to the return on investment which may be realized in a single proprietorship, partnership or profit-type corporation. In a co-op corporation, dividends on money invested are usually restricted to 8 percent or as prescribed by applicable state law. However, in a co-op corporation there are no limits on the returns or earnings which may be refunded to the patrons based on their volume of business with the cooperative.

Disposition of Net Earnings

Net earnings may be used as the individual wishes in a single proprietorship. In a partnership, net earnings are divided according to the original partnership agreement. In a profit-type corporation, net earnings after income taxes are distributed to stockholder-investors as dividends on stock shares or are kept as retained reserves for the corporation or some of both. In a co-op corporation, all the net earnings are prorated to the patrons or users on a patronage basis. If a co-op corporation fails to do so, then the portion not prorated is subject to federal and state income taxes as if the business were a profit-type corporation.

Although a cooperative does not earn money for itself, a successful farmer cooperative, for example, does earn money for its members by increasing their total net farm incomes. By reducing the cost of farm supplies purchased or by increasing the net return for farm products

---

[2]Sliger, B. F., "The American Cooperative Movement—What It Is and Isn't," *Proceedings of Tri-State Co-op Workshop*, Baton Rouge, La. July 1960. p. 94.

marketed, the farmer cooperative actually increases the net farm incomes of its members. In the case of household supplies purchased cooperatively, a successful cooperative reduces the cost of operating the household. As a part of the farm business of the members, the cooperative is like the farm tractor—it does not earn money for itself but for the farmer who owns and uses it.

When members purchase their supplies or market their products through their cooperative, they must pay the actual cost of the service performed by the cooperative. They share this cost on a patronage basis. When the "price" to members or patrons includes more than actual cost, a refund is made to each member proportional to his patronage. These refunds are made in order to bring the charges for the services of the cooperative down to actual cost to the members or patrons.

Owners' Liability

The single proprietor and the partners in a partnership have unlimited liability in the conduct of their businesses. If any losses, damage suits or other liabilities occur, they stand the full limit of these liabilities except for what may be exempted under applicable state laws. Both profit-type and co-op corporations have limited liability. That is, the owners are only liable to the extent of their equity in the corporations.

Liquidating the Business

In a single proprietorship, the death, disability, bankruptcy or retirement of the owner dissolves the proprietorship. In a partnership, the death of a partner, bankruptcy or decision to dissolve liquidates the partnership. In a profit-type or co-op corporation, bankruptcy or legal dissolution is the only means of liquidation.

Taxation of Net Earnings

Both single proprietors and partners are taxed on their net earnings at the individual income tax rate. A profit-type corporation pays income tax at the corporate rate. When dividends are paid out to stockholders, these persons are taxed at the individual rate. The cooperative, provided it meets certain rules and regulations, is taxed as if it were a partnership. The cooperative itself pays no income taxes if earnings are allocated to patrons or users of the business. The patrons pay income tax on these refunds at the individual rate. The subject of co-op taxation is quite technical and is discussed further in Chapters 18 and 19.

Differences Between the Profit-type and Co-op Corporation

From the preceding discussion, differences between the profit-type and co-op corporation are obvious in:
1. Recipients of goods and services.
2. Joining the business.
3. Control of the business.
4. Ownership of the business.
5. Return on investment.
6. Disposition of net earnings.
7. Taxation of net earnings.

TRUE COOPERATIVES VERSUS QUASI COOPERATIVES

At this point, we may restate the definition of a "true" cooperative as follows: "an association, usually incorporated, with economic aims formed by and for persons or corporations having common needs, having approximately equal voice in its management, making approximately equal or proportional contribution to capital and deriving proportional services and benefits from it."

In some cases, cooperatives may deviate somewhat from this definition, and in such cases, they may be termed "quasi cooperative." The most frequent deviation from true co-op principles occurs when member-patrons are not given full voting and control rights in a cooperative. Another type of deviation comes about when interest paid on capital is not limited, allowing the cooperative to gradually transform into a profit-type corporation seeking profit on capital investment rather than on patronage. Examples of quasi cooperatives are given in Chapter 8. A discussion of co-op principles is reserved for Chapter 9.

SOCIAL ASPECTS OF COOPERATIVES

Cooperatives are not primarily organized and operated to change society or to be social clubs. They are not social vehicles. If social

TABLE 2-1
Four Methods of Doing Business Under the Free Enterprise System

Phases	Single Proprietorship	Partnership	Profit-type Corporation	Cooperative
1. Why is the firm operated?	To buy, sell or produce goods and services.	To buy, sell or produce goods and services.	To buy, sell or produce goods and services.	To buy, sell or produce goods and services.
2. To whom are the goods and services rendered?	The public or non-owner customers.	The public or non-owner customers.	The public, incidentally to stockholders.	Chiefly its own members.
3. How is the firm started?	Decision of individual.	Agreement between associates who become partners.	Organization by associates who become stockholder-investors.	Organization by associates who become owner-members.
4. How does the firm become legal?	By the owner's attaining legal age and controlling the business.	By contract between two or more individuals, preferably written and recorded.	Usually incorporated under general laws giving corporations great freedom in their operations.	Usually incorporated under special laws requiring operation according to co-op principles.
5. Where is the business chartered?	No charter is required.	No charter is required. Partnership contract may be recorded.	Charter required. Only states can charter; no federal charter.	Charter required. States charter most cooperatives; some federally chartered.

(Continued)

TABLE 2-1 (Continued)

Phases	Single Proprietorship	Partnership	Profit-type Corporation	Cooperative
6. How does one get into the firm?	Starts business himself or buys it.	By consent of the partners and a new agreement.	By buying stock.	By meeting the qualifications for membership, obtaining approval by the board and doing business with the association.
7. Who controls the firm, selects the manager and makes policy decisions?	The individual.	The partners by agreement.	The board of directors elected by the stockholder-investors.	The board of directors elected by the member-patrons.
8. How is voting done?	None necessary.	Informal agreement; sometimes by vote of partners.	Usually one vote for each share of common stock.	Usually one member, one vote; sometimes by patronage.
9. Who owns the business?	The individual.	Two or more individuals.	The stockholders.	The member-patrons.
10. What do the owners put into the business?	The individual puts in personal effort and capital.	Each partner may put in capital or personal effort, or both.	Capital is supplied by investors seeking profits.	The members do business through the cooperative and put in funds or leave retains.
11. What returns can be received on the money invested?	Unlimited.	Unlimited.	Unlimited.	Usually limited to a maximum of 8 percent or as prescribed by state law.

(Continued)

TABLE 2-1 (Continued)

Phases	Single Proprietor- ship	Partner- ship	Profit-type Corporation	Cooperative
12. How may net earnings be used?	As desired by individual.	As agreed upon by partners.	As dividends to stockholders or as reserves, or both.	Prorated to patrons on patronage basis.
13. What is the owners' liability?	All property of indi- vidual, excepting legal exemptions.	All property of all partners, excepting legal exemptions.	Assets of the corporation.	Assets of the cooperative
14. How may business be ended?	Death, disability, bankruptcy or retirement of owner.	Death of any partner, bankruptcy or de- cision to dissolve.	Bankruptcy or legal dissolution of company.	Bankruptcy or legal dissolution of cooperative.
15. How are net earnings taxed?	As an individual.	As an individual.	At regular corporate tax rates.	As a partnership.

Source: American Institute of Cooperation, Washington, D.C.

changes do result from their organization and operation these are byproducts of their economic motivation.

It is true that in the early years of the American republic, many co-op endeavors were both economic and social. The quilting-bees, log rolling, cattle slaughter rings and other such ventures carried both an economic and social purpose. Most co-op groups in early America were never incorporated. They were informal associations without charters and bylaws and with no formal legal status.

The modern concept of cooperatives no longer includes such endeavors within the realm of economic cooperation. Nevertheless, most of the farmer cooperatives of today had their origins in informal, socio-economic groups which later developed more formal structures and followed advanced business procedures.

In nations whose economies are immature, cooperatives may likely play a larger social role than in mature economies. Governments in newly developed countries sometimes use the cooperative both as a social and economic vehicle for implementing economic development. In land reform and community services, cooperatives are used to bridge the transitional gap, socially and economically, from feudalism to democracy.

MYTHS ABOUT COOPERATIVES

Over the years, many myths about cooperatives have arisen. Many of these fallacies arose because the writers on cooperation were confusing cooperatives with religious and social movements, peasant revolts, politics and the "isms." They somehow failed to recognize the cooperative as a business type of organization with many of the shortcomings possessed by all business organizations. Some of these myths are now discussed.

Cooperatives for the Poor?

It is not necessary that a cooperative be comprised of the poor and the weak. Poverty and weakness are not essential criteria for the success of a cooperative. Nations with relatively high living standards and literacy rates contain wider co-op membership than nations with meager resources and high illiteracy rates.

Cooperatives Strive for Equality?

Cooperatives should not strive for equality but instead should strive for equity. It is not the purpose of a cooperative to make everybody equal; rather, it is to serve everybody equitably. Sometimes, equality and equity are the same, but not always. For example, should a cooperative charge the same price per sack for delivering five sacks of feed as for delivering 500? It costs less per sack to deliver 500 than it does five. One is a question of equality; the other is one of equity. To charge the same per sack would be equality but not equity.

The Cooperative a Labor Union?

A cooperative and a labor union are two different organizations. A cooperative is organized by entrepreneurs (capitalists) and/or by household firms. A labor union is organized in behalf of employees to bargain with employers or entrepreneurs. Therefore, the two are altogether different. In fact, cooperatives and labor unions may come into conflict whenever a labor union bargains for the employees of a cooperative with the co-op management. The cooperative in this case is the entrepreneur, or capitalist.

Labor unions are more compatible with consumer and housing cooperatives and with credit unions, for example, because union members participate in these cooperatives as householders and consumers, not as members of a labor union.

Also, a farmers' bargaining cooperative is different from a labor union. The former is a union of entrepreneurs, or capitalists; the latter is a union of employees of capitalists.

WHAT A COOPERATIVE IS NOT

At this point, we are not quite ready to present entirely what a cooperative is, but we can be sure of what a cooperative is not. It is not an economic system. It is not a movement, political or otherwise. It does not seek to overthrow or destroy capitalism; rather, it seeks to preserve capitalism. It is not a conspiracy to link all the cooperatives in one nation or in several nations into one economic movement. It is not a social movement. It is not a welfare scheme to give something to somebody. It is not a technique to replace government farm programs as presently constituted in many nations. It is not necessarily organized to help the poor; the rich use cooperatives too. It is not an automatic road to economic salvation; rather, it is a difficult economic institution to make function.

In the next chapter, the historical evolution of the cooperative is considered.

TOPICS FOR DISCUSSION

1. Name the four types of business organizations in a free enterprise economy.
2. Contrast these four types of business organizations according to each of the fifteen points presented in the chapter.
3. Name and discuss the seven essential differences between a profit-type and co-op corporation.
4. Distinguish "true" from "quasi" cooperatives.
5. What are some social aspects of cooperatives?
6. What are some of the myths about cooperatives?

SELECTED REFERENCES

1. Johnson, Counts, *Cooperatives Are a Vital Part of the American Business System,* Florida Council of Farmer Cooperatives, Winter Haven, Fla. June 1962.
2. Knapp, J. G., "Are Cooperatives Good Business?" *Harvard Business Review,* Cambridge, Mass. Jan.-Feb. 1957. pp. 57-64.
3. Loomis, C. P. and J. A. Beegle, *Rural Social Systems,* Prentice-Hall, New York, N.Y. 1950. pp. 641-650.
4. May, Mark A. and Leonard W. Doob, *Competition and Cooperation,* Social Science Research Council Bul. 25, New York, N.Y. Apr. 1937. pp. 62-71.
5. Phillips, R. and others, *Do You Know Your Cooperative?* Iowa Institute of Cooperation, Ames, Iowa. 1957. pp. 29-47.
6. Roy, E. P., "The Economic Truth About Cooperatives," *Catholic Rural Life,* Des Moines, Iowa. Oct. 1960. pp. 14-15.
7. Roy, E. P. and H. Braud, *Suggestions for Teaching Farmer Cooperation in Louisiana,* Depts. of Agr. Educ. and Agr. Eco., Louisiana State University, Baton Rouge, La. Feb. 1962. pp. 4-6.
8. U.S. Senate, *Definition of a Co-op Association,* Government Printing Office, Washington, D.C. Hearings of July 21, 1939, Parts 1 and 2.

CHAPTER 3 –

Historical Evolution

of the Cooperative

Cooperation touches no man's fortune, it seeks no plunder, it causes no disturbance in society, it gives no trouble to statesmen, it enters into no secret associations, it contemplates no violence, it subverts no order, it envies no dignity, it asks no favor, it keeps no terms with the idle and it will break no faith with the industrious. It means self-help, self-dependence and such share of the competence as labor, skill or thought can win and this it intends to have.
—George J. Holyoake

CONTRARY to popular belief, the co-op method of conducting business has a long and noted history. Over the centuries, the cooperative has evolved from a religion-oriented institution to a more formalized, business-oriented organization serving economic rather than spiritual needs.

EVOLUTION OF THE COOPERATIVE

The Ancient Egyptian Era

Cooperatives or quasi-cooperative structures were doubtless in existence, dating from the inception of the old Egyptian Empire, beginning approximately in the year 3000 B.C. As a result of their extensive investigations, two Egyptologists, Revillout of France and Lumbroso of Italy, point out that the craftsmen and artisans during the reign of the Pharaohs possessed a highly developed trade system which led to the establishment of associations charged with the regulation of the entire trade system. However, it is doubtful whether these organizations were established by the workers themselves for the purpose of safeguarding their trade interests or by the state for the purpose of serving its own ends. It can be assumed that the workers were never socially strong enough to allow themselves to create gilds (workers' associations) resembling those which existed during the Middle Ages in Europe. There is less reason to believe that the farmers and unskilled workers of ancient Egypt were able to form cooperatives for the improvement of their social conditions, because they were more or less enslaved servants forced to perform hard labor on the estates of the Pharaohs, of the temple priests and of other large estate owners. For this reason, they undoubtedly were incapable of achieving a great degree of social and economic liberty through the medium of cooperatives.

The Babylonian Era

It is safe to assume that cooperatives existed in ancient Babylonia where some agricultural leases had co-op features. The conclusion that the tenant system in agriculture of ancient Babylonia frequently

FIGURE 3-1

Archeologists and their helpers gather under the great rock front of the Temple of the Goddess of Athor. This temple was built by Ramses II. During the reign of the Pharaohs, associations were charged with the regulation of the entire trade system. (Courtesy, Wide World Photos)

assumed a co-op character can unquestionably be drawn from the famous Code of Hammurapi which, in addition to other types of tenant farming, provided for co-op tenant farming. The Code was proclaimed by the ancient Babylonian King Hammurapi some time during his 43-year reign between 2067 and 2025 B.C.

Under the laws of the Code, it was possible for a number of farmers to take over large estates on a co-op basis. These estates were then managed as common enterprises, or else they were parceled out to individual members of the cooperatives. Documents show that the tenant farmers in cooperatives kept strict account of their enterprises. If, instead of hiring themselves out to large estate owners, poor farmers were enabled by law to achieve economic freedom and independence, this can certainly be looked upon as an indication that co-op tenant farming could not have been a rare circumstance.

It can also be assumed that co-op undertakings were not lacking in Babylonian trade and commerce. The prevalence of credit transactions among the ancient Babylonians doubtless led to the creation of loan societies to assist the small farmers and craftsmen and sought to protect the weak and the poor against the injustices which were prevalent at that time among the rich and powerful. Fixed rates were determined for various forms of services, and these rates of legislation affected most branches of trade and commerce. Small industrial establishments existed side by side with larger shops operated by the rulers.

The Early Greek Era

There is no doubt that there were co-op societies among the ancient Greeks, for many of their burial benefit societies, created for the sake of their cult of the dead, soon became professional with economic aims. They had legal entity, could acquire property, could sue and be sued, and there are reasons to believe that they bore between themselves the nucleus of the Christian community. These religious associations resulted from a desire on the part of the members to be buried in accordance with the rituals of their religion.

Almost every Greek of the middle and lower classes of the population belonged to an association which assured its members of a burial place and a decent funeral and which furthermore was aimed at the promotion of mutual assistance. These religious and cultural associations, which were known as "Orglonen" and "Thiasi," were the forerunners of the subsequent professional and economic associations.

Some of these associations engaged in the wholesale purchasing of fuel and beverages. Others endeavored to extend aid to the poor and to temporarily impoverished members, while still others obligated their members to assist traveling members with information and care. A number of associations attempted to do all the foregoing services. Membership was open not only to free citizens but also to slaves and strangers; even women were admitted, which allows one to conclude that the associations were permitted to operate in freedom and safety. The affairs of the associations were taken care of by the members themselves, specifically by the monthly membership meeting which represented the highest administrative medium. Far reaching executive powers were placed in the hands of a trusted member. Once a year, a general assembly took place, followed by a festive banquet. The Greek associations were able to bring suit in court and were allowed to acquire real estate. There can be no doubt that during the rise of Christianity, many of these associations formed the nuclei for the formation of the Christian communities. It seems to be an established fact that in many localities of Asia Minor, Greece and Italy, the Christian church was founded on the basis of the religious burial associations, and it was in this form that it attracted its first followers.

Ancient Chinese Associations

Savings and loan associations, as we know this type of cooperatives today, first came into prominence in China during the Hon Dynasty 200 years before the Christian era, when Pong Koong, a rich and influential Chinese, instituted the first money lending society bearing co-op features.

Characteristic of these early Chinese associations was the fact that they were limited to a small group of members in a community, with no operating expense. For instance, a person who was in need of a loan would be required to call upon relatives and friends to form a society consisting of a definite number of members. Each member was required to contribute an equal sum to the fund. Stated quarterly meetings were held at the home of the president of the society, and each member was required to attend. At that time the various sums contributed to the fund were carefully checked and evaluated. At each properly notified meeting, the borrower was required to pay back into the fund an installment on the loan with interest at a rate per month previously agreed upon. The installment to the fund was to be equal to the amount contributed by each individual in the first instance. The interest was then divided equally among the members of the society. Also, at every duly notified meeting, each member was required to contribute to the fund an amount equal to that which he contributed at the first meeting.

In order to give all the members equal opportunity to borrow the collective amount thus formed, they were given a chance to bid competitively for the loan by the ballot-box method, the bids setting forth the rates of interest which the prospective borrowers were disposed to pay on the amount in question. The one making the highest offer was then declared to be the borrower of the loan.

Another regulation was that each member must be provided with a book in which the numbers of each attended meeting were recorded. Should any member be unable to contribute to the general fund at any one of the meetings the amount required from him, three days of grace were allowed him to raise his amount. At the expiration of that time, should he continue as a defaulter, he was required to pay a fine until the sum due was paid up.

From the foregoing regulations of the ancient Chinese lending associations, the following prominent features are recognized:

1. A limited society, all members contributing equal amounts.
2. Payment of dues and interest at stated intervals.
3. Equal division of profits.
4. Payment of the borrowed sum in installments at stated intervals.
5. Competitive bids for loans.
6. A system of fines for nonpayment of contributions to the fund.

The equality of payment by each member insured the most complete cooperation of the Chinese societies. Since voting was on a share basis, all had the same vote, because all members contributed equal amounts. As to division of the profits, according to shares, all received the same portion because of their equal contributions of capital.

The Roman Era

The cooperative craftsmen's organizations called "Collegia," which appeared as early as the beginning of Old Roman history, seem also to have arisen out of the religious associations. The ancient "Collegia" were first mentioned in the law of the Twelve Tables (451 to 449 B.C.), and history credits the legendary King Numa Pompilius with having established eight trade colleges, including those for shoemakers, potmakers, fullers, dyers, carpenters, coppersmiths, goldsmiths and flute players. As the crafts developed, the number of colleges increased correspondingly. The colleges were unlike the ancient gilds in that they possessed no legal facilities for settling questions regarding production, prices and labor relations. They were suspected by some of the Roman rulers of being the cradle of unrestrained conspiracies, were suppressed for a time and then later restored. When Julius Caesar came to absolute power, most of the colleges were again suppressed.[1]

The Early Christian Era

The birth of Jesus Christ during the reign of Augustus Caesar and the subsequent decline and fall of the Roman Empire constituted significant events in world history. Roman industry consisted of craftsmen who made their wares and sold them directly to consumers. Plantation agriculture, known as *latifundia,* was dominant. These larger estates had resulted because the small farmers were unable to compete with large landowners and left for the urban centers. Other peasant proprietors surrendered their land to wealthy landlords in return for the right to remain on the land as tenants although rental payments had to be made to the landlords. In some cases, the peasant tenants were given small plots for their own use. Agricultural cooperation had no basis upon which to develop and expand. The only instances of cooperation during the Roman Empire came from the artisans. Because they were organized in colleges, some co-op features existed. Funerary expenses of members were paid from funds obtained by common subscription; in other words, the arrangement was that of burial cooperatives. These artisan colleges under the reign of Emperor Aurelian, about 275 A.D., were the forerunners of the modern consumer cooperatives.

The Emperor Constantine in 313 A.D. won control and gave sanctions to the Christians for the first time. The exact role of Jesus Christ's teachings with regard to economic democracy and cooperation is cause for speculation.

---

[1]Weigandt, Harry, "Use of Mutual and Co-op Techniques in Business," *American Cooperation,* A.I.C., Washington, D.C. 1949. pp. 126-150.

Economist Genung concluded in this vein:

It was Christ who, at the very pinnacle of Roman power, effectively challenged the age-old slavery system. What was this particular kernel of Christian teaching? That man is not a slave. That man is responsible to God, through his God-given conscience, and not to any master, ruler or government. That man is the creation of God and is endowed thereby with a dignity which neither master nor government may impugn.

What, then, did it mean when the ruler was forced to yield a measure of personal freedom to his subject? It meant that the man could come and go freely, could speak freely, could work for himself and for pay—*could own things.*

That was the very essence of personal freedom: one could enjoy the fruits of his own labor, could own property. Private property! It was that right to be his own master, to work for himself or sell his own labor for pay, to acquire things that should belong to him exclusively.

The dignity of the individual, as set forth by Christ, cannot be realized without a private property system. It does not exist today in Russia nor in any other slave state. Freedom and private property are inseparable. The basic human right in a free society is the right to use or sell one's own labor and enjoy the fruits thereof as his own property.

Which means, per se, a free market for goods and services.[2]

The Barbaric Age

When the Roman Empire disintegrated (about 475 A.D.), a power vacuum developed in Europe which resulted in a condition of more or less general lawlessness. Robbery and pillage became rampant in the thinly populated areas. As a matter of self-protection, people had to live in communities. Except for the few port towns, the basis of most of the communities was the manorial system, headed by the lords of the manors, and is generally spoken of as "feudalism."

The community organizations under the manorial system became quite standardized and relatively simple. The community was built around two central centers of power and authority: (1) the manor house and (2) the church. The lord of the manor controlled the

---

[2]Genung, A. B., *Christianity and Private Property*, G.L.F. Co-op Exchange, Ithaca, N.Y. Not dated.

economic relationships, subject to a generally accepted "regulation" by church law, and the priest dominated the religious and social relationships of the entire community, including settling all disputes and establishing the rules governing the community.

Subject to the limitations of church law, the lord of the manor ruled supreme, and his authority was seldom challenged. Except for a small entourage around the lord, all the other members of the community were serfs, who swore loyalty to the lord; served as soldiers when required in either defensive or offensive military activities; devoted a specified amount of time in personal service to the lord, in cultivating the land reserved by the lord, in tending his stock or in some other economic service. The lord also received a share of the products of the serfs' labor.

Under feudalism, accepted customs largely served as laws. Each manorial estate was a law unto itself, and such government as it had was in the nature of a hereditary monarchy in the person of the lord of the manor.

In the manner now practiced, there was then no private ownership of land among the common citizens. The lord reserved certain areas for his private use; the serfs were allowed an area on which to build the huts in which they lived. The other land that was under the control of the lord—forests, pasture land, streams for fishing and farming land—was available for common use by members of the manorial community.

Farming was the major economic enterprise, and it was generally conducted as a group operation, the products of which were divided on the basis of custom. In the later stages, individual serfs were allowed to cultivate certain specific areas, and the use of this land was passed on to the serfs' heirs. As long as they remained loyal serfs, this arrangement stayed in force; however, they could not sell this land to anyone. They could only use it on a basis customary for the manor. In effect, the land was all owned by the lord of the manor.

The manorial system predominated in most of Europe for roughly a thousand years—from the fifth century through the fourteenth century. However, in parts of Europe, notably in Russia, it lasted into the early part of the twentieth century.[3]

The medieval manor and serf system with some of its collective

---

[3]Mastin, Orville, *History of Economic Development,* Unpublished manuscript, Denver, Colo. 1961.

means of farming could be considered the precedent for the communist collective farms of today except that the state is now the landlord.

The Rise of Islam

The Islamic faith began about 600 A.D. under the prophet Muhammad. His dissatisfaction with the conduct of trade and business in and around Mecca inspired him to seek solitude and reflect on the real purposes of life. In such endeavors, Muhammad received supernatural instructions which were embodied in the *Koran,* or the Islamic bible. At least one part of the *Koran* holds significance relative to cooperation. Wealth, for the mere sake of wealth, was opposed as a matter of faith. Extension of aid to economically weak persons also became part of the faith. The essence of Islamic teachings certainly lent strong support to the co-op idea. The cooperative was also looked upon as a unifying institution to better the economic, social and political conditions in the community.

The Middle Ages

The *gild* during the Middle Ages (500 to 1400 A.D.) resembled the modern trade union, for it was an association of craftsmen for the achievement of specific objectives. The chief objective was to secure the position of member craftsmen. Prices, hours of labor and quality of output were carefully prescribed.

These gilds had their original roots in the Roman industrial colleges. Gilds afforded a center of social activities and maintained common funds which were drawn upon to pay funeral expenses of their members, allowances to those physically incapacitated and grants to widows for a period of two years.

In a sense, the gilds of the Middle Ages anticipated the modern consumer cooperatives.

During the Middle Ages, the first agricultural cooperative venture was in the thirteenth century, when Swiss dairymen were reported to have made cheese cooperatively.

The Renaissance Period

The Renaissance Period covered the years from the fifteenth to the middle of the eighteenth century, or the recovery period following the Middle Ages. The Commercial Revolution was an integral feature

FIGURE 3-2

Mutual fire insurance cooperatives date back to the 1530's in London and Paris. This modern insurance cooperative is in Paris, France. (Courtesy, National Federation of Consumer Cooperatives, Paris, France)

of the Renaissance. Perhaps the most important step during this period was the development of the joint stock company, predecessor of the modern day corporation. Joint stock companies developed because of the need for large sums of capital for voyages of exploration and colonization, such as those of Columbus.

In a joint stock company, each subscriber received shares of stock and profits in proportion to the capital he contributed. A charter was received from the King which fixed responsibility, clearly stated rights and obligations and, above all, extended the protection of government to the recipients.

Among the types of co-op ventures during the Commercial Revolution were the mutual fire insurance companies organized around 1530 in London and Paris.

The German "Landschaften" System (1767)

Another example of adversity and the need for cooperation is the origin of the Landschaften system of Germany, dating back to one of the most critical periods in the history of Prussia following the Seven

Years' War of 1756 to 1763. Serious injury had been inflicted on the general prosperity of the country, leaving the landowners (belonging to the nobility) in critical financial circumstances due to the devastations brought about by the war. Agriculture was in a disastrous state, and the landowners lacked the means to carry out any reconstruction due to the difficulties in the way of procuring necessary capital. Credit could only be obtained from private individuals at a high rate of interest. There were at that time no institutions that could act as intermediaries between landowners seeking credit and capitalists seeking investment for their money.

Proposals for the creation of a credit system made their appearance, but the first to draw up a scheme of land credit which would enable the nobles to obtain the loans they needed was a Berlin merchant, Diederich Ernst Buhring. On February 23, 1767, Buhring requested an audience with Frederick the Great of Prussia to lay before that monarch his plan which was based on the premise that land represented the best conceivable form of a sound negotiable security. This plan was approved. In order for the system to be initiated, it was necessary to create, with the approval of the state authorities and of the persons in need of credit, a credit association, which on the basis of land mortgaged in its favor, issued mortgage bonds or interest-bearing land bonds payable to bearer. All lands belonging to the nobility were blanketed with a perpetual lien in favor of the association as a general security for any debentures it might issue. This association of the landowning nobility, formed for the provision of credit, was constituted in accordance with co-op principles, and the individual landowner was thus to figure in the eyes of the investors as a member of the whole landowning aristocracy.

This German Landschaften system became the forerunner of the federal land bank system such as is used in the United States.

The Industrial Revolution

Following the Commercial Revolution and the Renaissance Period came the Industrial Revolution in about 1750 A.D. The essence of this revolution was technological advance. Agricultural and communication improvements, development of capitalism and emergence of the modern factory were the key features of the Industrial Revolution. The revolution brought expanded production and mechanization, lowered prices, increased consumption and raised living standards.

Civil and economic liberties were expanded; feudal estates with peasantry were challenged. Mercantilism was demolished; the doctrines of laissez faire and free competition were in the forefront. These economic gains were not without their costs. The factory system led to exploitation of workers, creation of many social problems and abandonment of agriculture geared to self-sufficiency. Economic cycles of inflation and deflation occurred. Unemployment often visited many homes. Industrial accidents were frequent. Class conflicts became sharper and more violent.

At this point, two schools of thought emerged concerning the best way to solve the problems of the Industrial Revolution. One believed that the whole capitalistic system upon which the Industrial Revolution was based should be over-thrown and replaced by a system controlled by the state. In this group could be found Karl Marx, Friedrich Engels, and others. The other group believed in preserving the system which had produced such great accomplishments and in making any necessary changes within the structure of the system. In this group could be found the co-op pioneers we know today—the Rochdale weavers, Friedrich Raiffeisen and others. This ideological struggle continues to this day.

Penny Capitalists.—The Penny Capitalists actually preceded the Rochdale society in England. In 1769, in the village of Fenwick in Ayrshire, Scotland, a small group of weavers attempted to conduct business on a co-op basis. It was one of the earliest attempts at cooperation—a purchasing association for domestic products and handicraft supplies.

Because it was the weavers' own business enterprise they endeavored to make all possible savings, and resentful shopkeepers called them "Penny Capitalists."

Later, in 1794, other associations were organized for the purpose of purchasing at the lowest possible price the primary needs of home consumption. Most if not all these early associations failed.

Between the Penny Capitalist association in 1769 and the subsequent Rochdale cooperative in 1844, from 400 to 500 other co-op societies were in existence. However, between 1834 and 1844, cooperation in England was at a low ebb due to the collapse of a trade union scheme involving the co-op societies themselves. Thus, the Rochdale group was the starting point of a more realistic co-op orientation.

FIGURE 3-3

The original Toad Lane store of the Rochdale Society where modern cooperation began. (Courtesy, Co-operative Union, Manchester, England)

Rochdale Equitable Pioneers' Society.—In 1844, the Rochdale group in England pioneered what was to become a truly co-op type of business organization. There were 28 persons in the original group, ranging from flannel weavers to shoemakers. They were individual craftsmen or entrepreneurs who came together on Toad Lane to purchase supplies and consumer goods cooperatively. The original subscription was one English pound for one share of stock. The Rochdale experiment was organized under the following plan:

> Charles Howarth is the man who was probably responsible for the first draft of the policies and aims of the Society. They were sufficiently comprehensive and they provided:
>
> 1. The establishment of a store for the sale of provisions and clothing.
>
> 2. The building of a number of houses in which those members desiring to assist each other in improving their domestic and social conditions may reside.
>
> 3. The manufacture of such articles as the Society may determine upon, for the employment of such members as may be without employment, or who may be suffering in consequence of repeated reductions in wages.
>
> 4. The purchase of estates of land which shall be cultivated by the members when out of employment.

5. As soon as practicable, this Society shall proceed
to arrange the powers of production, distribution, education
and government, in other words, to establish a self-supporting
home colony of united interests.
6. That, for the promotion of sobriety, a Temperance
Hotel be opened in one of the Society's houses as soon as
convenient.[4]

Characteristics of the early Rochdale Co-op Society may be
summarized as follows:

1. Grew out of a need caused by unemployment.
2. Financed by money saved by members themselves.
3. Store only opened two nights a week at first.
4. In 50 years it had grown to 12,000 members and
annual business of $1,500,000.
5. Succeeded because they [the members] profited
from other peoples' mistakes.
6. Was politically and religiously neutral.
7. Charged current prices to avoid price wars.
8. Insisted on cash trading.
9. Insisted on frequent and regular audits of the books.
10. Controlled by a board of directors, elected by the
members.
11. Each member was allowed but one vote in all
elections.
12. Members furnishing capital were paid 5 percent
interest.
13. Refunded profits by patronage dividend.
14. Spent money to educate members and others.
15. Were content to operate within the capitalistic
system.

A further discussion of these Rochdale Principles is reserved for
Chapter 9.

Although the Rochdale group began operating in 1844, it was not
until 1852 that the British Parliament passed the Industrial and
Provident Societies Act. This legislation provided for the incorporation
of societies such as Rochdale but did not limit the liability of shareholders. An amendment to the Act, passed in 1862, did provide limited
liability. Afterwards, the progress of cooperatives was much more
rapid in Great Britain.

The Rochdale-type cooperative was introduced in the United States

---

[4]Chase, Stuart, *The Story of Toad Lane,* Cooperative League, Chicago, Ill. Not
dated. pp. 10-11.

FIGURE 3-4

Shown here are 13 of the 28 original Rochdale organizers. Charles Howarth, seated behind the desk, was responsible for the first draft of the aims of the society. (Courtesy, Office of Agricultural Publications, University of California, Berkeley, Calif.)

in 1863 at Lawrence, Massachusetts, and in 1864 in Philadelphia with the organization of a consumer cooperative known as the Union Cooperative Association No. 1 which had 24 members. It failed in 1866.

So far, we have attempted to trace the efforts which preceded and included the Rochdale Co-op Society in England. After Rochdale came what is considered to be the "modern era" of cooperation. Events of this era are considered in subsequent sections and chapters (see also Table 3-1).

EVOLUTION OF THE COOPERATIVE IN THE UNITED STATES[5]

Colonial Period to the Civil War

The Colonists, upon arrival in America, attempted some forms of communal or collective farming. Within a short period of time, these

---

[5]The instructor may choose to supplement this section by discussing the development of cooperatives within a particular state, region, province or nation.

attempts were abandoned in favor of private cultivation and ownership of what was produced. However, this did not restrain the Colonists from erecting community defenses from Indian attacks and from assisting each other in numerous undertakings, such as in land clearing, harvesting, barn raising and in many other joint activities.

In 1752, Benjamin Franklin became perhaps the first American cooperator with the organization of a mutual insurance cooperative called the Philadelphia Contributionship for the Insurance of Houses from Loss by Fire.

FIGURE 3-5

Oldest mutual insurance company, Philadelphia Contributionship for the Insurance of Houses from Loss by Fire, issued this fire mark, one of the first of its kind.

In 1794, cordwainers in Baltimore, Maryland, organized a co-op boot and shoe factory which was the forerunner of what are now called "workers' productive cooperatives."

About 1810, two dairy cooperatives were formed which are thought to be the first formal farmers' associations organized in the United States. One cooperative was located at Goshen, Connecticut, and the other at South Trenton, New York. Following these, many different commodity cooperatives were organized throughout the Northeastern States, Cotton Belt, Upper Mississippi Valley and Far West. They were mutual benefit enterprises operating without the advantage of special legislation. While many were short-lived, a few are still in existence.

The first mutual savings banks in the United States were organized in 1816, in Boston and Philadelphia, by community leaders who sought

TABLE 3-1

Historical Evolution of the Cooperative

Evolution of the Cooperative	Main Period of Development	Nature of Development
Ancient Egyptian Era	3100 to 1150 B.C.	Craftsmen and artisan associations.
Babylonian Era	3000 to 540 B.C.	Co-op tenant farming.
Early Greek Era	3000 to 325 B.C.	Burial benefit and craftsmen's societies.
Ancient Chinese associations	200 B.C.	Loan societies.
Roman Era	510 B.C. to 475 A.D.	Burial benefit and craftsmen's societies.
Early Christian Era	1 to 313 A.D.	Artisan societies with burial benefits.
Barbaric Age	476 to 700 A.D.	Co-op development stifled.
Rise of Islam	600 to 1490 A.D.	Cooperation stressed as part of the faith.
Middle Ages	500 to 1400 A.D.	Gilds developed. Cheese-making cooperative formed.
Renaissance Period	1400 to 1750 A.D.	Joint stock companies organized.
Industrial Revolution	1750 to 1944 A.D.	Mutual fire associations were begun. Mercantilism was demolished. Capitalism evolved and became modified:
(a) Penny Capitalists	(a) 1769 A.D.	(a) Weavers organized a consumer cooperative.
(b) Rochdale Society	(b) 1844 A.D.	(b) Modern era of cooperation began with consumer cooperatives. Farm and credit cooperatives were early developments.
(c) Raiffeisen Credit Societies	(c) 1860 A.D.	(c) Consumer credit unions began to be developed.
Atomic and Space Age	1945 A.D. to present	Second century of cooperation began with increasing emphasis on business aspects. Cooperatives became much more significant.

to provide a safe repository—and an interest-paying one—for the small savings of the wage earner. At that time, most commercial banks did not accept savings deposits, and no other type of thrift institution existed.

In 1824, Robert Owen's famed New Harmony, Indiana, settlement was attempted in the United States with unsatisfactory results. The Brook Farm (Fourier) experiment followed in 1841, and it too failed.

The first urban savings and loan cooperative in the United States was the Oxford Provident Building Association organized in Philadelphia in 1831. This cooperative was the forerunner of the vast savings and loan associations of today. In 1845, one year after Rochdale, a consumer cooperative was formed in Boston called the Workingmen's Protective Union. This cooperative was the forerunner of consumer cooperation in the United States. Farmers' mutual fire insurance companies were also organized in the 1840's.

In 1842, the Mutual Life Insurance Company of New York was chartered, marking the beginning of mutual life insurance as it is known today. The first policy was issued February 1, 1843.

In 1857, a co-op wheat elevator was organized in Dane County, Illinois. Later, co-op grain elevators were to become a significant facet of farm cooperation in the United States.

As early as 1850, mutual irrigation associations were formed in Utah and California. By 1860, there were 83 such associations in those two states.

Post Civil War to World War I

After the Civil War, consumer prices rose rapidly. This encouraged the formation of several hundred consumer cooperatives in the Middle West and Northeast, but by 1870 most of them had disbanded. The business decline and unemployment during that period hurt consumer cooperatives. Another phase of co-op development was the workers' productive societies which by 1887 numbered 135. However, by 1890, few of them remained.

In 1871, the Chicago Printers Co-op Association existed which served some of the economic needs of several small printers. In 1877, a group of New York City druggists pooled some of their drug orders to reduce costs. These two cooperatives are considered to have been the first businessmen's cooperatives in the United States.

By 1890, many farmers' mutual fire insurance companies had been formed. Some of these original mutuals expanded into wider insurance coverage and still exist today.

Beginning in 1871, the National Grange became very active in organizing local co-op buying and selling clubs among farmers. The co-op activities sponsored by the Grange expanded rapidly, reached a peak in about 1877 and then declined rapidly. In 1877, the Grange had over 30,000 cooperatives, with a membership of 2,500,000. The Grange cooperatives deteriorated because they gradually lost their co-op character and passed into private hands due primarily to the lack of adequate co-op statutes. The real significance of the Granger

FIGURE 3-6
Oliver Kelley, founder of the National Grange. (Courtesy, National Grange, Washington, D.C.)

period of co-op development was that farmers were provided with a plan of organization and were given an opportunity to demonstrate the value of group action in marketing and purchasing. Oliver Kelley was founder of the Granger movement.

Between 1880 and 1890, scattered cooperatives for marketing farm products were organized. Some of them are still in existence. A few examples include: co-op elevators established at Marcus, Iowa, in 1887 and at Rockwell, Iowa, in 1889; fruit marketing cooperatives in California, Florida, New Jersey and New York; livestock marketing cooperatives in the Middle West; a wool growers' cooperative in Indiana; and a tobacco growers' cooperative in New England. By 1890, there were about 1,000 active farmer cooperatives. Over 700 of these were handling dairy products; about 100, grain; and about 100, fruits and vegetables.

Between 1890 and 1915, the number of active local cooperatives increased to more than 12,000. Two general farm organizations, the National Farmers Union and American Society for Equity, stimulated this growth. Cooperatives became established in nearly all states and for the handling of all major farm products.

Several regional co-op federations were organized during this period. Examples of some of the earliest regionals include: Sunkist Growers of California, 1895; Chautauqua and Erie Grape Growers Cooperative Association of New York, 1897; and the Farmers Grain Dealers Association of Iowa, 1904. Several other regional cooperatives that are still in operation were organized during the period from 1910 to 1920.

FIGURE 3-7

The Sunkist Growers Cooperative of today had its origin in 1895 in California. (Courtesy, Sunkist Growers, Los Angeles, Calif.)

The period between the Civil War and World War I also saw the adoption of co-op statutes by state legislative bodies. A mutual co-op fire insurance law was passed in New York in 1857. Michigan passed a law authorizing "the formation of mechanics' and laboring men's cooperatives" in 1865 and amended it to include agricultural cooperatives in 1875. Other states passing early co-op laws include: Massachusetts, 1866; New York, 1867; Pennsylvania, 1868; Connecticut, 1870; Minnesota, 1870; New Jersey, 1875; California, 1878; Tennessee, 1882;

Ohio, 1884; Kansas, 1887; and Wisconsin, 1887. California recognized nonstock cooperatives by a law enacted in 1895.

In 1887, cooperative buying by retail grocers began in Baltimore, Maryland, with the organization of the Baltimore Wholesale Grocery Company. In 1888, the Frankford Wholesale Grocery Co-op in Philadelphia was formed.

The first co-op apartment in the United States came into being in the early 1880's in New York City. It was an outgrowth of the consumer co-op movement which developed in Europe during the early part of the nineteenth century. One of the earliest housing cooperatives was formed in 1882 under the name of The Barrington Apartment Association, and stated its purpose as: "purchasing, acquiring and improving real estate for residences, homesteads and apartment houses, to be leased and conducted by the corporation so formed and occupied by the stockholders thereof and others, and apportioning and distributing the same among the stockholders and members of the company."

The development of credit unions began in 1909 in Manchester, New Hampshire, with the organization of a credit union with Roman Catholic parishioners. Alphonse Desjardins of Quebec helped organize the first credit union in the United States. Massachusetts passed the first credit union act in 1909.

Post World War I to the "New Deal" (1933)

The development of farmer cooperatives during this period fits logically into five areas:

1. *Reorganization and consolidation of local cooperatives.* During this period most local cooperatives were reorganized under more modern state laws. While the number of local cooperatives decreased, the total number of members and volume of business increased due to expansion of individual cooperatives and consolidation. As compared to co-op marketing, co-op purchasing became increasingly important.

2. *Organization and expansion of regional cooperatives.* A great many new regional cooperatives, both in the marketing and purchasing fields, organized during this period. Regionals not only expanded in size but extended their business activities into fields further removed from the farm, such as processing and manufacturing.

3. *Formation of state-wide and national organizations.* Many

organizations for co-op education, public relations and legislative activity organized during this period. Examples at the national level included the American Institute of Cooperation, National Council of Farmer Cooperatives, the National Federation of Grain Cooperatives and the Cooperative League. State organizations initiated in this period included state councils of farmer cooperatives in a majority of the states. In 1919, the American Farm Bureau Federation was organized by several state federations which were then prominent in co-op purchasing and marketing.

4. *Development of many new laws affecting farmer cooperatives.* The legal framework for the organization and operation of cooperatives was clarified and improved during this period. Four important federal legislative acts were passed. They were: the Federal Land Bank Legislation of 1916, the Capper-Volstead Act of 1922, the Cooperative Marketing Act of 1926 and the Agricultural Marketing Act of 1929.

The land-grant colleges performed a vital role during this period in helping to establish farmer cooperatives especially through county agents in the agricultural extension services.

During this period various co-op incorporation statutes were enacted in all of the states and several territorial possessions of the United States.

5. *Development of a nucleus of consumer cooperatives in the Lake Superior region, especially by Finnish and Swedish groups.* While consumer cooperation has never expanded on a grand scale, experiences with it have been good. In 1921, the Pioneer Mutual Life Insurance Company became the first mutual group to issue accident and health insurance.

During this period, the Hoover Administration relied heavily upon the Federal Farm Board as a way of solving the economic problems of agriculture. Aaron Sapiro had laid the groundwork for the Federal Farm Board with his zeal and diligence in promoting centralized commodity associations organized on a regional and sometimes national basis. By 1925, 74 centralized cooperatives, with 880,000 members, were in existence.

The Federal Farm Board was created in 1929 under the Agricultural Marketing Act, with a revolving fund of $500 million to help stabilize prices. Since the Board had no authority to control supply, its success was short-lived. The Board's work with cooperatives had

FIGURE 3-8

The American Institute of Cooperation, organized in the 1920's, is a university without a campus. It coordinates and promotes education in cooperation. *(Courtesy, A.I.C., Washington, D.C.)*

long-range implications, however. The section of the Farm Board Act dealing with cooperatives expressed the desire of Congress to encourage the organization of producers into effective associations or corporations under their own control for greater unity of effort in marketing by promoting the establishment and financing of a farm marketing system of producer-owned and producer-controlled cooperatives and other agencies.

From the "New Deal" to World War II

With the arrival of Franklin Roosevelt and the "New Deal" in 1933, federal legislation with regards to cooperatives became abundant. For example, the Rural Electrification Act was passed in 1936 to aid rural areas in obtaining electricity cooperatively. A federal credit union act was passed which permitted the federal chartering of credit unions. Provisions for short-term agricultural credit on a co-op basis were enacted into law in 1933. The federal government enabled farmers to procure short-term credit cooperatively, and cooperatives themselves were provided a co-op banking system. The Marketing Agreements

Act of 1937 enabled farmers to vote-in marketing orders aimed at facilitating the marketing of milk, fruits and vegetables, among other commodities.

The passage of the Labor Relations Act (Wagner Act) in 1935 gave trade unionism legalized status and permitted collective bargaining between employees and employers. The rise of trade unions has been a big factor in co-op development, especially in group health plans, consumer cooperatives, mutual insurance, credit unions and co-op housing. There have been instances also where trade unionists have bought factories from their employers and operated them cooperatively.

Also, in 1932, the first Blue Cross plan was tried in Sacramento, California, with a group of hospitals. This was followed in 1937 by the appointment of the Blue Cross Commission and in 1939 by the organization of the first Blue Shield-type plan in California.

The first artificial breeding cooperative was organized in New Jersey in 1938.

One "New Deal" experiment with cooperatives dealt with the Farm Security Administration. The F.S.A. program resulted in the formation of over 17,000 cooperatives composed of small, low-income farmers using cooperatives for purchasing and servicing functions.[6] Because these cooperatives were under-capitalized, were poorly managed and had insufficient volume, most of them disappeared after World War II. Congressional disapproval of various F.S.A. cooperatives was also a factor.

The Federal Housing Administration (FHA) Act, while co-insuring private home loans, also provided means for co-op housing projects.

The Federal Savings and Loan Insurance Corporation insured savings deposits in building and loan associations and thus protected the depositors, many of whose accounts were of a modest sum.

As a result of these and other legislative acts, credit union, electric and telephone, farm credit, housing and other cooperatives were made possible within the framework of the free enterprise system. Consequently, cooperatives in the United States are now well balanced between farm and urban groups, although the cooperation between these groups has not developed to any extent.

In one significant aspect, the "New Deal" did not foster cooperatives. This was in acreage allotments and price support programs.

---

[6]Landis, B. Y., A Cooperative Economy, Harper & Bros., New York, N.Y. 1943. p. 61.

Whereas the Hoover Administration had relied heavily upon the Federal Farm Board and large-scale commodity co-op operations for stabilization of agriculture, the "New Deal" rejected this approach. It moved more in the area of direct federal intervention in acreage, output, marketing and price controls over agriculture. In retrospect, this was perhaps a fatal mistake. The federal government might have been better off and society might have been better served if less federal intervention had occurred and greater reliance had been placed on farmers' purchasing, marketing and servicing associations. Of course, this question will never be settled, and opinions differ on the probable results.

Post World War II to the Present

Between 1945 and 1955 farmer cooperatives in the United States showed only moderate growth. Reasons for this included: (1) inflationary times made for "easy" and "cheap" money; (2) farm prices rose faster than costs, and thus net incomes were good; (3) growth of federal price support programs lessened the need for farmer cooperation; (4) migratory shifts in farm population caused re-arrangement of rural society, making co-op organization difficult; and (5) more vocal antagonism against farmer cooperatives arose, especially on the income tax issue.

Since 1955, farmer cooperatives have demonstrated a better rate of growth. The co-op idea re-established itself as costs rose faster than prices; government programs became disillusioning, and new farmer leadership emerged. According to the Farmer Cooperative Service, the values of co-op marketings have increased at a faster rate than those of agricultural marketings of all farmers since 1954. Since 1952, the values of farmers' acquisitions of supplies and equipment through cooperatives have also increased at a faster rate than expenditures for supplies and equipment of all farmers.[7]

In the field of consumer cooperation, credit unions have continued to make rapid and sound growth, and the limits to their expansion are not yet visible. The growth of co-op housing was another outstanding accomplishment during this period. In 1947, the Health Insurance Plan (HIP) of Greater New York was organized providing a group practice medical plan for New York City employees.

---

[7]Gardner, K. B. and Anne Gessner, *Trends in Growth of Farmer Cooperatives*, FCS Gen. Rept. 110, Washington, D.C. Mar. 1963. p. v.

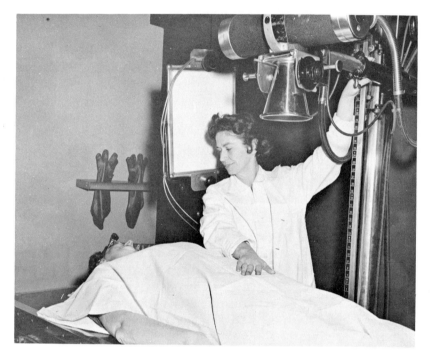

FIGURE 3-9

The Health Insurance Plan (HIP) of Greater New York provides many varied medical services for its patron-members on a self-help, voluntary basis. (Courtesy, Health Insurance Plan Co-operative, New York, N.Y.)

Perhaps the most significant co-op development since World War II has been the organization of retailer-owned wholesale cooperatives, such as co-op food, hardware, drug and lumber retailers. This development holds great potential for the future.

In summary, these trends in co-op development have become noticeable in the United States since World War II:

1. Increased use of highly skilled technical personnel as managers and employees.

2. Increased use of auxiliary departments in cooperatives (particularly in regionals) for servicing their main enterprises. Examples include auditing, traffic management, membership education, testing and laboratory services and marketing research.

3. Steady increase in co-op purchasing of farm supplies relative to co-op marketing of farm products.

4. Cooperatives, particularly regionals, adding more and more functions in the marketing system. Marketing cooperatives are processing farm products more completely and are carrying them nearer to the final consumer. Purchasing cooperatives are going into manufacturing and are carrying their activities nearer to the source of raw materials.[8]

5. Increased emphasis on farmers' bargaining cooperatives to enable farm groups to bargain more effectively with larger nonfarm buying groups.

6. The increased recognition given cooperatives by small businessmen. In earlier days, these men opposed cooperatives and regarded them as a threat. In recent years, they have come to see cooperatives as a bulwark against their possible liquidation and bankruptcy.

A more detailed discussion of the present scope of co-op activity in the United States is reserved for Chapters 6, 7 and 8.

In the next chapter, the important personalities in the development of cooperatives are considered.

TOPICS FOR DISCUSSION

1. Discuss the evolution of the cooperative during the Ancient Egyptian Era, the Babylonian Era, the Early Greek Era, the Ancient Chinese Era, the Roman Era, the Early Christian Era, the Barbaric Age, the Rise of Islam, the Middle Ages, the Renaissance and the Industrial Revolution.
2. Discuss the Penny Capitalists' and the Rochdale Pioneers' experiments.
3. Discuss the evolution of the cooperative in the United States from Colonial times to the present.
4. How have cooperatives fared in the United States since World War II?
5. Have farmer cooperatives kept pace with other agribusinesses during the last decade?

SELECTED REFERENCES

1. Adams, Herbert B., *History of Cooperation in the United States,* Johns Hopkins University, Baltimore, Md. 1888.
2. American Historical Association, *Why Co-ops?* Government Printing Office E.M. 23, Washington, D.C. Sept. 1944.

---

[8]Phillips, R. and others, *Do You Know Your Cooperative?* Iowa Institute of Cooperation, Ames Iowa. 1957. p. 32.

3. Bryngelsson, L. G., *A Survey of Consumer Cooperatives in the United States*, Ph.D. Thesis, City College of New York, New York, N.Y. 1941.
4. Cowling, Ellis, *Cooperatives in America*, Coward-McCann, Inc., New York, N.Y. 1938.
5. Landis, B. Y., *Bethlehem and Rochdale*, Cooperative League, Chicago, Ill. 1944.
6. Parker, Florence, *The First 125 Years*, Cooperative League, Chicago, Ill. 1956.
7. Scroggs, C. and M. A. Abrahamsen, *Agricultural Cooperation*, University of Minnesota Press, Minneapolis, Minn. 1957. pp. 3-56.
8. Staff, *Cooperation*, Wisc. Agr. Ext. Serv., Cir. 420, Madison, Wisc. Mar. 1952. pp. 20-47.
9. Staff, *Farmer Cooperatives in the United States*, FCS Bul. 1, USDA, Washington, D.C. Dec. 1955.
10. Warbasse, J. P., *The Cooperative Way*, Cooperative League, Chicago, Ill. 1946.
11. Watt, W. M., *Muhammad*, Oxford University Press, London, England. 1961.
12. Yaeger, J. F., *The First Thirty Years—Unico*, United Co-operatives, Inc., Alliance, Ohio. 1963.

CHAPTER 4 –

Important Personalities
in the Development
of Cooperatives

The people's welfare can best be secured by institutions organized by the people themselves, because these institutions are most likely to possess the characteristics that appeal to the people and therefore the stability necessary to perpetuate their services.

—Alphonse Desjardins
from Credit Union-North America,
Southern Publishers,
New York, N.Y.
1940. p. 81.

MANY PERSONS throughout the world have contributed to the development of cooperatives. Not everyone can be mentioned here. The selection of personalities presented in the following section is based on: (1) world-wide significance of their contribution to the co-op movement,[1] (2) uniqueness of their contribution and (3) permanency of their efforts.

CHARLES FOURIER (1772-1837)

Fourier was French, the son of a cloth merchant. During the Reign of Terror in France, he narrowly escaped the guillotine. During these troubled times, Fourier concentrated on the economic and social problems of the French people. As it was, Robert Owen, a contem-

---

[1] In this and other sections, the word *movement* is frequently used. The use of the word here denotes the "development of the co-op corporation." It does not mean, as used here, "a broad political foundation whose aims are to overthrow an existing system."

69

porary, was focusing on the ills of the Industrial Revolution in England at about the same time.

Fourier's proposals for reform consisted of many things, but essentially his plan was to organize communal associations covering three square miles each. These associations contained social centers, educational facilities and industry centers, among other things. Each member of an association had ownership of shares in the communal property. Fourierism was a plan for decentralizing large city populations and eliminating the attendant evils of urban life while escaping the isolation and drudgery of rural life at that time. There were to be, in essence, utopian communities.[2]

Fourier's plan was rather fantastic although it was tried in France, Holland and the United States—the Brook Farm near Cambridge, Massachusetts, and 40 other such utopian communities were organized and failed. Bad management, lack of funds and poor recruiting were responsible for the failure of these projects. Fourierism appealed to the many intellectuals of its originator's day and those subsequently. In a practical sense, his plan had little merit.

ROBERT OWEN (1771-1858)

Owen was born in Wales. At an early age he was made manager of a yarn mill. He later became wealthy in textile milling and other enterprises.

Owen's Co-op philosophy was not so wholesome as some writers have suggested. Owenism was more like socialism than true cooperation.

Owen developed the philosophy that the just price of a good was its cost. To charge more was unjust. Profits were the cause of overproduction and led to crisis. Money based upon the value of precious metals helped to confuse the relationship between the true values of goods in exchange. He advocated the organization of men in groups which should own and use in common all the instrumentalities of production necessary for the welfare of the members of each group. The ideal group, or community, should consist of from 500 to 3,000 people, placed on about 1,500 acres. All of the members of the community should live in one large quadrangular building, with public

[2]Bakken, H. H. and M. A. Schaars, *Economics of Cooperative Marketing*, McGraw-Hill, New York, N.Y. 1937. pp. 135-138.

kitchen and mess-room and with separate apartments for each family. The community should be mainly agricultural but should carry on a variety of occupations so as to be as nearly self-sufficing as possible. It should avail itself of the inventions, but without yielding to the factory system, and it should unite the advantages of country and town life. This system Owen eventually hoped would be embraced by the whole world.

At first his ideas were received with a good deal of favor, but this system tried both in England and America failed. Among such failures were the New Harmony Colony in Indiana and the Llano Colony near Leesville, Louisiana.

Owen did not accept the thesis that capitalistic cooperatives were

FIGURE 4-1

Robert Owen. (Courtesy, Co-operative Union, Manchester, England)

the true cooperatives. For example, he opposed the Rochdale Pioneers in 1844 whose principles later became the basis for capitalistic cooperatives. In commenting on the Rochdale co-op stores, Owen said:

> To my surprise I found their six or seven cooperative societies in different parts of the town, doing well, as they think, that is, making some profit by joint stock retail trading. It is, however, high time to put an end to the notion very

prevalent in the public mind that this is the social system which we contemplate, or that it will form any part of the arrangements in the New Moral World.[3]

In another instance, Owen said: "The trading associations that were buying and selling form no part of my cooperative scheme."[4]

Owen's legend in co-op history is difficult to analyze. Few of his principles were adopted; his social and economic reform plans failed.[5] One explanation for Owen's prominence in co-op literature is that he called attention to the abuses prevalent under capitalism. But, the remedies he proposed could have destroyed the system; therefore, his role in true cooperation has become tarnished.

N.F.S GRUNDTVIG (1783-1872)

Born in Denmark in 1783, Nikolai Frederick Severin Grundtvig studied theology and received his divinity degree in Copenhagen. His main contribution to cooperation was his inspiration for Danish folk schools which supply the enthusiasm for cooperatives in Denmark. These folk high schools provide a liberal education in literature, history and social economy. The basic background for successful cooperatives evolved from these schools, thus making Denmark one of the foremost co-op nations in the world.

Although Grundtvig himself did not formally organize Danish folk schools, he inspired Christen Kold and others in this organizational effort.[6]

LOUIS BLANC (1811-1882)

In 1848 at the age of 37, Louis Blanc, a Frenchman, proposed that industrial cooperatives be organized to alleviate the evils of the factory-type system in France and elsewhere. He deviated from the utopian, agrarian schemes of Fourier and Owen and insisted that workers own and control the tools, machines and other instruments of production. Realizing that workers would have difficulty in organ-

---

[3]Staff, *Cooperation*, Wisc. Agr. Ext. Serv., Circ. 420, Madison, Wisc. Mar. 1952. p. 34.
[4]Cole, Margaret, *Robert Owen of New Lanark*, Batchworth Press, London, England. 1953, p. 177.
[5]Owen did originate the co-op principle of a limited return on stock.
[6]Knudsen, J., *Danish Rebel*, Muhlenberg Press, Philadelphia, Pa. 1955. Ch. X.

izing these cooperatives, he advocated that government intervene and set up cooperatives and later withdraw when the workers became able to manage them. Blanc, therefore, was the father of the government-aid-to-cooperatives idea which has become so prevalent throughout the world. Blanc's thesis has been applied in the United States, for example, especially to the agricultural credit and rural electric cooperatives.[7]

HERMANN SCHULZE-DELITZSCH (1808-1883)

Hermann Schulze-Delitzsch was a German lawyer instrumental in organizing credit cooperatives for small businessmen, among other endeavors. He formed some 1,900 credit cooperatives in Germany during his lifetime. His organizing ability and zeal inspired Friedrich Raiffeisen to develop credit unions. Schulze-Delitzsch is also remembered as the founder of postal savings banks. In addition, he helped form consumer purchasing, accident, health insurance and, especially, wholesale buying cooperatives for small businessmen.

FIGURE 4-2
Hermann Schulze-Delitzsch (Courtesy, Central Union of German Consumers' Cooperative Societies, Hamburg, Germany)

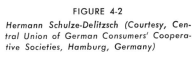

[7]Bakken and Schaars, *op. cit.* pp. 138-139, 141.

His basic economic beliefs concerning cooperatives were: (1) that patrons should control and capitalize their cooperatives, (2) that cooperatives should accept no charity and (3) that co-op growth should proceed slowly through self-help.

FRIEDRICH RAIFFEISEN (1818-1888)

The credit union idea was that of Raiffeisen, a German contemporary of Schulze-Delitzsch. Around 1860, economic conditions

FIGURE 4-3

Friedrich W. Raiffeisen. (Courtesy, Central Union of German Consumers' Cooperative Societies, Hamburg, Germany)

in Germany were catastrophic. The cities were crowded with unemployed. Men who before had been able to earn their bread with honest toil were reduced to begging, destitution and actual starvation. To make matters worse, a drought occurred and ruined two years' crops. In a desperate effort to keep their families together and continue living, these people had gotten themselves hopelessly in debt to usurious money lenders.

Raiffeisen, as Mayor of the country town of Flammersfeld, was desperate for a way to save his people from starvation. In the barren district of Westerwald, the usual meal that year was sauerkraut and a cup of chicory brew. The bits of dried-out land and the few starved animals the farmers had were most often forfeited to the money lenders. The people were in heavy debt which, together with the bad times, left them no way out. Raiffeisen appealed to the well-to-do of the community for financial help, but charity was merely a stop-gap.

Raiffeisen pondered over the problem for a long time and decided the only way was for the people to help themselves. So he set up his first credit union. His main idea was that only people who belonged to the credit union could borrow from it, that loans would be made only for provident and productive purposes, at low interest, and that a man's character was the most important security for his loan. He insisted that all the people in the credit union have a common bond of interest to hold them together. Credit unions throughout the world still operate on these principles today.

Raiffeisen traveled all over the country, talking with whomever he met about his new idea—in country inns, in the homes of the vil-- lagers, along the streets, with farmers in their fields. He shared the meager meals of the people, slept in hard beds, sacrificed his career, passed up financial gain and permanently ruined what little health he had left in order to spread the credit union idea. His name became a household word—throughout Germany he was known as "Father Raiffeisen"—and before he died he had organized 425 credit unions. Others carried on his work, and before the First World War, there were thousands of Raiffeisen banks flourishing in Germany.

Raiffeisen's fame has not been confined to Germany. In all parts of the world, credit unions are often referred to as the Raiffeisen credit societies. One significant principle which Raiffeisen also developed was the federation of local credit societies into a regional and hence into a national bank.

Raiffeisen is regarded as perhaps the foremost cooperator of all time.

ALPHONSE DESJARDINS (1854-1921)

Desjardins was born in the province of Quebec, Canada, in 1854. The matter of usury, or of charging high interest rates, gained his attention while working as a journalist. After making an exhaustive investigation of co-op credit systems in Europe, Desjardins established the credit union movement in Canada at Levis, Quebec, in 1900. For

FIGURE 4-4
Alphonse Desjardins. (Courtesy, Southern
Publishers, Kingsport, Tenn.)

his assistance in establishing 150 credit unions in cooperation with
the Catholic clergy, the Pope conferred knighthood upon him in 1913.

Desjardins was also instrumental in starting credit unions in the
United States. He assisted and inspired the first United States credit
union in Manchester, New Hampshire, in 1909.

SIR HORACE PLUNKETT (1854-1932)

Plunkett was born in Gloucestershire, Ireland, in 1854, the son of
Lord Doustany. During his youth, because of a frail constitution, he
emigrated to Wyoming where he became engaged in cattle ranching
and other farming pursuits. In 1889, he returned to Ireland to live
there permanently, although he made annual visits to the United
States thereafter.

The economic problems of the Irish farmers concerned him greatly,
and he endeavored to study the co-op method in the United States,
Western Europe and England. The Irish economic problems to which
he addressed himself were: (1) more land ownership for the farmers,
(2) better short-term credit, (3) more co-op marketing, (4) better
trained co-op personnel and (5) better agricultural education. These

problems were often confounded by religious and political differences which were reaching their peak at that time in Ireland.

Among his major accomplishments in Irish agricultural and co-op work were: (1) Head of the Irish Department of Agriculture for ten years; (2) sponsor of the Irish Agricultural Organization Society, which accounted for 1,000 co-op societies; (3) founder of the Horace Plunkett Foundation, which today serves as an educational agency for co-op development throughout the world; and (4) a member of Parliament for eight years.

Plunkett's work with agricultural cooperatives in Ireland centered

FIGURE 4-5
Horace Plunkett. (Courtesy, Basil Blackwell and Mott, Ltd., Oxford, England)

mostly around creamery cooperatives, although many other types also drew his attention and energy.

Although Plunkett was best known for his work in agricultural cooperatives, three other things should be mentioned: (1) his work in constructive administration as the creator of a new model of government in the field of agricultural and technical instruction, (2) his contribution to thought on the Irish political question and (3) his contribution to better Anglo-Irish-American relations.

Throughout his lifetime, Horace Plunkett was continually making contributions of great magnitude to both his home country and other countries. He fought ill health and much suffering through a long life. Through courage he almost always achieved his purpose, and he had the persistency to think things out. He sowed ideas in co-operation which are still growing.

E. A. FILENE (1860-1937)

Filene was an outstanding and successful businessman of Boston, Massachusetts. His business career was almost without parallel in the department store field. In later years, after taking exit from a business career, Filene took interest in the credit union movement. He became its most vigorous promoter in the United States, contributing more than $1 million in behalf of credit unions. Filene believed that the American of modest income could actually engage himself and his co-workers in a savings and loan business such as a credit union. He also believed that the credit union could not only teach economics to poor men but also could be an important cog in the credit wheel. Filene, who was adept in selecting able assistants, picked Roy F. Bergengren, a young Massachusetts lawyer, to aid in the organization and promotion of credit unions. This combination of leadership and zeal resulted in the formation of 2,200 credit unions in the United

FIGURE 4-6
E. A. Filene. (Courtesy, Credit Union National Association, Madison, Wisc.)

States by the year 1932.[8] It also resulted in the creation of CUNA, the Credit Union National Association, which is an educational agency.

Filene also believed in consumer cooperatives. He felt that the cost of distribution needed to be reduced similar to the economies achieved in mass production. Consumer cooperatives, in Filene's opinion, could provide one method of doing this job.

While many of his business associates did not share his ideas, Filene left an indelible mark upon what is today called "enlightened business management."

E. A. STOKDYK (1897-1946)

Stokdyk was born in Wisconsin of Dutch heritage. After graduating from high school with honors, he subsequently enrolled in the College of Agriculture at The University of Wisconsin. With a B.S. degree, he started his career as Extension Plant Pathologist at Kansas State College (now Kansas State University) in 1921.

During his first three years at Kansas State, Stokdyk made an impressive record in agricultural extension work as well as obtaining

FIGURE 4-7
E. A. Stokdyk. (Courtesy, Mrs. E. A. Stokdyk, Berkeley, Calif.)

[8]Johnson, Gerald W., *Liberal's Progress*, Coward-McCann, Inc., New York, N.Y. 1948. p. 217.

an M.S. degree in botany. In 1924, he shifted his extension work to agricultural marketing problems and likewise achieved recognition for his efforts in that field. Kansas State awarded him the Ph.D degree in 1929.

Because of his excellent scholastic abilities and knack for extension work, the University of California employed him as agricultural economist in 1929 to work particularly in co-op marketing. He stayed at that university four years, or until 1933, having distinguished himself in research and extension work and as an author and speaker.

With the enactment of the Farm Credit Act of 1933 and the establishment of the banks for cooperatives, Stokdyk was made president of the Berkeley, California, bank which serves California, Utah, Nevada and Arizona. After a five-year term in which he distinguished himself, Stokdyk took leave to become Deputy Governor of the Farm Credit Administration in Washington, D.C. At the end of 1939, he returned to the Berkeley Bank for Cooperatives as its president.

From 1940 to 1946, Stokdyk broadened the scope of his work by lecturing about cooperatives in various colleges, by helping to revitalize the American Institute of Cooperation and by providing a high degree of national leadership in co-op affairs. He became especially concerned with the poor image cooperatives displayed in the field of public relations.

Stokdyk made a strong impression on co-op developments in agriculture, not only in the western region, but throughout the United States as well.[9] He was a strong believer in the "pooling" and "revolving fund" methods used by co-op management. There is no doubt that Stokdyk would have contributed even more if his death had not come so soon, at the age of 49.

REV. M. M. COADY (1882-1959)

Father Coady was a native of the Margaree Valley of Nova Scotia, Canada. After graduating from the Urban College in Rome, he entered into teaching and organizational work. While meeting with a dozen or so adults in a community over a period of time, Father Coady was struck with the idea of merging adult education and co-op education. Consequently, this program of having mature citizens study

---

[9]Knapp, Joseph G., *E. A. Stokdyk—Architect of Cooperation*, American Institute of Cooperation, Washington, D.C. 1953.

FIGURE 4-8
Rev. M. M. Coady. (Courtesy, St. Francis Xavier University, Antigonish, Nova Scotia, Canada)

and learn together about cooperatives came to be known as the Antigonish Movement, named for the Diocese of Antigonish, Nova Scotia. The Antigonish Movement caused or had occasion to cause co-op organizations in the Maritime Provinces and in other parts of Canada. Cooperatives in such areas as fishing, farm supply, credit, marketing, consumer buying, processing, housing and insurance were organized through the efforts of Father Coady, A. B. MacDonald and Father J. J. Tompkins.

Among some of Father Coady's favorite expressions were these: "Poverty does not cause sin, but it may be a proximity for sin; therefore, if I must fight sin, I must also fight poverty." — "The people should become masters of their own destiny." — "Group action through cooperatives is the only way in which the people can still adhere to the principles of free enterprise while building a good society for themselves." — "Go home and find your lobster," meaning, "Tackle the problem nearest you."

Today, the St. Francis Xavier University and its Antigonish Movement are a mecca for cooperators throughout the world. The real significance of the Antigonish Movement was two-fold. It showed: (1) that people first have to understand their problems before a permanent solution can be found and (2) that poverty is no excuse for still further poverty. Self-help programs under the people's control could succeed.

AARON SAPIRO (1884-1959)

Sapiro was born in San Francisco, California, of the Jewish faith. He earned both a B.S. and M.S. degree at the University of Cincinnati. Later, Sapiro earned a law degree from the Hastings Law College at the University of California, graduating as valedictorian of his class.

Among his first jobs were those connected with the California Industrial Accident Board and the California State Market Bureau. Colonel Harris Weinstock, then head of the market bureau, had long taken an interest in Sapiro and had early recognized his speaking and organizing ability, his brilliant and analytical mind and his high character. It was Weinstock's idea that statewide marketing associations on a commodity basis needed to be organized in order to enhance farmers' bargaining power. Sapiro, as his legal counsel, rose to this occasion although Sapiro himself had no farm or co-op background.

During the years that he and others were organizing large-scale commodity marketing associations in California, Sapiro interested himself in all phases of their development. However, he specialized

FIGURE 4-9
Aaron Sapiro. (Courtesy, Wide World Photos)

in organizational structures and marketing contracts. This was to become the real source of his national and international fame.

He organized what was known as the Sapiro plan, or as we know it, the centralized-type of cooperative. It dispensed with the local association. The farmers became members directly of the centralized association through purchase of membership certificates or shares of stock and through signing long-term marketing contracts. Control and authority were centralized in the headquarters organization. Sapiro aimed at controlling such a large proportion of the market supply that cooperatives would have monopolistic power.

There was no better co-op organizer, speaker or lawyer than Sapiro in his era. In speaking to farmers, he reduced his economic philosophy to simple terms, namely, a monopolistic concept or enough control of the supply so as to fix or influence prices. While this concept was sound in theory, it became difficult to apply in practice with effectiveness.

His other contributions were in the realm of co-op financing and pooling schemes, adoption of uniform marketing statutes in various states and proper merchandising of farm produce all the way to market.

He dramatized the farmer's plight. He gave farmers the conception of doing things in a big way. Some of his economic thinking was naive, but his heart was in the right place. He was trying to develop equality for agriculture compared with other industries.

The major limitation of Sapiro-sponsored cooperatives was the lack of education which preceded their formation and the haste with which most were organized. Sapiro himself confessed to these limitations before his death in 1959.

Many of the Sapiro-type cooperatives still persist today in both the United States and Canada. For example, the Wheat Pools of Canada owe Sapiro a large measure of credit for inspiring this development. Sapiro would have to be termed the greatest single personality that farmer cooperatives have produced in the United States.

IVAN EMELIANOFF (1880-1960)

Emelianoff was born in Czarist Russia in 1880. He was educated in Russia, Yugoslavia and in the United States, receiving a doctorate of economics from Columbia University in New York. His career was varied. He was a professor of economics in Russian and Yugoslav universities as well as at Rutgers University in the United States. Ivan Emelianoff's experience with cooperatives dated back to 1917 to 1919 when he was a member of the Council of the Moscow Narodny Bank, the bank of 38,000 co-op organizations in pre-revolutionary Russia. He also served as president of a provincial bank and director of a co-op agency in London which served Russian cooperatives.

As a Russian who opposed the dominance of cooperatives by the state, his usefulness to the Communists was nil. For his Ph.D. thesis at Columbia University, Emelianoff composed his *Economic Theory of Cooperation*, which stands today as the most notable work in co-op theory. His experience with both state socialism and the free enterprise system provided him a unique background with which to cast properly the role of the cooperative in various economic systems. Emelianoff's strong defense of cooperatives within the capitalistic system was his greatest achievement. His exile from Russia gave him a better appreciation of capitalistic cooperatives as opposed to those Communist-dominated ones which he repudiated in his native land.

TOYOHIKO KAGAWA (1888-1960)

Kagawa was born in Kobe, Japan, the son of a parliamentary official. Both his parents died when he was four years old. At seventeen, his Buddhist uncle forced him to leave because Kagawa had adopted Christianity. He attended a Presbyterian college in Tokyo but withdrew when struck with tuberculosis. Isolating himself in the Tokyo slums, he remained eight years writing two books which drew attention to Japanese slum conditions, *Before the Dawn* and *Psychology of Poverty*. During his lifetime, Kagawa wrote more than 70 books.

In 1916, Kagawa came to the United States and attended Princeton Theological Seminary for two years. Upon his return to Japan, he organized both labor unions and farmer cooperatives, being responsible also for more friendly legislation toward Japanese labor unions.

Kagawa's subsequent achievements dealt with social welfare work; credit cooperatives; founding schools, hospitals and churches; and promoting a worldwide co-op movement for peace. He was twice president of the Japanese federation of consumer cooperatives.

In 1940, Kagawa was jailed by Japanese militarists because he opposed Japanese militarization and subsequent attack on the United

FIGURE 4-10
Toyohiko Kagawa. (Courtesy, Wide World Photos)

States. After World War II, he emerged as a key leader in the Japanese struggle for democracy.

In the next chapter, the worldwide status of cooperation is considered.

TOPICS FOR DISCUSSION

1. Discuss the main contributions of Fourier, Owen, Grundtvig and Blanc to the co-op idea.
2. Discuss the main contributions of the Germans, Schulze-Delitzsch and Raiffeisen, to co-op credit.
3. Discuss the work of Desjardins and Filene regarding credit unions.
4. What were Sir Horace Plunkett's contributions to cooperatives?
5. Discuss the religious roles played by Kagawa and Coady in co-op developments.
6. Discuss the roles played by Sapiro and Stokdyk in co-op marketing.
7. Discuss Emelianoff's contributions to the theory of cooperation.

SELECTED REFERENCES

1. Axling, William, Kagawa, Harper & Brothers, New York, N.Y. 1946.
2. Emelianoff, Ivan, Economic Theory of Cooperation, Edwards Bros., Ann Arbor, Mich. 1942.

3. Filene, E. A., *Next Step Forward in Retailing*, Kingsport Press, Kingsport, Tenn. 1937.
4. Franklin, Julia, *Selections from the Works of Fourier*, Sonnenschein & Co., London, England. 1901.
5. Holman, C. W., "Sir Horace Plunkett," *American Cooperation*, A.I.C., Washington, D.C. 1937. pp. 5-19.
6. Larson, Grace and H. E. Erdman, "Aaron Sapiro," *Mississippi Valley Historical Review*. Sept. 1962.
7. Loubere, Leo A., *Louis Blanc*, Northwestern University Press, Evanston, Ill. 1961.
8. Sapiro, Aaron, *Cooperative Marketing*, N.C. Agr. Ext. Cir. 110, Raleigh, N.C. July 1921.

CHAPTER 5 –

Cooperatives and
Their Worldwide Status

As fast as voluntary cooperation is abandoned, compulsory cooperation must be substituted.

—Herbert Spencer

In democratic countries the science of association is the mother of science; the progress of all the rest depends on the progress it has made. . . . If men are to remain civilized, or to become so, the art of associating must grow and improve.

—Alexis de Tocqueville

THERE ARE about 150 million persons in the world who are members of cooperatives. If we assume that each of these 150 million heads of households represent five persons, the total co-op family participation would be 750 million, or about 20 percent of the world's estimated 3.8 billion people.

The International Cooperative Alliance reports that, worldwide, co-op members belong to over 800,000 co-op societies. Co-op membership as a percentage of the population for various countries is estimated as follows:

Country	Co-op Members as Percentage of Population
Iceland	40.0
Finland	36.8
Denmark	31.7
Israel	29.0
Austria	27.6
Great Britain	25.4
Canada	18.8

Country	Co-op Members as Percentage of Population
Ireland	18.2
Cyprus	18.2
Sweden	17.7
France	13.8
Switzerland	13.8
Norway	11.3
United States	10.5
Italy	10.1

CANADA

Cooperation in Canada is primarily of two types: farmers' wheat pools in western Canada and credit unions and consumer cooperatives. Marketing cooperatives are considerably more important in Canada than are purchasing cooperatives, although the latter have been gaining rapidly in more recent years.

Local co-op associations in each of Canada's nine provinces have formed provincial associations or federations on a commodity-by-commodity basis. In turn, some of the provincial associations are affiliated into interprovincial associations.

The principal features of agricultural cooperation in Canada have been these:

1. Application of the principle of pooling, especially in selling grain.

2. Use of marketing contracts.

3. Organization on a commodity basis.[1]

The credit union movement in Canada in the provinces of Quebec and Nova Scotia has been among the most outstanding in the world. The influence of Alphonse Desjardins in Quebec and that of St. Francis Xavier University in Nova Scotia have contributed much to the co-op idea throughout the world. In particular, the adult education program of St. Francis Xavier with regards to co-op organization is outstanding. The heart of the program revolves around the premise that prospective cooperators need to be informed before the cooperative begins.

---

[1]Bakken, H. H. and Marvin Schaars, *Economics of Cooperative Marketing*, McGraw-Hill, New York, N.Y. 1937. p. 98.

FIGURE 5-1

In Canada, local associations have formed provincial federations which, in turn, have formed interprovincial associations as the one shown above. (Courtesy, Interprovincial Cooperatives, Ltd., Winnipeg, Manitoba, Canada)

Canadian cooperatives now number about 9,000, with a total membership of some 4.2 million members. About half of the co-operatives are credit, one-fifth are consumer and the balance are agricultural.

LATIN AMERICA

In 1948, there were 7,569 cooperatives in Latin America, with 2.3 million members. In 1963, their number more than doubled to 16,838, with a membership of over 5 million. *Brazil* reports 4,353 cooperatives; *Mexico*, 4,776; *Argentina*, 3,048. These three nations have about 90 per cent of the cooperatives in Latin America.

Among the more notable achievements are the Cooperative Cotia in Brazil and Puerto Rico Coffee Growers Cooperative. *Uruguay* and *Costa Rica* also have good marketing cooperatives.[2]

In *Chile*, a cooperative collected $200,000 from its members over a three-year period and proceeded to develop a housing and consumer co-op center. These and other co-op beginnings hold much promise for the people of Chile and other Latin American nations.

In *Puerto Rico*, there are 350 cooperatives, with a membership of over 130,000. Marketing cooperatives are very prominent.

In *Argentina*, the fourth largest wheat-exporting nation, local co-op

---

[2]Chaves, Fernando, "Latin American Co-ops," *News for Farmer Cooperatives*, Washington, D.C. June 1961.

FIGURE 5-2

Credit unions hold considerable promise in Latin America. Here a co-op member makes a deposit in a Peruvian credit union. (Courtesy, Farmer Cooperative Service, Washington, D.C.)

elevators exist, but no national federation. Cotton and dairy cooperatives are also present.

In *Peru,* over 200 credit union societies have developed largely through the efforts of the Catholic Church and some of its clergy, such as Father Dan McClellan. These credit unions have also led to housing cooperatives.

Mexico has made some noticeable strides in co-op organization in recent years, especially in marketing. It has also practiced a pseudo-cooperative type of farming on the Mexican *ejidos*. When these large estates were appropriated, they were made self-governing through elected committees and officers. Members farm the property collectively and are paid wages according to skill plus a share in the profits. The peasants live in single dwellings on a community-type basis. Some *ejidos* provide for individual plots and cultivation. Because illiteracy has been high on the Mexican *ejidos*, the National Bank of Ejido Credit in Mexico has served as a credit, technical and social advisor to the peasant groups.[3]

FIGURE 5-3

Potatoes are harvested at Chambi, Bolivia, where the people, with guidance from experts attached to the Phillapi project, have formed their own cooperative. (Courtesy, International Labour Office, Geneva, Switzerland)

[3]Digby, Margaret, *The World Cooperative Movement*, Hutchinson & Co., London, England. 1960. pp. 143-144.

FIGURE 5-4

Mexican villagers purchasing poultry feed at the depot of the Lake Patzcuaro Poultry Association, a village cooperative. (Courtesy, Food and Agriculture Organization, United Nations, N.Y.)

Co-op development in Latin America will probably increase substantially in the future as various countries seek ways and means of alleviating economic distress.

NORTHERN EUROPE

The five nations in this area are Denmark, Finland, Norway, Sweden and Iceland. This is probably the most highly developed, cooperatively speaking, of any area in the world. Practically every type of co-op organization possible has been utilized at some time or other. These

FIGURE 5-5

Rural electric cooperatives are greatly needed in Latin America. Here a workman in El Salvador fixes insulators to a transmission tower carrying power for new industries. (Courtesy, The World Bank, Washington, D.C.)

FIGURE 5-6

This modern department store in central Finland is one link of the co-op department store chain which covers the whole country. (Courtesy, Finnish Cooperative Wholesale Society, Helsinki, Finland)

countries are agricultural with some industrialization and a relatively high standard of living.

Denmark is a land of many small farms; thus the farmers have relied upon co-op businesses to expand the scope and scale of their farming activities. Danish co-op business societies consist of various commodity marketing associations, consumer stores, purchasing cooperatives and credit unions, among others. Cooperatives in Denmark are characterized by rather unique features, such as the fact that (1) each member must bear unlimited liability; (2) no incorporation is made; (3) cooperatives are organized on a commodity basis, and thus one person may belong to several cooperatives; (4) the use of membership contracts is universal; (5) the use of the nonstock cooperative predominates; (6) the system of pooling is universally adopted; and (7) education in cooperation is wide-spread. The Danish consumer cooperatives, with 2,000 locals, have a large membership, a close link with farmers' organizations and high sales per member, with a large proportion of the populace in consumer cooperatives.[4]

The *Finns* have the second highest percentage of the total popu-

---

[4]*Ibid.* p. 58.

lation in cooperatives. In a predominantly rural country, cooperatives play a significant role. Purchasing, credit, insurance, processing and sales associations comprise the bulk of Finnish cooperation. Dairy marketing cooperatives are particularly strong. Unlike Danish cooperatives, those in Finland trend more toward being multi-purpose, or combining marketing, purchasing and credit functions within one cooperative. Finland is also known for its co-op bus services, ferries and telephone service. The strong Finnish consumer cooperatives have their own wholesale society and some manufacturing facilities plus a co-op college for the instruction of co-op staffs. Finland, Norway and Denmark also jointly own the Scandinavian Wholesale Co-op Society, which purchases foreign goods on behalf of the member wholesale societies.[5] Finnish emigrants to the United States have played a large role in various co-op enterprises.

In *Norway*, cooperatives are somewhat less important than in other Northern European nations. The more significant ones are those for purchasing, processing and marketing. Milk and egg marketing cooperatives are especially prominent. Consumer cooperatives are quite strong. About one-third of Norway's population buys some foodstuffs at co-op stores. Fishery cooperatives are important also. Operating under federal marketing boards, they procure supplies, market fish and insure their vessels and engines cooperatively. Housing cooperatives are also important, comprising about 20 per cent of the national housing.

Swedish cooperatives have long been upheld as models representing what is often referred to as the "Middle Way."[6]

In agriculture, milk cooperatives predominate. In addition, cooperatives in poultry, forest products, livestock and fruit are common. Harmonious relations have existed between agricultural and consumer cooperatives.

It is in the field of consumer cooperation that Swedish cooperatives are strongest. Perhaps one factor in this strength has been the Swedish co-op policy of lowering prices at time of sale rather than charging the regular price and giving a patronage dividend later.

The most significant aspect of Swedish consumer cooperation is its *Kooperativa Forbundet*. This cooperative has deliberately chosen

---

[5]*Ibid.* p. 164.
[6]A term made famous by Marquis Childs, meaning a mixture of co-op and government enterprise, plus profit-type institutions.

FIGURE 5-7

A modern Swedish consumer co-op store. (Courtesy, Kooperativa Forbundet, Stockholm, Sweden)

expansion into commodities exhibiting monopolistic tendencies and has proceeded, on many occasions, to counteract these monopolies. It has over 1 million members out of the 7 million Swedish population.[7] Swedish emigrants to the United States have also played a significant role in American cooperation.

A summary of the extent of agricultural cooperation in the Northern European countries is shown in Table 5-1.

TABLE 5-1
Percentage of Agricultural Products Handled by Cooperatives in Northern Europe, 1960

	Denmark	Finland	Norway	Sweden
Milk	91	95	100	98
Cattle	45	70	59	83
Pigs	88	1	1	1
Eggs	40	54	67	65
Grain	—	30	2	70
Fertilizers	41	52	65	60
Feeding-stuffs	58	60	—	—
Machines	—	53	28	50

[1] No data.
[2] State-monopoly.
Source: International Federation of Agricultural
    Producers, Washington, D.C.

---

[7]Digby, *op. cit.* p. 58.

Iceland is the foremost co-op nation in the world. Its co-op activities are found in the fishing industry, consumer goods and services, farmers' purchasing and marketing, among other lines. The strongest feature of Icelandic cooperation is the uniting of local societies into one giant co-op federation capable of conducting manufacturing and foreign trade activities.

WESTERN EUROPE

The principal countries of Western Europe are Belgium, France, Spain, Holland, West Germany, Italy, Switzerland and Austria.

In *Belgium,* industrial workers have formed the nucleus for consumer cooperation. The local cooperatives are federated into a national society which acts as a wholesaler-supplier, promotes co-op education, provides benevolent services and is politically aligned with the Belgium Labour Party. Other features of Belgian co-operation are the agricultural credit and small entrepreneurial credit banks.

The *Dutch* cooperatives are particularly prominent in cheesemaking associations, agricultural credit and co-op auctions for the sale of perishable produce. Consumer cooperation is organized around the middle class of that country.

In *Spain,* the Civil War of the 1930's severely disrupted co-op developments. When the Fascists gained control, the consumer co-op movement, which had oriented itself to the left-wing, suffered much opposition. Other cooperatives not politically involved fared better. Digby cites the especially fine co-op achievements of the Spanish fishery cooperatives. This federation of local cooperatives has become highly integrated and performs a wide range of economic and social functions in behalf of Spanish fishermen. In the last few years, Spanish cooperatives have been gaining momentum and receiving less interference from the state.

In *Germany* and now *West Germany,* consumer cooperation began formally around 1890. It made wide-spread and vigorous growth until 1933 when Adolf Hitler came to power. The Nazis appropriated the consumer cooperatives for their own militaristic schemes, and the co-op structure was shattered. After World War II, the Allied Military Governments were receptive to the consumer cooperatives, and much of the pre-war achievements have been recovered. Attempts to develop liaison with consumer cooperatives in Communist East Germany have failed.

Credit and agricultural supply cooperatives are also important in West Germany. Both short-term and long-term credit societies originated in Germany. Raiffeisen and Schulze-Delitzsch developed short-term credit cooperatives while Buhring developed the Landschaften or land banks. The world owes much of its co-op credit success to these three German co-op pioneers.

Austria experienced the same war catastrophe as did Germany, and

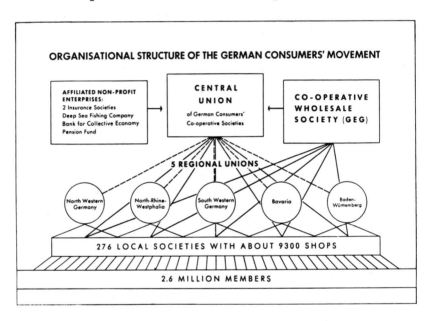

FIGURE 5-8

The German consumers' movement was re-established after World War II and is making fine progress. (Courtesy, Central Union of German Consumers' Cooperative Societies, Hamburg, Germany)

its co-op history is similar. Consumer cooperatives have been revitalized, and co-op housing has made some progress.

In *Switzerland,* cooperatives have been the beneficiary of the peaceful history of that country. In agriculture, co-op milk marketing is outstanding. There exists many joint relationships between agricultural and consumer cooperatives, such as in fluid milk marketing. One large agricultural co-op federation is engaged in purchasing supplies, marketing products and providing other services. In the service field can be found cooperatives engaged in insurance, credit and electric power, among others. Consumer cooperation is highly developed much on the same pattern and scale as in Scandinavia.

Italy experienced the same Fascistic take-over of cooperatives as did Germany. Although many of them retained their democratic structure, state domination was extensive. Much of this domination was accomplished by abolishing the boards of directors and installing managers appointed by the Fascist authorities. After World War II, however, the revival of true cooperation was relatively easy. The Italian consumer cooperatives have regained their pre-war achievements, although the movement is split into left- and right-wing factions. In agriculture, dairy and credit societies predominate. Credit banks for small entrepreneurs also exist. Two unique features of Italian cooperation are: (1) workers' productive cooperatives and (2) land cooperatives. The workers' cooperatives comprise craftsmen and highly skilled tradesmen who own and operate their own shops, factories or plants. After wages are paid, profits are divided on a mutual basis. The land cooperatives are an attempt by farmers to retain individual ownership of land while performing cultivation, harvesting, drainage and other functions cooperatively.

In *France*, cooperation has reached a high stage of development. In agriculture, dairy marketing cooperatives handle about half the production of French milk, both in fluid form and in processed dairy products. There are over 1,000 grain marketing cooperatives, with a membership of 1 million. Various wine associations perform finished-product marketing, storage or pressing functions, and some provide all of these. Agricultural credit societies on a local basis are federated into regional banks which provide credit facilities to French farmers. The American federal farm banking system resembles the French structure.

Consumer cooperation in France has a long history dating back to 1885. Both World Wars I and II set back the consumer cooperatives, but each time they have been re-organized and at present are strong. Because France is a rather large and diverse nation, regional federations developed, and these, in turn, united into a national federation. These consumer co-op federations provide consumer goods, educational and benevolent services, among other things.

The organization of trade workers and craftsmen into workers' cooperatives has been a special trait of French cooperation going back to Louis Blanc. Skilled tradesmen form a cooperative, establish a factory or plant, pay themselves wages according to some agreed-upon

FIGURE 5-9

A co-op super market in Saint Denis, France. (Courtesy, National Federation of Consumers' Cooperatives, Paris, France)

formula and divide the profits or losses among themselves. This type of cooperative differs from those in which each craftsman stays in his individual shop and cooperates with neighboring craftsmen in buying and selling.[8]

GREAT BRITAIN AND IRELAND

The *Irish* co-op movement produced an outstanding leader, Sir Horace Plunkett. Much has been done to promote cooperative creameries. Other Irish cooperatives are multi-purpose, marketing various farm products and selling farm and home supplies. There are relatively few consumer cooperatives. Credit societies are more numerous.[9]

Due to some hostility on the part of the Irish government, creamery cooperatives have lost some of their importance and are turning to wool marketing, livestock auction markets and farm supplies. It is their hope that these added functions will make up for the ground lost in milk marketing.[10]

In *Great Britain,* which includes England, Wales and Scotland,

[8]*Ibid.* p. 70.
[9]Bakken and Schaars, *op. cit.* pp. 99-101.
[10]Digby, *op. cit.* p. 117.

consumer cooperation is the outstanding feature of co-op development. Since the pioneer Rochdale Society of 1844, consumer cooperatives have increased in number to around 1,000, with a membership of 12 million, 25 percent of the entire population. The local consumer cooperatives handle groceries, meats, drapery, house furnishings, hardware, drugs and optical goods, among other items. Local societies are federated into two national societies, the British Cooperative Wholesale Society and the Scottish Cooperative Wholesale Society. These, in turn, cooperate in many undertakings. Together they own a total of 230 factories, with 75,000 employees, thereby manufacturing and processing many of the requirements of the two societies. Despite the great strides in British consumer cooperation, the retail societies handle only 15 percent of the grocery and 6 percent of the clothing and footwear retail volume in Britain.[11]

FIGURE 5-10

A co-op hardware and appliance store operated by the Dover Society. (Courtesy, Co-operative Union, Manchester, England)

[11]*Ibid.* p. 35.

Another strong aspect of British cooperation is the agricultural supply cooperatives, of which some perform marketing functions. Perhaps the weakest link in British cooperation is in the credit field. For example, no credit unions exist despite the fact that the British themselves were instrumental in credit union development in India. Agricultural credit societies are also rare. It was only in 1958 that a national agricultural credit organization was established through the efforts of the British Cooperative Wholesale Society and a group of large agricultural cooperatives.

THE MIDDLE EAST

Greece, Israel, Turkey and Egypt have experienced various phases of co-op development. In *Greece*, 8,800 agricultural credit societies, farm supply purchasing associations and marketing cooperatives predominate, with less emphasis on consumer and greater emphasis on credit cooperatives.

In *Israel*, there are about 2,600 cooperatives of various types. The labor co-op sector of the Israeli economy, in terms of the number of people it directly employs, conducts almost two-thirds of Israel's agriculture, a third of its building and public works, nearly a quarter of the industry and crafts and equally impressive proportions of the country's transport; communications; maritime industry; commerce, finance and insurance business; and various public services.

There are three main types of agricultural co-op settlement in Israel, all of which are alike with respect to basic co-op organization, but each of which makes its own specific contribution to co-op practice. The three types of settlement are: (1) the Kibbutz or collective settlement, (2) the Moshav or co-op smallholders' settlement and (3) the Moshav Shitufi, which combines the leading features of the other two types. Each individual settlement in Israel is registered as a co-op society, and each bears the triple aspect of a producers' cooperative, a marketing cooperative and a consumers' cooperative.[12]

Cooperation in *Egypt* in modern times began in 1909 under the leadership of Omar Loutfy. The passage of co-op acts in 1923 and 1927 aided co-op development.[13] When the Nasser government took

---

[12]Malkosh, Noel, *Cooperation in Israel*, General Federation of Labor (Histadrut), Tel Aviv, Israel. 1962. pp. 2-3, 27.
[13]Bakken and Schaars, *op. cit.* p. 107.

FIGURE 5-11
An annual meeting of a co-op society in Egypt. *(Courtesy, Co-operative Union, Manchester, England)*

charge in the 1950's, much federal resource was allocated to co-op development in agriculture, especially. While the Egyptian government concedes that federal control over the land reform cooperatives is apparent, the long-range goal is to withdraw this aid and permit the co-op members to manage their own affairs. Other types of cooperatives have traditionally had more managerial freedom. There are now about 4,300 cooperatives in Egypt, with a membership of 1 million. Of these, about 3,400 are agricultural and 250 consumer, and the balance involve various other co-op activities.

In *Turkey*, there are 2,100 cooperatives, with a membership of 1.25 million. Consumer associations are important. Government paternalism, as in Egypt, is expected to diminish as these cooperatives gain maturity. *Cyprus* and *Jordan* have some good co-op organizations. *Iran* and *Iraq* are making progress in their co-op development. Iran has a sound consumer co-op organization. It also has over 1,000 rural co-op societies.

AFRICA[14]

There are an estimated 13,300 cooperatives in Africa, with a total membership of 1.7 million members. The leading countries in terms of number of cooperatives are: Nigeria, Tunisia, the Cameroons, Uganda, Ivory Coast, Tanganyika, Algeria, Kenya, Union of South Africa, Ghana and the Sudan.

---

[14]Excluding Egypt, discussed under the Middle East section.

FIGURE 5-12

A village cooperative in Egypt owns and operates a threshing machine cooperatively. (Courtesy, Co-operative Union, Manchester, England)

The most important type of cooperative in Africa is engaged in the marketing, and sometimes processing, of agricultural produce. In many cases, too, supply and credit functions are linked with the marketing cooperatives, at least at the village level. There are a number of national or provincial co-op banks. Consumers' cooperation has been singularly unsuccessful in Africa. Co-op housing has had success in East Africa. Co-op insurance is successful in a few countries. A good foundation has been established for co-op methods, and the future holds considerable promise for their further development.[15]

INDIA

The most important phase of Indian cooperation is the Raiffeisen credit societies. In 1904, credit acts were passed allowing such credit societies to develop. There are now 150,000 village credit unions, with a membership of 10 million, yet only 5 percent of the rural Indian population is being served. Since deposits from the Indian villagers are meager, funds from provincial banks and the Reserve Bank of India must supplement. Other types of cooperatives consist of fluid milk marketing (in the larger cities), grain marketing, irrigation and some

---

[15]Staff, *The Cooperative Movement in Africa*, U.N. Economic and Social Council, United Nations, N.Y. Mar. 1962. pp. 2-3.

local consumer cooperatives. Workers' cooperatives for craftsmen engaged in making expensive shawls and brocades are also found. Digby reports that co-op consolidation of small land plots among certain villages has provided more efficient means of cultivation and raised productivity.[16]

FIGURE 5-13

A co-op society in Tanganyika helps celebrate its nation's Independence Day (Courtesy, Co-operative Union, Manchester, England)

The Indian government continues to support vigorously its co-op development program.

PAKISTAN

Cooperatives are significant in Pakistan. They include co-op banks, consumers' cooperatives, housing associations, farmers' and fishermen's

---

[16]Digby, op. cit. p. 164.

FIGURE 5-14

The Kaira District Cooperative Milk Producers' Union in India not only aids Indian farmers but also helps provide free milk to children in need. (Courtesy, Food and Agriculture Organization, United Nations, N.Y.)

cooperatives. In the future, co-op development is expected to increase.

THE FAR EAST

The countries included here are South Viet Nam, Ceylon, Thailand, Japan, Malaya, Burma, Formosa, the Philippines, Indonesia, and South Korea. Agricultural credit cooperatives are very prominent in Burma, Malaya, Thailand, Indonesia, the. Philippines, Ceylon and Formosa. Urban credit cooperatives are especially strong in Malaya. Consumer purchasing cooperatives are prominent in Ceylon, Malaya and Thailand. Marketing associations for various farm commodities are important in Thailand, Indonesia and the Philippines. Farm supply cooperatives are noted in Formosa, while fishermen's cooperatives are prominent in South Viet Nam and Hong Kong.

In *Japan,* cooperatives have had a long tradition. The Japanese militarists during World War II interfered with them, but the American occupational government under General MacArthur did much to restore cooperatives in Japan. Cooperation in Japan is strong in farm supplies (fertilizer), marketing of rice and raw silk, credit, consumer

FIGURE 5-15

This co-op society in Malaya is paying out its patronage refunds to members. (Courtesy, International Cooperative Alliance, London, England)

purchasing and fishermen's cooperatives. The co-op federated system predominates. There are some 11,000 farm cooperatives.

AUSTRALIA AND NEW ZEALAND

In *Australia,* co-op marketing predominates for exportable farm products, such as wool, wheat and dairy products. Through the use of "marketing boards," Australian producers voted upon themselves compulsory pooling, such as for eggs, wheat and other commodities. This continued up to the 1930's. World War II brought a return to the Australian Wheat Board and compulsory national marketing with the farmer cooperatives merely acting as agents.[17] Relations between Australian and English cooperatives in export-import trade have been good.

---

[17]*Ibid.* p. 131.

Consumer and farm supply cooperatives in Australia are well linked. Dairy marketing cooperatives predominate in *New Zealand*. Others for fruit, honey and wheat are also in existence. A considerable amount of the co-op meat and dairy output is destined for consumer cooperatives in Great Britain.

THE COMMUNIST BLOC

The nations in the Communist Bloc include all of Eastern Europe, Russia, China, Cuba, North Korea and various other satellite nations.

In Chapter 1 it was pointed out that the so-called cooperatives in the Communist Bloc nations are not cooperatives at all but arms of the state. The term *cooperative* is used by Communists to dignify their state enterprises with a respectable connotation. The official literature of the Communist Bloc nations concerning their so-called *cooperatives* is of questionable reliability. A summary of what transpires in a communist economy can be gleaned from the situation in East Germany:

FIGURE 5-16

In Thailand, workers are busy at the Napradoo Cooperative Rubber Factory. (Courtesy, Food and Agriculture Organization, United Nations, N.Y.)

The consumers' society in East Germany no longer pretends to be politically neutral. It openly supports communism and all important leaders are Communists. All important decisions and actions are ordered and directed by the Communist party and its instrument, the state. The consumers' society has lost its internal autonomy as well as its freedom of action. It has become the obedient servant of the Communist State.[18]

FIGURE 5-17

Technicians of local farmer cooperatives in Japan band together and visit members' farms, repairing their farm machinery. (Courtesy, Co-operative Union, Manchester, England)

Any omission of certain countries in the preceding sections does not imply that there are no co-op developments therein. Often, reports of co-op activity are slowly incorporated in the literature on cooperation.

[18]Hasselmann, E., *Consumers' Cooperatives in Germany*, Central Union of German Consumers' Cooperative Societies, Hamburg, Germany. Jan. 1961. p. 61.

In the next chapter, the scope of cooperation in the United States of America is considered.

TOPICS FOR DISCUSSION

1. Discuss the co-op developments in North, Central and South America.
2. What is the future for cooperatives in Latin America?
3. Why do the countries of Northern Europe lead the world in percentage of total business done cooperatively?
4. How have the Finns and Swedes, in particular, helped co-op development in the United States of America?
5. Discuss cooperation in Western Europe. How well have cooperatives in West Germany and Italy recovered from Fascist rule?
6. What lasting influence has the Rochdale Society had on co-op developments in Great Britain and the world?
7. Why do cooperatives hold so much promise in the Middle East, Africa and the Far East?
8. Discuss the fallacy of the so-called communist cooperatives.

SELECTED REFERENCES

1. Campbell, W. K. H., *Practical Cooperation in Asia and Africa*, W. Heffer & Sons, Cambridge, England. 1951.
2. Dankers, W. H., *Report of a Survey and Study Tour in Western Europe*, Minn. Agr. Ext. Serv., St. Paul, Minn. Sept. 1958.
3. Gorst, Sheila, *Cooperative Organization in the Tropical Countries*, Blackwell, Oxford, England. 1959.
4. Heckman, John and Anna Wheeler, *Agricultural Cooperation in Western Europe: Parts A, B, C,* FCS Gen. Rept. 4, USDA, Washington, D.C. June 1955.
5. Heikkila, R., *Finland—the Land of Cooperatives*, Institute of Cooperation, Helsinki, Finland. 1963.
6. Hough, Eleanor, *The Cooperative Movement in India*, Oxford University Press, London, England. 1959.
7. Staff, *Cooperatives in Canada*, Canada Dept. of Agri. Publ. 1119, Ottawa, Canada. Apr. 1962.
8. Staff, "Cooperatives in Other Lands," *News for Farmer Cooperatives*, FCS, USDA, Washington, D.C. Mar. 1958.
9. Staff, *Mission to India*, Nationwide Insurance Co., Columbus, Ohio. Feb. 1962.
10. Staff, *Report of Inquiry on Cooperative Enterprise in Europe*, Government Printing Office, Washington, D.C. 1937.
11. Valko, Laszlo, *Cooperative Ideas in the Eastern and Western Worlds*, Dept. of Agr. Eco., Washington State College (now Washington State University), Pullman, Wash. 1951.
12. Velie, Lester, "The Money Miracle of Father Dan," *Reader's Digest*. Apr. 1961. pp. 169-176.

CHAPTER 6 —

Scope of Cooperation
in the United States
of America

Cooperation is the means by which free men solve problems or tackle jobs too big for the individual.
—Dwight D. Eisenhower

Cooperative and mutual business has been a very important and constructive part of our free economy ever since Benjamin Franklin organized the first mutual insurance company in Philadelphia in 1752. It is one of the finest expressions of the American spirit. Here groups of people, faced with common needs, invest their capital and organize their own cooperatives to meet these needs. This is self-help at its best.
—John F. Kennedy

ACCORDING TO the Cooperative League, approximately 10 million families of a total of 52 million families in the United States own stock in publicly held, profit-type corporations. It is conservatively estimated that between 15 to 20 million families in the United States own co-op shares or investments. Thus, possibly twice as many families are involved in co-op ownership as in publicly traded, profit-type corporate ownership.

However, the dollar values of these respective investments are not in the same proportion. Investments in profit-type corporations far exceed investments in cooperatives, although precise data are not available.

In Tables 6-1 through 6-5 are presented data concerning the type and number of "true" and "quasi" cooperatives and total co-op memberships in the United States. A "true" cooperative is one which limits returns on capital; votes on the basis of one man, one vote and/or on patronage; and allocates all net earnings to its member-patrons. A "quasi" cooperative is one which meets at least one of these conditions but does not meet all three in a full and acceptable manner.

TYPES OF COOPERATIVES

The different types of cooperatives are grouped as follows: (1) agricultural producer cooperatives, (2) consumer-owned and operated cooperatives, (3) business-industrial associations, (4) workers' productive associations and (5) quasi cooperatives.

Agricultural Producer Cooperatives

The agricultural producer cooperatives number about 25,000 and account for about 32 percent of all cooperatives in the United States. The service cooperatives comprise over one-third of the agricultural

TABLE 6-1

Number of Cooperatives and Co-op Memberships,
Agricultural Cooperatives, United States

Type of Cooperatives	No. of Cooperatives		Co-op Memberships
Agricultural bargaining[1]	325		390,000
Agricultural credit:	2,090		1,136,280
Banks for cooperatives[1]		13	2,500[2]
Credit corporations[3]		21	[4]
Federal land banks[1]		779	379,940
Production credit associations[1]		487	518,840
Rural credit unions[1]		790	235,000
Agricultural marketing[1]	5,626		3,431,360
Agricultural services:	11,462		1,159,579
Artificial breeding[1]		47	675,000
Dairy herd improvement assoc.[1]		1,436	42,034
Grazing[5]		1,436	31,071
Irrigation[1]		7,729	161,679
Miscellaneous[5 6]		814	249,795
Farmers' fire mutuals[1]	1,600		3,000,000
Farm supply cooperatives[1]	3,206		3,634,690
Fishery marketing[5]	87		10,673
Indian enterprises[5]	219		12,520
Total	24,615		[7]

[1]Farmer Cooperative Service, USDA, Washington, D.C., and other sources.
[2]These 2,500 cooperatives serve 3,725,000 farmers.
[3]Farm Credit Administration, USDA, Washington, D.C.
[4]Data not available.
[5]Departments of Interior and Agriculture, Washington, D.C.
[6]Includes trucking, ginning, storing, grinding, freezing and other services.
[7]Memberships cannot be added due to duplications since one farmer may be a member of several cooperatives.

cooperatives. Marketing and farm supply cooperatives are next in importance (Tables 6-1 and 6-5).

In membership, the marketing cooperatives lead, followed by farm supply and credit. The 1959 Census of Agriculture reports 3.7 million farmers in the United States, yet the marketing cooperatives report a membership of about 3.4 million. This is because many farmers belong to more than one marketing cooperative as well as to other farmer cooperatives.

The twelve states with the largest number of farmer cooperatives are, in order of their importance: Minnesota, Wisconsin, Iowa, Texas, North Dakota, Illinois, California, New York, Nebraska, Kansas, South Dakota and Ohio. These twelve states have about two-thirds of all the farmer cooperatives in the United States.

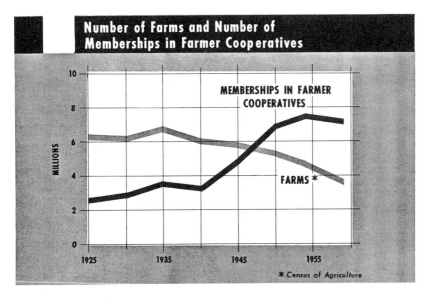

FIGURE 6-1

Although the number of farms and farmers is declining in the United States, membership in farmer cooperatives has increased. Therefore, the percentage of all farmers in cooperatives has risen considerably. (Courtesy, USDA, Washington, D.C.)

Farmer cooperatives have shown a generally upward trend in their relative importance in agriculture and the nation's economy since 1954. Since that year the value of products marketed by farmers through their cooperatives has increased at a faster rate than the value of agricultural

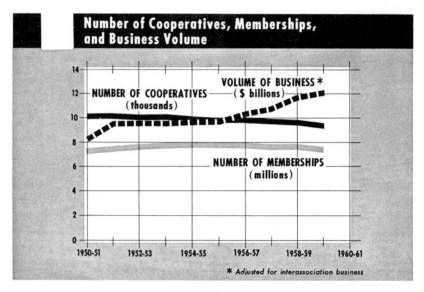

FIGURE 6-2
(Courtesy, USDA, Washington, D.C.)

FIGURE 6-3
(Courtesy, Agricultural Council of California, Sacramento, Calif.)

marketings of all farmers. Likewise, since 1952 the value of supplies and equipment that farmers purchase through their cooperatives has increased at a faster rate than similar expenditures of all farmers.

The index of co-op marketings rose rather steadily from 81.4 in 1950-51 to 119.4 in 1959-60. This is based on a 10-year average of net values of products marketed cooperatively, not including business between cooperatives. During the same period, the index of cash receipts of all farmers moved from 92.2 to 107.2 and showed numerous deviations.

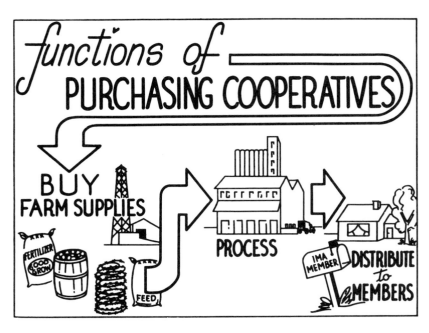

FIGURE 6-4
(Courtesy, Agricultural Council of California, Sacramento, Calif.)

Nine of 12 commodity groups showed improvement when their indexes of cooperative marketings were compared with corresponding indexes of cash receipts of all farmers from marketings of similar commodities. These nine groups included: cotton and its products, dairy products, fruits and vegetables, grain (including soybeans), nuts, poultry products, rice, sugar products and tobacco.

The three groups that showed little change were beans and peas (dry edible), livestock and livestock products and wool and mohair.[1]

The index for net values of farm supplies and equipment purchased through farmer cooperatives followed a similar pattern, rising from 81.1 in 1950-51 to 115.9 in 1959-60. Cash expenditures of all farmers showed less consistent growth. This index increased, with numerous deviations, from 101.3 in 1951 to a high of 110.2 in 1959 and then dropped to 106.6 in 1960.

Of the eight groups of farm supplies and equipment included in the analysis, cooperatives have made significant growth in six groups in recent years in relation to indexes of cash expenditures of all farmers for supplies and equipment. These six groups are: building materials, containers, fertilizer, petroleum products, seeds and sprays and dusts. Feed and farm machinery and equipment did not show such a consistently favorable position in recent years.[2]

Proportion of Supply Volume Purchased by Cooperative Patrons in Each Geographic Area, 1956-57

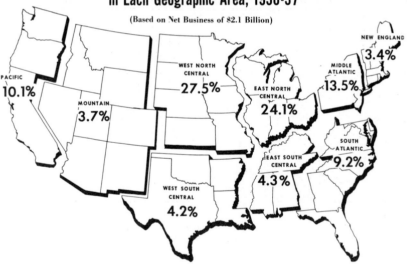

(Based on Net Business of $2.1 Billion)

NEW ENGLAND
3.4%

WEST NORTH CENTRAL
27.5%

MIDDLE ATLANTIC
13.5%

PACIFIC
10.1%

EAST NORTH CENTRAL
24.1%

MOUNTAIN
3.7%

SOUTH ATLANTIC
9.2%

EAST SOUTH CENTRAL
4.3%

WEST SOUTH CENTRAL
4.2%

FIGURE 6-5

Farmer cooperatives in the West and East North Central regions account for about half of all the co-op farm supply business done in the United States. (Courtesy, USDA, Washington, D.C.)

---

[1]Gardner, K. B. and Anne Gessner, *Trends in Growth of Farmer Cooperatives, 1950-60*, FCS Gen. Rept. 110, Washington, D.C. Mar. 1963.
[2]*Ibid.*

Proportion of Cooperative Marketing Volume Originating in Each Geographic Area, 1956-57

(Based on Net Business of $8.0 Billion)

FIGURE 6-6

Farmer cooperatives in the West and East North Central and Pacific regions account for about 65 percent of all the co-op marketing business done in the United States. (Courtesy, USDA, Washington, D.C.)

In 1961-62 farm marketing cooperatives did $10.2 billion in business; farm supply, $2.6 billion; and service, $302 million.

Various types of farmer cooperatives are discussed in the next chapter.

Consumer-owned and Operated Cooperatives

Of the over 77,000 cooperatives in the United States, about one-half are consumer-owned and operated (Tables 6-2 and 6-5). They constitute the largest single bloc of cooperatives. Over half of the consumer cooperatives are urban credit unions. Next in importance are mutual savings and loan associations, followed by mutual telephone associations and mutual insurances. Other important types are housing associations, consumer stores, rural electric cooperatives and mutual savings banks.

Proportion of Service Revenue Originating in Each Geographic Area, 1956-57

(Based on Total Revenue of $235 Million)

FIGURE 6-7

Farmer cooperatives in the West North Central, Pacific and West South Central regions account for about two-thirds of the co-op service revenues obtained in the United States. (Courtesy, USDA, Washington, D.C.)

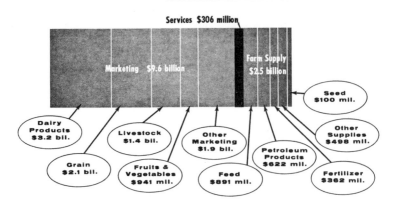

FIGURE 6-8

Marketing of farm products constitutes a far greater business volume than do farm supplies or services rendered. (Courtesy, Farmer Cooperative Service, Washington, D.C.)

TABLE 6-2
Number of Cooperatives and Co-op Memberships, Consumer Cooperatives, United States

Type of Cooperative	No. of Cooperatives	Co-op Memberships
College students[1]	500	50,000
Consumer stores[1]	1,050	750,000
Credit unions, urban[2]	20,710	14,065,000
Group health plans[1]	178	4,552,000
Housing associations[3][4]	1,334	120,000
Memorial associations[1]	100	100,000
Mutual insurances, co-op[1]	9	11,000,000
Mutual insurances, other[5]	2,600	[10]
Mutual life insurance, other[5]	158	67,200,000
Mutual savings and loan[6]	5,758	27,500,000
Mutual savings banks[7]	515	22,593,000
Mutual telephone[1]	3,630	500,000
Nursery schools[8]	820	24,600
Rural electric[1][9]	986	4,422,000
Utility cooperatives, other	[10]	[10]
Total	38,348	[11]

[1]Cooperative League of the U.S.A., Chicago, Ill.
[2]Credit Union National Association, Madison, Wisc.
[3]Foundation for Co-op Housing, New York, N.Y.
[4]*Statistical Abstract of the United States: 1962.*
[5]Insurance Information Institute, New York, N.Y.
[6]U.S. Savings and Loan League, Chicago, Ill.
[7]National Association of Mutual Savings Banks, New York, N.Y.
[8]American Council on Parent Co-ops, Pointe Claire, Quebec, Canada.
[9]National Rural Electric Cooperative Association, Washington, D.C.
[10]Data not available.
[11]Memberships cannot be added due to duplications.

Between 1951 and 1962, credit unions made a very rapid growth. They almost doubled in number, more than doubled their membership and increased their loan volume more than six times.

Mutual savings and loan and housing associations and mutual insurances also showed rapid growth during this period. This trend is continuing. There is also more interest in mutual telephone associations. Consumer stores, while not increasing very rapidly in number, have modernized their facilities and are demonstrating much vitality in certain key cities in the United States. Rural electric cooperatives continue to expand services to their membership.

Consumer cooperatives are discussed further in the next chapter.

Business-Industrial Associations

Data on business service and industrial cooperatives are obtained largely from the 1958 Census of Business. Certain limitations are apparent in these data, however: (1) The number of co-op establishments is reported rather than the number of co-op associations. In many cases, a co-op association may operate more than one establishment. (2) The number of firms in a cooperative is not reported by the Census of Business. This has to be estimated from various trade sources.

Nevertheless, over 6,000 business-industrial groups exist, which accounts for about 9 percent of the cooperatives in the United States. Approximately 600,000 firms belong to these groups, an average of about 100 firms per group (Tables 6-3 and 6-5).

Of the business-industrial associations operated cooperatively, about half are of the business service type. Almost half are wholesale cooperatives owned by retail firms. The remainder are nonfarm manufacturing and export associations (Table 6-3).

The growth rate, in these types of cooperatives, has been better for the co-op wholesales and business service groups than it has for the nonfarm manufacturing groups. The retailer-owned grocery co-op wholesales, in particular, have made an outstanding record. A further discussion of these cooperatives is given in Chapter 8.

Workers' Productive Associations

Unlike in the European countries, workers' productive cooperatives have never been too important in the United States. There was great interest in them before 1900 and again in the 1930's during the depression. At present, there are only about 12 such associations in the United States (Table 6-3).

A workers' productive association differs from a labor union in many ways. In a workers' cooperative, the workers are both the owners of and laborers in the plant. In a labor union, the workers do not own the plant but instead bargain with the owners over wages and working conditions. Labor unions are not considered as cooperatives because they represent employees, not employers. However, union members are important segments of consumer cooperatives.

A further discussion of workers' cooperatives is reserved for Chapter 8.

Quasi Cooperatives

There are an estimated 8,000 quasi cooperatives in the United States, or about 10 percent of all cooperatives in the United States (Tables 6-4

TABLE 6-3
Number of Cooperatives and Co-op Memberships, Business and Worker Cooperatives, United States

Type of Cooperative	No. of Cooperatives		Co-op Memberships
Business services[1][2][3]	3,359		505,787
Nonfarm manufacturing[3][4][5]	712		3,288
Retailer-owned wholesales[3][6]	2,478		82,932
Appliances, TV and radio		14	574
Automotive, all types		46	920
Drugs		26	10,000
Furniture and furnishings		24	2,400
Gasoline and petroleum		1,752	5,256
Grocery		262	45,000
Hardware		15	3,500
Lumber and building materials		55	5,500
Others[7]		284	9,782
Webb-Pomerene Associations[8]	30		296
Total	6,579		[9]
Workers' productive associations[10]	12		[11]
Total	12		[11]

[1]*Census of Business: Selected Services: 1958*, Government Printing Office, Washington, D.C. pp. 5-2 to 5-14.
[2]Includes advertising; office services and maintenance; news syndicates; employment agencies; research, development and testing laboratories; detective and protective agencies; management services; credit extension and credit bureaus; bank clearing houses; stock exchanges; transport and delivery cooperatives.
[3]Data also obtained from various trade associations and trade journals.
[4]*Census of Manufacturers: Summary Statistics: 1958*, Government Printing Office, Washington, D.C. 1961. pp. 3-2 to 3-55.
[5]Includes textiles and apparel; wood and wood products; printing and publishing; chemicals and allied products; building materials; metals and mining; machinery and equipment; and sales and marketing, among others.
[6]*Census of Business: Summary Statistics, Wholesalers: 1958*, Government Printing Office, Washington, D.C. 1961.
[7]Includes dry goods, apparel, footwear; bakery; various machinery and equipment; business and industrial supplies; chemical and wood products, among others.
[8]Federal Trade Commission, Washington, D.C.
[9]Memberships cannot be added due to duplications.
[10]Department of Labor and AFL-CIO, Washington, D.C. 1962.
[11]Data not available.

and 6-5). Quasi cooperatives are those which have at least one of the three basic co-op features but not all three, namely: (1) vote by one man, one vote or on patronage, (2) limit returns on invested capital and (3) allocate net earnings to member-patrons according to patronage. The principal deficiency of quasi cooperatives rests in voting procedures. Often, members are not given full and complete control over the organizations. However, conditions vary greatly among quasi cooperatives. Some are much closer to "true" cooperation than are others.

FIGURE 6-9

Blue Cross and Blue Shield plans provide millions of Americans with hospital and surgical-cost health protection on a privately operated basis. (Courtesy, National Association of Blue Shield Plans, Chicago, Ill.)

TABLE 6-4
Number of Cooperatives and Memberships, Quasi Cooperatives, United States

Type of Quasi Cooperative	Number	Memberships
Blue Cross associations[1][2]	77	57,408,000
Blue Shield plans[1][2]	69	47,095,000
Consumer rebate plans	8	[8]
Discount stores, closed-door[2][3]	47	3,500,000
Elementary and high schools[2][4]	587	151,937
Hospitals, nonprofit, private[5]	4,140	393,000[9]
Mutual funds[6]	170	5,300,000[10]
Soil conservation districts[7]	2,900	1,081,368
Others	10	[8]
Total	8,000	[11]

[1]Statistical Abstract of the United States: 1962.
[2]Data from trade associations.
[3]Fairchild Publications, New York, N.Y.
[4]Private Schools, Porter Sargent, Boston, Mass. 1961.
[5]Public Health Service, Washington, D.C., Vol. 7, Nov. 1961.
[6]Investment Company Institute, New York, N.Y.
[7]Soil Conservation Service, USDA, Washington, D.C.
[8]Data not available.
[9]Bed capacity only.
[10]Number of accounts only; individuals owning shares not known.
[11]Memberships cannot be added due to duplications.

The net effect of belonging to a "quasi" cooperative, however, is sometimes equal to belonging to a "true" cooperative. The Blue Cross and Blue Shield plans are good examples of how quasi cooperatives can contribute materially to the citizenry.

A further discussion of each type of quasi cooperative is reserved for Chapter 8.[3]

In the next chapter, agricultural and consumer cooperatives are discussed.

TABLE 6-5
Number of "True" and "Quasi" Cooperatives, by Groups,
United States

Group	Number	Percent of Total
Agricultural producer	24,615	31.7
Consumer-owned	38,348	49.4
Business, nonfarm	6,579	8.5
Workers' societies	12	.1
Quasi cooperatives	8,000	10.3
Total	77,554	100.0

Source: Tables 6-1 through 6-4.

TOPICS FOR DISCUSSION

1. Discuss the scope of agricultural producer cooperatives. What has been the trend in their growth?
2. Discuss the scope of consumer cooperatives. What has been the growth trend for them?
3. Discuss the scope of business and industrial cooperatives. Which type of co-op wholesale has demonstrated the fastest growth?
4. Discuss workers' cooperatives. Why are there so few such cooperatives in the United States?
5. Discuss quasi cooperatives. Why are they called "quasi"?

SELECTED REFERENCES

1. Lee, Henry, "Capitalists with the Common Touch," *Coronet*. Dec. 1960. pp. 128-132.
2. Phillips, C. F. and D. J. Duncan, *Marketing*, R. D. Irwin, Homewood, Ill. 1952. pp. 209, 223, 330 and 439.

---

[3]The instructor may, at this point, elect to discuss the status of cooperation in a respective community, county, state, province, nation or hemisphere.

3. Staff, *The Cooperative Movement and Present Day Problems*, International Labor Organization, Montreal, Canada. 1945.

4. Staff, *Cooperatives*, U.S.A., Cooperative League, Chicago, Ill. 1962.

5. Staff, *Health Insurance Data Sourcebook*, Health Insurance Institute, New York, N.Y. 1962.

6. Staff, *Rural Cooperatives in the United States*, Dept. of State, A. I. D., Washington, D.C. Apr. 1963.

7. Voorhis, Jerry, *American Cooperatives*, Harper & Brothers, New York, N.Y. 1961.

8. Weigandt, Harry, "Use of Mutual and Cooperative Techniques in Business Organization," *American Cooperation*, A. I. C., Washington, D.C. 1949. pp. 126-150.

CHAPTER 7 –

Agricultural and Consumer Cooperatives in the United States of America

Farmer cooperatives contribute to the material and spiritual prosperity of agriculture as well as to the total national economy. Farmer cooperatives, both large and small, are simply organizations of individual farmers which carry on essential functions needed by our farmers and by our society as a whole. Farmer cooperatives enjoy no special privileges or favors denied by law to any other group or organization which may elect to accept the same restrictions that are self-imposed by the members of cooperatives.

—J. G. Knapp,
Farmer Cooperative Service
Info. Leaflet 37, Washington,
D.C. Apr. 1963. pp. 2-3.

A cooperative is a business that's owned by its customers. It can be almost any kind of a business—a super market, an apartment building, a telephone system, an electric utility, a service station, an insurance company, a farm supply store, a grain elevator, a nursery school, a hospital and clinic. The important fact is—it's owned by its customers.

—Cooperatives, U.S.A.,
Cooperative League, Chicago,
Ill. 1963. p. 4.

TWO GROUPS OF COOPERATIVES are discussed in this chapter—the agricultural and consumer cooperatives. The agricultural group comprises about 32 percent and the consumer group 49 percent of all the cooperatives in the United States of America.

Part I

AGRICULTURAL COOPERATIVES

There are over 24,000 agricultural cooperatives in the United States. Each type of agricultural cooperative is discussed in some detail.

The service-type cooperatives number over 11,000; marketing, 5,600; supply, 3,200; credit, 2,100; and fire mutuals, 1,600. These are the principal types.

AGRICULTURAL BARGAINING
ASSOCIATIONS

There are about 325 agricultural bargaining associations in the United States organized on a co-op basis. These include 25 fruit bargaining co-op associations, 20 vegetable bargaining associations and 20 state Farm Bureau bargaining associations affiliated with the American Agricultural Marketing Association, an American Farm Bureau Federation subsidiary.[1] The other 260 bargaining associations are for milk, eggs, broiler chickens and sugar beets.

The Farmer Cooperative Service estimates that there are 9,500 farmer-members in fruit bargaining associations and 10,500 in vegetable bargaining associations.[2] There are an estimated 220,000 farmer-members in the other associations.

These bargaining associations are designed to bargain collectively with processors and dealers in these respective commodities. Items subject to negotiation usually include prices, method and time of payment, delivery conditions, grades, sizes and other related matters.

National Farmers Organization (NFO)

In addition to the associations discussed, there is the large National Farmers Organization (NFO) of Corning, Iowa. The NFO group has an estimated membership of 150,000 farmers.[3]

As previously mentioned, the main purpose of farmers' bargaining associations is to negotiate for prices and other marketing conditions with processors, buyers or handlers of farm produce. Unlike labor unions, which have the protection of the Wagner Act in collective bargaining, farmers' bargaining associations have relatively no legal compulsory power over produce buyers in bargaining collectively.

---

[1]Staff, *Proceedings of the 6th National Conference on Fruit and Vegetable Bargaining Cooperatives*, FCS, USDA, Washington, D.C. Jan. 1962. pp. 52-58.
[2]October 12, 1962, communication with Farmer Cooperative Service.
[3]Estimated from various trade sources. NFO has not released data on memberships.

A farmers' bargaining association must depend primarily on economic rather than legal persuasion.[4]

The NFO, unlike other farm bargaining groups, has resorted to supply withholding as a means of forcing collective bargaining on the part of produce buyers. Although temporary gains have been demonstrated by these tactics, the long-run gains are problematical.

Swanton summarizes the NFO objectives as follows:

> They would stabilize future prices by having sufficient production signed under a membership agreement so that processors cannot deal with farmers as individuals. Mere withholding of farm products from the market on the broad scale proposed is in line with union procedure and tactics. Such a program in the long-run could play into the hands of union organizers.[5]

If the Wagner Act were made to cover agricultural producers, collective bargaining by farmers with processors and buyers would no doubt accelerate. While the Capper-Volstead Act sanctions the interstate operation of bargaining cooperatives, it provides no legal cloak for farmers to bargain collectively with processors and other buyers. Despite various handicaps, farmers' bargaining associations promise to become more important in the future.

AGRICULTURAL CREDIT COOPERATIVES

There are some 2,090 agricultural credit cooperatives in the United States. These consist of 779 federal land bank associations, 790 rural credit unions, 487 production credit associations, 13 banks for cooperatives and 21 agricultural credit corporations.

Membership in these cooperatives totals about 1,136,000 farmers, although many farmers are members of two or more credit associations. However, of the 2,500 cooperatives served by the banks for cooperatives, another 3,725,000 farmers are indirectly benefited. Loans made to the 2,500 cooperatives aid individual farmer-members of these associations.

The co-op credit system in the United States is the marvel of world agriculture. It is a well-balanced system of credit extension, soundly

---

[4]Roy, E. P., *Alternative Bargaining Techniques for Broiler Growers*, La. Agr. Exp. Sta. D.A.E. Cir. 304, Baton Rouge, La. Apr. 1962.
[5]Swanton, Milo K., "Broad Aspects of Union Organization Among Farmers," National Council of Farmer Cooperatives Meeting, New Orleans, La. Jan. 11, 1961.

operated and now largely farmer-controlled. It is greatly responsible for the productive success of agriculture in the United States.

The co-op farm credit system in the United States is the marvel of world agriculture. Land banks and production credit associations are part of this system. (Courtesy, Farm Credit Administration, Washington, D.C.)

Federal Land Bank Associations

Farmers and ranchers, including part-time farmers, obtain land bank loans through local federal land bank associations. These associations, organized and chartered under the provisions of the 1916 Federal Farm Loan Act, as amended, are fully owned by their farmer-members. The associations, in turn, own all the stock of the federal land banks.

A farmer or rancher applies for a loan to the local association. The association's loan committee must unanimously approve each loan. The farmer or rancher who obtains a loan becomes an association member, buys capital stock in the association equal to 5 percent of the

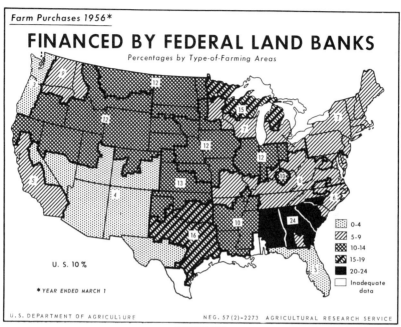

FIGURE 7-2
(Courtesy, USDA, Washington, D.C.)

FIGURE 7-3
(Courtesy, Farm Credit Administration, Washington, D.C.)

loan and pledges the stock with the association as collateral. The association buys an equal amount of capital stock in the land bank, and such stock is pledged with the bank as collateral.

Loans are made to farmers on farm real estate up to 65 percent of appraised value. Terms of the loans are not less than 5 years nor more than 40 years. Interest rates are around 5½ to 6 percent. There are about 380,000 loans outstanding in the amount of $3.2 billion. These long-term loans, at relatively low rates of interest, comprise approximately 20 percent of the existing farm mortgage loans in the United States.

Production Credit Associations

In 1933, the production credit associations were created because private lending agencies, including those which discounted their loans with the federal intermediate credit banks, were not able fully to meet farmers' short-term credit needs.

The PCA's saved many farmers from bankruptcy in the Depression by providing a source of short-term credit. Of the total government capital once invested in PCA's, about 99.8 percent has been rapid, with resultant ownership passing to the farmers themselves. All but seven of the PCA's in the United States are now completely farmer-owned.

Production credit associations make short-term loans to farmers for production purposes, such as purchase of livestock, feed, seed, fertilizer and other farm supplies. Most of these loans are written to mature within one year, although they may extend for seven years (for equipment and improvements), with specified annual payments required. Under a production credit association's budget plan, money is advanced to the farmer as he needs it, and repayments are made throughout the year as the farmer's income is received. Thus, he pays interest on each borrowed dollar only for the exact number of days he uses it. "PCA loans" comprise about 14 percent of the short-term farm credit in the United States. Commercial banks, processors, merchants and dealers are other principal short-term lenders.

Banks for Farmer Cooperatives

The Farm Credit Act of 1933 provided that a bank for cooperatives was to be chartered and organized by the Farm Credit Administration in each of the 12 cities in which a federal land bank was located and that the bank for cooperatives was to serve the same territory as the land bank.

A thirteenth bank, called the Central Bank for Cooperatives, was headquartered at Washington. The district banks were designed to serve the needs of cooperatives in their areas. The Central Bank was empowered to (1) make loans to co-op associations, (2) make loans to the district banks for cooperatives, (3) buy from and sell to any regional bank for cooperatives or intermediate credit bank various types of commercial paper and (4) borrow from and discount or rediscount paper with any or all such banks.

The 12 district banks for cooperatives lend only to farmer cooperatives, not to individual farmers.[6]

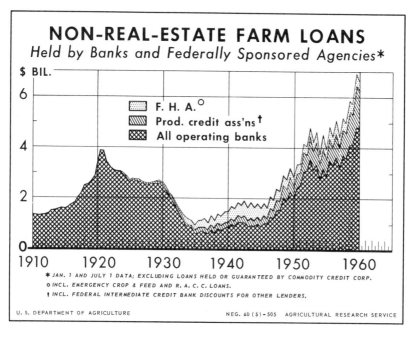

NON-REAL-ESTATE FARM LOANS
*Held by Banks and Federally Sponsored Agencies**

F. H. A.°
Prod. credit ass'ns †
All operating banks

* JAN. 1 AND JULY 1 DATA; EXCLUDING LOANS HELD OR GUARANTEED BY COMMODITY CREDIT CORP.
° INCL. EMERGENCY CROP & FEED AND R. A. C. C. LOANS.
† INCL. FEDERAL INTERMEDIATE CREDIT BANK DISCOUNTS FOR OTHER LENDERS.

U. S. DEPARTMENT OF AGRICULTURE   NEG. 60 (5) - 505   AGRICULTURAL RESEARCH SERVICE

FIGURE 7-4
(Courtesy, USDA, Washington, D.C.)

Rural Credit Unions

Rural credit unions are similar to the PCA's in that only short-term credit is extended. Rural credit unions are homogeneous in their mem-

---

[6]Staff, *The Cooperative Farm Credit System*, FCS Cir. 36-A, USDA, Washington, D.C. Dec. 1959. pp. 1-4.

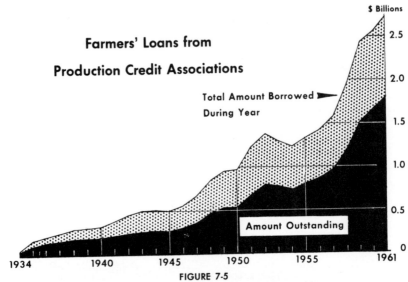

FIGURE 7-5

(Courtesy, Farm Credit Administration, Washington, D.C.)

bership, are usually small and obtain funds primarily from members' deposits or savings. They also are usually operated in conjunction with a farmers' supply or marketing cooperative.

The Middle West has the largest proportion of rural credit unions. North Dakota leads with 74.

Agricultural Credit Corporations

Cooperative agricultural credit corporations are found in cotton, livestock, poultry and fruit and vegetable enterprises, among others. These credit cooperatives take the notes pledged them as collateral for monies loaned to farmers and discount these notes with the intermediate credit banks. In this manner, short-term funds flow more freely to farmers and aid them in financing crop and livestock production. Feeding of livestock in the Middle West and Far West is often financed through the medium of cooperative agricultural credit corporations.

AGRICULTURAL MARKETING COOPERATIVES

Some 5,600 farm marketing cooperatives in the United States serve over 3.4 million farmers. Two of every three farmers in the United States market produce through some cooperative.

Agricultural marketing cooperatives are organized for the collective marketing of members' produce. Depending upon the nature of this produce, they may engage in the co-op marketing of cotton, dairy products, fruits and vegetables, grain, dry beans, rice, livestock, nuts, poultry products, tobacco and wool, among other produce. They market about one-fourth the value of all farm products in the United States.

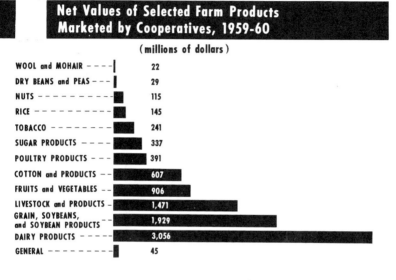

Net Values of Selected Farm Products Marketed by Cooperatives, 1959-60

(millions of dollars)

WOOL and MOHAIR ‒ ‒ ‒ ‒	22
DRY BEANS and PEAS ‒ ‒ ‒	29
NUTS ‒ ‒ ‒ ‒ ‒ ‒ ‒ ‒ ‒	115
RICE ‒ ‒ ‒ ‒ ‒ ‒ ‒ ‒ ‒	145
TOBACCO ‒ ‒ ‒ ‒ ‒ ‒ ‒ ‒	241
SUGAR PRODUCTS ‒ ‒ ‒ ‒	337
POULTRY PRODUCTS ‒ ‒ ‒	391
COTTON and PRODUCTS ‒ ‒	607
FRUITS and VEGETABLES ‒ ‒	906
LIVESTOCK and PRODUCTS ‒	1,471
GRAIN, SOYBEANS, and SOYBEAN PRODUCTS ‒ ‒	1,929
DAIRY PRODUCTS ‒ ‒ ‒ ‒ ‒	3,056
GENERAL ‒ ‒ ‒ ‒ ‒ ‒ ‒ ‒	45

FIGURE 7-6
(Courtesy, USDA, Washington, D.C.)

These marketing cooperatives range in size from small local organizations to powerful centralized groups which have sales representatives in numerous markets and handle considerable portions of the respective agricultural produce. Many marketing cooperatives engage in processing of commodities produced by the members, such as freezing and canning, butter-making and other forms of processing. Many have developed great volume and strength.

Between 1950 and the early 1960's the number of agricultural marketing cooperatives declined, as many associations merged and smaller ones liquidated. With the decrease in the number of farmers in the United States, co-op membership also declined. However, it is believed that the proportion of farmers belonging to marketing cooperatives increased.

Despite the declines in co-op numbers and in membership, co-op business volume in 1961-62 was over 50 percent greater than in 1950-51. Sales per cooperative increased steadily year-by-year between 1950 and the early 1960's (Table 7-1).

TABLE 7-1
Number, Membership and Business Volume of
Agricultural Marketing Cooperatives, U.S.A.

Period	Number of Cooperatives	Member- ship (Number)	Total Business Volume ($)(000,000)[1]	Business Volume per Cooperative ($)
1950-51	6,519	4,117,950	6,361.8	975,886
1951-52	6,594	4,229,125	7,376.7	1,118,699
1952-53	6,501	4,247,035	7,365.8	1,133,026
1953-54	6,457	4,273,050	7,338.8	1,136,565
1954-55	6,330	4,213,485	7,424.7	1,172,938
1955-56	6,284	4,223,260	7,495.2	1,192,743
1956-57	6,284	4,121,700	7,998.9	1,272,899
1957-58	6,119	3,879,675	8,283.1	1,353,669
1958-59	6,042	3,860,950	9,070.2	1,501,192
1959-60	5,828	3,621,900	9,329.9	1,600,875
1960-61	5,727	3,473,425	9,636.3	1,682,609
1961-62	5,626	3,431,360	10,160.4	1,805,972

[1]Excludes intercooperative business; thus, net sales.
Source: Farmer Cooperative Service, USDA, Washington, D.C.

Dairy products account for roughly one-third of co-op marketings. Next in importance are the marketings of grain and soybeans, followed by livestock and livestock products. Other important co-op marketings are fruits and vegetables, cotton and cotton products, poultry products, sugar products and tobacco.

AGRICULTURAL SERVICE COOPERATIVES

Included in agricultural service cooperatives are artificial breeding and dairy herd improvement associations; irrigation and grazing associations; and trucking, storing, grinding, freezing and other servicing organizations. These service cooperatives number over 11,000 in the United States, with a farmer membership of over 1 million.

Artificial Breeding Associations

Artificial breeding associations provide dairymen and cattlemen with the best sires possible. Any one indivdual husbandman could not afford to purchase and maintain expensive sires, but cooperatively the cost per service call is nominal. Although only 47 cooperative bull studs are indicated, these centralized associations serve a total of 1,500 local associations located throughout the United States.

Dairy Herd Improvement Associations

"Cow testing" has been practiced in the United States since 1905 when the first dairy herd improvement association was formed in Michigan. The purpose of testing is to determine the quantities of milk and butterfat produced by each cow in each member's herd. A supervisor keeps feed, production, income and breeding records on each cow. He spends one day a month with each herd, supervises the milking and prepares reports on the performance of each cow. With such information, unprofitable cows can be eliminated.

The services and expenses of a D.H.I.A. tester or supervisor are shared on a co-op basis among the dairymen in the association.

Irrigation Associations

Co-op or mutual irrigation companies supply water for about 30 percent of all the land irrigated in the United States.

The mutual irrigation company is a voluntary association of persons producing farm products under irrigation. Its purpose is to obtain and distribute irrigation water at cost for use primarily on lands of its owner stockholders or members. Since irrigation water is supplied to the members at cost, these associations reduce the cost of production and increase returns from farm operations.

Grazing Associations

In addition to 90 National Forest Grazing Advisory Boards, there are 742 national forest livestock associations and 24 national grassland co-op grazing associations. The Bureau of Land Management, Department of Interior, reports another 580 grazing associations, with a membership of about 10,500 individuals. The combined number of grazing associations is 1,436, with 31,071 members. Grazing associations are formed to allow grazing of federal lands. The federal government charges certain fees for grazing these public lands. In Utah, these fees have averaged about 5 cents per acre over all lands grazed.

FIGURE 7-7

Irrigation cooperatives began with the Mormons in Utah. They make a significant contribution to agriculture in the western United States, particularly. (Courtesy, Bureau of Reclamation, Department of the Interior, Washington, D.C.)

Miscellaneous Services

In the miscellaneous category of service cooperatives are found the various associations organized to provide farmers with essential services such as trucking, storing, grinding, etc. While the number of and membership in these cooperatives declined between 1950 and 1961, the business volume per cooperative more than tripled (Table 7-2).

FARM SUPPLY COOPERATIVES

Unlike farm marketing cooperatives, the farm supply ones have increased both in number and membership. They are becoming more significant because farmers are becoming more commercial and rely more heavily on purchased inputs.

FIGURE 7-8

Grazing associations enable ranchers to pool their resources in obtaining the most economical operations for grazing sheep and cattle especially in the western United States. (Courtesy, Bureau of Land Management, Department of the Interior, Washington, D.C.)

TABLE 7-2
Number, Membership and Business Volume of Agricultural Service Cooperatives, U.S.A.[1]

Period	Number of Cooperatives	Member- ship (Number)	Business Volume[2] ($) (000)	Business Volume per Cooperative ($)
1950-51	262	94,280	99,958	381,519
1951-52	261	102,030	114,480	438,621
1952-53	249	89,230	141,750	569,277
1953-54	241	82,030	157,802	654,780
1954-55	227	67,880	195,522	861,330
1955-56	235	64,865	214,880	914,383
1956-57	234	61,920	234,629	1,002,688
1957-58	233	63,595	246,964	1,059,931
1958-59	229	54,075	272,866	1,191,555
1959-60	220	51,090	298,177	1,355,350
1960-61	214	49,795	305,600	1,428,037
1961-62	207	44,190	302,102	1,459,430

[1]Services include trucking, grinding, storing, ginning and others. Freezer locker cooperatives are omitted in this tabulation.
[2]Excludes intercooperative business.
Source: Farmer Cooperative Service, USDA, Washington, D.C.

Total business volume of the farm supply cooperatives in the United States increased 50 percent from 1950 to the early 1960's. Sales per cooperative increased from $513,372 in the 1950-51 period to $798,920 in the 1961-62 period (Table 7-3).

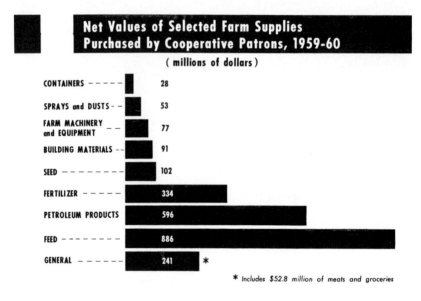

Net Values of Selected Farm Supplies Purchased by Cooperative Patrons, 1959-60

(millions of dollars)

CONTAINERS – – – – –	28
SPRAYS and DUSTS – –	53
FARM MACHINERY and EQUIPMENT – –	77
BUILDING MATERIALS – –	91
SEED – – – – – – – –	102
FERTILIZER – – – – –	334
PETROLEUM PRODUCTS	596
FEED – – – – – – – –	886
GENERAL – – – – – –	241 *

* Includes $52.8 million of meats and groceries

FIGURE 7-9
(Courtesy, USDA, Washington, D.C.)

The leading farm supply item handled is feed, followed by petroleum, fertilizer, other supplies, seeds, building materials, farm machinery and equipment and sprays and dusts. Meats and groceries (consumer items) are also handled by some farmer cooperatives, especially in the North Central states.

Although there are associations principally engaged in farm supplies, a considerable number of marketing cooperatives also handle supplies. Of the approximately 10,000 farmer cooperatives in the United States engaged in purchasing and marketing, about 70 percent sell some supplies. In addition, about 20 percent of the farm supply cooperatives market some farm products.

FARMERS' FIRE MUTUALS

Farmers' fire mutuals number about 1,600 in the United States, with a policyholder membership of 3 million.

TABLE 7-3
Number, Membership and Business Volume of
Farm Supply Cooperatives, U.S.A.

Period	Number of Cooperatives	Member- ship (Number)	Business Volume ($)(000,000)[1]	Business Volume per Cooperatives ($)
1950-51	3,283	2,878,890	1,685.4	513,372
1951-52	3,324	3,032,550	1,918.7	577,226
1952-53	3,378	3,138,820	2,013.8	596,152
1953-54	3,374	3,252,860	1,978.1	586,277
1954-55	3,346	3,322,490	2,021.6	604,184
1955-56	3,375	3,443,610	2,046.1	606,252
1956-57	3,373	3,489,425	2,145.9	636,199
1957-58	3,383	3,543,185	2,187.5	646,615
1958-59	3,387	3,643,525	2,371.1	700,059
1959-60	3,297	3,600,465	2,408.2	730,422
1960-61	3,222	3,679,675	2,472.3	767,318
1961-62	3,206	3,634,690	2,561.3	798,920

[1]Excludes intercooperative business.
Source: Farmer Cooperative Service, USDA, Washington, D.C.

A farm mutual is a company which has more than 50 percent of its insurance on farm property. It is estimated that more than 80 percent of the insurance held by farm mutuals is strictly on farm property; the remainder is mostly on rural nonfarm property.

Originally all farmers' mutual fire insurance companies operated on a post-assessment basis. Each time a member suffered a fire loss to insured property, his claim was paid out of a pro rata assessment of the members. This was a logical development from the log-rolling and barn-raising period of informal mutual fire insurance. When the membership became too large for all to enter into the physical rebuilding, a cash assessment was made. At first, an assessment was made after each fire loss, but this also became burdensome to the companies; most mutuals have shifted to the advance assessment plan. This assessment is an estimate of the coming period's costs, based on past years of experience. Reserve funds enable the mutuals to make up for heavy loss or build up strength in periods of low fire loss.[7]

FISHERY MARKETING

Congress has encouraged the organization and operation of fishery

---

[7]Lance, B. P. and J. C. Thompson, *An Economic Analysis of Farmer Mutual Fire Insurance Companies of Georgia*, Ga. Agr. Exp. Sta. Bul. 88, Athens, Ga. Dec. 1961. pp. 6-7.

FIGURE 7-10

Cooperatives are most vital to fishermen because "one man against the sea" does not fare as well as a "group of men against the sea." Fishery cooperatives are engaged in marketing fish, purchasing supplies and repairing boats, among other services. (Courtesy, Department of Commerce and Industry, Baton Rouge, La.)

marketing cooperatives by enacting what is popularly called the Co-op Fishery Marketing Act of 1934. The Act, however, does not provide for their incorporation. This must be done on a state basis.

There are now 87 fishery marketing cooperatives in the United States, serving about 10,673 fishermen (Table 7-4).

INDIAN ENTERPRISES

Data on Indian cooperatives are not adequate, yet 219 associations are known to exist, serving about 12,500 members. The Office of Indian Affairs in the Department of Interior is charged with a credit program for Indian cooperatives. This office cooperates with 58 of these associations, primarily marketing.

FIGURE 7-11

On Indian reservations in the United States, cooperatives help in marketing wares, purchasing supplies and extending credit, among other services. (Courtesy, Arizona Highways, Phoenix, Ariz.)

Part II

CONSUMER COOPERATIVES

There are over 38,000 consumer cooperatives. Urban credit unions number about 21,000; mutual savings and loan associations, about 5,750; mutual telephone associations, 3,630; housing associations, about 1,335; and consumer stores, about 1,050. The remainder consists of many different types of consumer cooperatives.

COLLEGE STUDENT COOPERATIVES

College student cooperatives number about 500, with 50,000 student members located at both large and small colleges and universities. College cooperatives predominate on the Pacific Coast and in the Middle West. Room, meals, laundry and books are their main concerns. In some cases, college fraternity and sorority groups have formed pur-

TABLE 7-4
Number of and Membership in Fishery Cooperatives, U.S.A.

State	Number of Cooperatives	Total Number of Members	Members per Cooperative
Alaska	22	3,432	156
Arkansas	2	156	78
California	14	1,523	109
Florida	7	126	18
Louisiana	3	106	35
Maine	8	443	55
Maryland	2	90	45
Massachusetts	4	678	170
Michigan	1	16	16
Minnesota	3	260	87
New Jersey	3	112	37
Ohio	2	19	10
Oregon	2	121	60
Rhode Island	1	116	116
Texas	1	[1]	[1]
Washington	11	3,466	315
Wisconsin	1	9	9
Total	87	10,673	123

[1]Data unavailable.
Source: Fish and Wildlife Service Leaflet 292, Department of Interior, Washington, D.C. 1961.

chasing associations in order to buy food and household supplies more economically.

Student cooperatives have from their inception achieved substantial reductions in the cost of living for their members. Since all or a large part of a cooperative's work is performed by members, cash operating costs are low. Members agree to devote four to six hours a week to kitchen work, cleaning, repairing and serving. In addition to comparatively lower initial charges, often a third lower than in other student living units, surpluses are frequently available either for patronage refunds or for improvement and expansion.

To an extent that some visitors from abroad have found it hard to comprehend, students have been willing to allocate savings for purposes that would benefit future generations of students more than themselves. Cooperatives that began with nothing have in this way accumulated property worth hundreds of thousands of dollars. Of course, patronage refunds have been voted also. Sometimes the savings are divided between refunds and a permanent reserve fund. Oberlin College offers an example of another type of expense structure, since co-op rates there

FIGURE 7-12

Many students in the United States could not afford college if it were not for cooperatives. This college student cooperative is at a midwestern university. (Courtesy, Cooperative League, Chicago, Ill.)

are the same as rates in the college dormitories. The Oberlin cooperators, however, have received patronage refunds amounting to about $100 per member per school year in recent periods.[8]

Patronage refunds at some student cooperatives have gone as high as 13 cents per dollar spent at the cooperative. Often, these patronage refunds are paid in stock shares, with the cooperatives retaining them for expansion.

---

[8]Beall, Hayes, "Student Cooperatives in the United States," *International Cooperation*, London, England. Oct. 1955.

CONSUMER RETAIL COOPERATIVES

Consumer retail cooperatives may be classified into two groups: (1) consumer stores and (2) consumer service cooperatives.

Consumer Store Cooperatives

According to the Census Bureau and the Cooperative League, there are an estimated 1,050 consumer co-op stores, serving some 750,000 members. These cooperatives operate approximately 2,400 retail units. Food and fuel stores, building materials and hardware stores, eating establishments and general merchandise stores are the more important types. There are generally two classes of consumer co-op stores: (1) those in rural areas where retail facilities are sparse, such as in the upper portions of Michigan, Minnesota and Wisconsin, and (2) those in large urban centers, such as Chicago, San Francisco, Los Angeles, New York and Washington, D.C.

Rochdale-type cooperatives were the forerunner of much that is now called modern cooperation. Consumer-owned stores are in reality Rochdale-type cooperatives. By joining together many consumer households, even if small in terms of individual purchasing power, consumer-owned cooperatives can successfully and efficiently serve their needs.

One of the most successful consumer retail cooperatives is the Greenbelt Consumer Services in Maryland. It operates food stores, pharmacies, furniture stores and service stations. It has about 23,000 members, with a capital stock of about $2 million.

Another successful consumer-owned cooperative is the Consumers Cooperative of Berkeley, Inc., Berkeley, California. To belong to this cooperative involves purchase of a membership share. At Berkeley, such a share costs $5.

Shareowners are entitled to rebates on all purchases. They deposit cash register receipts bearing their membership numbers into boxes at store locations. The total volume of purchases by each member is tabulated at the end of the cooperative's fiscal year, and refunds are determined. The refunds are applied to a consumer-member's share in the cooperative until the member has a $100 investment.

Meanwhile, the member's ownership shares earn 4 percent interest. They are redeemable for full cash value if a member moves or decides to withdraw from the organization at any time. To some extent, these

FIGURE 7-13

Consumer co-op stores help lower retail prices for food, drugs, etc., in both urban and rural areas. (Courtesy, Greenbelt Consumer Services, Beltsville, Md.)

refunds to members are like the trading stamp refunds awarded by some retailers.

The Hyde Park Co-op Society in Chicago is another fine example of a consumer retail cooperative.

Some cooperators have been disappointed by the lack of growth in consumer cooperation. However, Voorhis and others have recognized the reasons for this apparent lack of expansion: (1) Nationally integrated chain store systems provide intense competition. (2) Consumers have difficulty in getting together and subscribing enough capital. (3) Securing and retaining good management personnel have been difficult for some consumer cooperatives.[9]

Consumer Service Organizations

The service associations present as varied a field of activities as do the distributive associations. They provide such services as housing (in

---

[9]Voorhis, Jerry, *Cooperatives Look Ahead*, Public Affairs Committee, New York, N.Y. July 1952. pp. 12-13.

FIGURE 7-14

Consumer cooperatives perform many services for their member-patrons. Better nutrition through meal-planning for families is one of them. (Courtesy, Consumers Cooperative of Berkeley, Inc., Berkeley, Calif.)

the form of apartments or furnished rooms), meals, laundry work, transportation, automobile repair, recreational facilities, cold-storage facilities, lawn mowing and baby-sitting, among others.

The Census Bureau reports 698 consumer service establishments, with gross receipts of about $30 million annually.

Since consumers are increasingly in need of home, personal and repair services of all kinds, this phase of consumer cooperation will continue to grow in the years ahead.

One type of consumer service association which has rendered good service is the American Travel Association. Organized by various co-op groups, it serves to coordinate travel services for Americans going abroad and for foreigners visiting the United States.

Another example of a nonprofit consumer service organization is Consumers' Union. The purposes of Consumers' Union, as stated in its charter, are to provide for consumer information and counsel relating to consumer goods and services, to give information and assistance on all matters relating to the expenditure of the family income, to initiate and to cooperate with individual and group efforts seeking to create and maintain decent living standards. There are about 1 million subscribers to its monthly *Consumer Reports.*

Another well-known service corporation operating on a non-profit basis is the American Automobile Association, which was incorporated in Connecticut on April 29, 1910. This organization has no stockholders. Its membership consists of over 7 million motorists and car-owners throughout the country, and its revenues, derived chiefly from membership dues, are used to provide special services for its members, including some forms of insurance and legal assistance, emergency road service, maps and travel service.[10]

CREDIT UNIONS (URBAN)

Credit unions are the most numerous type of cooperatives existent in the United States. There are about 20,700 "urban" credit unions plus 790 rural credit unions. The urban credit union membership is over 14 million, with savings of $5.7 billion.[11] Credit unions conduct about 10 percent of the customer credit business in the United States and are growing faster than other consumer finance institutions.

Credit unions are simply short-term credit institutions in which savings of members are pooled and loaned to the same or other members on a nonprofit basis. About half of the credit unions in the United States are state-chartered, while the other half are federally-chartered. There is very little difference among credit union charter laws.

The usual process is for a rather homogeneous group of workers, farmers, church members, etc., to come together, pool savings and lend these savings to members of said group. A credit committee drawn from the membership passes on loan applications. Other important personnel are the board of directors, office manager, supervisory or auditing committee and education committee. By law, maximum interest on loans is one percent per month on the outstanding balance. Many unions charge less, and some even refund part of the interest charges at year's end. Competitive rates of interest are paid on savings deposited in the union.

---

[10]American Automobile Association, Washington, D.C. Oct. 26, 1962.
[11]*Credit Union National Association Yearbook,* Madison, Wisc. 1962.

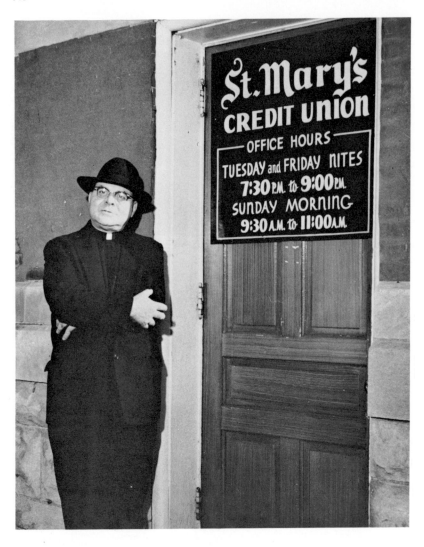

FIGURE 7-15

Credit unions in both urban and rural areas aid in reducing the cost of credit. Various church, professional, occupational and labor union groups, among others, help sponsor these credit societies. (Courtesy, National Catholic Rural Life Conference, Des Moines, Iowa)

Credit unions were the first lending agencies to insure their borrowers' lives for the amount of their loans. Most carry this insurance.

FIGURE 7-16

Filene House in Madison, Wisconsin, named in honor of E. A. Filene. It serves as headquarters of the Credit Union National Association, which assists credit unions in many parts of the world. (Courtesy, CUNA, Madison, Wisc.)

Thus, when a borrower dies or is permanently disabled, his loan is automatically paid. The debt dies with the debtor.

Most credit unions also insure their members' lives for the amount of their shares, up to $2,000. When a member dies, his family receives his share plus an equal sum from group insurance. Credit union members pay nothing additional for either borrowers' or life savings insurance.

In order to provide stability, some credit unions organize a joint stabilization fund. Unions joining the fund pay a small percentage of their membership savings into it. This fund helps credit unions which dissolve to pay out their members' deposits more quickly. Also, the fund can be enlarged and made to self-insure members' deposits from loss, since federal savings deposit insurance is not permitted for credit unions. Legislation has been introduced in Congress on several occasions to provide for federal savings and loan insurance for credit unions, but this legislation has never been enacted. Proponents maintain that credit union depositors need this protection so as to be more competitive with savings and loan associations and commercial banks. Opponents maintain that credit unions are already in strong competitive position and that such legislation would cause credit union management to become lax in its fiscal management. In any case, there is a precedent for having such insurance through a federally-chartered corporation.

GROUP HEALTH PLANS

There are approximately 1,300 voluntary insuring organizations which provide Americans with health insurance. Included in this total are 819 insurance companies issuing health insurance policies, 77 Blue Cross plans, 69 Blue Shield plans and over 300 independent-type plans of which about 170 are co-op group medical practice plans. Only the latter type plans are discussed here. The Blue Cross and Blue Shield plans are considered under quasi cooperatives in the next chapter.

Co-op Medical Practice Plans

Prepaid co-op group health plans include those that are consumer-sponsored, such as cooperative, labor, employer, fraternal and community sponsored.

A typical co-op health plan is one in which a group of people pay agreed-upon monthly dues to an association which they control and receive in return agreed-upon medical services through a staff of doctors and nurses giving part or all of their time to the care of that particular group. Within this broad definition there have developed many different types of plans.

These co-op plans do not, as do other cooperatives, pay patronage refunds to their members. Instead, they operate as nearly at exact cost as possible, and if a surplus is shown, the benefits are broadened, the monthly dues reduced, the staff enlarged or its compensation increased. Such plans stress prepayment, group practices, comprehensive and preventive care and democratic control.

Though they differ widely in nature and scope, the plans have these common features:

1. Members or subscribers prepay the cost of health care, usually through monthly payments.

2. Family doctors and specialists work as a group-practice team to share the knowledge and facilities needed for complete care.

3. The plans seek to prevent, as well as to diagnose and treat, illness and to rehabilitate patients. The cooperatives call members in for

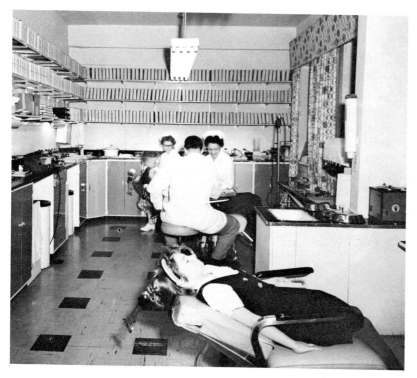

FIGURE 7-17

Co-op medical practice plans allow members to prepay for their health care, hire doctors and specialists, operate medical facilities and provide health care at cost. (Courtesy, Group Health Association, Inc., Washington, D.C.)

checkups, mail them advice on keeping healthy and follow up treatment with phone calls.

4. They provide service at cost. Medical staff members are paid as they and the plan's administrators agree.

5. Each plan's policies, financing and administration are controlled by or in the interests of consumers of health services.

Among the more successful plans in the country are the Group Health Cooperative of Puget Sound; the Group Health Association of Washington, D.C.; the Health Insurance Plan of Greater New York; and the Labor Health Institute of St. Louis. These co-op health facilities are distinguished from nonprofit community, governmental or church-sponsored health facilities.

As part of the group health plan, some cooperatives operate hospitals and clinics. The oldest rural co-op hospital in the United States is the Community Hospital of Elk City, Oklahoma, which is owned by the Farmers Union Cooperative Hospital Association.

HOUSING ASSOCIATIONS

Some 1,335 housing associations, with 120,000 members, are existent in the United States. Under the Federal Housing Acts, Sections 207 and 213, co-op housing projects are availed FHA-insured-type mortgages. The activity under these two sections has been as follows:[12]

Section 207

Projects completed (number)	1,455
Units (number)	171,618
Amount ($) (000)	1,749,714

Section 213

	Sales-type Cooperative	Management-type Cooperative
Projects completed (number)	1,316	326
Units (number)	32,423	46,941
Amount ($)	391,479,247	582,203,459

In all, there are two types of housing cooperatives: sales-type and management-type. The sales-type is one which constructs dwellings but dissolves upon completion and sale of dwellings to individual owners. The blanket mortgage which FHA has insured is replaced by individual mortgages as each unit is sold. The management-type continues in existence for the purpose of managing the property after construction is completed. If a sales-type cooperative is used, only single-family dwellings can be financed under 213. If a management-type cooperative persists, then either multiple- or single-family units may be financed under 213.

Most housing cooperatives today arise out of sponsoring organizations. The tasks of land purchase, architectural design, financing, incorporation, organization and construction are too difficult for a group of families to master on their own. Sponsors include churches, trade unions, veteran's groups, private foundations, other cooperatives—any organization interested in better housing at lower cost.

---

[12]Communications with Federal Housing Adm., Washington, D.C. Nov. 15, 1962.

When a family joins a housing association, a down-payment on its home is required. This varies, depending largely on construction costs and type of financing. The family also makes regular monthly payments. These include its share of principal and interest on the cooperative's mortgage, taxes, insurance, reserves, maintenance and perhaps utilities. Usually each family is responsible for maintaining the interior of its home; the cooperative, the exterior.

After meeting expenses each year, what's left belongs to the co-op

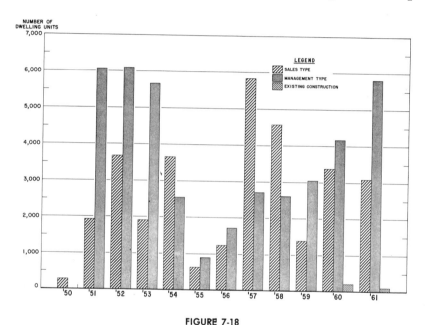

FIGURE 7-18

Co-op housing projects insured under Sections 207 and 213 of the Federal Housing Acts. (Courtesy, Federal Housing Administration, Washington, D.C.)

members. They may put this into reserves, improve services or reduce charges. Members establish policies and elect directors. The directors, in turn, hire a manager or name a management committee to handle day-to-day details.

By meeting known needs on a nonprofit basis, cooperatives have reduced housing costs by 15 to 20 percent, compared with similar rental housing. In addition, each family may deduct from taxable income its share of the cooperative's interest and property tax payments, just as an individual homeowner would.

Through their housing cooperatives, families find it easy to work together in joint purchase of fuel, milk, equipment and landscaping and in such joint ventures as swim clubs, insurance groups, camps, credit unions, nursery schools, libraries, sitter swaps, health plans and social clubs.

When a member leaves, the cooperative resells his share to the incoming owner at a price determinable under the bylaws. No change is needed in the title, mortgage or insurance. Co-op resale fees are quite nominal.

MEMORIAL ASSOCIATIONS

Some 100 memorial associations, with 100,000 members, are known to exist in the United States.

These associations are of three types: (1) those which contract with mortuaries for necessary services for their members, (2) those which recommend but do not sign contracts with mortuaries and (3) those which operate cooperatively by prepaying burial costs over a period of time and/or operating their own mortuaries on a co-op basis.[13]

MUTUAL INSURANCES

All insurance is essentially a co-op activity. It involves the pooling of the savings of a considerable number of people so as to spread the risks in the common hazards of life. No one person can have an insurance company; only a large number of persons can make possible a successful one. Insurance is conceived to provide people as members of a group with greater security than they can possibly gain individually.

Mutual insurance companies are among the oldest types of cooperative found in the United States. Mutual insurance is provided for life, liability, marine, fidelity, fire, casualty, automobile and for other needs. A mutual insurance company enables each policyholder in the company, rather than investors, to own the company. After all operating expenses are met and necessary reserves made, whatever is left is refunded pro rata to policyholders. It should be mentioned, however, that stock insurance companies often likewise pay dividends to their policyholders on the basis of "participating" policies.

---

[13]Nora, Fred, *Memorial Associations,* Cooperative League, Chicago, Ill. 1962.

Three types of mutual insurance companies are discussed: (1) co-op mutual insurance, (2) other mutual insurance (excluding life) and (3) mutual life insurance.

FIGURE 7-19

One of the co-op mutual insurance companies in the United States is Nationwide Insurance Co., Columbus, Ohio.

Co-op Mutual Insurance

There are nine co-op mutual insurance companies serving about 11 million policyholders. Co-op mutual insurance is similar to other mutual insurances except that, in a co-op mutual, the policyholders are given greater opportunity to control their company. Co-op mutuals will hold district and area meetings over a wide territory to see that each policyholder has an opportunity to cast a vote for members of the board and for other matters.

Co-op mutual insurance companies have assets of over $400 million with an annual premium income of $375 million. Nationwide Mutual Insurance Company of Columbus, Ohio, is a good example of a co-op insurance company.

Other Mutual Insurances

In addition to farmers' fire mutuals and mutual life insurance companies, there are about 2,600 mutual casualty[14] insurances for liability, fidelity, urban fire, burglary, automobile, marine and other insurable losses. Mutual insurances of this type are provided for both consumers or households and employers or entrepreneurs.

Although the mutual property and casualty companies account for 2,600 of the 3,500 companies in this field, they account for about $4 billion of the total $14 billion in insurance premiums. Mutual casualty companies are necessarily smaller than stock firms because many restrict their business to groups with mutual undertakings.

Mutual Life Insurance

In the mutual life insurance field, some 158 mutuals report a total of about 67 million policyholders in the United States. These 158 mutuals hold 60 percent of the life insurance in force, while 1,322 stock life insurance companies hold the other 40 percent. On a premium-collected basis, the mutuals collect about $12 billion as against $8 billion for stock companies.[15]

---

[14]"Casualty" may include automobile liability, workmen's compensation, personal liability, damage or loss to property, accident, travel, burglary, fidelity and surety. In this sense, mutual casualty insurance would include practically all insurance other than life.

[15]American Mutual Insurance Alliance, Chicago, Ill. Nov. 13, 1962.

FIGURE 7-20

Mutual insurance has a major role in the underwriting of risks such as for Chase Manhattan Plaza in New York City. Dominating the plaza and the revitalized area is the new Chase Manhattan Bank Building towering 60 stories as a landmark in mutual insurance service both on the national and world scenes. (Courtesy, American Mutual Insurance Alliance)

Life insurance companies are under the supervision of the state in which they are incorporated and the states in which they do business. One of the requirements of such supervision is that the reserves accumulated on level-premium insurance be of a certain minimum size, which is considered enough to meet the future claims against these reserves. Thus companies that conduct their business on the level-premium plan and maintain reserves at least equal to the minimum requirements are known as *legal-reserve companies*.

The legal-reserve companies may be separated into *stock* and *mutual* companies on the basis of who controls them and who takes the profits or sustains the losses. The stock company is organized as a private enterprise by individuals who contribute the capital required and receive stock in the venture. On this stock they expect to receive profits just as in any other business undertaking. The stock company is controlled by the stockholders who run the business for their own profit as investors. Any profits accruing to the business as a result of its operations are theirs to divide, and likewise, they must sustain any losses which may be experienced. The policies issued by a strictly stock company are known as *non-participating* policies, since the policyholders have no participation in the profits.

In a strictly *mutual company* there is no capital stock and thus there are no stockholders. Those insured own all of the assets and control the organization for the benefit of themselves as policyholders. The endeavor of a mutual company is to provide insurance for its members at cost. If the full annual premiums are not used, the balance at the end of the year is returned to the policyholders. This type of insurance is spoken of as *participating*.

Not all the legal-reserve companies fall strictly into these two classes, because some organizations, known as *mixed companies*, have capital stock and still offer participating policies. In these the rate of dividends to stockholders is limited, and any remaining profits are distributed among the policyholders.

In summary, a mutual life insurance company has no stockholders and no "profits" in the usual sense of the word. The funds which are left over after making benefit payments, setting aside reserves for future obligations, meeting the costs of doing business and retaining a reasonable amount for future contingencies, are returned as dividends to policyholders.

Mutual Insurances and Co-op Principles

The main criticism of mutual insurance in regard to co-op principles rests in the lack of control by policyholders over the mutual companies.

There are certain factors which are responsible for this, however. First, some state laws do not permit policyholders who live outside the state of incorporation to vote. Second, proxy voting, when permitted, allows certain individuals to control a large bloc of votes. Third, most mutual companies operate nationwide thus making it difficult to have adequate policyholder control. Fourth, notices of annual meetings are often obscured on the policy itself, causing the policyholder to overlook the date of the annual meeting, especially when no reminders are sent to him.

MUTUAL SAVINGS AND LOANS

There are an estimated 5,758 mutual savings and loan associations compared with 600 stock savings and loan in the United States. The mutual associations have over 27 million accounts.

The differentiation as between mutual and stock associations is that the former has no proprietary interest represented by common stock or its equivalent. The stock association, on the other hand, has such stock, and it is known variously as guaranty, permanent or permanent reserve stock. This type of capital is authorized in some 18 states of the union.

Savings associations are unique among financial institutions in that the major emphasis of their investment program is upon home mortgage loans. In fact, a full 85 percent of the assets of savings associations are channeled back into the community as home mortgage credit. Savings and loan associations finance nearly 45 percent of all homes purchased every year in the United States. They are the nation's biggest single home mortgage lenders.

Interest income received is spent as follows: 21.7 percent for operating expenses, 2.4 percent for interest on borrowed funds, 13.7 percent to reserves and 62.2 percent to depositors.[16]

Savings associations are locally managed and governed by a board of directors made up of locally prominent business leaders. These institutions operate either under a federal government charter, issued by the Federal Home Loan Bank Board in Washington, D.C., or under a state charter issued by the state in which they are located.

The combined savings in all associations is over $80 billion.

---

[16]*Savings and Loan Fact Book: 1962*, Chicago, Ill. pp. 100-101.

FIGURE 7-21

Mutual savings banks are another type of credit institution which helps finance homes and provide safe depositories for members' savings. (Courtesy, National Association of Mutual Savings Banks, New York, N.Y.)

MUTUAL SAVINGS BANKS

There are 515 mutual savings banks in the United States, with an account membership of over 22 million. In addition, there are 512 branches of these banks.

The first mutual savings bank was incorporated in Boston in 1816 as the Provident Institution of Savings. Since that time mutual savings banks have increased to the present number of 515 located in the New England states, Indiana, New Jersey, New York, Ohio, Pennsylvania, Washington, Wisconsin, Delaware, Maryland, Minnesota, Oregon and Alaska.

"Mutual" means that a bank is organized to accommodate and reward the savings of its depositors. There are no stockholders to claim a portion of the bank's earnings. The interests of the depositors are paramount. Those who serve as trustees of a mutual savings bank, and thereby establish its policies, may not profit personally from any of the bank's operations or investments, except to the same extent as all other depositors. Earnings, after operating expenses are paid and reserves are set aside to protect depositors, are distributed regularly to the depositors in the form of interest credited to their accounts.[17]

The aggregate savings of mutual savings banks total over $41

---

[17]Staff, *Mutual Savings Banks*, National Association of Mutual Savings Banks, New York, N.Y. 1962. p. 3.

billion, approximately half that of building and loan associations. Mutual savings banks hold only 13 percent of the home mortgage loans in the United States, but they hold about 60 percent of such mortgages in the eastern United States. Dividends on deposits average about 3.7 percent, slightly lower than the average 4.1 percent paid by building and loan associations, but higher than commercial banks.

NURSERY SCHOOL COOPERATIVES

There are an estimated 820 co-op nursery schools in the United States, with a student membership of 25,000. In these schools, parents pay tuition as well as volunteer aid as teachers' assistants and in

FIGURE 7-22

Pre-schoolers begin their long climb toward maturity in a co-op nursery school where outdoor play and indoor activity each has its role in a child's introduction to learning. Mothers' participation in the program has the dual benefit of cutting costs and acquiring teaching and guidance skills under trained supervision. (Courtesy, Cooperative League, Chicago, Ill.)

performing other duties. Committees elected by parents administer the school cooperatives on a nonprofit basis.

RURAL ELECTRIC COOPERATIVES

Electric power cooperatives number about 985 in the United States, with a membership of 4.4 million. They serve about 75 percent of all farm families in the United States.

Of the 985 co-op electric distributing systems, only 68 of them generate all or most of their own electricity. Therefore, one main weakness of the rural electric cooperatives is their large dependence on others for their power source. On a percentage basis, the rural electric associations generate only 18 percent of their electricity, obtain 43 percent from private power companies, 32 percent from federal power facilities and 7 percent from other public power sources (Table 7-5).

The job of rural electrification is not quite complete, as shown in Table 7-6. In addition to extending service to all farms in the United States, there remains the perhaps bigger job of promoting greater use of electricity especially in farm work mechanization and in rural homes.

The question of rural electric cooperatives versus investor-owned utilities in relation to farm electrification has become very controversial. For a discussion of the position of rural electric cooperatives, see Clapp,[18] and for the position of the investor-owned utilities, consult the Edison Electric Institute report.[19]

TABLE 7-5
Co-op Electricity: Generation, Consumption and Rates

Item	1960	1955	1950
Electricity generated, kilowatt hours (000)	4,921,797	3,254,592	1,076,946
Electricity sold, kilowatt hours (000)	27,268,625	15,738,772	6,883,939
Percent generated	18.1	21.0	15.6
Average monthly residential consumption, kilowatt hours	357	242	147
Average revenue from residential users, cents per kilowatt hours	2.49	2.98	3.63

Source: *Cooperatives, U.S.A.*, Cooperative League, Chicago, Ill. 1962. p. 23.

[18]Clapp, Norman, *Crisis in Rural Electrification*, REA, USDA, Washington, D.C. Oct. 1961.
[19]Staff, *Rural Electrification in the United States*, Edison Electric Institute, New York, N.Y.

FIGURE 7-23

Rural electric cooperatives are local, privately owned business institutions. Some of them are joining together to generate their own electricity. (Courtesy, National Rural Electric Cooperative Association, Washington, D.C.)

TABLE 7-6
Number of Farms and Percentage of Farms
Electrified, U.S.A.

Year	Number of All Farms (000)	Number of Farms Electrified (000)	Percent of Farms Electrified
1935	6,812	744	10.9
1940	6,097	1,853	30.4
1950	5,382	4,154	77.2
1960	3,710	3,578	96.4

Source: *Cooperative Digest,* Ithaca, N.Y. Feb. 1961. p. 20.

Telephone Mutuals

Telephone mutuals with line and switchboard services number 3,630, with a total membership of about 500,000 customer-owners. The oldest active rural telephone cooperative is the Clarksville, Illinois, Community Telephone Company organized in 1890. In addition, there are some 20,000 other mutuals that provide lines only which connect through switchboards owned by other companies.

These mutuals play an important role in rural areas and provide an essential service. Exchanges are usually small, covering only a local area, although recent consolidations point to fewer but larger exchanges serving a wider area and giving better service. Some of the telephone cooperatives, but not all, borrow funds from the Rural Electrification Administration. Others use private sources of financing.

However, the job of providing telephones to every American home is far from over. According to the 1960 Census, 30 percent of the rural homes in America and 19 percent of the urban homes have no telephone service. Those in urban areas without telephones could have connection but perhaps for economic reasons do not. Most of the 30 percent in rural areas without telephones simply have no facilities for connection. Cooperatives can perform a useful service in the future by providing such telephone service.

UTILITY COOPERATIVES

Besides irrigation water, rural electric, telephone and soil conservation districts, there are co-op drinking water, natural gas, fire protection, sewerage, railroad and intra-urban transport districts, among others.

Cooperatives are playing a decreasing role in utility services except for electricity, telephone, irrigation and drainage. Investor-owned companies (with monopoly grants), public agencies (police juries, municipal governments) and quasi-public bodies are assuming the major role in providing these other utility services. This is because patronage of some utility services must be mandatory, not voluntary, to guarantee the economic success of the services. Only government bodies can implement mandatory patronage; cooperatives cannot.

In some rapidly growing suburban areas where utility services are scarce, cooperatives have been formed to provide water, sewerage, trash collection and fire-fighting services.

In the next chapter, cooperatives other than farmer and consumer are discussed.

TOPICS FOR DISCUSSION

1. Name and discuss five types of agricultural cooperatives.
2. Which types of agricultural cooperatives are increasing and which are decreasing in importance?

3. Name and discuss five types of consumer cooperatives.
4. Which types of consumer cooperatives are increasing and which ones are decreasing in importance?
5. Can you think of some other types of farmer and consumer cooperatives not mentioned in this chapter?

SELECTED REFERENCES

1. Bainbridge, John, *The Story of Mutual Fire and Casualty Insurance,* Doubleday & Co., New York, N.Y. 1952.
2. Bodfish, H. M., *History of Building and Loan Associations in the United States,* U.S. Building & Loan League, Chicago, Ill. 1931.
3. Bogardus, Emory, "Why Consumers Cooperate?" *Sociology and Social Research.* Vol. 26. 1942. pp. 352-363.
4. Bowen, E. R., *The Cooperative Organization of Consumers,* Cooperative League, Chicago, Ill. 1957.
5. Brainerd, J. G., *Consumers' Cooperation,* American Academy of Political and Social Science, Philadelphia, Pa. May 1957.
6. Childs, Marquis, *The Farmer Takes a Hand,* Doubleday & Co., New York, N.Y. 1952.
7. Danenberg, Elsie, *Get Your Home the Co-op Way,* Greenberg Publishers, New York, N.Y. 1936.
8. Jewett, Alyce and E. C. Voohries, *Agricultural Cooperatives: Strength in Unity,* The Interstate Printers & Publishers, Inc., Danville, Ill. 1963.
9. Laidlaw, A. F., *Consumer Cooperative Movement,* Warbasse Memorial Library Association, New York, N.Y. June 1962.
10. Muller, F. W., *Public Rural Electrification,* American Council on Public Affairs, Washington, D.C. 1944.
11. Myrick, Herbert, *Cooperative Finance,* Orange Judd Co., New York, N.Y. 1912.
12. Orcutt, W. D., *The Miracle of Mutual Savings,* Bowery Savings Bank, New York, N.Y. 1934.
13. Pursell, Arthur, *Keys to Effective Rural Credit Unions,* FCS Info. 19, USDA, Washington, D.C. Nov. 1961.
14. Rowlands, D. T. and others, *Current Developments in Housing,* American Academy of Political and Social Science, Philadelphia, Pa. Mar. 1937.
15. Sherman, F. J., *Modern Story of Mutual Savings Banks,* Little & Ives Co., New York, N.Y. 1934.
16. Slattery, Harry, *Rural America Lights Up,* National Home Library Foundation, Washington, D.C. 1940.
17. Staff, Bureau of Labor Statistics Bulletins:
    (a) 750—*Directory of Consumer Cooperatives.* 1947.
    (b) 859—*Developments in Consumers' Cooperatives.* 1946.
    (c) 896—*Nonprofit Housing Projects in the U.S.* 1947.
    (d) 971—*Consumers' Cooperatives.* 1949.

(e) 1093—*Housing Cooperatives in the U.S.* 1951.
(f) 1158—*Consumer Cooperatives in the U.S.* 1954.
(g) 1211—*Consumer Cooperatives.* 1957.
18. Staff, *Credit Unions,* National Catholic Rural Life Conference, Des Moines, Iowa. Apr. 1961.
19. Staff, *Mutual Savings Banking,* Prentice-Hall, New York, N.Y. 1962.
20. Vogel, H. N., *The Co-op Apartment,* Libra Publishers, New York, N.Y. 1960.
21. Warbasse, J. P., *Cooperative Medicine,* Cooperative League, Chicago, Ill. 1951.

CHAPTER 8 —

Business, Worker and Quasi
Cooperatives in the
United States of America

A "cooperative" is, in essence, simply an effort of a group of individuals to combine together for the purpose of establishing a business, to produce, or buy, or sell a commodity or service. City consumers have gotten together to buy goods and sell them. Businessmen have formed mutual fire insurance companies. Individuals join together to buy life insurance through a mutual company. Farmers join together to buy goods they use in production or to sell things they grow. People who save money may put their funds in a mutual savings bank. All of these are forms of "cooperatives." They are forms of private enterprise.

The general principle should be recognized that if a cooperative enterprise, or any other legitimate form of enterprise, can make a place for itself in the United States by its efficiency, it should not be handicapped by government. On the other hand, no form of business enterprise should be given special advantages, which put its competitors in an inferior position before the law or require such competitors to assume an unfair share of the burden of supporting governmental costs. The real problem is to see to it that regulations and laws which affect business operators apply equally to all forms of business, regardless of whether sole proprietorship, partnership or corporation, and regardless of whether the corporations formed are on a stock or cooperative basis.

—*Staff, Cooperatives in Relation to Other Forms of Business Enterprise, National Association of Manufacturers, New York, N.Y. p. 1.*

BUSINESS COOPERATIVES AND
NONPROFIT ASSOCIATIONS

BUSINESS COOPERATIVES and nonprofit associations are classified into three groups: (1) business services; (2) nonfarm manufacturing, marketing and supply services; and (3) retailer-owned wholesale cooperatives.

BUSINESS SERVICE COOPERATIVES
(NONFARM)

Very diversified types of cooperatives are found in the nonfarm business world. These include cooperatives for transport and delivery, bank clearing houses, credit bureaus, credit corporations, communication, testing and research, repair services, personal services and many others.

There are an estimated 3,359 business service nonprofit associations operating along co-op lines, with a membership of about 506,000 firms.

Transport and Delivery

It is estimated that there are about 175 delivery and transportation cooperatives of all types in the United States, with a membership of 36,138 firms.

One procedure is for smaller suppliers and merchants to form a shipping cooperative so that carload lot shipments from major supply centers can be obtained. Profit at the end of the year is distributed pro rata to member-patrons. Membership fees range from $50 to $500. Freight costs range from 20 to 40 percent less than on individual shipments. Businesses in freight associations include department stores; restaurants; furniture stores; florists' shops; wholesale drug, jewelry, clothing and other retailers and wholesalers. In all, there are an estimated 138 *shipping* cooperatives serving some 24,000 firms.[1] Also, many of these individual members represent multiple-establishment firms, such as chain stores and retail organizations having more than one store in a locality, which would mean that this total of 24,000 would be materially increased.

Representatives of national merchandising groups estimate that over 800,000 individual business units are either shipping or receiving freight through the facilities of nonprofit shipping associations.[2]

There are 34 cities in the United States in which a total of some 170 merchants have banded together for the purpose of forming and operating mutual delivery associations. Instead of each merchant delivering his own goods, the stores act collectively through a cooperatively owned and operated delivery service. The advantage of

---

[1]Communication with Vendors Consolidating Co., New York, N.Y. Oct. 10, 1962.
[2]Communication with National Conference of Nonprofit Shipping Associations, Inc., Atlanta, Ga. Nov. 9, 1962.

this plan is that it enables a store to reduce its package delivery cost in an area where it has relatively few customers. The only disadvantages involved are shuttling of packages between stores and occasional differences in personnel policy.

Since many retail stores of all types buy merchandise in less-than-carload lots, cooperative pooling of orders and shipments is one method which is being used to reduce shipping costs. The co-op technique has considerable value to these retail stores. Manufacturers like to deal with co-op groups because they are able to sell in larger volumes while, at the same time, shipping costs are reduced to the individual stores.

Perhaps the best known mutual enterprise in the freight transport field is the Railway Express Agency, reorganized in 1928, which consists of 61 railroad companies operating for mutual benefit. If each railroad attempted to operate such a freight operation individually, the costs

FIGURE 8-1

Railroad companies find it more economical to operate a consolidated freight service than for each to operate this service individually. (Courtesy, REA Express, New York, N.Y.)

and duplication of service would be wasteful. The REA serves 23,000 communities in the United States and combines air, truck and rail service to provide efficient freight transport. Door-to-door delivery is provided within published limits. Worldwide international service is also provided.

Another type of mutual enterprise in the railroad industry is the joint operation of bridges, freight terminals, passenger depots and tracks by two or more rail lines.

In the truck transportation field, moving van lines have formed cooperatives for long distance hauling. Member companies take care of their own short distance hauls but pool the long distance jobs. The co-op van lines perform the dispatching, insurance and unification functions of their member-agents. Any surplus at the end of the year is prorated to member-agents on a patronage basis.[3]

Many taxi associations in large American cities are cooperative. Taxi drivers share income above expenses, elect their board of directors, provide group health and life insurance and perform other services cooperatively, such as operating paint shops. Each co-op member provides or invests in a vehicle.

The retail florists throughout the United States operate an association which serves customers by delivering flowers locally when ordered by a person outside the city.

Before the establishment of Florists' Telegraph Delivery Association, for example, florists sent flowers out-of-town for their customers by physically shipping them by parcel post or express. By 1910, it was evident that shipping was inadequate because of the growth of America and the perishable nature of flowers. A new plan was initiated. When customers wanted flowers sent to another town, a florist wired a colleague in that city and asked him to deliver the flowers from his stock. To expand this service and guarantee quality and quick delivery to the public, 22 florists gathered in Rochester, New York, in August of 1910 and organized F.T.D. They adopted a constitution and bylaws, set down strict requirements for membership, elected officers and established a trust fund to assure payments to one another for flower orders they exchanged. F.T.D. had 315 members in 1911 and had grown to 1,200 by 1920. Today, more than 11,000 florists in the Americas are members.[4]

---

[3]Communication with Allied Van Lines, Chicago, Ill. Oct. 9, 1962.
[4]*F.T.D. Fact Sheet,* Detroit, Mich. Sept. 17, 1962. pp. 1-2.

News Collection and Dissemination

The Associated Press is a nonprofit organization. It is wholly independent and operates without subsidy, interference or influence by any government. AP's annual budget, now more than $40 million, is the highest in the news agency field. Its members spend many times this figure for collecting local and regional news which is then supplied

FIGURE 8-2

Newspapers and other news media could not very well gather news individually. Instead, they rely on The Associated Press. (Courtesy, Wide World Photos)

to The Associated Press. As a member or subscriber, the newspaper or broadcasting station obtains the benefits of not only a worldwide staff of expert newsmen and photographers but of vast transmission facilities which speed the news. Some 475,000 miles of leased wire carry the AP report in the United States alone, serving 1,750 newspapers and 2,300 radio and television stations.[5]

───────────

[5]Communication with The Associated Press, New York, N.Y. Oct. 10, 1962.

Credit-type Associations

Credit associations for businesses are of two types: (1) credit bureaus for screening credit applicants and (2) credit corporations to finance accounts receivables and, in some cases, facility financing.

The retail credit bureaus operated in most cities are organized and operated by member retail merchants and others who use the credit bureaus as clearing houses on consumer credit information.

Business corporations often form co-op finance companies which jointly relieve the member companies from carrying accounts receivables and thereby provide them with more operating capital. Net earnings are prorated to each company according to the volume of business done by that company. In other cases, the functions and services of a credit department are centralized and owned by a group of stores in order to reduce costs.

Bank Clearing Houses

Bank clearing houses number 283 in the United States, with a membership of 1,749 bank firms. A clearing house association is an organization of banks designed to promote in every possible way the

FIGURE 8-4

Banks in an area usually operate a clearing house so that check transactions can be cleared among the banks after the day's business. (Courtesy, Chamber of Commerce, Baton Rouge, La.)

mutual interests of the members. The most common of these mutual services is that of *clearing* checks.

The leading states in number of bank clearing house associations are Pennsylvania, California, Ohio, Texas and Illinois.

Research and Testing

Research and testing organizations number 24, with an estimated membership of 8,920 firms. Individual manufacturers who make use of testing facilities are charged for the time of engineers assigned to an investigation, construction work done, materials used, preparation of the report, etc. Such research and testing organizations are nonprofit.

Advertising and Sales

Sales, advertising and promotion cooperatives are estimated at 20, with a membership of 200 firms.

Automobile, appliance and other types of dealers handling the

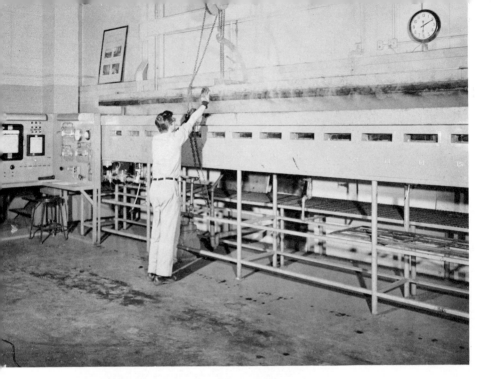

FIGURE 8-5

Manufacturing companies often jointly own and operate testing laboratories to determine the quality of their products. The spread of fire on paints, plastics, veneers, etc., is determined in this furnace. (Courtesy, Underwriters' Laboratories, Inc., Chicago, Ill.)

same brand of product in a trade area often organize nonprofit advertising and promotional associations. This effort enables them to pool resources and minimize promotional costs in a given area.

Other Business Services

Realtors have organized associations which maintain multiple listings of homes for sale so that each realtor-member may sell the listed property.

In some cities, merchants own parking lots in common due to the increasing need for downtown parking and the high price of land in these areas. The city of Philadelphia, for example, has such a plan in operation. The city acquires land either by purchase or condemnation and constructs a completely equipped parking lot, including paving, lighting, fencing, attendant's booth and striping, for use of shoppers, merchants and area visitors.

The merchants' group is required to form a nonprofit corporation, which leases the lot from the city and establishes an escrow fund as a guaranty in meeting rental payments. The amount of the fund is based on $63 per thousand of the city's total investment. The fund is established in a savings bank, and interest accrued reverts to the merchants.

Following construction of the lot, the land is reappraised for its reuse value, and 4 percent of this figure constitutes the annual rental. Leases are drawn for 25 years in five-year segments, with an option to renew at the end of each five-year period.

Some lawyers' groups have formed purchasing associations to reduce costs of supplies and equipment needed for their offices. The same holds true for other professional groups.

Better business bureaus in many cities operate on the cooperative technique. Various firms pay membership fees and hire a staff through their boards of directors to eliminate deceptive business practices in the community. These bureaus are operated as nonprofit organizations.

In many instances, retail stores form cooperatively-owned buying offices which procure merchandise for the member stores more economically.

Stock Exchanges and Boards of Trade

There are 13 stock exchanges registered under the Exchange Act, of which the New York and American Stock Exchanges are the largest. These exchanges are organized and operated on a mutual benefit basis. Seats are sold and purchased according to the bylaws. Members are regulated directly by the exchanges.[6]

The exchanges themselves are not operated for profit. Each member has one vote. An initiation fee is usually charged when a member is admitted.

One such exchange has been described as follows:

> The Exchange is a rather unusual form of enterprise. It doesn't try to make a profit, and it isn't a charitable organization. It is a voluntary association of brokers.
> The Exchange needs enough income each year to operate its extensive market facilities and pay salaries and wages. This requires an annual budget of approximately twenty-three million dollars.[7]

Stock exchanges obtain income both from transaction charges and members' annual dues or assessments. For example, the present annual

[6]*Security and Exchange Commission Annual Report,* Government Printing Office, Washington, D.C. 1962.
[7]*Understanding the New York Stock Exchange,* New York Stock Exchange, New York, N.Y. 1963. p. 14.

dues on the American Stock Exchange are $500 per member.[8] If the dues are not needed to meet the operating costs of the exchange, the $500 assessment is classed as a "capital contribution" which is used for capital improvements.

Any person desiring a seat on an exchange must arrange to purchase it from another member and be approved by the exchange's board of directors. During 1961, the price of a seat on the American Stock Exchange reached $75,000.[9]

The American, New York and Midwest Stock Exchanges have a combined membership of about 2,263. The membership in the remaining ten exchanges is 761; thus over 3,000 members are on all 13 stock exchanges. In addition, there are "associated" and "allied" types of membership with no voting rights.

Also subject to regulation by the Securities and Exchange Commission are boards of trade. At present, the Chicago Board of Trade with its 1,402 members is the only one so regulated. Boards of trade are similar to stock exchange operations as far as mutual features are concerned.

NONFARM MANUFACTURING, MARKETING AND SUPPLY ASSOCIATIONS

It is estimated that there are about 712 nonfarm industrial associations, with over 3,000 firms engaged in manufacturing, supply and marketing. These are more prominent in coal and iron ore mining, petroleum operations, steel-making, glass-making, aerospace, chemicals, building materials, etc.

The Census Bureau data on nonfarm industrial associations contain three limitations: (1) The number of establishments rather than number of firms is reported. (2) Cooperatives as a legal type of organization are reported together with "other legal" types. (3) The number of firms belonging to an association is not reported. This number has to be estimated from trade sources.

Some reasons for the development of cooperatives among industrial firms are as follows: (1) to increase consumer demand or to extend the market for the products of the cooperating companies, (2) to

---

[8]*Staff Report on the American Stock Exchange,* Securities and Exchange Commission, Washington, D.C. Jan. 3, 1962. p. 3.
[9]*Ibid.* p. 7.

work together in order to thwart the expansion in use of substitutes for their products, (3) to compete more effectively with chain organizations and larger-scale businesses, (4) to gain the benefits of national advertising and publicity in cases where such a national program by an individual firm is out of the question and (5) to cooperate in product testing and development, research, better warehousing and distribution services.

Most state laws permit a minimum of three corporations or persons to form a nonprofit corporation. When a few corporations go into a joint venture, a partnership effect is usually created. Joint venture nonprofit corporations are spreading rapidly occasioned by higher capital requirements and the need for covering larger territories. The main obstacle to these nonprofit ventures is the possibility of antitrust violations. Since industrial companies in any one line are few, any combination might unduly restrict competition.

Fusfeld, in his study of 75 joint ventures in the iron and steel industry, expressed his concern over antitrust violations as follows:

> If we are committed to a policy of competition in the American economy, quasi-mergers, like joint subsidiaries, should immediately be suspect, especially when they involve large firms in the same industry. And if we are committed to dispersal of economic power rather than its concentration as an essential element of political democracy, the interest groups that can be fostered by joint subsidiaries should not be tolerated.[10]

Some joint ventures, although of a corporate structure, are taxed as partnerships. In this instance, their status is parallel to that of farmer cooperatives, for example, which are corporate bodies but are taxed as partnerships.

Purchasing Cooperatively

Cooperative purchasing by nonfarm businesses of an industrial character is wide-spread and becoming more important.

For example, 150 iron and steel scrap companies have created a national supply cooperative which purchases gasoline, oil, tires and steel strapping for its member firms. Membership investment is $200 per firm.

---

[10]Fusfeld, D. R., "Joint Subsidiaries in the Iron and Steel Industry," *American Economic Review.* Vol. 48, No. 2. May 1958. p. 587.

Coupled with the importance of keeping high-priced jets earning back their cost and keeping passengers happy, airlines find it highly expensive to stock enough spare parts at airports around the globe to prevent groundings. To solve this problem, airlines are turning increasingly to co-op parts pools at global way stations, letting one set of parts protect several lines which formerly stocked complete sets on their own.

Parts pooling was started in 1949. It developed slowly, restricted mostly to the remote outposts of the international airlines. But with the coming of jets and the critical economic need to keep them flying, the practice has expanded rapidly. One airline official estimates that $25 million to $30 million in parts are being pooled today, compared with only $1 million in 1960.

All lines sharing a part, including the owning line, prorate its cost, depreciated over a set period, such as five years. The "users" pay out their share in weekly installments over the five years. If the part is put into use, it must be returned or replaced within a week.

Manufacturing and Mining

Cooperative manufacturing and mining activities among industrial companies is gaining particularly in those lines in which risks are exceptionally large, where large capital requirements exist or where market demand is not yet well established. Among the principal enterprises containing cooperative efforts are printing and publishing, chemicals and allied products, wood and wood products and machinery and instruments.

Steel companies, under the "captive mining" or cost-company ruling of the Internal Revenue Service, often organize corporations which mine and otherwise handle coal and ores exclusively for participant companies on a nonprofit basis. In this sense, such ventures are akin to farmer cooperatives. The participant companies subscribe capital and share costs in proportion to the use they make of such a "captive" company. The operating corporation under such agreements has no profits or funds of its own; they belong to the participating companies. In filing its annual corporation income tax return, the operating company is likened to a nonexempt farmer cooperative.

At least one drawback to such enterprises is the antitrust impli-cation; the purpose of such ventures ought not to restrict competition or enable price collusion. When the purpose is exclusively "cost reduction," antitrust violations are not so likely or so suspect.

Marketing Cooperatively

Cooperative marketing activities among industrial companies include the following: (1) joint advertising and promotion programs; (2) development of one, uniform product label or brand; (3) co-operative development, testing and distribution of new industrial products; (4) joint ownership of research facilities; and (5) marketing or merchandising industrial products jointly.

Cooperative marketing and sales programs in industry involve chemical products, steel and steel products, tile, silk, glycerine, concrete blocks, machinery of various types, display fixtures, brick and other building materials and coal, among others. One principal co-op activity among oil companies is the joint use of pipelines. Many pipelines are jointly owned.

In one instance, metalworking firms operate a marketing cooperative which obtains contracts for its member firms. It costs up to $400 per month to be a member, plus up to 5 percent commission on each sale. Each shop is inspected to see that it can meet the cooperative's standards. Large defense contractors find that this cooperative is a good place through which to subcontract jobs they need to have done.

Researching Cooperatively

Most small and medium sized companies need the fruits of research, but feel they cannot afford the seed.

The conventional approach may be prohibitively expensive. At least six or eight scientists and technicians are required to conduct even a small research project. The minimum cost of an effective program is $30,000 to $45,000 per year per researcher, including salaries, standard equipment and supplies.

But there is a way out. A company can buy the same services for as little as $2,000 to $4,000 a year via co-op research. Many companies are using the approach to learn more about the basics underlying their manufacturing processes, to improve their products and operations and to develop new products.

In other ways, several oil companies may organize a co-op oil well data system. Available data on all the oil wells in a certain area are put on computer tape and data processed electronically regarding

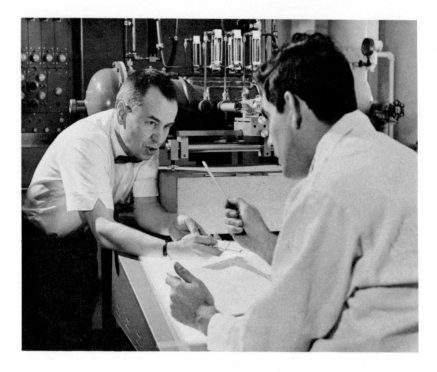

FIGURE 8-6

Most industrial firms recognize the need for research and development but sometimes cannot afford it individually. By cooperatively operating research and development centers, each member company benefits. (Courtesy, Aerospace Corporation, El Segundo, Calif.)

certain phases of oil production. The cost of this central computer operation is shared jointly.

In still other instances, small companies desiring national defense contracts find it better to form nonprofit combines to accumulate sufficient capital and talent in order to properly service these contracts.

Educating Cooperatively

Industrial firms use the nonprofit trade association technique on a vast scale. Trade associations perform many functions for their members, some of which constitute cooperative efforts.

Besides conducting educational and informational programs for members, trade associations may provide various insurance benefits. Some research and quality standardization programs are conducted cooperatively, as well as various management development programs.

Credit and accounting services may also be included. In some instances, trade association headquarters have evolved into purchasing associations which pool orders from members to buy in large quantities and at a cost savings.

RETAILER-OWNED WHOLESALE COOPERATIVES

The Department of Commerce reports 7,005 wholesale co-op establishments in the United States, with total sales of approximately $9 billion per year (Table 8-1). These establishments are owned by some 2,500 wholesale cooperatives serving 82,000 member retail firms. The annual payroll alone of the co-op wholesales amounts to $285 million. The number of co-op wholesales is less than the number of establishments because some co-op wholesales may operate more than one wholesale establishment.[11]

TABLE 8-1
Number of Wholesale Establishments, by
Legal Form of Organization, U.S.A.

Legal Form of Organization	Number of Establish- ments	Percent of Total
Profit-type corporations	162,184	56.7
Partnerships	37,601	13.1
Single proprietorships	78,428	27.4
Cooperatives	7,005	2.4
Other legal forms	778	.4
Total	285,996	100.0

Source: *1958 Census of Business.* Vol. III. p. 5-2.

It is apparent that retail lines vary in their adoption of the wholesale co-op techniques. Lumber and building material retailers have the highest proportion of memberships in co-op wholesales, followed by drug stores, grocery stores, department stores and hardware dealers. Shoe retailers have the least membership (Table 8-2).

---

[11]*Statistical Abstract of the U.S.* 1962. p. 842.

TABLE 8-2
Number of Retail Establishments, by Type
of Establishment, U.S.A.

Type of Retail Establishments	Total Number	Number in Wholesale Cooperatives	Percent of Total
Grocery	287,572	45,000	15.7
Drug stores	56,009	10,000	17.9
Furniture and home furnishings	50,729	2,400	4.7
Hardware	34,858	3,500	10.0
Lumber, bldg. materials	30,177	5,500	18.2
Shoes	23,847	232	1.0
Bakeries	19,034	1,000	5.3
Fish and seafood	4,458	315	7.1
Department stores	2,761	388	14.1
Total	509,445	68,335	13.4

Source: *Statistical Abstract of the U.S. 1962.* p. 831.

Operating Conditions of Wholesale Cooperatives

Wholesale cooperatives that are retailer-owned are governed by stockholder members elected by their fellow retail members. Voting control is vested in the retail merchants who are stockholders. All members, both large and small, are treated fairly. Earnings and savings are distributed as patronage dividends in proportion to the amount of business done with and through the warehouse by the individual retailer. Retailer cooperatives seek to keep their retail members competitive with any and all other operators in their trading areas. They engage in group buying, promoting, advertising and distributing. The sales program in the ordinary wholesale house is almost entirely eliminated in the successful retailer cooperative, for the reason that buying and distribution are chiefly for members only. Thus the wide-spread sales effort which is so costly in the general operation of a wholesale house is eliminated.

Other important ways in which the retailer cooperatives reduce the cost of operation are by rigid credit controls and the elimination of bad debt losses; large-scale purchasing; coordinated advertising and promotion; virtual elimination of selling expenses, commissions and travel costs; elimination of wholesale operating profit; speedy turnover and smaller inventories; and coordinated retail store merchandising practices. Their objective is to furnish retail goods for resale at as nearly production cost as possible. Purchasing agreements or contracts similar to those used in farmer cooperatives are sometimes employed.

Appliance, TV and Radio Wholesales

There are an estimated 14 retailer-owned appliance, radio and television dealer wholesales, with an individual dealer membership of 574. The largest cooperative of this kind has 145 member stores which do more than $100 million of business annually in six states and the District of Columbia.

The main obstacle to co-op appliance groups has been the lack of sufficient number of dealers handling identical "brands" in a certain locality. For this reason, appliance cooperatives have a better chance for success in large metropolitan areas, such as New York, Chicago and Los Angeles. Various impediments exist against appliance cooperatives, but these can be solved if member-owners are willing to work together to achieve a common goal, namely, the survival of the smaller appliance dealer.

Bakery Cooperatives

There are also in existence purchasing cooperatives serving the retail bakery trade, and their experience has proven that where retailers combine their buying power, results can be both practical and profitable.

The best known bakery-owned cooperative is Quality Bakers of America Cooperative founded in 1922 and presently having a membership of 130 plants. This cooperative originated and promotes the "Miss Sunbeam" bread label, which provides a uniform bread label and national advertising for that label. It has been especially helpful in reducing the trend to chain-store bread labels. Other achievements of Quality Bakers of America Cooperative have been: (1) adoption of uniform cost accounting procedures among bakery members, (2) purchasing of supplies cooperatively, (3) joint sales promotion and (4) provision of much other management, marketing and engineering information.[12] There are other examples of bakery cooperatives.

---

[12]Graf, George, "A Slingshot for David," National Canners Association Convention, Chicago, Ill. Feb. 22, 1959.

FIGURE 8-7

Bakers throughout the United States, through a cooperative, have established the well-known "Miss Sunbeam" bread label. (Courtesy, Quality Bakers of America Cooperative, New York, N.Y.)

Dry Goods, Apparel and Footwear

These types of wholesale business cooperatives merely act as purchasing agents for their members and as such do not take title to the commodities from the manufacturers. The title of a commodity passes directly from the manufacturer or processor to the cooperative's members. The expenses of the operation of the cooperative are borne by assessments made upon the members in proportion to the volume of business done by them with the cooperative.

There are six retailer-owned shoe buying syndicates. The independent shoe retailer is rapidly disappearing. Advent of chain shoe retailers and discount shoe stores has created a competitive environment difficult for the independent to meet. Independent shoe retailers have little alternative but to form cooperatives in order to survive.

As in the case of other independent retailers, men's wear retailers, children's wear and women's wear shops are actively seeking the co-op route as a means of bolstering their economic position against chain stores and discounters. The advantages of cooperatives in the apparel field are obvious: (1) better bargaining with manufacturers, (2) co-op delivery, (3) centralized alteration department, (4) factoring of accounts receivables, (5) group promotion and advertising, (6) interchange of merchandise and (7) automatic data processing in a central location to serve small stores.

Drug Wholesales

The Federal Wholesale Druggists' Association, with headquarters in New York City, was organized in 1915. This association is representative of the co-op wholesale distribution type in the drug field. Groups of this kind operate on the basis that after all expenses have been paid, the savings in distribution are returned pro rata to stockholder-druggists.

Local drug cooperatives vary considerably in number of members and business volume. For example, members may be required to purchase a share of stock for $200 plus $300 for built-up reserves. This money is held by the cooperative for anticipated bad debts, and no member may own more than one share of stock. Sales of drugs are made at prices below those of other wholesalers. Refunds are held for 18 months for operating purposes, then are paid back to the members at 3-month intervals. The directors meet monthly. Dividends are paid on stock, and patronage refunds are paid to members and nonmembers. Nonmembers may use such refunds to buy a share of stock.

Another co-op wholesale drug house, Celo Labs of Burnsville, North Carolina, serves 47 consumer cooperatives and group health plans, as well as individuals through mail order. It has been a factor in reducing drug costs.

Furniture and Furnishings

There are 24 retailer-owned furniture wholesales, with a store membership of 2,400. Their aggregate retail sales are about $1 billion per year. This is about 20 percent of national retail furniture sales. Most of these co-op wholesales developed since 1953 when smaller, independent retailers were in a cost-price squeeze. The most important functions of these cooperatives are: (1) advertising services, (2) pool car shipments, (3) co-op buying and (4) merchandising programs.

Views differ as to the role of co-op groups in furniture and furnishings. Some retailers anticipate a large increase in the number of these co-op groups. Others see less growth because furniture and

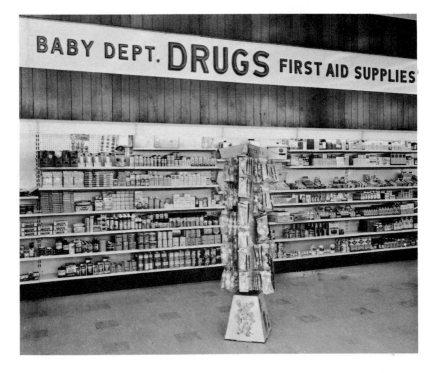

FIGURE 8-8

Independent druggists often form cooperatives to better compete with chain-owned drug houses and discount drug operations. (Reprinted by permission of Drug News Weekly, copyright, Fairchild Publications, New York, N.Y.)

FIGURE 8-9

Gasoline and petroleum cooperatives are becoming important factors in this business. They not only own service stations but also other petroleum facilities. (Courtesy, Greenbelt Consumer Services, Beltsville, Md.)

furnishings, for the most part, are not mass-consumed items like food, drugs or even appliances. Nevertheless, some co-op furniture groups have made striking successes. One group of furniture dealers, by co-operating, has made savings in freight costs, carried less inventory, obtained more selling space in stores and exchanged management ideas with fellow co-op members.

Gasoline and Petroleum Cooperatives

Cooperatives refine lubricants, as well as fuels, and operate several lube oil blending and grease compounding plants. They refine and distribute heating oils and liquefied petroleum gases such as propane and butane.

Since World War II, cooperatives have achieved a measure of vertical integration in the petroleum industry. Collectively, they refine as much petroleum fuels as they distribute wholesale, though they produce only 13 percent of the crude oil they refine.

Cooperatives have oil leases in nine states and two Canadian provinces, with estimated reserves of 32 million barrels of crude oil. They own a working interest in 3,249 wells, which in 1961 produced

7,683,000 barrels of oil. Co-op refineries have a combined through-put capacity of 161,100 barrels of crude oil a day. They have 1,815 miles of pipelines to gather crude oil into these refineries and own 895 miles of refined product pipelines.

Slowly, cooperatives are gaining increased control over the crude oil they need to operate their refineries. In the five years from 1956 to 1961, the ratio of crude oil produced to refinery capacity rose from 10 to 13 percent.[13]

Grocery Wholesales

There are 262 retailer-owned wholesales, with a membership of about 45,000 grocers. Their rapid growth in recent years is due mainly to the need for larger-scale buying to match giant corporate food chains. Other small grocery stores have joined profit-type wholesales in a voluntary self-help program, a quasi cooperative set-up. Independent retailers belonging to voluntary and co-op groups have increased their share of food store sales from 29 percent in 1947 to 49 percent in 1961, making them the biggest single bloc in the nation's food retailing structure.

The cooperatives' share of all business of grocery wholesalers advanced from 7.0 percent in 1939 to 10.2 percent in 1948 to 23.0 percent in 1958. At the same time the share of business carried on by general-line grocery wholesalers dropped from 62.9 percent in 1939 to 61.2 percent in 1948 to 40.0 percent in 1958.

Retailer-owned grocery wholesales follow many of the popular co-op principles: cash selling; one man, one vote; and dividends on patronage. Membership per cooperative is usually large. Such organizations are named Associated Grocers, Independent Grocers, United Grocers and Affiliated Food Stores, among others. Since each cooperative is chartered under state law and often confines its operations locally, duplications of co-op names are numerous.

Retailer-owned wholesale cooperatives usually supply their members with dry groceries and frequently with frozen food and other products, as well as with warehousing and other merchandising services.

Nearly all retailer-owned cooperatives take the corporate form. A few are nonstock corporations, but most have both common and

---

[13]*Cooperatives, U.S.A.*, Cooperative League, Chicago, Ill. 1962. pp. 43-44.

preferred stock. Debt securities are also found in their capital structures. Active retailer-members are required to make cash deposits equal to the average of their purchases for from 1 to 4 weeks. Capital is also raised by withholding patronage dividends.

Cooperatives have salaried general managers, responsible to the directors. Such a manager may also be an officer or director of the corporation. The manager often suggests to the members sources of supply for products not handled by the cooperative.

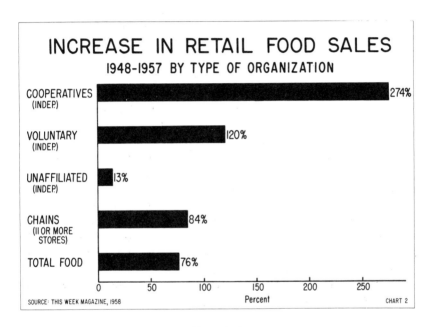

FIGURE 8-10
(Courtesy, This Week Magazine)

Another technique being developed in the grocery field is a national co-op buying group which purchases supplies such as paper sacks, shopping carts and cash registers for member food stores and other types of stores. Each store member of the group pays a fee according to the size of savings made. Surpluses are distributed periodically according to the volume of business conducted with the group. Buying groups for stores enable the smaller retailer to reduce his operating costs and become more competitive with the larger retail chains.

Hardware Wholesales

There are an estimated 15 co-op hardware wholesales, with 3,500 member firms in the United States.

The independent hardware retailer is in much the same position as the independent druggist and groceryman. With the advent of chain stores, discount houses and buying clubs, the independent hardware owner faces shrinking profit margins and loss of some customer loyalty. Cooperatives offer him an opportunity to remain independent while strengthening his competitive position. In addition to cooperatives, many independent hardware owners join voluntary wholesales, in which an independent hardware wholesaler takes a group of retail stores under his "wing" to afford them a better competitive position.

Independent hardware dealers have formed co-op wholesales by investing in common stock (usually $100 per share) and in preferred stock. Each member usually has only one vote regardless of size of store. Instead of paying annual cash patronage dividends, co-op wholesales will issue rebate notes paying 5 percent interest with a maximum due date of 10 years. If the dealer needs cash, he can usually redeem these notes sooner. Interest on common and preferred stock may be paid annually also.

In addition to low prices, participation in cooperatives assures overnight delivery, since goods are warehoused centrally. Besides, there are no minimum order requirements. Thus, the dealer can hold his inventory down and in turn step up his turnover, which has spelled increased profits for participating stores.

Probably the most important aspect of the co-op venture is the merchandising help it offers the dealer.

Lumber and Building Material Groups

There are some 55 lumber and building material wholesale groups serving some 5,500 retailers.

It is customary for retail lumber dealers to purchase one share of voting stock in a cooperative, usually at $100. They elect a board of directors and operate like other farm and nonfarm cooperatives.

Generally, these cooperatives handle items which retail lumber dealers formerly purchased in less-than-carload-lot (LCL) quantities. They also purchase materials outright for members, and these are then shipped directly from manufacturers to members.

Interest dividends on stock are paid and patronage dividends are refunded to member firms.

WEBB-POMERENE ASSOCIATIONS

The Webb-Pomerene Act of 1918 permits domestic firms to form export trade associations and exempts such associations from prosecution under the Sherman Act. There are 30 such associations serving 296 firms.

While Webb-Pomerene associations are for marketing purposes, many retail business firms are pooling their resources to buy foreign-made products much more cheaply than if they bought as individual firms. Such a cooperatively operated agency keeps retailer-members informed as to available goods, prices, shipment dates, etc. The position of the individual retailer is thereby strengthened in competition with companies large enough to import goods on their own.

WORKERS' PRODUCTIVE COOPERATIVES

It is estimated that there are only about a dozen workers' productive cooperatives in the United States. These cooperatives are comprised of craftsmen, unionists and technicians who own the plants in which they work. These differ from "labor unions" in which the workers are employees of management and do not own controlling interests in the plants. In the past, workers' productive cooperatives have existed in the manufacture of cigars, glass, apparel, building products, pottery, bakery goods, coal and seafood packing, among other industries.

There is a growing tendency for labor unions or workers themselves to purchase plants which are closing for various reasons in order to preserve the jobs of the plant workers. However, workers usually proceed with much caution because the danger of economic failure is great. If a corporation itself could not make a profit, the workers' co-op group will likewise face a tough economic situation.

In other cases, workers can create new jobs for themselves by working cooperatively. In a plywood manufacturing cooperative, for example, a worker buys-in as a working share. Once he has a working share he is permitted to work in the cooperative, and each worker works his allocated number of days at the specific job to which he is assigned. Every worker makes an identical amount of money during the year. The manager is hired just as it is done in any other cooperative. The manager is not a member. Neither is the controller, usually, nor any of the office staff. Earnings are shared among the workers according to the amount of work they put into the cooperative.

QUASI COOPERATIVES

Quasi cooperatives, as defined previously, are those which have at least one element of the co-op business method but not all three elements, such as: (1) one man, one vote or patronage voting control, (2) limited returns on invested capital and (3) refunding of surpluses to member-patrons on a patronage basis.

Blue Cross Associations

At the present time the Blue Cross plans are the most widely used type of prepaid hospital service. At least one Blue Cross organization operates in nearly every state. The programs in different parts of the country vary in detail of set-up and operation. They are alike in basic structure and methods, however.

The American Hospital Association adopted the term "Blue Cross" in 1938 to designate any prepaid hospital service plan which met the standards established by the Association. These standards were slightly modified in 1946. At present they are as follows:

1. Representation of hospitals, the medical profession and the general public on the governing boards.

2. Nonprofit sponsorship and control.

3. Free choice of hospital and physician with opportunity for all hospitals of standing in the area to become member-hospitals.

4. Benefits guaranteed by member-hospitals.

5. Sound accounting practices and adequate statistical records.

6. No interference with professional relationships.

7. Compliance with principles governing the organization and operation of Blue Cross plans, as established by the American Hospital Association.

8. Other principles include adequate general or contingency reserves, equitable payments to hospitals, dignified promotion and administration, sound enrollment practices and interplan coordination.

By the end of 1960, 77 Blue Cross organizations had been formed in the United States. They covered 57.4 million subscribers.[14][15]

Blue Cross plans are chartered under respective state laws, are nonprofit, provide free choice of hospitals by subscribers and each subscriber is protected under an indemnity schedule outside the plan's service area. In addition, some Blue Cross plans offer surgical coverage. The Blue Cross receives premium payments from its subscribers which are pooled; from this pool the plan pays each hospital for the care provided its subscribers. The hospitals bill the plan, not the patients, and the plan pays the hospitals directly with no money going through its subscribers. If the plan offers surgical coverage, payment can be made directly to the subscriber who, in turn, pays the physician, or it may be paid directly to the physician.[16]

Blue Shield Plans

These plans are designed primarily to help cover surgery and anesthesia expense, although a few go so far as to include hospitalization expense.

There are about 70 Blue Shield plans covering 47.1 million persons in the United States.

Blue Shield plans are nonprofit, and in most cases the majority of the board of directors are physicians, not laymen. Usually, a plan covers an entire state. Both group and individual enrollment is usually permitted. Premiums charged are set from time to time as financial conditions require.

The main weakness of the Blue Cross and Blue Shield plans, from a co-op standpoint, is their proxy voting which each subscriber usually consents to at the time he joins. This proxy allows a small group or a board of directors to determine policy and control the affairs of the plans. If voting were made more democratic, these plans would be truly cooperative.

Consumer Rebate Plans

While no precise data are available concerning consumer rebate plans, it is generally conceded that they are numerous. One procedure

---

[14]Johnston, Helen, *Cooperation for Rural Health*, FCS Misc. Rept. 123, USDA, Washington, D.C. Sept. 1948. pp. 5-6.
[15]*Statistical Abstract of the U.S. 1962.* p. 478.
[16]Holman, E. J. and G. W. Cooley, "Voluntary Health Insurance in the U.S.," *Iowa Law Review.* Winter 1950. Vol. 35. pp. 183-208.

is for an ordinary profit-type corporation to pledge, in advance of beginning such a plan, to refund a certain amount or an amount according to formula. This rebate is therefore tax deductible for the corporation. The consumer pays no income tax on the rebate because the saving is for household expenses.

The most famous consumer rebate plan was the one used by Henry Ford in 1914. Henry Ford promised to refund $50 to each purchaser if Ford sold 300,000 cars the next year. A total of 308,000 cars were sold, or 39 percent more than in 1913-14. Ford paid $15,411,000 in cash to his customers. Next year Ford cut prices $50 a car and abandoned the consumer rebate idea.

A more recent case involved American Motors. Under this plan, if car sales of the company rose above 10 percent for any given month as compared with the same month one year previous, the customer would receive a $25 U.S. savings bond. If sales increased by a percentage over 20, commensurate bond payments would be paid. The plan was basically similar to the Ford Plan of the decade following 1910. Consumer rebates of this type are tax deductible provided the plan is announced publicly before any rebates are allowed and assuming other pertinent conditions are met.

Another type of consumer rebate or purchase discount involves a "buying membership" plan. For a $10 fee, the shopper is given a membership card and a quarterly directory in which participating merchants are listed, together with the discount they have agreed to give all persons presenting the card. The directory is broken down geographically to provide the consumer a convenient guide in shopping in specific cities within an area.

Another plan provides that retail stores pay a small fee to a central office which then mails out this list of stores to consumers, who also pay a small fee. The consumers are able to get various discounts from these listed stores.

Still another plan involves pharmacies and labor union members. For a small annual fee, each union member is given a membership card which qualifies him for discounts on drug purchases. It is estimated that for a $2 annual fee, each union member and his family may save about $50 per year in drug costs.

Closed-Door Discount Stores

Discount stores are generally defined as general-line retail stores which follow a management and pricing policy based on low-markups.

These stores may be distinguished from conventional retailers whose management and pricing policy are not based essentially on low-markups but on service, credit extension and conventional markups, sometimes following fair-trade pricing and manufacturers' suggested retail prices.

Discount stores are of two types: (1) open-door and (2) closed-door. The open-door discounter trades with the general public similar to a conventional retailer. The closed-door discounter confines his trade to consumer-groups, such as municipal, state and/or federal employees. Also, consumer membership in closed-door discounters is usually evidenced by an annual membership fee or subscription. Closed-door discounters may be chartered as profit or nonprofit corporations.

At the end of 1961, there were about 47 closed-door discount firms in the United States, with a membership of over 3 million. These 47 firms were operating 122 stores, or an average of about 3 stores per firm and 42,553 members per firm. They operate in 34 states. Closed-door discounters operate stores that are larger than open-door stores.

Leading states in number of all discount stores are New York, Ohio, California, Pennsylvania, Illinois, Texas and Massachusetts.

The number of paid memberships in closed-door discounters has been rising fast in recent years. At least one discounter reports a gain of about 600,000 paid-in members in one year alone.

Elementary and High School
Associations

Elementary and high school associations number about 585, with a student membership of over 151,000.

The largest concentration of nonprofit schools is in the eastern United States. Of the 587 nonprofit schools about 283, or half the number, are located in Connecticut, Massachusetts, New York, New Jersey and Pennsylvania. California with 45 is also important in this regard. These six states also have half of the enrolled student membership, or about 80,000. These nonprofit schools do not include denominational schools.

While the principal emphasis in the United States has been on public schools and public education, there are indications that a nonprofit school system privately operated has some merits. For example, Act 257 of the 1958 Louisiana legislature enables five or more parents of school children to organize elementary and high school

cooperatives. So far, about 36 such cooperatives have been organized, having a student membership of over 6,500.

Nonprofit Medical Care Institutions

Out of a total of 31,723 medical care institutions in the United States, 4,140 are nonprofit; 474 are federally owned; 3,593 are state, city and county owned; 2,248 are church owned; 19,156 are profit-type and 2,112 are unclassified.

Of the 4,140 nonprofit hospitals, about half contain less than 50 beds. The average bed capacity per hospital is 93. In all, the nonprofit institutions have a total bed capacity of about 393,000.

The accreditation of nonprofit institutions is high. Although they account for only about 13 percent of all institutions, they represent 38 percent of all those accredited. Profit-type institutions which account for about 60 percent of all institutions represent only 5 percent of those accredited.[17]

---

[17]Osato, Sylvia, *Number and Type of Medical Care Institutions in the U.S.*, Public Health Service, Washington, D.C. Vol. 47, Nov. 1961.

Mutual Funds

There are about 170 mutual funds in the United States, with total assets of $22.8 billion. Some 5.3 million accounts are in mutual funds. However, one person may hold more than one account. Thus, the number of shareholders would be considerably less.

Open-end investment companies are popularly known as mutual funds. The terms are interchangeable.

Unlike closed-end companies which generally have a fixed number of shares outstanding, the number of shares outstanding of mutual funds may be constantly changing. All mutual funds stand ready at any time to redeem outstanding shares — generally at asset value — when presented by investors. These companies therefore are called "open-end" because the number of their shares is not fixed but may decrease as shares are redeemed. In addition, most mutual funds continuously offer new shares to investors at a public offering price based upon current net asset value. Thus, the total number of shares outstanding in such companies may increase or decrease.

Mutual fund shares are usually available from investment dealers. In most cases the offering price to the public includes a distribution charge. A prospectus for each fund, which must be given to prospective purchasers, describes this charge.[18]

Under the Internal Revenue Act, the companies that pay at least 90 percent of their earnings to shareholders are not taxed on the earnings distributed to shareholders. The shareholders pay income tax on the part of the payment that is designated as investment income, and pay a capital gains tax on the remainder. In this regard, mutual funds are taxed similarly to cooperatives. Mutual funds now distribute over $1 billion annually in earnings, of which about half is from investment income and half from realized capital gains.

Mutual funds make the owning of stocks safer by spreading investments over a number of carefully selected and managed stocks in several different kinds of businesses. Mutual funds may vary in their purposes. Some funds are geared to "growth" stocks, others to stocks with good dividend records, while still others may have varying objectives.

---

[18]*Investment Companies Fact Book,* Investment Company Institute, New York, N.Y. pp. 6-7.

Soil Conservation Districts

The Soil Conservation Service is responsible for carrying out a national program of conservation for land and water resources. The Service assists 2,900 soil conservation districts and other cooperators in bringing about physical adjustments in land use to conserve soil, water and plant resources; establish a permanent and balanced agriculture; and reduce damage by floods and sedimentation. Special drainage, irrigation, flood prevention and watershed protection activities are developed and carried out in cooperation with soil conservation districts, watershed groups and other federal and state agencies. Some 1.1 million farmers are served within these 2,900 districts.

Farmers organize soil conservation districts under state laws. The federal government assists them financially and technically in carrying out water and soil management practices.

ECONOMIC COOPERATION AMONG GOVERNMENTS

CARE

The Cooperative for American Remittances Everywhere (CARE) ships individual food packages to persons and provides many other services, the cost of which is paid for by donors in the United States. CARE operates as a private, nonprofit cooperative food and service distributor with the sanction and cooperation of the various governments.

CARE was organized in 1945 by 22 private groups interested in post-war European relief. The groups represented two major divisions: organizations with their own operating relief programs overseas and those with overseas interest but without general relief operations. They represented labor, cooperative and nationality groups—people with widely different interests and activities.

One-third of all donated funds now go into self-help projects.

The World Bank

The World Bank for Reconstruction and Development had its origin under Articles of Agreement drawn up by the United Nations Monetary and Financial Conference at Bretton Woods, New Hampshire, in July 1944.

The Bank is owned by its member countries as stockholders, and its membership consists of 68 countries of world-wide representation. The capitalization of the Bank is derived from capital shares subscribed by these member countries, purchasable only by members and transferable only to the Bank. As of 1959 the total subscribed capital amounted to the equivalent of $18.6 billion.

Voting power in the World Bank is alloted on the basis of stock shares, with the nations supplying the most capital having the largest number of votes. The United States, the United Kingdom, France and Germany have about 55 percent of the stock and of the votes.[19]

The World Bank makes loans to various countries of the world in assisting with their economic developments. These are loans, not grants, and are repaid to the Bank with interest. The lesser-developed countries have benefited from loans made possible by the capital contributions from the more highly developed countries.

Customs Union

Sovereign states, provinces and nations may also utilize the co-op techniques in establishing customs unions or "common markets." In this manner, each governmental unit cooperates by lowering its tariffs against goods produced in another country within the customs area. This leads to freer trade, higher living standards and stronger economies for all governmental units concerned.

In the next chapter, the Rochdale Principles are discussed in terms of modern cooperation.

TOPICS FOR DISCUSSION

1. Discuss the scope and nature of business service cooperatives.
2. Discuss the scope and nature of nonfarm manufacturing, marketing and supply associations.
3. Discuss the scope and nature of retailer-owned wholesale cooperatives. What kind of potential do these cooperatives have for small businessmen?
4. What are Webb-Pomerene associations?

---

[19]Staff, *The World Bank*, Washington, D.C. June 1960. p. 127.

5. Why have workers' productive cooperatives played such a minor role in American business?

6. Discuss the scope and nature of quasi cooperatives. Why are they called "quasi"?

SELECTED REFERENCES

1. Cook, Hugh and others, *Cooperative Arrangements Among Small Processors of Farm Products,* Wisc. Agr. Exp. Sta. Bul. 243, Madison, Wisc. June 1963.

2. Eldridge, Seba, *Development of Collective Enterprise,* University of Kansas Press, Lawrence, Kans. 1943.

3. Foth, J. H., *Trade Associations,* Ronald Press, New York, N.Y. 1930.

4. Goldman, Franz, *Voluntary Medical Care Insurance in the U.S.,* Columbia University Press, New York, N.Y. 1948.

5. Hales, Charles, *The Baltimore Clearing House,* Johns Hopkins Press, Baltimore, Md. 1940.

6. Meissner, F., "Closed-Door Discount Stores," *Journal of Retailing.* Vol. 38. Fall 1962. p. 17.

7. Miller, R. W. and H. R. Grossman, "The Nonprofit Corporation or Association in the Non-agricultural Field," *Law and Contemporary Problems,* Duke University, Durham, N.C. pp. 463-472.

8. Myers, James, *Labor and Co-ops,* Cooperative League, Chicago, Ill. 1949.

9. O'Leary, Edmund, *Cooperative Wholesaling in Grocery Distribution,* The Ohio State University Bur. of Bus. Research, Columbus, Ohio. Apr. 1942.

10. Pink, Louis, *The Story of Blue Cross,* Public Affairs Committee Pamphlet 101, New York, N.Y. 1945.

11. Schmedel, S. R., "Appliance Dealers Join Buying Co-ops," *Wall Street Journal,* New York, N. Y. July 10, 1963.

12. Slawson, H. H., "Businessmen's Cooperatives," *America.* Oct. 4, 1950.

13. Staff, *Small Business Problems in Food Distribution,* House of Representatives Rept. 2234, Washington, D.C. 1960.

14. Stewart, M. S., *The Role of Investment Companies,* Public Affairs Pamphlet 221, New York, N.Y. 1955.

15. Walter, J. E., *Role of Regional Security Exchanges,* University of California Press, Berkeley, Calif. 1957.

16. Weiss, E. B., *Death of the Independent Retailer,* Doyle Dane Bernbach, Inc., New York, N.Y. 1963.

17. Williams, Marc, *Flowers-by-Wire,* Mercury House, Detroit, Mich. 1960.

CHAPTER 9 –

The Rochdale Principles
and Modern Cooperatives

A good principle, not rightly understood, may prove as harmful as a bad principle.

—Milton

Important principles may and must be flexible.

—Abraham Lincoln

MUCH OF THE LEGISLATION dealing with cooperatives in the United States was no doubt influenced by the Rochdale Society which began in England in 1844. It is necessary at this point to review the Rochdale Principles to determine whether these principles are still valid.[1] It must be remembered that Rochdale was a retail cooperative selling mostly consumer goods, such as food, clothing, etc. It is difficult to see how any set of principles designed for a retail cooperative could be generalized for all types of cooperatives. The Rochdale Pioneers themselves never ordained a set of co-op principles. In time, their policies and practices became crystallized into a code which most cooperators throughout the world came to accept. It may be well at this point to evaluate the Rochdale Principles over a century after the founding of the Rochdale Society.

1. OPEN MEMBERSHIP

The Rochdale Pioneers wanted an open co-op society—anyone, man or woman, at least up to a fixed number, could join the society on equal terms with the original members. They wanted no discrimination on political, religious or racial grounds. Their only basis for rejecting a member was bad character or bad habits.

---

[1] The ten so-called Rochdale Principles evaluated here reflect the popularly held beliefs as to what these principles comprised.

This Rochdale principle has been widely misinterpreted. A cooperative might not effectively operate on a principle of *open membership.*
Membership in a cooperative has to be applied for, documented or
proved as to qualification and must be approved by the board of directors on a majority vote. A board might reject a membership application
on many grounds. State co-op laws do not legally force cooperatives to
accept any and all memberships submitted to them. There are many
cases in which cooperatives have closed membership; that is, a processing association might have all its capacity committed to present members—for example, a raw sugar mill cooperative. Cooperatives such as
irrigation and livestock breeding associations have to operate on a
restricted membership basis in order to maintain service which will be
satisfactory to the membership.

One reason open membership has been popular is because many
retail cooperatives have sought to expand business volume rapidly and
have chosen not to screen their member applicants very closely.

The principle of open membership, while a good one, has to be
qualified. In all cases, however, membership or withdrawal from membership is voluntary. Whenever compulsion or coercion is employed,
as in communist collectives, no true cooperative can exist. It would
become an arm of the state.

In summary, a cooperative ought to be very careful in admitting
members. These principles should be followed:

1. A cooperative should have intelligent membership of efficient
persons who recognize the need for organization and who will contribute to the objectives of the cooperative.

2. A cooperative should expel irresponsible individuals, chronic
kickers and agitators.

3. Membership should be limited by receiving applications only
during specific periods.

4. Membership should never be automatic. It should be processed
carefully.

2. ONE MAN, ONE VOTE

The Rochdale Pioneers felt that the person, rather than his stock
investment, should be the basis of voting.

This Rochdale Principle is not universal. There are now at least four
ways of voting in a cooperative instead of one method, as follows:

1. One man, one vote.

2. Vote according to patronage on a dollar volume or on some other basis but with a limitation on votes cast.

3. One man, one vote plus additional votes based on patronage, on shares of stock or on some other basis.

4. Vote acording to shares of stock. Mississippi co-op law provides for an option of voting according to shares of stock, for example.

The Rochdale societies themselves have partially abandoned the one man, one vote principle. According to Digby, societies that make up the British Cooperative Wholesale Society hold one vote per society at quarterly meetings plus additional votes in proportion to their patronage with the B.C.W.S.[2] A limit on voting power is usually stipulated, however.

Emelianoff made a thorough analysis of the one man, one vote principle. He concluded that the one man, one vote principle is not necessary to have a true cooperative. His analysis showed that the equal vote concept is a special case—only when the cooperators are economically equal. If the co-op members are not economically equal, then proportional voting based on patronage would be more equitable. He wrote:

> Cooperators vote equally in their associations because they are, for all practical purposes, economically equal, not because they strive for economic equality. There cannot be a more striking and persuasive illustration of this fact than the very case of the Rochdale Pioneers themselves, who were perfectly equal . . . in their poverty.[3]

In practice, the one man, one vote principle works against the larger patron. However, since 32 of the 50 state co-op incorporation laws for agriculture stipulate voting only on the basis of one man, one vote, it might require a long period of time before changes are made in state incorporation laws. Some 18 states do permit voting on a basis other than one man, one vote, such as on the basis of acres or trees owned, etc., or on some other indicator of patronage such as dollar volume.

The related question of proxy voting is an interesting one. Co-op principles usually stipulate that no proxy voting be used. However, state laws vary. Some laws permit proxy voting while others do not. If per-

---

[2]Digby, Margaret, *The World Co-op Movement,* Hutchinson & Co., London, England. 1960. p. 41.
[3]Emelianoff, Ivan, *Economic Theory of Cooperation,* Edwards Bros., Ann Arbor, Michigan. pp. 195-196.

mitted, proxy voting is usually well regulated under a cooperative's bylaws.

3. CASH TRADING

The Rochdale Pioneers had this rule because credit evils were rampant in England during the Industrial Revolution. In recent years, consumer cooperatives in England have themselves started selling on credit. Most students of cooperation now agree that *cash trading* is an operating practice, not a co-op principle. Emelianoff concluded in this vein.

In the United States, most farm supply cooperatives sell on credit, yet they are still true cooperatives. Many of them were forced into

FIGURE 9-1

Selling for cash, while not regarded as a true co-op principle is often a good business prin-ciple to follow. Credit sales, if made, should be carefully controlled. (Courtesy, Consumers Cooperative of Berkeley, Inc., Berkeley, Calif.)

credit selling by their competition. In Chapter 15, this problem will be dealt with further.

4. MEMBERSHIP EDUCATION

The Rochdale Pioneers desired to further co-op knowledge since so few understood what cooperation was all about.

While membership education is a noble objective, it is not considered a co-op principle as such. If all the cooperatives in the world were to be asked about member education, they would probably reply that they do some of it. There is no precise basis for judging what is and what is not member education. All cooperatives would agree that membership education should be penetrating enough that each member recognizes fully his rights and responsibilities to his business.

5. POLITICAL AND RELIGIOUS NEUTRALITY

The Rochdale Pioneers wanted to keep clear of political and religious entanglements. They had enough problems dealing in economics. However, in later years the Rochdale-type societies in England violated this principle by forming a cooperative political party which, at times, has joined the British Labour Party in politics. Cooperatives in various other countries have also entered into the political arena.

As can be noted, political neutrality is really not a principle because many cooperatives in many parts of the world have joined various political groups. It is a recommendation rather than a principle.

Religious neutrality is likewise not a principle. A church-sponsored credit union is not likely to admit members from another church or denomination, yet it is still a cooperative. Again religious neutrality is simply a recommendation.

It is well to point out, however, that political activity is dangerous for all cooperatives. A far better recommendation is that cooperatives stress better citizenship, voting on election day and more civics education in schools, without actually offering or endorsing political candidates. Another fault of co-op political activity is that a cooperative's own membership may be divided on political candidates; therefore, dissension and conflict are likely to arise. While political neutrality is not a test of cooperation, it is a sound policy to follow.

FIGURE 9-2

Membership education, while not regarded as a true co-op principle, is still urgently neces-sary if cooperatives are to reach their full potentials. (Courtesy, Florists' Telegraph Delivery Association, Detroit, Mich.)

6. NO UNUSUAL RISK ASSUMPTION

The Rochdale Pioneers did not have an abundance of capital. Therefore, they were conservative in their approach and rightfully felt that no unusual risks should be assumed.

While this is often a good approach, it cannot be considered a principle because there is no precise measure of "risk" or of "unusual risk." By merely opening their Toad Lane store, the Rochdale Pioneers had already made an unusual risk assumption in terms of the conditions of the Industrial Revolution.

The best which can be stated here is that co-op management usually tends to the "conservative" and attempts to avoid strictly "speculative" ventures.

7. LIMITED INTEREST ON STOCK

The Rochdale Pioneers believed that interest on stock investment should be limited. This idea had been gotten from Robert Owen. Five percent was thought to be the maximum rate that should be paid on stock investment.

This tenet qualifies as a principle considerably better than do the others, although 5 percent should not be construed as being part of the principle. The rate itself depends on the supply and demand for money in a certain country at a certain period of time. In the United States, the maximum usually specified is 8 percent, while in other countries it may be more or less, depending.

Emelianoff does not wholly agree with this principle. He argues that it is a special case. When stock investment and a member's patronage are not the same proportion of the total, interest on stock serves to rectify inequalities. He argues that if each member had the same proportion of stock as he had of patronage, then there would be no reason to pay any interest whatever on stock. The member would simply get

FIGURE 9-3

Limited interest on stock or equity capital is a common co-op principle. This is to prevent capital investment and returns on investment from becoming the sole objective of a cooperative. (Courtesy, National Association of Mutual Savings Banks, New York, N.Y.)

his interest on stock as part of the patronage dividend. In other words, in such a case, interest on stock would have no significance.[4]

In more recent years "interest on stock" has been changed to "interest on capital" since so many cooperatives are not organized on a stock share basis. In such a case, interest may be paid on the money invested regardless of the form in which it is invested.

The principle of limiting interest paid on capital is a good one because a cooperative is organized to serve its patrons, not investors. If patrons are also investors, they will not mind a limit on interest paid on capital.

"Paying interest on stock" poses still another problem with regards to common and preferred stock. Many cooperatives do not pay interest on common stock because each member has only one share. On preferred stock, where members hold varying amounts, interest is usually paid. Thus, we see that this circumstance supports Emelianoff's theory that if each patron has an equal amount of stock investment, it is useless to pay interest. Interest is paid on stock or equity because not all members have invested equally in stock or equities.

8. GOODS SOLD AT REGULAR
RETAIL PRICES

There are at least two distinct pricing policies a retail cooperative may follow: (1) selling at the same price at which other retailers are selling or (2) selling at the cooperative's true cost. The Rochdale Pioneers believed in (1), while many other cooperatives have followed (2), especially the Swedish cooperatives. In the United States, it is estimated that the majority of retail cooperatives follow (1), with a minority following (2).

A retail cooperative which follows a "price maintenance" policy does so for these reasons: (1) Its management is fearful of retaliation by profit-type businesses or of price wars. (2) Its management may feel that a larger net savings will remain at year's end thus easing capital requirements and enhancing management stature. (3) Its management may feel that nonmembers should not be given benefits of low prices. (4) Its management cannot predict costs of operation in advance.

A retail cooperative which follows a "low price" policy does so for

---

[4]*Ibid.* p. 183.

these reasons: (1) Its management may want to disturb the price structure. (2) Its management may want to encourage more members to join because of its low prices. (3) Its management may feel that a dividend is already paid when low prices are charged. (4) Its management is able to estimate all the costs of operation in advance and may feel that needed capital can be raised in other ways.

The Rochdale Pioneers adopted this practice because they did not want to upset the price structure in England at that time. If they had lowered prices, the other retail shops would have retaliated against the Rochdale group by selling below cost for awhile or by using other retaliatory measures.

This is really not a co-op principle but a business policy which can be changed from time to time as economic conditions demand. The significant point is whether cooperatives wish to pass-on the dividend day-by-day or in a lump sum at year's end.

9. LIMITATION ON THE NUMBER OF SHARES OWNED

The Rochdale Pioneers desired to limit the control over shares owned by any one member.

As a universal principle, such a rule is weak because it fails to cover the nonstock cooperatives which have no shares to sell. If voting is going to be restricted to one man, one vote, there is not much danger from shareholders. There also cannot be any danger in regards to paying too much interest on stock since this is usually limited by law. The dangers are therefore illusory.

However, in practice, this Rochdale Principle has been widely accepted. For example, in federal credit unions in the United States there is a limitation on shares owned per member, or no more than 20 percent of the total.

10. NET MARGINS DISTRIBUTED ACCORDING TO PATRONAGE

The Rochdale Pioneers decided to pay all their operating costs and interest on shares invested, and whatever was left was to be prorated to patrons according to the volume of business each had done with the

FIGURE 9-4

The most universal co-op principle is the refunding of any excess income over costs to patrons in proportion to their patronage or use of the association. (Courtesy, National Association of Mutual Savings Banks, New York, N.Y.)

society. It is believed that, at first, Rochdale did not have nonmember business as cooperatives have today.

This Rochdale Principle is the most secure and everlasting of all their principles. *It is perhaps the only real and universal co-op principle.*

Some authorities argue that health insurance associations do not pay patronage dividends and thus might be excluded as cooperatives. Nevertheless, these patronage dividends exist despite the fact that they may be used in ways other than cash refunds.

SUMMARY OF ROCHDALE PRINCIPLES

The following Rochdale Principles may be rejected *prima facie* as being nonprincipled:

3. Cash trading.
4. Membership education.
5. Political and religious neutrality.
6. No unusual risk assumption.
8. Goods sold at regular retail prices.

The following Rochdale Principles may be accepted with reservation and qualification:

1. Open membership.
2. One man, one vote.
7. Limited interest on stock.
9. Limitation on the number of shares owned.

The following Rochdale Principle is accepted as a co-op principle without reservation or qualification:

10. Net margins distributed according to patronage.

The International Cooperative Alliance, which is an international association of the more important national co-op associations, has likewise rejected cash trading, educational promotion and political and religious neutrality as basic co-op principles. It accepts open membership, democratic control, patronage refunds and limited interest on capital as tests of a true cooperative. Voluntary affiliation and freedom from state control have also been added as criteria for a true cooperative.[5]

Schaars concludes that:

> If I were to name the principles, not practices if you please, which I feel any organization must include in its set-up to be a true cooperative, be it a grocery store company, a rural electric cooperative or a cooperative milk plant, I would list only three. These I call the "hard-core" underlying principles of cooperation. They are:
>
> 1. Services at cost to member-patrons.
> 2. Democratic control by member-patrons.
> 3. Limited returns on equity capital.[6]

The legal definition of a cooperative varies greatly. Legislators have wrestled with this problem for many years, yet no definite conclusions are in sight. Even co-op scholars and researchers differ among themselves concerning the definition of a "true cooperative." Nevertheless, there is general agreement with Schaars's conclusion that a "true" cooperative is one which provides: (1) service at cost, (2) democratic control by member-patrons and (3) limited returns on equity capital. As stated before, a "quasi" cooperative is one which meets at least one of these three specifications but not all three of them.

---

[5]Odhe, Thorsten, *Cooperation in World Economy*, International Cooperative Alliance, London, England. Not dated. p. 8.
[6]Schaars, Marvin, "A Look at Principles," *News for Farmer Cooperatives*, FCS, Washington, D.C. Apr. 1963. p. 8.

Federal legislation as it affects cooperatives in the United States of America is the subject of the next chapter.

TOPICS FOR DISCUSSION

1. Enumerate the commonly accepted Rochdale Principles.
2. Discuss the strength and weakness of each principle.
3. Which of the Rochdale Principles are truly principles?
4. Which three principles have come to be accepted as "hard-core" co-op principles?
5. Devise a list of additional co-op principles which might be considered valid in this modern era of cooperation.

SELECTED REFERENCES

1. Bakken, H. H., *Basic Concepts, Principles and Practices of Cooperation,* Mimir Publishers, Inc., Madison, Wisc. 1963.
2. Bakken, H. H., "Rochdale Principles Constitute Business Strait Jacket," *Western Producer,* Saskatoon, Saskatchewan, Canada. Aug. 24, 1961. p. 5.
3. Erdman, H. E. and J. M. Tinley, *Principles of Cooperation,* Calif. Agr. Exp. Sta. Bul. 758, Berkeley, Calif. Feb. 1957.
4. Lambert, Paul, *La Doctrine Cooperative,* National Federation of Consumer Cooperatives, Paris, France. 1959.
5. Lowrie, Alyce, "One Man, One Vote?" *Cooperative Digest,* Ithaca, N.Y. Oct. 1961. pp. 11-12.
6. Mann, M. G., Jr., "Competition vs. Cooperation," *Carolina Cooperator,* Raleigh, N.C. May 1963.
7. Nourse, Edwin G., "Economic Principles of Cooperation," *Agricultural Cooperation,* University of Minnesota Press, Minneapolis, Minn. 1957.
8. Olsen, H. M., *Some Principles and Practices of Farmer Cooperatives,* The Interstate Printers & Publishers, Inc., Danville, Ill. 1961.
9. Roy, E. P., "A Re-appraisal of Co-op Principles," *Cooperative Digest,* Ithaca, N.Y. Mar. 1960. pp. 6 and 18.
10. Schaars, Marvin, "Basic Principles of Cooperatives," *Agricultural Cooperation,* University of Minnesota Press, Minneapolis, Minn. 1957.
11. Schaars, Marvin, "Farmer Cooperatives—What They Are and What They Are Not," *News for Farmer Cooperatives,* FCS, Washington, D.C. Mar. 1963.
12. Staff, *What Is a Co-op?* FCS, Bul. 6, USDA, Washington, D.C. Not dated.
13. Thompson, Jack C., *Organizational Structure for a Cooperative,* Ga. Agr. Exp. Sta. Bul. 105, Athens, Ga. June 1963.

CHAPTER 10 –

Federal Legislation Affecting
Cooperatives in the
United States of America

. . . In its full and complete significance the idea of democracy is participation by the people in all the vital and important social processes. These processes, when broken down into the concrete, are the economic, political and cultural forces that are to be found everywhere. In a democratic society the control of these processes is not the privilege of any one class, but of the people as a whole. It isn't enough that the people participate in one of them or even some of them. Neither is it sufficient that this participation be partial or grudgingly allowed to them. Thus it follows that economic group action is implicit in the very idea of democracy; and cooperation aims to realize this democracy by placing the country and its economic forces in the hands of our own people. If there is any virtue, therefore, in our democratic ideals and principles, it must be agreed that cooperatives promote the common good. This is the real test of a democratic movement.

—Dr. M. M. Coady

LEGAL BASIS FOR COOPERATION

THE VARIOUS federal and state laws dealing specifically with cooperatives have been designed to legalize cooperative action, to provide means of incorporating associations, to provide rules by which such associations will operate on a cooperative basis and to promote cooperatives as a method enabling entrepreneurs and consumers to compete on a more satisfactory basis with others in the economy.

Perhaps the most important of the laws are those legalizing farmer cooperatives. Throughout history the rights of producers to form associations for the purchase of supplies have seldom been questioned. The right, however, to act together in marketing their products was not legally established in this country until after 1900. For centuries the common law, established by common usage and court decisions, looked unfavorably on anything that appeared to restrain trade. Against this background of opposition to the restraint of trade and as partnerships, corporations and joint-stock companies grew larger and trading more complex, Congress in 1890 passed the Sherman Antitrust Act.

Sherman Antitrust Act (1890)

The Sherman Antitrust Act was passed by Congress at a time (1890) when cooperatives were in their infancy. Considering the generally prevalent disdain for trusts and combinations, it was natural that the courts of the country should interpret co-op associations in the spirit of the antitrust law. The first section of this Act read as follows:

> Every contract, combination in the form of trust or otherwise, or conspiracy in restraint of trade or commerce in any Territory of the United States or of the District of Columbia, or in restraint of trade between any such Territory and another, or between any such Territory or Territories and any State or States or Foreign nations, is hereby declared to be illegal. Every person who shall make any such contract or engage in any such combination or conspiracy shall be deemed guilty of a misdemeanor, and, on conviction thereof, shall be punished by fine not exceeding $5,000 or by imprisonment not exceeding one year, or by both said punishments in the discretion of the court.

From 1890 to 1910, the United States Supreme Court consistently ruled that restraints of trade, whether reasonable or unreasonable, were prohibited by this Act. But after 1910 the so-called rule of reason became the criterion of infractions. Mere size and method of organization were not indications in themselves that trade was being restrained. Action, rather than size, was questioned. As the large-scale co-op associations grew to an extent that they sold products from all parts of a state and interstate, they were vitally interested in knowing their status under the Sherman Act. Decisions of the courts soon showed that cooperatives had a precarious standing under this law and were easily adjudged as combinations in restraint of trade. During the period 1890-1910, directors and officers of selling cooperatives were indicted in five states under state antitrust laws and in Louisiana under the Sherman Act.

Gradually, however, more courts rendered decisions favoring farmer cooperatives, and as additional states passed laws providing for such organizations, public policy as to the desirability of these cooperatives became clear. Federal laws were effective in establishing this policy on a national basis. The first of these was embodied in the Clayton Act of 1914.

Clayton Act (1914)

Co-op leaders desired a definite statement in the laws which would exempt them from the provisions of the Sherman Act. In 1914 the Clayton Act was passed and exempted agricultural and horticultural organizations instituted for the purpose of mutual help. Section 6 of this Act included the following provisions:

> That the labor of a human being is not a commodity or article of commerce. Nothing contained in the antitrust laws shall be construed to forbid the existence and operation of labor, agricultural, or horticultural organizations, instituted for the purposes of mutual help, and not having capital stock or conducted for profit, or to forbid or restrain individual members of such organizations from lawfully carrying out the legitimate objects thereof; nor shall such organizations, or the members thereof, be held or construed to be illegal combinations or conspiracies in restraint of trade, under the antitrust laws.

It will be noted that this provision simply exempted the nonstock, nonprofit cooperatives but did not clarify the status of the capital stock associations. Since a large number of farmers' organizations had capital stock, and others were interested in organizing with capital stock, there arose a persistent demand that a definite federal law be enacted which would legalize both types of associations. Precedents had already been set by the passage of many state cooperative laws. It should not be inferred from the wording of this Act that farmers' nonstock associations were permitted to engage in illegal business operations; it simply expressed the opinion of Congress that the organizations per se were not illegal and were not to be dissolved if they met the conditions specified in Section 6. To further clarify the status of agricultural marketing cooperatives (engaged in interstate commerce) and to allow the existence of associations organized with capital stock, the Congress in 1922 passed the Capper-Volstead Act.

Capper-Volstead Act (1922)

The Capper-Volstead Act clarified the Clayton Act. Capper-Volstead is frequently referred to as the "Magna Carta" of farmers' cooperatives. It makes legal an association of farmers for the purposes of marketing whether incorporated or not and whether with or without capital stock provided:

1. It is operated for the mutual benefit of its members as producers.

2. It conforms to one or both of the following requirements:

(a) No member is allowed more than one vote because of the amount of stock or membership capital he may own, *or*

(b) Dividends on capital stock or membership capital do not exceed 8 percent per year.

3. The association does not deal in products of nonmembers to an amount greater in value than such as are handled by it for members.

While the Capper-Volstead Act reaffirmed the right of farmers to associate, it did not embrace all agricultural cooperatives but only those engaged in marketing agricultural products.

With the passage of the Capper-Volstead Act the uncertainty of the capital stock associations was removed. This law was quite different from the Clayton Act in that it definitely authorized the association of

FIGURE 10-1

President Harding signing the Capper-Volstead Cooperative Marketing Law, February 18, 1922. The signing was witnessed by the authors of the bill and by representatives of Farmers' Union, American Farm Bureau, National Grange and National Board of Farm Organizations. (Courtesy, Farm Credit Administration, Washington, D.C.)

agricultural producers. The Clayton Act was primarily designed to permit the organization of laborers for their mutual benefit and merely included, as an afterthought, the nonstock, nonprofit associations of agricultural producers. The Clayton Act, however, is not repealed by the passage of the Capper-Volstead Act. The Capper-Volstead Act does not permit co-op marketing associations to conduct their businesses as monopolies in restraint of trade. The Act permits the organization of producers of agricultural products to engage in interstate commerce and defines the method of organization of such associations.

The Capper-Volstead Act is not a law under which marketing associations may be chartered. It merely permits such organizations to exist without, by their mere existence, being considered in violation of the federal antitrust laws. It does not allow them to adopt practices not permitted other types of business organizations. Thus cooperatives are subject to investigation and prosecution for unfair competition, price-fixing agreements with third parties and other illegal actions restraining or monopolizing trade. Because of the federal government's authority to control interstate commerce, it is essential that marketing cooperatives engaged in handling products in interstate trade abide by its provisions.

The regulatory powers under the Capper-Volstead Act were given to the Secretary of Agriculture. If he has reason to believe that an association monopolizes or restrains trade in interstate or foreign commerce to the extent that it raises unduly the price of any agricultural product, he may issue a complaint against the association. If the Secretary believes after a hearing that the association has monopolized or restrained trade, he may issue an order directing the association to cease and desist. The order, if not obeyed, is enforceable by the federal district court in the district in which the association has its principal office.

No complaint has ever been issued by a Secretary of Agriculture under the Act. But, if the Secretary of Agriculture does not act to restrain monopoly, then the Justice Department can bring its own case under the Sherman Act or Clayton Act.

It is interesting to note that the Capper-Volstead Act may have been weakened by a ruling of the United States Supreme Court on May 2, 1960, in the case of *Maryland-Virginia Milk Producers Association.*

These points appeared clear from the Court's decision:

> 1. The general philosophy of Section 6 of the Clayton Act and the Capper-Volstead Act is simply that individual farmers

should be given, through agricultural cooperatives acting as entities, the same unified competitive advantage and responsibility available to businessmen acting through corporations as entities.

2. While Section 1 of the Capper-Volstead Act immunizes farmer cooperatives against prosecution in carrying out "the legitimate objects" of "collectively processing, preparing for market, handling and marketing" products through common marketing agencies and the making of "necessary contracts and agreements to effect such purposes," the Court in effect said that if a cooperative engages in what the Court regards as predatory practices in carrying out its "legitimate objects" then the cooperative is not protected from antitrust prosecution.

3. The Court indicated that even where a cooperative enters into lawful contracts and business activities, it may still make up a "pattern of conduct unlawful under the Sherman Act."

4. The Court indicated that the purchase of another business by a farmer cooperative in an above-the-board business transaction would be a violation under Section 7 of the Clayton Act if the result of the transaction "may be substantially to lessen competition, or to tend to create a monopoly." Apparently in the Court's view the Capper-Volstead Act under such circumstances gives an agricultural cooperative no rights or protection antitrust-wise whatsoever. It appears that Section 7 of the Clayton Act would be absolutely controlling, the Capper-Volstead Act notwithstanding.[1]

Another notable case involving a cooperative and the antitrust laws was *The Associated Press* vs. *United States* (1945). This was a civil action wherein the United States successfully enjoined The Associated Press from combining cooperatively to violate the Sherman Antitrust Act. In the majority opinion, Justice Hugo Black significantly pointed out: "We need not again pass upon the contention . . . that because AP's activities are cooperative, they fall outside the sphere of business . . . when Congress has desired to permit cooperatives to interfere with the competitive system of business, it has done so expressly by legislation."[2]

FEDERAL FARM CREDIT LEGISLATION

Cooperative federal farm credit legislation embodies the Federal

---

[1]*Legal-Tax Memorandum*, N.C.F.C., Washington, D.C. Vol. IX, No. 4. May 5, 1960.
[2]Hanna, John, "Antitrust Immunities of Cooperative Associations," *Law and Contemporary Problems*, Duke University, Durham, N.C. Summer 1948. p. 490.

Farm Loan Act of 1916, the Intermediate Credit Act of 1923 and the Farm Credit Act of 1933 as amended.

These three acts are the cornerstones of what is universally considered to be the best farm credit system in the world. A large portion of the farmers in the world are plagued by high interest rates, unavailability of credit and misuse of credit. The American farmers, on the other hand, enjoy the benefits of a model credit system which within a few years will be totally owned by farmers.

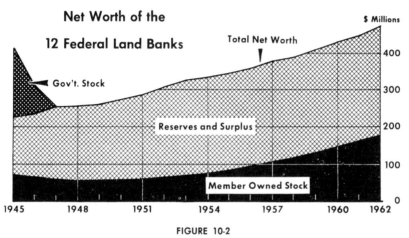

FIGURE 10-2

The government capital in the federal land banks was completely retired in 1947. The land bank associations now own the land banks. (Courtesy, Farm Credit Administration, Washington, D.C.)

Federal Farm Loan Act (1916)

The first land bank association was chartered on March 27, 1917, under the provisions of the Federal Farm Loan Act of 1916. The number of associations increased to about 5,000 in the early thirties. The depression of the thirties rendered many of these associations insolvent, and over 50 percent suffered some impairment of their capital with the result that the whole system has been reorganized since 1933.

These land bank associations are cooperatives dealing in mortgage credit. A borrower becomes a member by purchasing stock in an association to the extent of 5 percent of his loan. The association in turn takes stock in the Federal Land Bank for an equivalent amount. The stock is retired at par upon full repayment of the loan if the capital of the local association is not impaired. Loans are made for terms up to a maximum of 40 years and up to 65 percent of the appraised normal agricultural value of the farms.

The federal land bank associations make only loans approved by appraisers of the district federal land bank and borrow the entire amount of a loan from it. The district land bank in turn secures funds by floating bond issues sold to the general public.

The 12 district land banks were originally capitalized by the federal government. These banks became fully owned by the federal land bank associations in 1947. The banks have repaid to the government all of the initial capital provided under the provisions of the Federal Farm Loan Act of 1916 and the additional capital stock of $125 million and paid-in surplus of $189 million provided during the severe depression of the early 1930's.

Intermediate Credit Act (1923)

The Intermediate Credit Act of 1923, which provided for the establishment of 12 intermediate credit banks, was designed to provide a permanent and dependable source of funds through which local lending organizations could finance livestock feeding and breeding, crop production and marketing. It also provided for capital needs—for example, buildings, major equipment and mechanization of farm operations. The banks do not make direct loans to individuals, nor do they accept deposits or otherwise engage in a general banking business.

The lending functions consist of purchasing loans made for agricultural purposes and making loans to production credit associations and various types of agricultural financing institutions, including commercial banks.

Eligible to do business with the Federal Intermediate Credit Bank are: production credit associations, banks for cooperatives, national banks, state banks, trust companies, agricultural credit corporations, incorporated livestock loan companies, savings institutions and rural credit unions.

Until January 1, 1957, all of the capital stock of the Federal Intermediate Credit Bank was owned by the federal government. The Farm Credit Act of 1956 provided for the gradual retirement of this government capital through purchases of capital stock by the production credit associations and the payment of patronage refunds to the users in capital stock and participation certificates.

How Farmers in each of 12 Districts Share in Control of Cooperative Farm Credit System

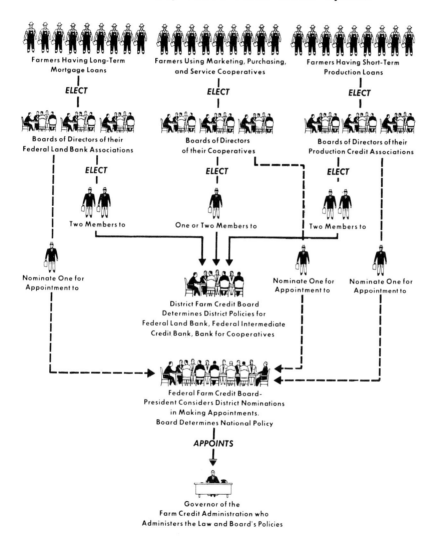

Farmers Having Long-Term
Mortgage Loans

Farmers Using Marketing, Purchasing,
and Service Cooperatives

Farmers Having Short-Term
Production Loans

ELECT

ELECT

ELECT

Boards of Directors of their
Federal Land Bank Associations

Boards of Directors
of their Cooperatives

Boards of Directors of their
Production Credit Associations

ELECT

ELECT

ELECT

Two Members to

One or Two Members to

Two Members to

Nominate One for
Appointment to

Nominate One for
Appointment to

Nominate One for
Appointment to

District Farm Credit Board
Determines District Policies for
Federal Land Bank, Federal Intermediate
Credit Bank, Bank for Cooperatives

Federal Farm Credit Board—
President Considers District Nominations
in Making Appointments.
Board Determines National Policy

APPOINTS

Governor of the
Farm Credit Administration who
Administers the Law and Board's Policies

FIGURE 10-3

The Farm Credit Act of 1955 transferred control of the Farm Credit Administration from the federal government to the elected representatives of those who use the services of the production credit associations, national farm loan associations and banks for cooperatives. (Courtesy, Farm Credit Administration, Washington, D.C.)

FARM CREDIT ACT (1933)

The Farm Credit Act of 1933 provided for the establishment of 12 regional banks for cooperatives and one central bank for cooperatives to make loans to farmer cooperatives. It also created the production credit associations. The PCA's were formed for the purpose of extending short-term credit to farmers and ranchers who would belong to these associations. As a result, the credit acts enabled land bank associations, co-op banks and production credit associations to serve farmers' credit needs through a system of district banks supervised by the Farm Credit Administration.

The Farm Credit Act of 1955 provided a comprehensive plan for the cooperatives using the services of the banks to build up their investment in these banks and for the gradual retirement of the government-owned capital.

A further discussion of PCA's and banks for cooperatives is reserved for Chapter 13.

EXTENT OF GOVERNMENT CAPITAL
IN FARM CREDIT SYSTEM

The federal land banks and land bank associations do not have any

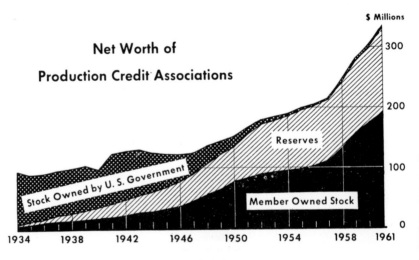

FIGURE 10-4

The production credit associations are almost entirely owned by farmer-members. (Courtesy, Farm Credit Administration, Washington, D.C.)

federal government capital left in them. The intermediate credit bank capital is gradually becoming farmer-owned. Production credit association capital is practically all farmer-owned. The government capital in banks for farmer cooperatives is gradually being replaced by cooperative-owned capital (Table 10-1).

CO-OP AGRICULTURAL MARKETING ACTS

Five agricultural marketing acts applicable to cooperatives are discussed.

Cooperative Marketing Act (1926)

The Cooperative Marketing Act of 1926 directed the establishment in the Department of Agriculture of a division authorized to promote the knowledge of co-op principles and practices and to cooperate with educational and marketing agencies, cooperatives and others in promoting such knowledge.

Another section of this Act provided that cooperatives may acquire,

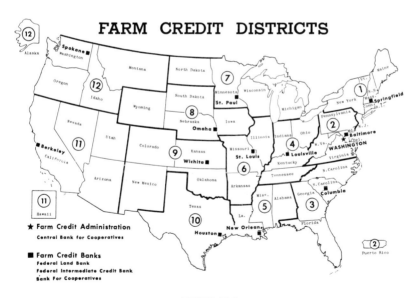

FARM CREDIT DISTRICTS

★ Farm Credit Administration
  Central Bank for Cooperatives

■ Farm Credit Banks
  Federal Land Bank
  Federal Intermediate Credit Bank
  Bank For Cooperatives

FIGURE 10-5

There are 12 Farm Credit Districts in the United States. (Courtesy, Farm Credit Administration, Washington, D.C.)

TABLE 10-1
Government- and Farmer-owned Capital and Distribution of Earnings in Cooperative Farm Credit System

Banks and Associations	Peak Capital Owned by U.S. Government		June 30, 1962 Capital Owned by		Earned Net Worth	Dividends and Patronage Refunds to Members to June 30, 1962	Franchise Taxes and Dividends Paid to U.S. Government to June 30, 1962
	Amount	Date	U.S. Government	Farmers and Farmer Cooperatives			
Federal land banks	$313,942,505	6-30-39	—	$175,617,230	$298,150,510	$174,472,344	—
Federal land bank associations	—	—	—	175,697,590	94,926,396	84,953,362	—
Federal intermediate credit banks	101,389,120	6-30-62	$101,389,120	40,524,780[1]	75,067,039	27,435,317	$18,383,119
Production credit associations	90,106,775	11-30-34	465,000	202,364,149	153,455,773	20,913,198	57,759
Banks for cooperatives	178,500,000	2-28-54	94,837,500	66,989,259	105,653,708	32,983,387	14,677,483
Less: intercorporate items	—	—	—	214,352,575	—	174,472,344	—
Net total	$683,938,400	—	$196,691,620	$446,840,433	$727,253,426	$166,285,264	$33,118,361

[1]Includes $1,789,435 in participation certificates owned by financing institutions other than production credit associations.
Source: Farm Credit Administration, USDA, Washington, D.C.

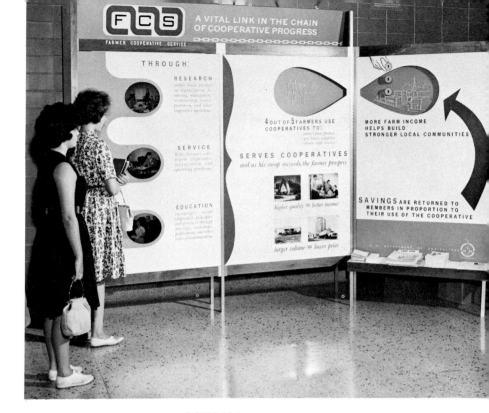

FIGURE 10-6

The Farmer Cooperative Service in the United States Department of Agriculture does research, service and educational work for farmer cooperatives. (Courtesy, Farmer Cooperative Service, Washington, D.C.)

exchange, interpret and disseminate past, present and future crop, market, statistical, economic and other similar information by direct exchange between such associations or federations thereof and/or by and through a common agent created or selected by them.

Although the agency responsible has been shifted several times, the Department of Agriculture has continued to carry out these functions since the passage of the Cooperative Marketing Act. The division now carrying them out is known as the Farmer Cooperative Service of the United States Department of Agriculture.

Agricultural Marketing Act (1929)

The Agricultural Marketing Act of 1929 provided for: (1) the creation of the Federal Farm Board of eight members with the Secretary of Agriculture as an ex-officio member, (2) the appointment of commodity committees to advise the Board, (3) a revolving fund of $500 million from which loans could be made to cooperatives, (4) the establishment of stabilization corporations for the handling of surplus agricultural commodities, (5) price insurance to cooperatives and (6) the creation of producer-controlled clearing houses.

While the Federal Farm Board attempted to stimulate the growth of farmer cooperatives, it was not too successful in this effort, nor was it successful in dealing with depressed farm prices. With the passage of the Agricultural Adjustment Act of 1933, some of the activities of the Farm Board were transferred to other agencies, and others were discontinued. Some of its remaining funds were used to capitalize the banks for cooperatives. The Farm Board as such no longer functions.

Perishable Agricultural Commodities Act (1930)

This Act was preceded by the Produce Agency Act of 1927 which made it a misdemeanor, punishable by fine or imprisonment, or both, for any person who receives fruit, vegetables, dairy or poultry products or other perishable products to be sold for somebody else to make fraudulent accounting or false or misleading statements, with an intent to defraud, or to dump produce without good cause.

As the Act applied only to the handling and disposition of products received in interstate trade for sale on consignment, some persons believed that further regulatory measures should be enacted to apply to all types of contracts involving the purchase, sale and consignment of fruit and vegetables.

After several years of study by members of the industry and legislators, the *Perishable Agricultural Commodities Act* became law in 1930. It was designed to suppress unfair and fraudulent practices and to promote more orderly marketing of perishable agricultural commodities in interstate and foreign commerce. It applies to all persons doing business as commission merchants, dealers or brokers who handle fresh or frozen vegetables in interstate or foreign commerce, except if a commodity is of an individual's own raising or purchased in small quantities solely for sale at retail. These merchants, dealers or brokers must hold licenses issued by the Department of Agriculture or be subject to fines. License fees are deposited in a special fund and used to defray the expense of administering this Act, the Produce Agency Act and the Export Apple and Pear Act.

The Perishable Agricultural Commodities Act prohibits such unfair practices as rejection without reasonable cause (goods might otherwise be rejected if prices are falling fast); failure to deliver without reason-

FIGURE 10-7

The Aquatic Products Act is for fishery cooperatives what the Capper-Volstead Act is for farmer cooperatives. (Courtesy, Louisiana Wildlife and Fisheries Commission, New Orleans, La.)

able cause; making false or misleading statements (for example, untrue statements made to induce a person to make a contract he would not make if he knew the true details); making incorrect accountings or consignments; failure to pay promptly for commodities purchased or received on consignment; misrepresenting the grade, the quality condition, or state or country of origin; and altering federal inspection certificates.

Cooperatives dealing interstate-wise in fresh fruit and fresh vegetable marketing are subject to the licensing and other provisions of the P.A.C. Act. The Secretary of Agriculture administers the provisions of this Act.

Aquatic Products Act (1934)

This Act was passed June 25, 1934, and authorizes the formation of cooperatives among fishermen in catching, producing, preparing for market, processing, handling and marketing their products in interstate commerce. The Secretary of Commerce is given the authority to supervise the activities of these associations particularly if any monopolistic devices are created or tend to be created. Other sections of the Act are comparable to the Capper-Volstead Act of 1922 insofar as one man, one vote is required and, if not mandatory, then interest paid on stock or capital should not exceed 8 percent per year. Not more than 50 percent of the business can be conducted with nonmembers.

Agricultural Marketing Agreements Act (1937)

This Act authorizes the Secretary of Agriculture to enter into marketing agreements and/or orders with processors, producers, associations of producers or cooperatives and with others engaged in the handling of specified agricultural products (milk, certain fruits and vegetables) if said action will prove beneficial in the orderly marketing of farm products. These marketing agreements and orders are exempt from the antitrust laws. The Act has been amended at various times to enlarge the number of commodities subject to marketing agreements and orders.

Many orders are in effect with respect to marketing of farm produce. The orders do not fix prices, but limit the quantity, grade or size of the commodity that may be handled. An order may provide for the appor-

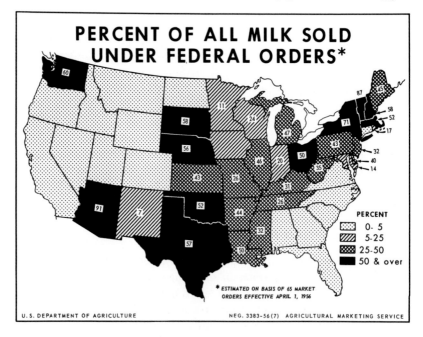

FIGURE 10-8

Federal milk marketing orders, for example, allow dairy cooperatives to vote on behalf of their producers, pool returns and provide other services for their producers. (Courtesy, USDA, Washington, D.C.)

tionment of the total quantity to be handled among handlers or producers. The orders generally contemplate the issuance of regulations at intervals during the marketing period. A surplus pool may also be established under an order.

Certain pre-existing practices of cooperatives are specifically recognized as rights under terms of the 1937 Act. These are, principally, the rights: (1) to vote on behalf of their producers, (2) to pool returns and (3) to provide specified services for their producers that otherwise would be performed by the Market Administrator.[3]

FEDERAL REGULATORY ACTS

Other acts of a regulatory nature dealing with cooperatives, directly or indirectly, are the Federal Trade Commission Act of 1914, U.S. Warehouse Act of 1916, the Packers and Stockyards Act of 1921, Grain Futures Act of 1922, Securities Act of 1933, Motor Carrier Act of 1935 and the Robinson-Patman Act of 1936.

Federal Trade Commission Act (1914)

The FTC is charged with enforcement of the provisions of the Clayton Act, Robinson-Patman Act, Webb-Pomerene Act, the Federal Trade Commission Act and other similar regulatory acts.

To safeguard further the operation of competition, Congress in 1914 established the Federal Trade Commission and charged it with the duty of stopping the use in interstate commerce, by persons, partnerships or corporations, of unfair methods that suppress or injure competition. By such means it was felt that monopolies could be checked in their incipiency. Monopoly-breeding methods in business have been stopped in numerous cases prosecuted by the Commission.

The original Sherman Act and the Federal Trade Commission Act, followed by a series of supplemental acts of Congress, stand in recognition of the importance of competition in commercial activities. Under them, competing manufacturers or sellers are not permitted to agree or to conspire among themselves to fix prices or to limit the amount of production so as to keep prices high through artificially created scarcities or to divide territory so as to avoid competing with one another.

---

[3]Krause, S. F. and J. M. Cowden, *Evaluating Dairy Co-ops*, FCS Bul. 14, Washington, D.C. Sept. 1962. pp. 36-37.

Likewise, a manufacturer or distributor is not permitted to injure, prevent, or destroy competition by discriminating in price among his competing dealers or in the services he furnishes to them for promoting the resale of his products. Nor is he permitted to lessen competition materially by requiring them not to handle the products of competitors. A corporation may not limit competition substantially by buying up its competitors, and it may not have one or more persons serve at the same time on its own and its corporate competitor's board of directors, unless both are comparatively small concerns.

Implemented by such laws is the basic principle that sellers have no right through monopolistic practices or combinations in restraint of trade to deprive purchasers of the benefit of competition as a governing influence in sales transactions. The view is generally accepted that the driving force of competition in the distribution of goods from producer to consumer will bring to the buyer the greatest abundance and variety of merchandise at the lowest price and with the best quality for the money.

Congress also enacted the policy, enforced by the Federal Trade Commission, that competition, although free, shall not be allowed to degenerate into or become corrupted by practices that are tinged with elements of deception, bad faith or fraud, whether brought about by misrepresentation on the part of the seller or by his concealment or nondisclosure of material facts which tend to mislead or deceive the buyer. A great variety of selling practices of this sort has been ruled unlawful by the Federal Trade Commission.

The Wheeler-Lea Amendment of 1938 has strengthened the FTC by giving it stricter enforcement powers especially in the area of advertising.

The FTC is sometimes involved with milk cooperatives in cases of alleged unfair trade practices. In one case the FTC held that the co-op association had used its power and strength and its control of milk producers to compel, by threats and intimidation, processing plants in that state to purchase from it all of their milk.

Warehouse Act (1916)

Congress passed the United States Warehouse Act in 1916. It applies only to staple and unprocessed agricultural commodities, not to semi-manufactured and manufactured goods derived from agricultural products.

It authorizes the Secretary of Agriculture to set up standards for the inspecting and grading of farm commodities and to issue licenses to warehousemen. But these actions are not mandatory; warehousemen decide for themselves whether to apply for licenses and place their operations under the supervision of the Department. The Secretary is not required to license any warehouseman unless he finds that the warehouseman can comply with the regulations. He is authorized to examine the operations of the warehouseman after licensing as often as he deems necessary; if it is found that the warehouseman is not complying with the law and regulations, he can suspend or revoke the license.

This Act permits grain elevators, for example, to store agricultural commodities in federally licensed warehouses and use the warehouse receipts as collateral for obtaining working capital. This is very beneficial to both private and co-op elevators.

Packers and Stockyards Act (1921)

The Packers and Stockyards Act was enacted in 1921. Extensive Congressional investigations had shown that the large meatpackers owned dominant interest in major stockyards and thereby exercised considerable control over the market agencies to which producers consigned their livestock. Charges were made at Congressional hearings that the packers assessed unreasonable marketing charges against patrons of public markets, discriminated between them in the furnishing of stockyard facilities and services, attempted to influence the movement of livestock to market, tried to control the prices received by producers for their livestock and engaged in other unfair and monopolistic practices.

The passage of the Act signaled the end of a long fight by livestock producers' organizations to obtain, through federal legislation, an effective means of regulating in the public interest the practices of meatpackers engaged in interstate operations and the marketing of livestock through public stockyards.

The Act and regulations issued under its authority provide, among other things: (1) that the services and facilities furnished consignors of livestock to public stockyards shall be adequate and (2) that the yardage, commission, feed and other charges assessed by stockyard companies and market agencies shall be reasonable and applied on a nondiscriminatory basis.

FIGURE 10-9

In 1927 Congress sanctioned the right of farmer cooperatives to be represented on boards of trade and exchanges. (Courtesy, Chicago Board of Trade)

The Act assured cooperatives the right to transact business in the central market exchanges even though they may pay patronage refunds.

Grain Futures Act (1922)

Transactions in commodity futures on boards of trade are regulated under the Commodity Exchange Act, the amended name of the Grain Futures Act of September 21, 1922. Congress found, in the enactment of this regulatory legislation, that transactions and prices on boards of trade are susceptible to speculation, manipulation and control and that regulation of such trading is conducive to the protection of interstate commerce and the national public interest.

The Act prohibits the manipulation of the price of wheat, cotton, rice, corn, oats, barley, rye, flaxseed, grain, sorghums, millfeeds, butter, eggs, Irish potatoes, wool tops, all fats and oils, cottonseed meal, cottonseed, peanuts, soybeans and soybean meal. Also, the legislation prohibits an "attempt" to manipulate the price of any of those commodities in interstate commerce or for future delivery on a board of trade. A corner or an attempt to corner is likewise prohibited.

In 1927 Congress enacted a statute forbidding boards of trade and exchanges (except markets designated as contract markets) on which agricultural products are bought and sold to exclude the duly authorized representatives of any lawfully formed and conducted co-op association "composed substantially of producers of agricultural products," provided such association complies with certain prescribed conditions. The Act further provided that no rule of a board of trade should be construed to prevent the payment of patronage dividends by a co-op association of producers.

Securities Act (1933)

The Securities Act of 1933, which requires the registration of securities offerings, also requires the filing of full information with respect to an offering and the company that is making it. In addition, this Act provides for true and accurate information to be furnished to shareholders. It has a constant impact upon most open-end investment companies, which generally are constantly offering shares to the public and hence are in continuous registration under the law.

Under the Securities Act mutual finance and tax exempt farmer cooperatives are exempted from registration of securities in interstate commerce:

> ". . . any securities issued by a building and loan association, homestead association, savings and loan association, or similar institution, substantially all the business of which is confined to the making of loans to members (but the foregoing exemption shall not apply with respect to any such security where the issuer takes from the total amount paid or deposited by the purchaser, by the way of any fee, cash value or other device whatsoever, either upon termination of the investment at maturity or before maturity, an aggregate amount in excess of 3 percentum of the face value of such security), or any security issued by a farmers' cooperative association as defined in paragraphs (12), (13) and (14) of Section 103 of the Revenue Act of 1932." Nonexempt farmers' cooperatives must register their securities.

The Securities and Exchange Commission, Washington, D.C., administers the various securities acts.

Rule 235 of the SEC does provide a clear exemption for stock or other securities representing memberships in a co-op housing association provided the cooperative meets certain provisions.[4]

---

[4]General Rules and Regulations, SEC, Washington, D.C. 1962. p. 13.

Motor Carrier Act (1935)

Exemption from economic regulation was provided for motor carriers by Congress under the Motor Carrier portion of the Interstate Commerce Act. Part II, Sec. 203(b) is of particular interest to farmer cooperatives. That section reads in part as follows:

> (4a) Motor vehicles controlled and operated by any farmer when used in the transportation of his agricultural (including horticultural) commodities and products thereof, or in the transportation of supplies to his farm; or
>
> (5) Motor vehicles controlled and operated by a cooperative association as defined in the Agricultural Marketing Act, approved June 15, 1929, as amended, or by a federation of such cooperative associations, if such federation possesses no greater powers or purposes than cooperative associations so defined.
>
> (6) Motor vehicles used in carrying property consisting of ordinary livestock, fish (including shell fish), or agricultural (including horticultural) commodities (not including manufactured products thereof), if such motor vehicles are not used in carrying any other property, or passengers, for compensation.

Section 204 relative to driver qualifications and maximum hours of service of employees and safety of operation or standards of equipment does apply, however, to trucks owned and operated by co-op associations. Trucks controlled and operated by "cooperative associations" meeting the definition in the Agricultural Marketing Act of 1929, as amended, are exempt from economic regulation by the federal government. No operating authority is required from the Interstate Commerce Commission for the operation of such trucks in interstate commerce.

Retail merchants and others who form shipping associations cooperatively may come under Section 402(c) of the Interstate Commerce Act, as follows:

> The provisions of this chapter shall not be construed to apply (1) to the operations of a shipper, or a group association of shippers, in consolidating or distributing freight for themselves or for the purpose of securing the benefits of carload, truckload or other volume rates.

Robinson-Patman Act (1936)

This Act was designed to prevent business firms from discriminating between customers. While transactions by cooperatives with third parties are covered by the Act, it specifically provides that patronage refunds paid by cooperatives to members do not represent discriminations.

The Robinson-Patman Act prohibits discrimination in price between purchasers of commodities of like grade and quality. To accomplish this, certain discriminations in price and advertising and brokerage allowances have been made unlawful. This law requires a seller to treat all of his customers equally, or at least on proportionately equal terms. It applies to every transaction of interstate commerce, and it applies indirectly to intrastate sales. Those responsible for the management of cooperatives engaged in buying or selling goods in interstate commerce should become familiar with the provisions of this Act and endeavor to keep up to date with the rules and regulations imposed by the agency responsible for its administration. Milk cooperatives are especially concerned here. Wholesale cooperatives have from time to time run into difficulty under this Act.

OTHER FEDERAL LEGISLATION APPLICABLE TO COOPERATIVES

Hatch Experiment Station Act (1887)

The oldest continuous link between the USDA and the land-grant colleges and universities is the partnership established between state and federal scientists engaged in agricultural research. The Hatch Experiment Station Act of 1887 provided for the annual appropriation of federal grants to the college departments known as agricultural experiment stations. USDA administers these funds through its Cooperative State Experiment Station Service. Research on problems faced by farmer cooperatives often come under this program.

Smith-Lever Act (1914)

The Extension Service was established in 1914 by the Federal Smith-Lever Act. It is financed cooperatively by the federal, state and county governments, thus the name Cooperative Extension Service. Although it varies from state to state, at present the federal government pays about 40 percent of the cost of extension work. State governments pay about 35 percent and the counties about 25 percent. The land-grant colleges and county extension agents have worked closely with farmers

FIGURE 10-10

The land-grant college experiment stations often work closely with farmer cooperatives and their members in solving economic and technological problems.

in the organization and operation of cooperatives since the passage of this Act.

Webb-Pomerene Act (1918)

The Webb-Pomerene Act was passed for the purpose of allowing domestic firms to form export associations in order to compete more effectively in foreign trade.

The heart of the Webb-Pomerene Act is the provision that nothing in the Sherman Act is to be construed as declaring illegal "an association entered into for the sole purpose of engaging in export trade and actually engaged solely in such export trade, or an agreement made or act done in the course of export trade by such association, provided such association, agreement, or act is not in restraint of trade within the United States, and is not in restraint of the export trade of any domestic competitor of such association."

Some associations divide their export business among the members in predetermined proportions, or quotas, agreed upon by the members.

For this purpose, the capital-stock holdings of the members may serve as a basis, or the volume of export business over some past period, or perhaps periodical reports by the members as to amounts available for export.

Other functions that have been adopted by the export associations include standardizing products for export and improving the quality of the goods; maintaining inspection services, employing claims agents and settling disputes over export sales; establishing rules and regulations for packing and shipping the goods; arranging for freight rates, cargo space and shipping dates; consolidating the shipments of the members; taking out insurance, etc.

Federal Home Loan Act (1933)

The federal authority for chartering savings and loan associations is provided by the Home Owners' Loan Corporation Act of June 13, 1933. The Federal Home Loan Agency administers this Act under the Federal Home Loan Bank Board.

FIGURE 10-11

The agricultural extension services also assist cooperatives in many ways. Here an extension worker interviews consumers in a grocery store which is a member of a co-op wholesale. (Courtesy, La. Agr. Ext. Serv., Baton Rouge, La.)

FIGURE 10-12

The Taylor Grazing Act enables ranchers to graze their stock on certain federal lands. (Courtesy, Bureau of Land Management, Department of the Interior, Washington, D.C.)

The Federal Savings and Loan Insurance Corporation insures members' deposits up to $10,000. Under the provisions of Title IV of the National Housing Act, the Corporation was established in 1934 for the insurance of savings accounts in all federally-chartered savings and loan associations and such state-chartered institutions and co-op banks as apply and qualify for membership.

Each of the states also provides for the chartering and supervision of savings and loan associations. There are about two state-chartered associations for every one federally-chartered.

Taylor Grazing Act (1934)

This Act authorizes the Secretary of Interior to establish grazing districts which are not in national forests, national parks or Indian reservations and which in his opinion are chiefly valuable for grazing livestock and raising forage crops.

Before any grazing district is created in any state, a hearing is held in that state to determine its feasibility. If found feasible, the Secretary promulgates rules and regulations for furthering the objectives of the Act, namely: (1) to regulate occupancy and use, (2) to preserve the land from abuse, (3) to develop the range in an orderly manner and (4) to protect and rehabilitate the grazing areas.

Grazing permits are issued by the Secretary to individuals, groups, associations or corporations authorized to conduct business under the laws of the state in which the grazing district is located.

The permits issued are for a period of not more than 10 years, subject to renewal. The Secretary also sets the grazing fees.[5,6]

Federal Credit Union Act (1934)

Congress passed and President Roosevelt signed the Federal Credit

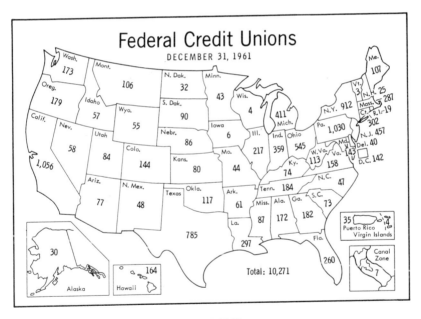

FIGURE 10-13

Federal credit unions are chartered under a 1934 act. They constitute about half of all credit unions in the United States. (Courtesy, Bureau of Federal Credit Unions, Washington, D.C.)

---

[5]Bureau of Land Management, *Taylor Grazing Act of 1934, with Amendments,* Dept. of Interior, Washington, D.C. 1962.
[6]B. L. M., *Grazing Regulations for the National Land Reserve,* Dept. of Interior Cir. 2075, Washington, D.C. Jan. 1962.

Union Act on June 26, 1934. The Act was designed to establish a Federal Credit Union System, to establish a further market for securities of the United States and to make available to people of small means credit for provident purposes through a national system of co-op credit, thereby helping to stabilize the credit structure of the United States.

The Bureau of Federal Credit Unions is the administrative agency in the Department of Health, Education and Welfare. It audits and supervises all federal credit unions.

Social Security Act (1935)

The Social Security Act provides, among other things, for old-age benefits or pensions and indirectly for unemployment insurance. To provide revenue to cover the benefits and insurance, certain taxes are imposed.

Cooperatives and their employees are concerned with two sections of the Act: (1) the old-age, survivors' and disability insurance system (OASI) and (2) unemployment insurance.

OASI Tax.—Work for a nonprofit organization exempt from income tax under Section 501 or Section 521 of the Internal Revenue Code of 1954 (except religious, charitable, scientific, literary and educational organizations; organizations testing for public safety; and community chests) is covered unless:

> A.   The pay for the work is less than $50 for a calendar quarter; or
> B.   The work is excluded by some other provision of the Social Security Act.[7]

In effect, employees of cooperatives are covered. Both employers and employees contribute to the OASI program. Wages up to $4,800 per year are taxed.

Unemployment Insurance Tax.—The unemployment insurance program provides partial income replacement for a limited period to persons who become unemployed. It is a state administered program with federal participation. The Federal Unemployment Tax Act taxes all employers in commerce and industry who employ 4 or more workers during 20 or more weeks of the year at the rate of 3.1 percent on the first $3,000 wages paid to each of their workers in a year.

---

[7]*Social Security Handbook*, Dept. of Health, Education and Welfare, Washington, D.C. p. 113.

If a state has an unemployment insurance law that meets the basic provisions of the federal law, employers can credit their state taxes against 90 percent of the federal tax. In order that employers may continue to obtain the tax offset provided in the federal law, the state unemployment insurance system must continue to conform to the general requirements in the federal law. This offset also extends to the taxes an employer is excused from paying by provisions of state law varying the tax rate in accordance with the employer's experience with unemployment. This is called "experience rating" and is provided for in all states.

In many states, the law applies to employers who have less than four employees and to employers who are engaged in types of work not covered by the federal law. In three states, employees also are taxed.

Each state specifies in its laws:

1. Who may receive unemployment benefits.
2. How each worker can qualify for benefits.
3. The amount of the weekly unemployment benefit.
4. The maximum number of weeks for which unemployment benefits may be paid.

The state unemployment insurance agency makes the rules for the payment of benefits, handles the claims of unemployed workers and decides in each case whether the claimant is entitled to unemployment benefits.[8]

The Federal Unemployment Tax Act does not provide for the election of coverage by nonprofit religious, charitable, scientific, literary or educational organizations; services performed for such organizations are specifically exempt for federal unemployment tax purposes. Services for certain voluntary beneficiary associations are likewise exempt.

Wage and Hour Law

If a cooperative meets the coverage specifications of the Wage and Hour Law, its employees must be paid the minimum wage specified and be provided with all other benefits named under this law, such as overtime payments and suitable working conditions, among others. Employment conditions for women and children are also covered under the law.

---

[8]*Ibid.* p. 227.

The employer-employee relationship is clear in all cooperatives except workers' productive societies, in which "employees" are also "employers" or owners of the businesses. The United States Supreme Court in one case ruled that a cooperative of knitwear homeworkers constitutes an employer-employee relationship and is therefore subject to the Fair Labor Standards Act. Three justices dissented from the majority opinion, saying that a workers' co-op society is a true cooperative and "a true cooperative does not automatically become the employer of its members in the commonly understood sense of these terms."

Soil Conservation Act (1935)

The Soil Conservation Service develops and carries out a national soil and water conservation program through local soil conservation districts created and managed by farmers and ranchers under state law. In addition it carries out the Department of Agriculture's responsibilities in watershed protection, flood prevention projects and river basin investigations; administers the Great Plains Conservation Program and the National Cooperative Soil Survey; makes and coordinates snow surveys and water supply forecasting in the western states; helps develop the annual Agricultural Conservation Program; and gives technical assistance to farmers in this and other Department programs.

Today the soil conservation district is the central source of help and information about soil and water conservation in nearly every community in the nation. All 50 states have soil-conservation-district-enabling acts. Districts, numbering more than 2,900, cover 92 percent of the land in farms and 96 percent of the farms in the United States. Twenty-four states plus the Virgin Islands and Puerto Rico are completely blanketed by districts.

Rural Electrification Act (1936)

The Rural Electrification Administration was created by executive order on May 11, 1935, but not established by law until May 20, 1936, with the passage of the Norris-Rayburn Act. The REA is authorized "to make loans to persons, corporations, states, territories and subdivisions and agencies thereof, municipalities, people's utility districts and cooperative nonprofit or limited-dividend associations organized under the laws of any state or territory of the United States, for the purpose of financing the construction and operation of generating plants, electric transmission and distribution lines or systems for the furnishing of electric energy to persons in rural areas who are not receiving central-station service." Contrary to wide-spread beliefs, the REA also loans money to electric companies other than cooperatives.

On October 28, 1949, REA was authorized to make loans for the purpose of improving and extending telephone service in rural areas. Under this authority, provided by Congress in an amendment to the Act, REA is empowered to make loans to existing companies and to cooperative, nonprofit, limited-dividend or mutual associations.

District of Columbia Consumers' Cooperatives Act (1940)

This Act passed in 1940 permits five or more persons or two or more associations to incorporate for the purpose of acquiring, producing, building, operating, manufacturing, furnishing, exchanging or distributing any type or types of property, commodities, goods or services for the primary and mutual benefit of their patrons as ultimate consumers.

Incorporators need not be residents of the District of Columbia; therefore, the Act has a "federal" or "interstate" status.

Under this Act, citizens of any state can form consumer cooperatives or housing associations, among other types, but not co-op credit or insurance businesses.

Federal Housing Act (1948, 1950 and 1961 Amendments)

The first step taken to provide federal assistance to privately financed nonprofit housing cooperatives was in the form of amendments to Section 207 of the Housing Act of 1948. Under this legislation the FHA was authorized to insure long-term high-percentage mortgage loans to nonprofit housing cooperatives at moderate interest rates.

The program was relatively successful considering the many obstacles that had to be overcome. Co-op housing by its very nature places a burden upon groups of people of modest means, engaged in all types of work, who are inexperienced and uninformed concerning porblems of real estate and building. Section 207(f) contained no provision for furnishing technical advice and assistance to such groups. Another obstacle was the hesitancy of lenders to finance cooperatives. Valuable experience gained in two years of operation led to the passage of a new section in the Housing Act of 1950.

Section 213 of Title II authorizes the FHA to insure mortgages, including construction advances, on co-op housing projects of eight or more dwelling units.

The mortgagor must be (1) a nonprofit co-op housing corporation or trust, the permanent occupancy of the dwellings being restricted to members of the corporation or beneficiaries of the trust (management-type project), or (2) a nonprofit corporation or trust organized for the purpose of building homes for members (sales-type project), or (3) a corporate investor regulated by the FHA Commissioner which under-

FIGURE 10-14

Various federal housing legislation enables families to own and operate co-op housing projects. (Courtesy, Fund for Urban Improvement, Inc., New York, N.Y.)

takes the construction of a management-type project and certifies to the Commissioner its intention of selling the project to a co-op group within two years after completion.

The mortgage on a sales-type project contains provision for the release of the individual properties from the blanket project mortgage. Mortgages covering the individual dwellings may be insured under Section 213.

Management-type cooperatives may use insured mortgages to finance the purchase and rehabilitation of existing housing.

Section 213 authorizes the FHA to furnish technical advice and assistance in the organization of cooperatives and in the planning, development, construction and operation of co-op housing projects.

Section 231 of the Act passed in 1961 authorizes the FHA to insure mortgages on rental housing projects of eight or more living units especially designed for use by persons 62 years of age or older. Section 221 provides for direct federal loans to housing cooperatives at below-market interest rates.

The maximum mortgage amounts for a nonprofit mortgagor are 100 percent of estimated replacement cost for new projects and 100 percent of estimated value for rehabilitated projects.

The mortgage may include commercial and special facilities adequate to serve the occupants of the project.[9]

Granger-Thye Act (1950)

Under Section 18 of this Act, the Chief of the Forest Service is empowered to recognize a local advisory board with respect to the management and administration of the grazing resource of a national forest.

The grazing permittees petition the chief for such a board following the provisions specified in the Act. The chief then rules on this petition as to whether to accept it or reject it. Functioning of such a board is comparable to an ordinary co-op association.

In addition, the Great Plains and western lands now known as national grasslands display the results of one of the biggest land rehabilitation projects of all time. There are 18 of these national grasslands, covering 3.8 million acres in 11 states. They support about

---

[9]Staff, *Cooperative Housing*, FHA 3239, Washington, D.C. Sept. 1961.

200,000 head of livestock annually and also provide a habitat for many wild animals and birds.

Now under the management of the Forest Service, these lands are administered for the same multiple uses as the national forests. In addition to the public grazing, they offer camping and picnicking, hunting and fishing opportunities, protection against erosion for many critical watersheds and even some timber.

FIGURE 10-15

Cotton cooperatives, under the price support programs, merchandise their members' cotton to obtain maximum returns.

Federal Farm Price Support Programs

Cooperative participation under farm price support programs can be classified under three headings: (1) price-stabilization-type cooperatives, (2) warehousing cooperatives and (3) merchandising cooperatives.

Price-stabilization-type cooperatives include most of the organizations which make price supports, especially on tobacco, available to farmers. The Commodity Credit Corporation makes loans to the tobacco cooperatives, which in turn make advances to the growers. Practically all the tobacco marketing associations are cooperating with the federal government in making tobacco price supports available to growers. In fact, many associations were organized for this purpose. Services performed by the associations include receiving, redrying, packing, storing and marketing tobacco consigned to them under the price support program. Contracts are entered into with warehouses, redriers and others to perform such services as the cooperatives do not perform. Each grower who places tobacco under loan usually becomes a member of a grower's association, which makes the loan under contract with the Commodity Credit Corporation.

The next group of cooperatives that participates in the price stabilization programs is warehousing cooperatives. The main relationship of these cooperatives with the Commodity Credit Corporation exists in providing warehouse space for members. This enables members to take out price support loans with the Commodity Credit Corporation. Some of the large grain organizations fall into this category. They usually provide marketing services for their members, but in their relations with the Commodity Credit Corporation, only the warehousing aspects of their operations are involved. These cooperatives render an invaluable service to members and the Commodity Credit Corporation in providing the storage which is necessary before price supports can be obtained. They have also been able to effect substantial savings on storage services for their members.

The third classification is the merchandising cooperative which takes out price support loans in its own name, determines when and in what quantities commodities shall be pledged to the government and when and in what quantities such commodities shall be redeemed from the loan. The provisions of the price support programs permit this type of participation by cotton, rice, edible bean, dairy and soybean cooperatives. Other commodities may not be pledged to the Commodity Credit Corporation in the name of the cooperative.

Consumer Protection Legislation

Many federal laws and regulations have been passed to protect consumer interests. The most outstanding of these are: (1) Meat

FIGURE 10-16

The federal poultry products inspection program protects consumers. There are a host of other federal inspection programs which protect consumers. (Courtesy, Watt Publishing Co., Mount Morris, Ill.)

Inspection Act (1906); (2) Insecticide Act (1910), later replaced by the Insecticide, Fungicide and Rodenticide Act; (3) Grain Standards Act (1916); (4) Federal fruit and vegetable grading for quality and condition (1922); (5) Cotton Standards Act (1923); (6) Tobacco Inspection Act (1935); (7) Food, Drug and Cosmetic Act (1938); (8) Wool Products Labeling Act (1940); (9) Fur Products Labeling Act (1951); and (10) Poultry Products Inspection Act (1959).

In addition, the Federal Trade Commission attempts to regulate unfair and deceptive advertising and trade practices. The Sherman, Clayton and Robinson-Patman Acts have as their ultimate objective the preservation of competition in business which will lead to fair and reasonable prices thus protecting the consumer.

The Public Health Service of the Department of Health, Education and Welfare establishes uniform sanitary codes used by local health departments in the control of the sanitation of restaurants and has a comprehensive program to reduce or prevent pollution of the nation's waters.

INTERNAL REVENUE AND OTHER ACTS

Various Internal Revenue Acts beginning in 1913 and up to the present have dealt with cooperatives and their tax status. This is the subject of Chapters 18 and 19.

Federal excise taxes on machinery, trucks, gasoline, lubricating oils, tires, tubes and some consumer goods (furs, jewelry, cosmetics, luggage and handbags) must be collected and remitted by retail cooperatives to the federal government.

FEDERAL CHARTERING OF COOPERATIVES

Although many federal laws have been passed concerning cooperatives, only six give authority to charter cooperatives, as shown in Table 10-2.

The types of cooperatives which may receive federal co-op charters only are the federal land bank associations, the production credit associations and the banks for cooperatives.

TABLE 10-2
Roster of Federal Laws Chartering Cooperatives

Year Adopted	Title of Act	Type of Cooperative
1916	Federal Farm Loan Act	Land bank associations
1933	Farm Credit Act	PCA's and banks for cooperatives
1933	Home Owners' Loan Corporation Act	Savings and loan associations[2]
1934	Federal Credit Union Act	Credit unions[2]
1940	District of Columbia Cooperatives Act[1]	Consumer cooperatives[2]
1950	Granger-Thye Act	Empowers recognition of certain grazing associations

[1]Although not a federal act, its scope is nationwide.
[2]State statutes also provide for their chartering.

In addition, credit unions, certain grazing associations and savings and loan associations may receive either federal or state charters as they may elect.

Consumer cooperatives also have the option of chartering under their respective state laws or chartering under the District of Columbia

Cooperative Act although the latter is not in reality a federal charter. In practice it serves as one.

COOPERATIVE LAW IN OTHER COUNTRIES

The legal aspects of cooperation in other countries are covered by Valko,[10] Barnes,[11] Digby[12] and Francis.[13]

Co-op legislation in the various states of the United States is the subject of the next chapter.

TOPICS FOR DISCUSSION

1. Discuss the Sherman Act and its effects on cooperatives.
2. How did the Clayton Act amend the Sherman Act, and how did the Capper-Volstead Act amend the Clayton Act?
3. Discuss the various federal acts regarding farm credit.
4. Discuss the five marketing acts and their effects on cooperatives.
5. Enumerate and discuss briefly the seven federal regulatory acts.
6. Discuss the Federal Credit Union Act and the Rural Electrification Act.
7. Enumerate other federal acts of importance to cooperatives.
8. Which types of cooperatives can be federally-chartered?

SELECTED REFERENCES

1. Brooks, Neil, *Legal Aspects of the Federal Marketing Orders for Agricultural Products,* USDA, Washington, D.C. Not dated. pp. 12-13.
2. Danenberg, Elsie, *Get Your Home the Co-op Way,* Greenberg Publishers, New York, N.Y. 1949.
3. Dankers, W. H., *Legal Requirements for Cooperatives,* Minn. Agr. Ext. Serv. Cir. 245, St. Paul, Minn. Jan. 1945.
4. DeWolfe, Mildred, *For-Hire Motor Carriers Hauling Exempt Agricultural Commodities,* ERS Rept. 585, USDA, Washington, D.C. Jan. 1963.
5. Evans, Frank and E. A. Stokdyk, *Law of Agricultural Cooperative Marketing,* Lawyers Co-op Publishing Co., Rochester, N.Y. 1937.

---

[10]Valko, L., *International Handbook for Co-op Legislation,* Washington State College (now Washington State University), Pullman, Wash. 1954.
[11]Barnes, W. S., *American Cooperation,* Washington, D.C. 1950. pp. 387-395.
[12]Digby, Margaret, *Co-op Law at Home and Abroad,* King & Son, London, England. 1933.
[13]Francis, W. B., *Canadian Co-op Law,* Carswell & Co., Toronto, Canada. 1959.

6. Fletcher, L. B., "Farm Co-ops: How Special a Status?" *Iowa Farm Science*, Ames, Iowa. June 1961.

7. Jensen, A. L. and others, *Cooperative Corporate Association Law*, American Institute of Cooperation, Washington, D.C. 1950.

8. Mischler, R. T. and L. S. Hulbert, *Legal Phases of Farmer Cooperation*, FCS Bul. 10, USDA, Washington, D.C. Jan. 1958.

9. Mueller, W. F. and J. M. Tinley, *Membership Marketing Contracts*, Calif. Agr. Exp. Sta. Bul. 760, Berkeley, Calif. Mar. 1958.

10. Nourse, E. G., *The Legal Status of Agricultural Cooperation*, Macmillan, New York, N.Y. 1928.

11. Packel, Israel, *The Law of Cooperatives*, M. Bender & Co., Albany, N.Y. 1956.

12. Purdy, H. L. and others, *Corporate Concentration and Public Policy*, Prentice-Hall, New York, N.Y. 1942.

13. Saunders, J. J., "The Status of Agricultural Cooperatives Under the Antitrust Laws," *Federal Bar Journal*. Vol. 20, No. 1. p. 35.

14. Staff, "Agricultural Cooperatives and the Antitrust Laws: Clayton, Capper-Volstead and Common Sense," *Virginia Law Review*. 1958.

15. Staff, *Antitrust Laws*, N.A.M., Washington, D.C. Apr. 1955.

16. Staff, *Cooperative Marketing*, FTC, Washington, D.C. 1928. Chapter 13.

17. Staff, *Farmer Cooperatives in the U.S.*, FCS, Bul. 1, USDA, Washington, D.C. Dec. 1955.

18. Staff, *Federal Credit Union Act*, Supt. of Documents, G.P.O., Washington, D.C. 1959.

19. Staff, *Moody's Bank and Finance Manual*, Moody's Investor Service, New York, N.Y. 1961.

20. Staff, *Preloan Procedures for Rural Telephone Co-ops*, REA, Bul. 320-1, USDA, Washington, D.C. Feb. 1962.

21. Stanton, Beryle, *The Way Farmer Cooperative Service Works*, FCS Info. 36, USDA, Washington, D.C. Mar. 1963.

CHAPTER 11 –

Cooperatives and State
Legislation in the
United States of America

They ought not to await the event to know what measures to take; but the measures which they have taken ought to produce the event.

—Demosthenes

STATE LAWS APPLICABLE TO COOPERATIVES

THE LEGAL BASIS for co-op organization in the United States began in 1865 in Michigan when an act was passed authorizing the formation of mechanics' and laboring men's cooperatives. In 1875, this act was amended to include agricultural and horticultural associations.

In 1866, Massachusetts passed an act permitting the formation of mechanical, manufacturing and agricultural cooperatives. Several other states patterned their acts on the Massachusetts act including, for example, Pennsylvania (1868), Minnesota (1870), Connecticut (1875), California (1878), New Jersey (1887) and Ohio (1884).

In 1887, Wisconsin, Kansas and Pennsylvania passed co-op association acts.

Between the passage of the Sherman Act in 1890 and the Clayton Act in 1914, only a few states enacted co-op statutes. These included, for example, California (1895), Minnesota (1897—creamery associations), Alabama (1909), Wisconsin (1911), Nebraska (1911), Indiana (1913) and Colorado (1914).

The Wisconsin law (1911) was particularly significant because it recognized three basic co-op principles: (1) limitation of capital holdings, (2) democratic voting and (3) patronage refunds.

Between the passage of the Clayton Act in 1914 and the Capper-Volstead Act in 1922, several states enacted co-op statutes. These included, for example, North Dakota (1915), Florida (1917), New Mexico (1915) and Texas (1917).

Because the Clayton Act had not dealt with the stock cooperatives and since the co-op statutes in various states contained considerable ambiguity and variations from sound co-op principles, the United States Department of Agriculture drafted a "model law" in 1917 for farmer cooperatives. In drafting this bill the experiences of states that had already incorporated certain specific features in their laws were considered.

The bill, which was to serve as a model, included provisions for the incorporation of either capital stock or nonstock associations and provided for marketing agreements and for penalties in the event of breach of contract. Other provisions relating to voting, ownership of stock and distribution of patronage dividends were included. The Department's bill found ready acceptance by numerous states during the years 1917 to 1921. It also had its effect upon the wording of the Capper-Volstead Act of 1922.

At about the time the federal Capper-Volstead Act was enacted, the state legislature of Kentucky passed the Bingham Cooperative Marketing Act (1922). This Act became a model for many co-op statutes enacted in other states.

The influence of Aaron Sapiro on state co-op marketing statutes cannot be minimized. His stress upon marketing associations and marketing contracts influenced many state legislatures to pass specific statutes providing for the incorporation of such associations. This is the reason why many of the states have at least two statutes on the incorporation of farmer cooperatives. One is for farmer cooperatives generally, while the other is more specifically for marketing cooperatives.

In the organization of consumer and business cooperatives, the state laws authorizing the incorporation of such cooperatives are not so uniform as they are in the case of farmer cooperatives. Some states have broad statutes authorizing the incorporation of cooperatives which may engage in any type of commercial transaction. In states where there is no specific statute authorizing the formation of consumer and business cooperatives, such cooperatives are generally formed under the General Corporation Act of the state.

Although there are wide variations in the provisions of the co-op laws of the different states, they generally specify the following:

1. Minimum number of members required to incorporate.

2. Conditions to be included in the articles of incorporation and bylaws.

3. The state official or department with which the articles of incorporation are to be filed.

4. Fees required.

5. General powers, rights and obligations of the co-op members.

6. Voting rights of stockholders and members.

7. Terms and conditions of membership.

8. Nonmember relationships.

9. General provisions with respect to distribution of savings or net margins.

10. Capital structure (stock or nonstock) and interest rate to be paid on capital.

In Table 11-1 are presented the various state statutes regarding cooperatives. An "X" indicates that a specific law has been passed for that type of cooperative. An "*" indicates that while no specific statute is available, the cooperative may be chartered under some other accommodating statute. Then, a limited discussion of different types of cooperatives is presented in connection with the legislation appropriate to them.

Agricultural Cooperatives

All 50 states have laws designed especially for the incorporation of agricultural cooperatives.

No other type of cooperative has as good a legal basis for chartering as does the farmer cooperative. Much credit in this respect is due to the United States Department of Agriculture, various farm organizations, co-op councils and others that provided the leadership in getting adequate and uniform farm co-op statutes in each of the 50 states.

Agricultural Credit Corporations

Agricultural credit corporation statutes are infrequent because farmers can adequately organize, under federal law, into production credit associations and credit unions to supply their short-term credit needs.

TABLE 11-1
Status of State Co-op Incorporation Laws, by States, U.S.A.[1]

Type of Co-op Incorporation Law

State	Agr. Assoc.	Agr. Credit Corp.	Consumer Co-op	Credit Union	Fishery	Fraternal Benefit Society	Group Medical[2]	Hospital Service Assoc.	Housing Assoc.[3]	Memorial Cemetery Assoc.	Mutual Insurance[4]	Mutual Savings Banks	Nonprofit Co-op Corp.	Rural Electric	Savings & Loan	Telephone Mutuals	Utility Co-op[5]	Workers' Productive Co-op[6]
Alabama	X	X	X	X		X	R	X	X	X	X		X	X	X	X	S	X
Alaska	X	X	X	X	X	X			X	X	X	X	X	X	X	*	I, S	X
Arizona	X			X		X	M	X		X	X		X	X	X	*	I, S	
Arkansas	X	X	X	X		X	N		LD		X		X	X	X	X	I, S	X
California	X		X	X	X	X	R	X	X	X	X		X	*	X	*	I, S	X
Colorado	X		X	X		X	M		X	X	X		X	*	X	*	I, S	XW
Connecticut	X		X	X		X	O	X	LD	X	X	X	X	X	X	*	S	X
Delaware	X			X		X	N	X	LD		X	X	X	*	X	*	I, S	
Florida	X	X	X	X		X	M	X	X	X	X		X	X	X	*	I, S	XW
Georgia	X			X		X	M	X	X	X	X		X	X	X	X	S	
Hawaii	X		*	X	X	X	M	X	X	X	X		X		X	*	S	
Idaho	X	X	X	X		X	M	X	X	X	X		X	*	X	*	I, S	X
Illinois	X	X	X	X		X	N		X	X	X		X	*	X		I, S	X
Indiana	X		X	X		X	M	X	X	X	X	X	X	X	X	X	S	XW
Iowa	X		X	X		X	M	X	X	X	X		X	*	X	*	S	X

X–Applicable state law empowering specific charter.

[1]Interpretation of these statutes is based on the author's judgment and does not necessarily reflect interpretations that might be made by others.

[2]N–none, R–restrictive, M–mandatory, and O–open.

[a]Charter may be accommodated under another available statute.

[3]LD–Limited-dividend housing statutes might be used.

[4]One or more types of mutual insurance.

[5]I–irrigation, S–soil conservation district.

[6]W–workers' productive cooperatives specified.

(Continued)

TABLE 11-1 (Continued)

Type of Co-op Incorporation Law

State	Agr. Assoc.	Agr. Credit Corp.	Consumer Co-op	Credit Union	Fishery	Fraternal Benefit Society	Group Medical[2]	Hospital Service Assoc.	Housing Assoc.[3]	Memorial Cemetery Assoc.	Mutual Insurance[4]	Mutual Savings Banks	Nonprofit Co-op Corp.	Rural Electric	Savings & Loan	Telephone Mutuals	Utility Co-op[5]	Workers' Productive Co-op[6]
Kansas	X		X	X		X	R	X	X	X	X		X	X	X	*	I, S	X
Kentucky	X		X	X		X	M	X		X	X		X	X	X	X	S	X
Louisiana	X	X		X	X	X	R	X		X	X		X	X	X	*	S	
Maine	X			X		X	R	X	X	X	X	X	X	*	X	*	I, S	X
Maryland	X		X	X	X	X	O	X		X	X	X	X	X	X	*	S	
Massachusetts	X		X	X		X	R	X	X	X	X	X	X	*	X	*	S	X
Michigan	X	X	X	X		X	R	X	X	X	X	X	X	*	X	X	S	XW
Minnesota	X	X	X	X		X	R	X		X	X	X	X	*	X	*	I, S	X
Mississippi	X	X	X	X		X	O	X			X			X	X	*	S	
Missouri	X		X	X		X	N	X		X	X		X	X	X	X	S	
Montana	X	X	X	X		X	R		X	X	X		X	X	X	X	I, S	X
Nebraska	X	X	X	X		X	N	X	X	X	X		X	X	X	*	I, S	XW
Nevada	X	X		X		X	N		X	X	X		X	*	X	*	I, S	X
New Hampshire	X			X		X	M	X	LD	X	X	X	X	*	X	*	S	
New Jersey	X		X	X		X	M	X	LD	X	X	X	X	*	X	*	I, S	X
New Mexico	X	X	X	X		X	O	X	X	X	X		X	X	X	*	I, S	
New York	X	X	X	X		X	O	X	X, LD	X	X	X	X	X	X	*	S	XW
North Carolina	X		X	X		X	O	X	X	X	X		X	X	X	X	I, S	X
North Dakota	X		X	X		X	M	X	X, LD	X	X		X	*	X	*	I, S	XW
Ohio	X		X	X		X	M	X	X, LD	X	X	X	X		X	*	S	XW

(Continued)

TABLE 11-1 (Continued)

State	Agr. Assoc.	Agr. Credit Corp.	Consumer Co-op	Credit Union	Fishery	Fraternal Benefit Society	Group Medical[f]	Hospital Service Assoc.	Housing Assoc.[g]	Memorial Cemetery Assoc.	Mutual Insurance[h]	Mutual Savings Banks	Nonprofit Co-op Corp.	Rural Electric	Savings & Loan	Telephone Mutuals	Utility Co-op[i]	Workers' Productive Co-op[j]
Oklahoma	X		X	X		X	O			X	X		X	X	X	X	I, S	X
Oregon	X	X	X	X	X	X	O		X	X	X	X	X	*	X	*	I, S	X
Pennsylvania	X		X	X		X	M	X	X	X	X	X	X	X	X	*	S	
Rhode Island	X		X	X		X	M	X	X		X	X	X		X	*	S	
South Carolina	X		X	X		X	R	X	LD		X		X	X	X	*	S	X
South Dakota	X		X			X	O	X		X	X		X	X	X	*	I, S	X
Tennessee	X		X	X		X	M	X	LD	X	X		X	X	X	*	S	
Texas	X	X		X		X	O	X		X	X			X	X	X	I, S	
Utah	X			X		X	N	X			X		X	*	X	*	I, S	
Vermont	X		X	X		X	R	X	X	X	X	X	X	X	X	*	S	X
Virginia	X	X	X	X	X	X	M	X		X	X		X	X	X	X	I, S	X
Washington	X	X	X	X	X	X	O		X	X	X	X	X	*	X	*	I, S	X
West Virginia	X	X	X	X		X	R	X		X	X	X	X	*	X	*	S	
Wisconsin	X	X	X	X		X	X	X	X	X	X	X		*	X	*	I, S	X
Wyoming	X			X		X	N	X		X	X			*	X	*	I, S	X
District of Columbia	X		X	X		X	X	X	X	X	X		X		X	*		

Sources: Interstate and Foreign Commerce Committee, *Group Health Inquiry—Part VI*, U.S. House of Representatives, Washington, D.C.
Ostrolenk, B., *Literary Development of Cooperative Principles and Data*, Series A, Part I, W.P.A., New York, N.Y. Mar. 1939.
Parker, Florence, *The First 125 Years*, Cooperative League, Chicago, Ill. 1956.
Rural Electrification Administration, Washington, D.C. 1962.
Staff, *Organization and Management of Co-op and Mutual Housing*, BLS Bul. 858, Dept. of Labor, Washington, D.C. 1946.
Staff, *Consumers' Cooperative Statutes and Decisions*, U.S. Dept. of Labor, Washington, D.C. 1937.

FIGURE 11-1

Agricultural cooperatives have available the most comprehensive set of statutes for incorporation. These statutes are provided in all 50 states of the United States. (Courtesy, Southern States Cooperative, Richmond, Va.)

However, agricultural credit corporation laws are useful state statutes because, in the future, credit needs of farmers will become more acute and agricultural credit corporations will become more important. This is especially true in the case of vertical integration and contract farming.

Consumer Cooperatives

Although consumer co-op legislation is not so comprehensive as for farmer cooperatives, the status of consumer co-op statutes is nevertheless adequate. Only the states of Arizona, Delaware, Georgia, Indiana, Louisiana, Maryland, Mississippi, New Hampshire, Texas, Utah, West Virginia and Wyoming do not have a specific consumer co-op statute.

This does not preclude the organization of consumer cooperatives in the aforementioned states, however. At least two alternatives are available: (1) organize a consumer cooperative under the general in-

FIGURE 11-2

Consumer cooperatives have specific incorporation statutes available to them in 38 of the states. (Courtesy, Hyde Park Cooperative Society, Chicago, Ill.)

corporation law as a nonprofit corporation or (2) organize under the District of Columbia Consumer Co-op Act.

Credit Unions

State credit union legislation is very adequate and comprehensive. Edward Filene and Roy Bergengren and the Credit Union National Association are largely responsible for this. Only the states of Alaska, Delaware, Hawaii, Nevada, South Dakota and Wyoming have no state credit union statutes. This is not a serious handicap, however, because credit unions in those states can be chartered federally under the Federal Credit Union Act.

Both state and federal credit union acts are quite similar. Also, state credit unions can usually be converted to federal unions, and vice versa.

Fishery and Seafood Cooperatives

Two items should be mentioned regarding fishery and seafood cooperatives: (1) Only coastal states bordering on the Atlantic or Pacific Ocean or on the Gulf of Mexico are interested in them. (2) The Aquatic Marketing Act of 1934 is for fishermen what the Capper-Volstead Act is for farmer cooperatives. In other words, the 1934 Act gives state fishery cooperatives legal protection in interstate commerce.

Only Alaska, California, Hawaii, Louisiana, Maryland, Oregon, Virginia and Washington provide specifically for fishery and seafood cooperatives. However, fishery cooperatives may be organized also under the nonprofit provisions of the general corporation law or the nonprofit co-op corporation acts.

Fraternal Benefit Societies

All the states except Hawaii have statutes enabling fraternal benefit societies. These societies consist of lodge, secret order, religious, lay and fraternal bodies wishing to provide mutual services and benefits for their own groups.

Group Medical Practice

Group medical practice includes those plans in which consumers (unionists, farmers) organize to provide group medical, surgical and hospitalization coverage on a prepaid basis under their own control. Physicians are employed by the co-op groups to look after the health of their members. This is considerably different from the Blue Shield plans which are physician-controlled and administered although operated on a nonprofit basis.

Group health and Blue Shield plans are locked in a tough fight to determine whether financial control of these medical care plans will rest with doctors or with laymen or jointly with both. Blue Shield plans are aimed primarily at *curative* medicine while group medical practice is aimed at *preventive* medicine. Involved in this struggle are the issues of (1) corporate practice of medicine and (2) the physician-patient relationships.

The status of state legislation permitting co-op group health plans versus Blue Shield plans is interesting and complex. To clarify the legal issues involved in physician-subscriber medical care plans and to promote their organization, three states have passed enabling legislation: Illinois, Massachusetts and Wisconsin. These acts state, in substance, that a medical care prepayment plan is not essentially insurance nor is it the corporate practice of medicine. These are excellent laws.

Those states with "open acts," or acts not designed for either physician or consumer control are: Connecticut, Maryland, Mississippi, New Mexico, New York, North Carolina, Oklahoma, Oregon, South Dakota, Texas and Washington.

Those states with "restrictive acts," or acts which allow for physician control by precluding lay plans are: Alabama, California, Kansas, Louisiana, Maine, Michigan, Minnesota, Montana, South Carolina, Vermont and West Virginia.

States with "monopoly or mandatory" acts containing provisions for exclusive physician control plans thereby eliminating both consumer plans and other profit-type plans are: Arizona, Colorado, Florida, Georgia, Idaho, Iowa, Kentucky, New Hampshire, New Jersey, North Dakota, Ohio, Pennsylvania, Rhode Island, Tennessee and Virginia.

The states with no legislation in this area are: Arkansas, Delaware, Indiana, Missouri, Nebraska, Nevada, Utah and Wyoming. Court cases have recently indicated that consumer plans are possible in Missouri and Nebraska.[1]

---

[1]*Health Inquiry,* Government Printing Office, Washington, D.C. 1954. pp. 1779-1785.

There have been many attempts by various groups to charter under statutes favorable to group medical practice. In Louisiana, by using Act 254 of 1914 (a non-trading corporation act), a very successful group medical practice plan has evolved in the absence of a favorable statute.

Hospital Service Associations (Blue Cross)

Thirty-seven states have enacted special state laws which enable Blue Cross plans to be exempt from regular insurance laws, free them from maintaining high reserves and relieve them of paying taxes. However, in most, if not all, states, Blue Cross plans are chartered and regulated by the Insurance Commissioner rather than by the Corporation Commissioner.

The principal weakness in Blue Cross plans is the lack of effective control by subscribers to such a plan. A small group usually attends meetings and controls its affairs. An inbred management not especially accountable to subscribers often lessens the essential co-op features of the plan.

Housing Cooperatives

The chartering of housing cooperatives is a rather new field, and many states have not adequately provided for these cooperatives. In the future, activity in this field is expected to increase substantially.

States with adequate co-op housing statutes are approximately the same states with consumer co-op statutes. In addition to these states, there are some others with "limited-dividend" co-op housing statutes.

The latter laws permit a state, or city within the state, to make low interest mortgage loans of up to 90 percent of a project's construction costs to builders who agree to a limit of 6 percent profit on their investment. Equity provided by the sponsor of the project makes up the remaining 10 percent of the cost. A law authorizes the appropriation of state funds for financing. Under this program, tax exemption and tenant income limits are fixed as in the other city and state middle-income housing laws. In addition, the permanent financing of the project is furnished by the state or the city at the rates it pays on the sale of housing bonds to the public (about 3 percent), plus a charge for the cost of borrowing, with small amortization.

In those states with no co-op housing statutes, prospective home-owners might incorporate under the District of Columbia Consumer

Co-op Act. However, such a cooperative will become "foreign" to the state in which it is physically located. Housing cooperatives may charter in some states under the general incorporation law.

Memorial Associations

Included under memorial association laws are the (1) "cemetery acts" which provide that groups of people may organize to own and maintain cemetery plots in common and (2) burial associations which cover the cost of funeral benefits and conduct of religious services on a mutual basis.

All states provide for either or both cemetery and burial associations except Arkansas, Delaware, Georgia, Hawaii, Mississippi, New Mexico, Rhode Island, South Carolina and Utah. Even in these states, however, a fraternal benefit group organized under the fraternal society acts can satisfy the needs of cooperators. Some religious denominations (Catholic) administer cemetery associations to which church members subscribe on a quasi-cooperative basis.

Mutual Insurances

Each of the 50 states has one or more statutes for chartering mutual insurance associations. However, not all of the states provide for the incorporation of any and all types of co-op mutual insurance. Admittedly, the mutual insurance field is very broad. It includes mutual fire, lightning, tornado, cyclone, hail, windstorm, livestock, employers' liability, workmen's compensation, life, accident, health, burglary, robbery, auto, fidelity, surety, marine, plate glass and farm machinery insurance, among others.

Before a particular mutual insurance cooperative is organized, the statutes of the home state need to be carefully analyzed.

Mutual Savings Banks

There is no federal statute for chartering mutual savings banks, although bills have been introduced into Congress to allow for this. Therefore, only state statutes apply in this case. Only the states of Alaska, Connecticut, Delaware, Indiana, Maine, Maryland, Massachusetts, Minnesota, New Hampshire, New Jersey, New York, Ohio,

Oregon, Pennsylvania, Rhode Island, Vermont, Washington and Wisconsin provide for the incorporation of mutual savings banks.

After receiving a charter permitting organization of a bank, the corporators may apply for insurance of deposits through the Federal Deposit Insurance Corporation. The corporators elect a board of trustees to establish bank policies, and the board, in turn, selects officers to operate the bank. The primary function of mutual savings banks is to promote thrift by encouraging personal saving. In addition to regular savings accounts, mutual savings banks offer special accounts, such as Christmas and vacation clubs, school savings and investment accounts. More than 300 mutual savings banks in Massachusetts, New York and Connecticut offer Savings Bank Life Insurance, a low-cost family protection offered over the counter and without agents' fees. Other services generally offered include money orders, travelers' checks, payroll savings accounts, banking by mail, safe deposit boxes and, of course, mortgage loans.

Nonprofit Co-op Corporations

Co-op corporations in the business and industrial field, except for credit, banking and insurance cooperatives, charter either under the general incorporation law as nonprofit corporations or under a nonprofit co-op corporation statute.

Chartering Cooperatives Under the General Incorporation Law.— Many co-op leaders believe that cooperatives should never charter except under specific co-op statutes. They recall the Grange cooperatives of the 1880's which deteriorated into profit-type corporations in the absence of specific co-op statutes. However, in recent years, more co-op leaders are coming to the viewpoint that the general incorporation law can be used to charter cooperatives successfully.

Satterfield, a noted lawyer and authority on co-op corporations, advocates greater use of the general corporation law for chartering cooperatives:

> Laying aside historical significance and theory, consideration of the hard facts of present-day financing and business reveals the following advantages arising from the flexibility of use of general corporation laws for the organization of cooperatives:
> 1. Under the general corporate form, the cooperative would not have the status of an exempt cooperative under the

federal income tax law. Nevertheless, its charter and bylaws
may carry a legally enforceable obligation to handle its business at cost and to refund to its patron-stockholders the difference between the amount received and the actual cost of doing
business. This will entitle the corporation to exclude from its
gross income all patronage refunds paid or payable under the
rules similar to those applicable to cooperatives organized as
nonexempt cooperatives under special state statutes. However,
under the general corporate form there is no maximum upon
the amount of fixed dividends which may be payable upon the
different forms of stock. On the other hand, as is true of all
entities of a cooperative nature which are not exempt cooperatives, the dividends upon capital stock may be paid only with
tax paid money and hence should be held to as low a percentage as possible.

2. The use of this form results in the ability to authorize
the issuance of all forms of corporate stock permissible under
the general statutes. This may include preferred stock of all
kinds, with limited dividends cumulative or noncumulative as
desired. Dividends may be limited to any percentage of par
value which may be desired, with or without a callable feature.
Such preferred stock may have no voting power (under most
state statutes) or may have voting power equal to that of the
common stock. Payment of dividends may be given preference
over the payment of patronage refunds in order to make the
investment more attractive.

3. The extent of the participation in the management of
the corporation by various classifications of stockholders may
be varied. This is sometimes material in maintaining compliance with special definitions contained in federal or state
statutes. As an illustration, common voting stock may be
divided into classes such as Class A common stock with a par
value of $5 per share (20 votes for each $100 invested), Class
B common stock with a par value of $100 per share (one vote
for each $100 invested) and Class C common stock with a
par value of 10 cents per share (1,000 votes for each $100
invested). Again we are dealing with the hard facts of modern
business as distinguished from the theory of "democratic control, one member = one vote."

4. Under this form of organization different classes of
common stock may perform different functions in the allocation to stockholders of the services or goods furnished to the
corporation. The charter or bylaws may provide preferred
patronage rights with each class of stock whereby each
[stockholder] is permitted to purchase a named quantity of
the products of the corporation or a fixed amount measured
by the market price thereof. Thus, the extent of a stockholder's
right to receive goods or services furnished by the corporation

would be proportionate to his investment in stock. This also may be varied as to particular products. For instance, if a manufacturing cooperative manufactures anhydrous ammonia, ammonium nitrate and mixed fertilizer, it may have three classes of stock. Class A stock would carry with it preferred patronage rights for the purchase of anhydrous ammonia only. Class B stock would carry with it preferred patronage rights for the purchase of ammonium nitrate only. Class C stock would carry with it preferred patronage rights for the purchase of mixed fertilizer only. Thus, in one corporate organization, the stockholder may in effect invest in the different manufacturing enterprises carried on by such corporation.

5. Another illustration of the flexibility of the use of the general corporate form is that the preferred stock, the certificates of participation and certificates of indebtedness may be callable or not as provided in charter or bylaws or as provided in the trust indenture under which the certificates are issued.

6. Another flexible feature of the use of the general corporate form is the ability of the corporation to enter into contracts with nonmembers or nonstockholders whereby such persons will receive patronage refunds. There is no requirement that the corporation pay patronage refunds to nonstockholder-patrons on the same basis as stockholder-patrons, nor is there any requirement that nonstockholder-patrons be treated with complete uniformity. The freedom of contract inherent in general corporate entities is present.

7. By the use of general corporate form the charter or bylaws may contain restrictions upon the purchase or transfer of stock. In most states it may be provided that stock may be transferred to or held only by agricultural producers or some other class of persons. The provisions setting up preferred patronage rights also may restrict the use of such rights in such a way as to prevent the effective transfer of the stock contrary to the policy of the company. For instance, it may be provided that all preferred patronage rights will cease when the stockholder ceases to be an actual agricultural producer or that the preferred patronage rights will be no greater than the amount of the production of the company actually used by the stockholder on his own property. Through these means the agricultural integrity of the corporation may be preserved, for, if the common stock dividend rate is low, the major advantage of ownership is the use of the right to purchase the products or services of the corporation through the preferred patronage rights.

8. Under the general corporate form the original corporation in its charter may permit the organization of any number or type of subsidiaries. These may be wholly or partially

owned and controlled by the parent corporation. They may be used as adjuncts to the business of the parent corporation or for an entirely separate purpose.

There are a number of disadvantages to the general corporate form which are readily discernible and which should be taken into consideration prior to making the determination to set up a cooperative in the form of a general business corporation. These include, of course, the fact that the entity is subject to all of the regulatory statutes affecting general corporations such as Blue Sky laws, the Federal Security Acts, the antitrust laws without limitation, and certain relatively small corporate taxes from which cooperatives in some states are exempt such as franchise taxes, privilege taxes, fees paid in connection with compliance with Blue Sky laws, etc.[2]

Nonprofit Co-op Corporation Statutes.—All of the states except Georgia, Hawaii, Mississippi, Texas, West Virginia and Wyoming have specific nonprofit co-op corporation statutes applicable to business and industrial cooperatives.

The Virginia Act passed in 1914 is typical of such acts:

> Any number of persons, not less than five, may form a corporation, with capital stock, for the purpose of conducting any agricultural, dairy, mercantile, merchandise, brokerage, manufacturing or mechanical business on the cooperative plan.

Finally, there is always the opportunity to incorporate cooperatives under the laws of any state which has a liberal statute. Then, cooperatives might qualify to do business in their own home states but as "foreign" corporations. Care should be exercised, however, in following this procedure. Legal counsel should be retained.

Rural Electric Cooperatives

Although the passage of the Rural Electrification Act did much to encourage rural electric cooperatives, the Act itself did not provide for their incorporation. State statutes only enable incorporation. The REA itself in its early years was most helpful in encouraging the states to adopt uniform co-op statutes.

In Arizona, California, Colorado, Idaho, Illinois, Iowa, Kansas,

---

[2]Satterfield, J. C., "The Co-op in Our Free Enterprise System," N.C.F.C. Meeting, Jan. 10, 1961. New Orleans, La.

FIGURE 11-3

The rural electric cooperatives are state-chartered, not federally-chartered. Most of the states have adequate incorporation statutes. (Courtesy, National Rural Electric Cooperative Association, Washington, D.C.)

Maine, Michigan, Minnesota, Nebraska, Nevada, New Hampshire, Ohio, Oregon, Utah, Washington and Wisconsin, rural electric cooperatives can charter under the nonprofit co-op corporation statutes. In Delaware, New Jersey, Vermont, West Virginia and Wyoming, they may be incorporated under the general incorporation law.

In Arizona, California, Nebraska and Washington, they may be incorporated also under the utility district statutes (Table 11-1).

In most states, rural electric cooperatives have been able to charter so as to obtain freedom from public service commission regulations.

Savings and Loan Associations

Of the total savings and loan associations in the United States, 70 percent are state-chartered. All of the 50 states have appropriate savings and loan statutes. However, state laws vary in some of the details; therefore, thorough study of the state statutes is recommended. For example, 18 states permit stock savings and loan associations in addition to mutuals.

Like the commercial banking structure, savings associations operate within a dual system of charters and supervision. The state-chartered institutions function within a legal framework administered by the supervisory authorities of the respective states. Those with federal charters, which were authorized by the Home Owners' Loan Corporation Act, are subject to the supervision of the Federal Home Loan Bank Board.

In most states, an association with a state charter can convert to a federal charter, and vice versa. Whether the association is state or federal, it may elect to insure its accounts up to $10,000 with the Federal Savings and Loan Insurance Corporation.

Telephone Mutuals

Not many states have enacted specific statutes for the incorporation of mutual telephone cooperatives. Those states with specific statutes are Alabama, Alaska, Arkansas, Georgia, Indiana, Kentucky, Michigan, Missouri, Montana, North Carolina, Oklahoma, Texas and Virginia. In Florida, South Carolina, West Virginia and Wyoming, mutual telephone cooperatives may be organized under the general incorporation law. In the balance of the states, they may be incorporated under the nonprofit co-op corporation law unless otherwise prohibited.

Telephone companies are, in many states, regarded as public utilities or common carriers and, as such, are subject to regulation by state commissions. A number of states exempt from such regulation associations operating as pure mutuals (i.e., serving members only and having no predetermined rates but assessing all members their pro rata share of the cost of operation); service extended to even one nonmember subjects an association to regulation by the state commission. Some of the regulations imposed by these state commissions also place obstacles in the way of completely cooperative practice. Thus, in states where operating territory is apportioned company by company and exclusive rights are given therein, state commissions generally require the companies to serve all applicants for service whether they are stockholders or not.

In some cases the companies are specifically prohibited from making any distinction in the rates charged to members and to nonmembers.

The result is that where nonmembers can get the same service as members and at the same rate, there is little inducement to take out membership in the telephone cooperative. Such has been the effect of this that in states where this regulation is in force, many associations have a greater number of nonmember than member subscribers.

As is evident, therefore, the rate of observance of the co-op principles among the telephone associations is dependent to a considerable extent upon these legal and regulatory requirements.[3]

Since the REA Act was amended in 1949 enabling it to make loans to telephone cooperatives, a renewed interest in them is developing. It can be expected that those states without co-op telephone statutes will consider adopting them in the future.

Utility Cooperatives

Utility cooperatives considered here are broadly classified into two types: (1) irrigation mutuals and (2) soil conservation districts.

Irrigation co-op statutes are quite numerous, being on the law books of 28 states. In states without such statutes, irrigation mutuals may be incorporated under the general corporation law.

All the states have enabling statutes providing for soil conservation districts. This was accomplished since 1935 when the Soil Conservation Act was first passed by Congress.

Workers' Productive Cooperatives

Although workers' productive cooperatives are not so important now than in decades past, the state statutes with regard to them are better than expected. These statutes consist of two types: (1) those that are broad enough in their coverage to provide for workers' productive cooperatives and (2) those that are specifically for workers' cooperatives.

Unusual State Co-op Laws

In Table 11-2 is presented a list of unusual state co-op laws passed for some specific purpose or under some unusual circumstance. However, this list does not exhaust all the unusual co-op laws passed by various state legislatures.

---

[3]Parker, Florence, *Consumers' Cooperation in the U.S.*, BLS Bul. 659, Dept. of Labor, Washington, D.C. Aug. 1938. pp. 198-199.

TABLE 11-2
List of Unusual State Co-op Laws, Selected
States, U.S.A.

State	Co-op Law Provides For:
Arizona	A scientific research co-op corporation.
Florida	A sponge cooperative.
Louisiana	Elementary and high schools on a co-op basis, Act 257, 1958.
Nevada	Co-op historic and literary societies.
North Dakota	Teaching about cooperatives in colleges and high schools (not mandatory).
Ohio	Farm laborers' associations.
Oklahoma	Physicians' and dentists' mutual insurance association.
South Dakota	Dental health insurance.
Tennessee	Sheepowners' mutual to protect sheep from dogs.
Vermont	Railroad cooperatives.
Wisconsin	Mandatory teaching about cooperatives in high schools.

Summary of State and Federal Incorporation Laws

In Table 11-3 is presented a summary of incorporation statutes covering both state and federal laws for each type of cooperative.

TABLE 11-3
Applicable Chartering Statutes for Cooperatives,
by Type of Cooperative

	Cooperative Can Incorporate Under	
Type of Cooperative	State Statutes	Federal Statutes
Agricultural bargaining	Yes[1]	No[2]
Agricultural marketing	Yes[1]	No[2]
Artificial breeding	Yes[1]	No
Bank for farmer co-ops	No	Farm Credit Act, 1933
Business service	Yes[3]	No
Consumer	Yes[4]	D.C. Consumer Co-op Act, 1940[5]
Credit corporation, farm	Yes[1] [3]	No
Credit union	Yes[6]	Federal Credit Union Act, 1934
Dairy herd improvement	Yes[1]	No
Educational	Yes[7]	No
Farm supply	Yes[1]	No
Federal land bank	No	Federal Farm Loan Act, 1916
Fishery	Yes[3]	No[8]
Grazing	Yes[1] [9]	No[10]

(Continued)

TABLE 11-3 *(Continued)*

Type of Cooperative	Cooperative Can Incorporate Under	
	State Statutes	Federal Statutes
Group health	Yes[3]	D.C. Consumer Co-op Act, 1940
Housing	Yes[3]	D.C. Consumer Co-op Act, 1940
Indian enterprise	Yes[1 3]	No
Irrigation	Yes[3]	No
Memorial association	Yes[3]	No
Mutual insurance	Yes[3]	No
Mutual savings and loan	Yes	Home Owners' Loan Corporation Act, 1933
Mutual savings bank	Yes[3]	No
Mutual telephone	Yes[3]	No
Nonfarm, nonprofit business	Yes[3]	No
Production credit association	No	Farm Credit Act, 1933
Rural electric	Yes[3]	No
Soil conservation district	Yes[3]	No
Utility	Yes[3]	No
Wholesale, retailer-owned	Yes[11]	No
Workers' productive society	Yes[3]	No

[1]Under agricultural association acts.
[2]Capper-Volstead Act controls if the cooperative conducts business interstate-wise.
[3]See Table 11-1 for states with specific statute. May incorporate under specific co-op statute or sometimes under the general corporation law.
[4]Except in 12 states; see Table 11-1.
[5]While this Act is not a federal statute, it has interstate scope.
[6]Except in six states; see Table 11-1.
[7]Almost all states have some type of nonprofit educational society statute.
[8]Aquatic Marketing Act of 1934 controls if business is interstate.
[9]Only North and South Dakota have specific co-op grazing statutes.
[10]Granger-Thye Act of 1950 empowers federal government to recognize grazing association, but it does not charter them as such.
[11]A few states have specific statutes for retailer-owned wholesale cooperatives. Otherwise, they incorporate under the nonfarm, nonprofit business association statutes or the general corporation law.

OTHER STATE STATUTES APPLICABLE TO COOPERATIVES

Cooperatives chartered under state statutes must comply with other legislation and regulations, although not every cooperative is affected in the same way or to the same extent.

Filing Annual Reports

Some state laws require cooperatives to file annual financial reports with a certain department official(s), usually the State Treasurer or Corporation Commissioner. In all states, it is a good precaution to file a copy of the cooperative's audit report with the Corporation Commissioner unless he specifically declines to accept such a report.

Nondiscrimination Against Co-op Members

At least two states, California and New Jersey, have passed laws which make it illegal for anyone to interfere with a farmer's right to join a farmer cooperative or to discriminate against farmers who do join.

The California bill makes it unlawful for any processor, handler, distributor or his agent to:

1. Interfere with, restrain, coerce or boycott farmers who want to join bargaining associations.

2. Discriminate against farmers on price or other terms of buying farm products because they belong to co-op bargaining associations.

3. Pay or loan money to farmers to lure them out of bargaining associations.

4. Maliciously or knowingly give false reports about the finances, management or activities of a bargaining association.

Violations are misdemeanors punishable by a fine of not less than $50 nor more than $500.

Right-to-Do-Business Laws

There are some states in which a cooperative organized in some other state and having the word *cooperative* in its name may not do business as a foreign corporation. The reason is that in some states the co-op statute prohibits the use of the word *cooperative* by any corporation except one organized under that statute. Thus, when a cooperative has incorporated in a state which makes the use of the word mandatory, it sometimes finds it cannot be admitted to do business in certain other states.

One apparent choice for a cooperative desiring to do business on a national basis is to incorporate in a state which does not require the use of the word *cooperative* as a part of the corporation name and then to adopt a name which does not include the word.

Usually, a foreign cooperative is authorized to do business in a state upon issuance of a certificate of authority to that effect by the Secretary of State. In order to procure such a certificate, the cooperative shall make application therefor to the Secretary of State. Such application is made on forms prescribed and furnished by the Secretary of State and is executed in duplicate by the cooperative by its president or a vice president and by its secretary or an assistant secretary and verified by one of the officers signing such application.

State Antitrust Laws

In the standard cooperative marketing acts under which most of the farmer cooperatives are organized is a provision reading like the one in the Virginia Act: "No association organized under this Chapter shall be deemed to be a combination in restraint of trade or an illegal monopoly; or an attempt to lessen competition or fix prices arbitrarily, nor shall the marketing contracts or agreements between the association and its members, or any agreements authorized in this Chapter, be considered illegal or in restraint of trade."

Such state statutory provisions quite clearly establish farmers' rights to organize cooperatives within the laws of their states but have no effect on federal antitrust acts.

Although state antitrust cases do not arise frequently, cooperatives should comply carefully with any existing state antitrust statutes. Forty states have antitrust laws.

State Bureaus of Markets

Most states have some type of agency, usually under the State Commissioner of Agriculture, which aids in organizing and, in some cases, financing agricultural marketing cooperatives. In addition, some states have a farmers' market agency by which the state and farmers cooperatively organize and operate public markets for farm produce.

State bureaus of markets or marketing commissions may do one or more of the following:

1. Conduct a market news and information service.
2. Inspect and grade farm products.
3. Perform various diagnostic and regulatory functions.
4. Assist farmer cooperatives in marketing, in financing and in other ways.

State Marketing Orders

Some states have made provisions for state marketing orders for various farm products, such as for milk, fruits and vegetables. California is the leading state in this regard, but more and more states are enacting marketing order legislation.

Cooperatives usually play an instrumental role in calling for an order, testifying at hearings, voting in bloc, proposing amendments to orders and assisting state officials in administering these orders.

State Securities Registration
("Blue Sky" Laws)

A cooperative should ascertain if any plan which it intends to follow in obtaining capital is subject to the "Blue Sky" laws of a state in which sales or contracts will be made. "Blue Sky" law is a popular name for an act providing for the regulation and supervision of investment securities sold to the public.

1. States with enabling legislation are shaded.
2. Commodities under federal order regulation are listed in the state in which the order is located.
   (An order covering onions in Texas has recently been added.)

FIGURE 11-4

More and more states are adopting marketing orders to improve the marketing of farm produce. Cooperatives play a vital role in the development and operation of state marketing orders.

Generally speaking, co-op corporations are not subject to the laws regarding the type and amount of stock and other securities that may be sold and the registration of these securities. This is because cooperatives are selling securities to a closed group in order to do business for themselves. Not all types of cooperatives are necessarily exempted from "Blue Sky" laws.

Regulatory Commissions

In the case of telephone, irrigation, rural electric and insurance cooperatives, these may be subject to state regulatory commissions which fix telephone, electricity and other rates. State laws vary widely on this point from no regulation to full-fledged regulation. Consult the appropriate state regulatory commissions for details and retain legal counsel.

State Motor Carrier Acts

Bowser, in his study of state motortruck exemptions, found the following:[4]

Exemption Category	Exemption Granted Yes (No. of States)	No
Farmer cooperative associations	18	32
Agricultural commodities	35[1]	15
Farm vehicles	44[1]	6

[1]Some "yes" responses were qualified.

Statutory Reserves

Many states have legislation which clearly specifies the nature of financial reserves and manner in which they are to be created. For example, the law may state that 10 percent of the annual net savings be allocated to "general reserve" until the amount therein is equal to but does not exceed 50 percent of the paid-in capital. Credit unions and other types of financial cooperatives are carefully audited on statutory reserves for compliance with state law.

The insurance mutuals are also closely supervised as to statutory reserves and protection for policyholders.

Unemployment Insurance

Each state computes its own unemployment insurance tax rates depending upon the ratio existing between the balance in the unemployment compensation trust fund and the net taxable wages paid employees. In addition, most states have a merit system which adjusts rates for individual firms.

Cooperatives covered under unemployment insurance laws and

---

[4]Bowser, W. C., Jr., *State Motortruck Exemptions*, FCS Rept. 60, USDA, Washington, D.C. Apr. 1963.

regulations may obtain detailed information from the Office of Employment Security in their home states.

Workmen's Compensation Laws

Workmen's compensation laws ensure prompt medical care and cash benefits to a worker when he is injured in connection with his job, or cash benefits to his dependents if he is killed.

In over half of the states, these laws are mandatory for all employers covered by the law. In the remaining states, an employer may elect not to come under the system, but in such cases he is not permitted to use the defense against workers' claims that he would have had under common law. Employers meet the cost of workmen's compensation by insurance. Employers usually have two choices—to insure with a private insurance company or to self-insure. In some states there is a third choice—that of insuring with the state. In a few states, all employers are required to insure with the state.

State Tax and Revenue Laws

Cooperatives chartered under state law need to examine possible

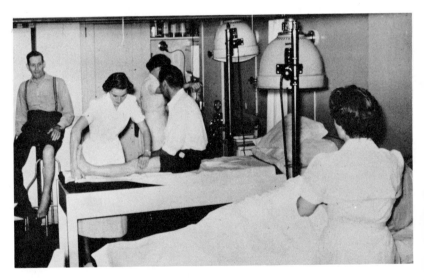

FIGURE 11-5

Most states require workmen's compensation coverage for co-op employees. It is a wise policy to provide such coverage whether a state requires it or not. (Courtesy, American Mutual Insurance Alliance)

compliance with some or all of the following revenue and tax laws and regulations: (1) state corporation income tax; (2) state, county and local property taxes; (3) state, county and local sales taxes; (4) business permits, licenses or fees; (5) domestic franchise tax; (6) tax on vehicles, movables, inventories, etc.; (7) inspection and regulatory fees and reports; (8) payroll taxes; (9) excise taxes; (10) annual corporation or license fee; (11) state unemployment insurance tax; (12) state gaso-

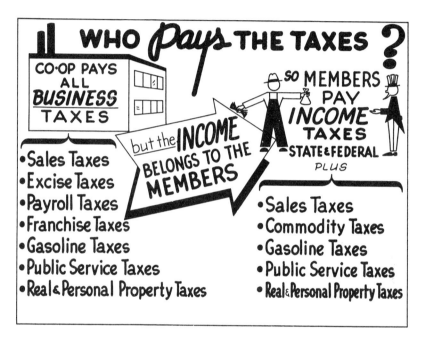

FIGURE 11-6

Cooperatives pay all the taxes other businesses do. In the case of corporate income taxes, cooperatives may exclude from their taxable income bona fide patronage refunds made to their patrons. (Courtesy, Agricultural Council of California, Sacramento, Calif.)

line and fuel taxes; (13) highway use tax; (14) health and sanitation permits; (15) workmen's compensation; (16) gross receipts tax; (17) capital stock and stock transfer tax; and (18) stock dividends tax, among others.

States differ in their requirements; therefore, it is imperative that appropriate state statutes be consulted regarding these and other laws and regulations.

Bonding of Co-op Employees

Some states have statutory provisions requiring the bonding of all persons handling money in a cooperative. Credit unions and other financial cooperatives are the ones most often specified in such legislation. Farmers' marketing and purchasing associations are usually not included thereunder. They should require such employees to be bonded as a matter of good business practices.

In the next chapter, the matter of organizing cooperatives is considered.

TOPICS FOR DISCUSSION

1. Examine the scope of state incorporation statutes for various types of cooperatives.
2. Why have agricultural co-op statutes been adopted in each of the 50 states?
3. Discuss some of the complexities in chartering group medical cooperatives.
4. In your opinion, is a federal act for chartering mutual savings banks needed?
5. Discuss Satterfield's approach to the chartering of cooperatives under the general corporate law.
6. Discuss some of the other state laws and regulations affecting cooperatives.
7. Familiarize yourself with the co-op statutes applicable to your state, province or nation.

SELECTED REFERENCES

1. Alanne, V. S., *Fundamentals of Consumer Cooperation,* Cooperative Publishing Co., Superior, Wisc. 1941.
2. A. M. A., *Voluntary Prepayment Medical Benefit Plans,* American Medical Association, Chicago, Ill. 1954.
3. Anderson, O. W., *State Enabling Legislation for Non-profit Hospital and Medical Plans,* University of Michigan, School of Public Health, Ann Arbor, Mich. 1944.
4. Bowen, E. R., *The Cooperative Organization of Consumers,* Cooperative League, Chicago, Ill. 1957.
5. Collins, John R., "Symposium on Co-ops," *Wisconsin Law Review.* No. 4. July 1954.
6. Golman, Franz, *Voluntary Medical Care,* Columbia University Press, New York, N. Y. 1948.

7. Hansen, Horace, "Laws Affecting Group Health Plans," *Iowa Law Review.* Vol. 35. 1950. pp. 209-236.
8. Klem, Margaret, "Recent State Legislation Concerning Prepayment Medical Care," *Social Security Bulletin X.* Jan. 1947. pp. 10-16.
9. Mischler, R. J. and J. F. Donoghue, *State Statutes Authorizing Assistance to Farmer Cooperatives,* FCS Info. 22, USDA, Washington, D.C. Dec. 1961.
10. Reed, L. S., *Blue Cross and Medical Service Plans,* U.S. Public Health Service, Washington, D.C. Oct. 1947.
11. Roy, E. P., *Handbook for Farmers' Co-op Corporations,* La. Agr. Exp. Sta. D. A. E. Circ. 294, Baton Rouge, La. Oct. 1961.
12. Somers, H. M., *Doctors, Patients and Health Insurance,* Brookings Institute, Washington, D.C. 1961. Chapters 15 and 16.
13. Staff, "Cooperation in Medicine," *Minnesota Law Review.* Vol. 35. pp. 373-395.
14. Turney, J. R. and H. H. Ellis, *State Water-Rights Laws,* ERS Pub. 921, USDA, Washington, D.C. Dec. 1962.

CHAPTER 12 –

Organization of Cooperatives

He who would catch fish must first venture his bait.
—Benjamin Franklin

Educate about cooperatives before you organize a cooperative; educate during and after you organize; and then educate some more.
—Anonymous

If you want an orchard tomorrow you must plant the trees today.
—Anonymous

The journey of a thousand miles begins with one pace.
—Lao-Tsze

IN ORGANIZING A COOPERATIVE, the following sequence of events usually occurs: (1) the idea, (2) organizing committee, (3) surveys, (4) general meeting, (5) drafting and adopting articles, bylaws and agreements, (6) obtaining legal status, (7) election of board and (8) steps after chartering.

THE IDEA

The idea for a cooperative may originate from several sources, among which are: (1) experiences of other cooperatives, (2) suggestions from co-op specialists, (3) trade sources, including journals, (4) individuals in the community proposing a cooperative as a solution to some existing problem, (5) community and/or area surveys dealing with economic development or other management or marketing problems, (6) addresses by co-op specialists or co-op leaders on the possibilities of cooperation, (7) essay contests and other educational activities dealing with cooperatives and (8) organizational efforts of larger cooperatives, especially regional associations wishing to extend operations in a virgin area.

ORGANIZING COMMITTEE

After an idea is born, some mechanism must be at hand to nourish this idea to fruition. Each situation differs in regard to co-op organization, but generally it is wise to have more than one person assume some leadership in seeing whether such organization is feasible. Alternative methods of implementing an organizing committee are as follows: (1) Civic, business or other organization leaders may assume leadership and utilize the existing structure of their organizations to provide an organizing committee. (2) An informal group of three to five responsible citizens of the community may serve as this organizing committee. (3) A formal association may be organized to sponsor community activities and, as part of this work, serve as an organizing committee. (4) Educational groups such as young farmer groups within the Smith-Hughes program may serve as an organizing committee. (5) Rural development associations operating within the program of the agricultural extension service may serve as an organizing committee. (6) The board of directors of an existing cooperative and/or a co-op trade association may serve as an organizing committee.

FIGURE 12-1

An organizing committee is usually necessary to coordinate all the details in organizing a cooperative. (Courtesy, Cooperative League, Chicago, Ill.)

The organizing committee should determine potential membership, plant and equipment needed, financial plans and policies and should obtain legal aid.

ECONOMIC SURVEYS

The organizing committee usually has the responsibility to conduct an economic survey. It rarely can do the whole job itself. Assistance from various sources is usually required. Possible sources of help in conducting economic surveys are: (1) land-grant colleges and universities, (2) various agencies of the state and federal government, (3) co-op councils, leagues and trade associations, (4) private research and consulting firms and (5) state and regional cooperatives.

Type and Depth of Surveys

Some type of economic survey ought to precede the organization of any cooperative. Of course, the kind and depth of the survey will vary depending upon the type of cooperative to be organized. As a practical guide, however, the following points are considered basic to any co-op survey:

1. Are there any controllable costs which upon analysis can be reduced through joint cooperation or group effort?
2. Can group rather than individual effort effect a more orderly and more profitable movement to market?
3. Will management "know-how" and experience be enhanced and multiplied by a free pool of the experience of many?
4. Can any intangible benefits be achieved through group action which are impossible under individual action?
5. There is strength in unity and size. [Of] how much value is such strength in negotiating, bargaining or gaining cooperation from suppliers or buyers?
6. How much independence of action must be sacrificed by participation in group action?[1]

Using these six basic questions as guide lines, those interested in the cooperative, or a committee thereof, might consider drafting specific questions which, when answered, will reveal whether the coopera-

---

[1]Graf, George, "A Slingshot for David," National Canners Association Convention, Chicago, Ill. Feb. 22, 1959.

tive should be organized. Examples of specific questions that might be asked of each prospective cooperator are:

1. Itemize your total fixed and operating costs of doing business during the last fiscal year and relate these costs to your volume of business so as to obtain unit costs. Assuming you joined a cooperative and your business volume remained the same, would unit costs decline and, if so, by how much? Would price received per unit increase? Would volume (V) times price (P) or gross income (GI) minus cost (C) yield a higher net income (NI) in a cooperative than otherwise?

2. During the last three years, could a cooperative have promoted more orderly purchasing and/or marketing, and how much additional net income would this have yielded?

3. What present steps are being taken to up-grade management skill in your business? What has this cost? Could a cooperative provide this same management skill and training at lower cost or more skills at the same cost?

4. Does your business have any brand image, or do you attempt to differentiate your product? Could a cooperative buy supplies or market products under its own brand? How much more net income would this yield?

5. Can you efficiently obtain accounting, legal, research and credit services for your firm and at what cost? Could a cooperative effect savings in these categories or obtain better services for the same cost?

6. Consider the fact that in joining a cooperative you will have to invest: (a) time and (b) money. Can you expect to benefit by shifting some of your time and money to the cooperative? If so, how large a benefit in dollars?

7. What is specifically wrong with the current economic situation in your line of business—poor services, facilities lacking, too much or too little competition, margin or prices too low or costs too high? Could a cooperative help in one or more of these situations?

8. Would you consider changing your purchasing and/or marketing patterns if a cooperative were formed? Would this cause you any losses and, if so, for how long a time? Would you expect some type of economic retaliation by others?

9. Are you informed about co-op methods of business? If not, would you attend educational meetings prior to organization?

10. Do you expect to be in the same business 10 years hence? If so, what factors do you feel will cause you the greatest concern

during the next decade? Would a cooperative be of any benefit in meeting these problems?

FIGURE 12-2

(Courtesy, Agricultural Council of California, Sacramento, Calif.)

FIGURE 12-3

(Courtesy, Farm Credit Administration, Washington, D.C.)

When individual replies to the survey are summarized, the survey coordinator should ask these questions:

1. What will be the annual operating cost of the cooperative considering variable costs, interest costs and depreciation of fixed facilities? How much volume of business or how many units of product are expected? What is the estimated unit cost of operation? Is this expected volume of business purely an estimate or are there marketing and/or purchasing agreements to back up this estimate?

2. What kind of revenue schedule is expected for the volume of business anticipated? Does this leave any net margins? If not, the calculations should be extended for the next three years and analyzed again. Is there still a deficit?

3. Considering the expected volume of business and estimated costs of operation, do these costs take into account "services" to which members are accustomed? If not, can these services be eliminated without harming the interest of members?

4. Considering the facilities and operating capital required, is enough capital available? If not, what are the credit sources available?

FIGURE 12-4

(Courtesy, Agricultural Council of California, Sacramento, Calif.)

Can some items be rented instead of purchased? Can a suitable site be obtained?

5. Can management be found to staff the cooperative adequately and at what cost?

Economic Analysis of Need
(Hypothetical)

In Table 12-1 a hypothetical situation is assumed depicting the present financial status of 10 farmers individually producing and marketing fresh vegetables. Their aggregate output is 2,000 units which brought $40 per unit, or the "going market price." It cost $61,750 to produce and market the crop, leaving an aggregate net income to management of $18,250, or about $9.13 per unit. However, 6 of the 10 farmers either lost money or had no returns to management.

Could a cooperative help and by how much?

We will assume that the 2,000 units are still produced on 10 farms but are now delivered to the cooperative. Of the total cost (producing and marketing), marketing costs represent 20 percent, or $12,350. Suppose the cooperative can make a 5 percent net saving in marketing costs, or $617.50. Suppose the cooperative can save 3 percent of the production costs, or $1,482, in reducing fertilizer, hamper and chemical costs. Suppose the cooperative, by pooling the vegetables and timing the marketing of them, achieves a net 2½ percent increase in revenue, or $2,000. We now estimate a total net saving of $618 + $1,482 + $2,000, or about $4,100 on 2,000 units, or an extra $2.00 per unit saved. Consequently, we could expect that the four previously prosperous farmers would become more prosperous, and of the six "unprofitable" farmers, two would be making money while the other four would reduce their losses. The normal expenses of handling and marketing would be transferred from the middlemen to the cooperative but would not have been eliminated.

In most types of businesses, economies to scale are evident; namely, the larger the volume handled, the lower the unit cost, down to a point. At that point, costs per unit remain stable over a wide range of output and then costs per unit will tend to rise (Figure 12-5). This principle is most basic in organizing a cooperative.

A study of the feasibility of a co-op store, processing plant, etc., needs to include an analysis of economies to scale. It will reveal to the prospective member how important his patronage is, will project possible savings to be made and will indicate the financing required.

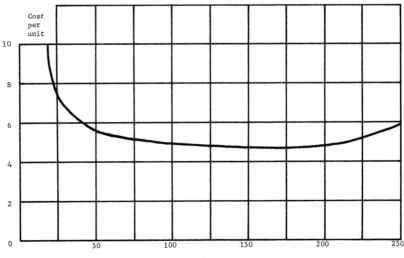

FIGURE 12-5

The larger the volume handled, the lower the unit cost, down to a point. From that point, cost per unit remains stable for awhile, then usually rises.

TABLE 12-1

Hypothetical Situation Involving 10 Individual
Farmers Producing and Marketing Vegetables Before
and After Co-op Organization

Farmer No.	Units	Total Cost ($)	Cost per Unit ($)	Revenue ($)[1]	Net Income Before the Cooperative ($)	Net Income After the Cooperative ($)
1	200	7,500	37.50	8,000	+ 500	+ 900
2	100	4,500	45.00	4,000	− 500	− 300
3	150	6,000	40.00	6,000	0	+ 300
4	50	2,500	50.00	2,000	− 500	− 400
5	250	8,750	35.00	10,000	+ 1,250	+ 1,750
6	100	4,500	45.00	4,000	− 500	− 300
7	100	4,500	45.00	4,000	− 500	− 300
8	400	10,000	25.00	16,000	+ 6,000	+ 6,800
9	150	6,000	40.00	6,000	0	+ 300
10	500	7,500	15.00	20,000	+12,500	+13,500
Total	2,000	61,750	30.88	80,000	+18,250	+22,250

[1]$40 per unit is the assumed price.

FIGURE 12-6

Before accepting members into a cooperative, care should be exercised by the board of directors to see that each member accepted is able to make a definite contribution to the welfare of the whole co-op group. (Courtesy, Consumers Cooperative of Berkeley, Inc., Berkeley, Calif.)

Patronage is of critical essence to a co-op association, more so than its capitalization. If members agree to patronize their cooperative and confirm this agreement with a marketing and/or purchasing contract, as it may apply, then the capitalization is easier than would otherwise be the case. This is especially true in the borrowing of funds.

In addition, with an assured patronage, capitalization may proceed on the basis of retains per ton, bushel, pound, dozen, etc. In this way, the cooperative may be adequately capitalized over time, if not initially.

Therefore, the basic point in any economic survey should revolve around *patronage*—buying from, selling to or servicing with the cooperative. Unless a sound patronage basis is created, a cooperative has little chance for success.

Survey of the Members

In addition to the economic analysis concerning the prospective cooperative, the survey coordinator should make some analysis of the prospective members themselves. An analysis based on these points is recommended.

1. Are the prospective cooperators efficient in their present line of business? Are they morally responsible, and do they have good character?

2. Are they educated as to co-op principles and methods?

3. Are they financially solvent and responsible?

4. Are they willing and able to provide leadership when called upon?

5. Are they able to weather difficulties and strife without complaint?

6. Are they willing to sacrifice some of their individual action for the benefit of the whole group?

7. Are they looking toward the future and not fighting the battles of the past?

8. Are they the type of people that we would want as partners in business?

9. Are they willing to sign and abide by a marketing and/or purchasing agreement?

10. Are they willing to finance and invest in proportion to their use of the cooperative?

Affirmative answers to all 10 questions would enhance the success of the cooperative provided its "economic" feasibility has been recommended.

GENERAL MEETING

In order to publicize the results of the survey, a mass meeting for all prospective cooperators should be held. Everyone should be given due notice of the meeting. In order to encourage attendance, a speaker possessing knowledge of cooperatives and having respect of the cooperators should be invited. Visual aids and other devices should be employed to present the survey data in an effective way. Both the advantages and disadvantages of a cooperative plus some concrete and specific proposals for organizing, operating and financing should be presented.

After all sides of the question have been presented, the assembly chairman should ask the meeting for a motion to organize, postpone or terminate action. If the motion to organize carries, the chairman may elect to appoint committees for certain specific jobs, such as financing, membership, charter, etc. Preparing the legal documents prior to a formal chartering is an immediate task. Competent legal and tax consultants should be retained at this point in the organization of a cooperative.

DRAFTING THE LEGAL DOCUMENTS

Organization Agreements

While the prospective members of a cooperative are being contacted about joining, the use of an organization, marketing or purchasing agreement is highly recommended. Many persons are agreeable to joining a cooperative in principle, but when formal steps are taken to organize, some will hesitate. The organization agreement sets down in writing what the cooperative proposes to do and how. In this way, the organization agreement provides a quick and reasonable indication of how many people are serious about a cooperative and how many just want to talk about it. Furthermore, the organization agreement requires a pledge of money toward capitalizing the cooperative. For a copy of an organization agreement, consult Farmer Cooperative Service Bulletin 10, pages 309 to 311.

Articles of Incorporation

After drafting the organization agreement, the articles of incorporation are drafted next.

What is the legal relationship between the law under which a cooperative is incorporated, the cooperative's articles of incorporation and its bylaws?

The law outlines the general powers, privileges, requirements and organizational structure for cooperatives incorporated under it. The articles of incorporation are written to fit a particular cooperative and are more specific than the law. The articles must not be in conflict with any provision of the law. The bylaws contain still more detail and must not conflict with any provision in the articles of incorporation or the law.

In case of legal questions, the articles of incorporation take precedence over the bylaws, and the law under which the cooperative is incorporated takes precedence over the articles of incorporation. A sample set of articles of incorporation for a farmer cooperative may be obtained by consulting Farmer Cooperative Service Circular 18. The services of a competent attorney, experienced in co-op work, should be retained to aid in drawing up the articles of incorporation.

It is noted that the following decisions need to be made before the articles of incorporation are finally completed for filing purposes:

1. A minimum number of incorporators must be obtained and a statute selected for incorporation.

2. A name and domicile for the cooperative must be chosen.

3. The duration of the cooperative must be specified.

4. The number and length of terms of directors must be specified.

5. The type of capital structure must be specified whether stock or nonstock.

Drafting Bylaws

Bylaws are the operating rules of the cooperative, and they explain more fully the articles of incorporation. In some cases, they are drafted together with the articles of incorporation, while in other cases they may be drafted and filed 30 to 60 days after the articles. Amending the bylaws is a considerably easier matter than amending the articles. This is why the articles should be general in nature while the bylaws may be much more specific. For a set of bylaws accompanying the articles of incorporation, see Farmer Cooperative Service Circular 18.

For sample copies of articles and bylaws, consult the reference sources cited in Table 12-2.

OBTAINING LEGAL STATUS

Procedures for incorporation vary from state to state: An attorney should be consulted for the correct procedure. However, generally the incorporators take the original copy of the articles of incorporation to the county seat and have it recorded with the County Recorder or Clerk. The County Recorder certifies a carbon copy of the documents which are then forwarded to the State Recorder, Secretary of State or Corporation Commissioner. Fees for recording and filing are charged both by the county and state. Fees may vary from $5 to over $50 depending upon state law. For example, chartering of a credit union under The Federal Credit Union Act requires a $20 investigation fee, plus a $5 chartering fee. Chartering under most state laws, the fees run from $10 to $25.

Usually, 30 days after the charter has been granted by the state, a set of bylaws must be adopted by the membership and one copy forwarded to the State Recorder.

TABLE 12-2
Sources of Information on Articles and
Bylaws for Cooperatives

Type of Cooperative	Source of Information
Consumers' cooperative, buying club and memorial association	Bureau of Labor Statistics Bul. 1024, Dept. of Labor, Washington, D.C.
Credit union	Credit Union National Association, Madison, Wisc.
Farmer supply and marketing cooperative	Farmer Cooperative Service Circular 18, USDA, Washington, D.C.
Federal land bank association	*National Farm Loan Associations,* Kansas Agr. Exp. Sta. Cir. 374, Manhattan, Kans. Mar. 1960.
Fishery cooperative	Fish and Wildlife Service, Dept. of Interior, Washington, D.C.
Group health plan	*Co-op Medicine,* Cooperative League, Chicago, Ill. pp. 72-75.
Housing association	*The Co-op Apartment,* Libra Publishing Co., New York, N.Y. pp. 92-119.
Mutual savings bank	National Association of Mutual Savings Banks, New York, N.Y.
Retailer-owned wholesale	*Retailer Cooperatives,* Harper & Brothers, New York, N.Y. 1937. pp. 42-49.
Rural electric and telephone	National Rural Electric Co-op Association, 2000 Florida Ave., N.W., Washington, D.C.

The cooperative should provide every member with a copy of both the articles of incorporation and the bylaws. An amendment to the articles of incorporation requires recommendation by the board and approval by the general membership and filing of such amendments with the County Clerk where the original incorporation occurred and also with the Secretary of State or State Recorder.

Amendments to the bylaws require membership approval only and need not be filed.

ELECTING THE BOARD AND
ITS OFFICERS

The articles of incorporation will stipulate how many board members are to be elected and their terms of office. The board itself usually elects its officers.

Qualifications for membership on the board may be incorporated in the articles but such restrictions should be kept at a minimum. Terms of board members should be staggered so that experienced members remain on the board while new board members are getting experience.

A further discussion of boards of directors is found in Chapter 16.

STEPS AFTER CHARTERING

After its officers are elected, the board should take the following steps as quickly as possible (not necessarily in this order):

1. Elect committees of the board, especially an executive committee.

2. Select the depository bank and complete fund raising, if not previously accomplished.

3. Select management personnel and decide on salaries, job specifications and working conditions.

4. Arrange for the necessary bonding of board officers and co-op employees.

5. Obtain workmen's compensation coverage for the manager and hired employees and business liability coverage.

6. Secure bookkeeping services and set up an accounting system.

7. Decide upon credit and pricing policies.

8. Decide upon purchasing, marketing and servicing policies.

9. Decide upon building, equipment, trucking and warehousing policies.

10. Develop an educational and training program for board members, employees and co-op members.

All of these steps are discussed in more detail in Chapters 13 through 17.

ECONOMIC LIMITATIONS OF COOPERATIVES

There are definite economic limitations to what cooperatives can do.

1. Cooperatives cannot always return the highest price for products nor furnish supplies and services at the lowest cost. Their desire to do this and their ability to do it are two different things.

2. Cooperatives cannot control the supply or the demand for products. They cannot hold out for "cost of production plus a profit."

3. Cooperatives cannot raise substantially the price of a product when the supply on the market exceeds the demand for it.

4. Cooperatives cannot sell ordinary quality products at top market prices or buy top quality supplies at cheap prices.

5. Marketing cooperatives which sell large quantities at wholesale cannot get as high unit prices as individual farmers who sell at retail.

6. Cooperatives may "replace" middlemen, but most of the jobs these men do must still be done. While cooperatives often find ways to make savings and to eliminate unnecessary handling, the cost of necessary operations accounts for much of the price spread between the producer and consumer. The profit portion is much smaller than most people think.

7. Another limitation is that cooperatives cannot deliberately enter lucrative fields of enterprise outside the scope of their charters. If they did so, they would run the risk of charter revocation. A farmer cooperative cannot venture into aerospace work unless it can prove that this work has a direct connection with the farming activities of its members. But, profit-type corporations can allocate their money and talent into any field they consider most lucrative so as to maximize net profits.

8. Purchasing cooperatives cannot retail supplies and provide retail services at wholesale prices.

9. Cooperatives can make savings only when they bring about economies, eliminate unnecessary services and operate efficiently. Members help reduce operating costs by patronizing their cooperatives. A cooperative does not make savings just by being a cooperative. Economics must always accompany enthusiasm.

ECONOMIC POTENTIALS
FOR COOPERATIVES

Cooperatives have an opportunity to rectify some economic imperfections, but especially important is their potential to solve price-fixing. By solving or attempting to solve price-fixing problems, cooperatives can render a great service not only to their patrons but to the capitalistic system as well.

Competition developed by cooperatives is a different kind of competition from that developed by other corporations. On the marketing side, a cooperative seeks a higher price for its members, yet its competition is different because of its obligation to market the whole crop over a long period of time and to return the full price to the farmer-patron. In the same manner, a supply cooperative is a buyer of products for farmers and not a seller of products to farmers. Its price objective is exactly opposite that of other corporations selling to farmers. Large-size operations by cooperatives increase competition rather than decrease it.

In fields where they are strong enough to make their effectiveness felt, cooperatives help to curb monopolistic practices among other types of enterprise by establishing a yardstick of quality and price that others must meet in order to compete effectively. As their purpose is to render service to their patron-owners and not to make a profit, they are less likely to engage in monopolistic practices; and where they are strong enough to exert adequate competitive influence, they make it very difficult for other types of business to engage in price-fixing and other abuses of free enterprise.

COSTS VERSUS RETURNS OF CO-OP MEMBERSHIP

Membership in a cooperative is never "all gain" and "no loss." Co-op margins are refunded to members both when they are positive and negative. Let us hypothesize how a prospective co-op member might evaluate his joining or not joining a cooperative:

Possible gains:

1. Lower costs of marketing, purchasing and servicing operations.

2. Payments based on quality delivered, better quality of items purchased and better servicing.

3. Social satisfaction of working together with others.

Possible costs:

1. Investment in the cooperative is required. Opportunity cost of this investment may be high. In other words, could the dollars invested in a cooperative return more money elsewhere (in farming operations, a tractor, more land, better livestock)?

2. Managerial decisions might be limited. After joining the cooperative, freedom of going to another buyer, supplier, etc., might be restricted for a period of years.

3. Responsibilities of ownership. In a cooperative, the member is not simply a buyer or seller but its owner. As owner, one must attend many meetings, serve on boards and committees, etc., usually with small, if any, compensation.

There are many other "gains" and "costs." Each prospective member, by placing a dollar value on these, can evaluate whether the "gains" equal or exceed the "costs." Additionally, there are short-run and long-run implications in making these evaluations.

ECONOMIC-LEGAL STRUCTURE OF COOPERATIVES

Several items of an economic-legal nature are of interest concerning the organization of cooperatives.

The structure of cooperatives may consist of: (1) independent, local units, (2) co-op federations, (3) centralized cooperatives and (4) combinations of (2) and (3).

Independent, Local Cooperatives

Independent, local cooperatives stand alone in their purchasing, marketing and servicing activities. The number of strictly independent locals is declining.

The advantages of an independent, local cooperative are as follows:

1. Members all know one another.

2. All have the same marketing and production problems.

3. The business is usually easily understood and conducted by the patrons.

4. Members have confidence in the local manager whom they know and regularly meet.

5. The association is on a more democratic basis.

6. It is an effective means of extending marketing and production information.

7. Services are usually improved and as a result the members' wholehearted support and loyalty are enlisted.

The disadvantages of independent, local cooperatives are the advantages of federated and centralized cooperatives, considered next.

Co-op Federations

Federated associations are organized on a "bottom up" plan of organization. Individuals are members of local associations, and locals are members of the overhead federated association. A federation is a cooperative of existing local associations.

Ordinarily it is customary for federations to be established after local associations have been operating for some time. They are therefore considered as being built from the "bottom up."

Patrons do not hold direct memberships in federated cooperatives; instead, the local cooperatives are members of federated cooperatives. Federated cooperatives are controlled entirely by the locals. Usually, the president or the general manager of a local cooperative serves as the voting delegate to the federation meetings.

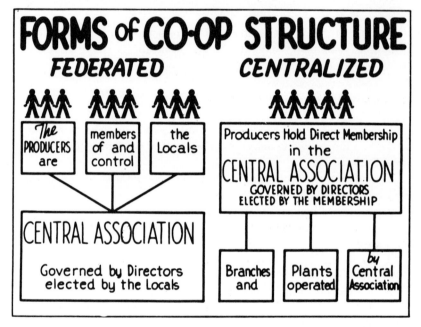

FIGURE 12-7

Both "federated" and "centralized" co-op structures are used throughout the world. Each has advantages and disadvantages. (Courtesy, Agricultural Council of California, Sacramento, Calif.)

The advantages of a federation are as follows:

1. A republican form of government is followed.

2. Authority, control, interest and responsibility rest in the locals at all times.

3. Federation is built from the ground up in which the importance of self-governing local associations is recognized.

4. There is relatively greater ease of keeping contact with the membership through long established local and district association.

5. It can provide better service, products, etc., than strictly local associations.

6. Financing a venture is simplified since stock can be sold at local levels.

7. Fewer errors will be made since the establishment of a federation is usually a slow, evolutionary process.

The disadvantages of federations are the advantages of centralized cooperatives, considered next.

Centralized Associations

The centralized association, unlike the federated association, dispenses with autonomous local associations. Control and authority are centralized in the headquarters' organization whereas in the federated association control is decentralized in the autonomous local associations.

Usually a large proportion of the volume has to be signed up before the centralized association starts functioning. Members' products are received, sorted, graded, pooled and prepared for sale to market operators at warehouses or local packing houses operated, owned or leased by the central association, not by the local farmers who deliver these products. The association is also in charge of all functions incident to the market distribution of its members' products or to the supplies purchased for its members. It is structured from top to bottom.

Patrons are direct members of centralized cooperatives. If a centralized cooperative operates local units, these local units are subject to control directly through the board of directors and manager of the regional, rather than by the members who patronize each local.

The advantages of a centralized association are:

1. It is usually organized in a relatively short time.

2. It is valuable in cases in which a strong central control is advisable.

3. It assures reduced costs and more economical use of byproducts.

4. The "bottom-up" method of organization is a slow process, and if local initiative is depended upon, few if any large-scale associations will be organized.

5. Definite plans can be drawn in advance for the sound method of building and modifying the organization.

6. Better bargaining power, especially for marketing associations, can be attained.

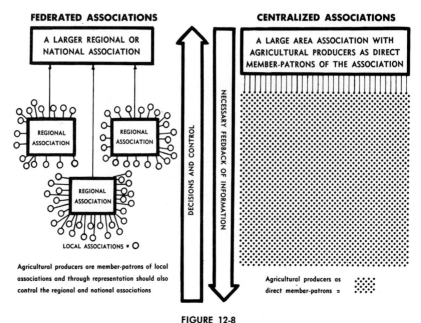

FIGURE 12-8
(Courtesy, W. H. Dankers, University of Minnesota, St. Paul, Minn.)

7. Local associations and facilities are sometimes unable to handle products economically.

The disadvantages of a centralized cooperative are centered around its lack of membership contact; members' feeling of belonging to an impersonal, distant business; and usually more iron-clad membership agreements.

A comparison of a federated versus centralized structure especially for marketing cooperatives is shown in Table 12-3.

TABLE 12-3
Comparison of Federated and Centralized Cooperatives

Item	Federated	Centralized
1. Membership	Patrons in locals, locals in districts, districts in central associations.	Patrons directly in central associations.
2. Primary objective	To lower costs and obtain the best market prices.	To control prices through control of major amounts of market supplies.

(Continued)

TABLE 12-3 *(Continued)*

Item	Federated	Centralized
3. Methods of achieving objectives	Render the most efficient services.	Gain control of the bulk of the crop and use such control as an effective bargaining weapon.
4. Authority	Rests with local associations.	Rests with central headquarters.
5. Voting	Patrons vote in locals, locals in district associations, districts in central associations.	Patrons vote in voting districts, and district delegates vote in the central associations.
6. Contractual arrangements	Contracts not considered absolutely essential.	Contracts are a vital part of the organization.
7. Title to products	Patrons may retain title.	Association usually takes title to commodities.
8. Pooling arrangements	Pools are local and for short duration.	They are ordinarily co-extensive with the entire membership area.
9. Price and sales policy	Usually emphasizes market services, development of markets and quality improvement.	Greater emphasis placed on control of large portion of the crop.
10. Control of volume	No set percentage of crop is necessary to start.	Usually a high percentage (75% or more).
11. Marketing practices	Most grading, packaging and storing left to the locals.	Central associations establish grades, pack, time of sales, price and all marketing functions.
12. Nonmember business	Many locals handle non-member business.	Nonmember business is usually not handled.
13. Financial form of organizations	Favors capital stock associations.	Partial to nonstock membership associations.
14. Ownership	Locals own their own facilities	Centralized associations own or lease facilities.

Source: Adapted from *Economics of Cooperative Marketing*, p. 224.

Combination of Centralized and Federated Structures

In some cases, large regional cooperatives may have a dual structure involving both federated and centralized types. Such a cooperative may operate through local co-op affiliates which represent a federated structure. In addition, it may have a centralized structure in which individuals are directly members of the cooperative. These individuals may be served by franchised agents. Although this dual type of structure appears cumbersome, in practice it has proven flexible and efficient in some areas of the United States.

It is a unique feature of this combination type to witness the franchising of a local profit-type corporation or proprietorship which

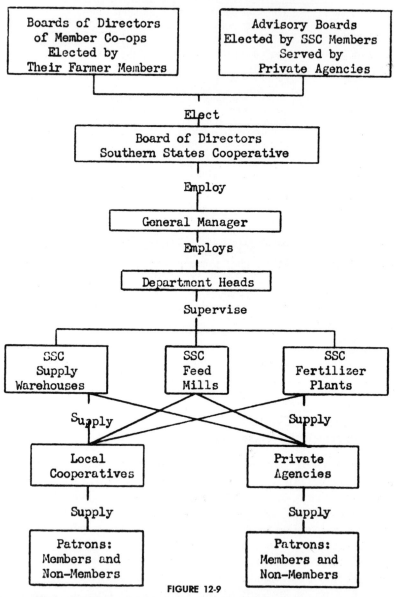

DIAGRAM OF SOUTHERN STATES COOPERATIVE
AS A CENTRALIZED-FEDERATED COOPERATIVE

FIGURE 12-9

Some regional cooperatives use a dual-structure—federated and centralized combined—as shown above. (Courtesy, Southern States Cooperative, Richmond, Va.)

serves local members according to its franchise agreement with the regional association. These arrangements are discussed more fully in a subsequent section of this chapter.

One major problem in this type of cooperative is voting rights. Shall local cooperatives and individuals who are members of the overhead cooperative each have one vote apiece? One solution has been to allow one vote to each cooperative and to each individual, plus additional votes based on the volume of business each conducts with the overhead association.

Super-Federations

In addition to the structures already mentioned, very often two or more co-op federations and/or centralized associations will come together and form a super-federation. These super-federations are organized primarily for large-scale mining, manufacturing and industrial purposes. Large-scale associations in two or more nations often federate into an international co-op association, such as the Scandanavian Wholesale Society, International Cooperative Petroleum Association, among many others.

SINGLE-PURPOSE VERSUS MULTI-PURPOSE COOPERATIVES

There has long been a controversy among co-op leaders regarding single-purpose versus multi-purpose cooperatives. Some contend that supply cooperatives should also market products and marketing cooperatives should sell supplies. Others contend that cooperatives should limit themselves to one function as do the various credit and housing associations.

These questions cannot be satisfactorily answered until the economic circumstances facing each cooperative are analyzed. Generally speaking, however, multi-purpose cooperatives seem to be more successful than single-purpose ones. Basically, this is due to spreading overhead costs over a greater business volume.

Normally, the advantages of single-purpose cooperatives are:

1. Common interests of the membership are recognized.

2. Handling unrelated commodities requires additional facilities, and specialized labor and greater capital investments.

3. There are limits to the capacity and efficiency of the management.

FIGURE 12-10

Some cooperatives are single-purpose, operating in only one commodity (apples, above). Such cooperatives have to be large-scale in order to afford competent management and make savings for members. (Courtesy, American Fruit Grower, Willoughby, Ohio)

The multiple-commodity cooperative has many advantages over the single-commodity cooperative. It does away with the problem of setting up several cooperatives in the same area. Possibly it can add scale without increasing overhead. It makes for year-round use of facilities and management. In this type of cooperative, a failure of one commodity does not necessarily mean total failure. The cooperative can still rely on some of the other commodities that have had a more successful year.

Many single-purpose cooperatives are operating only seasonally, perhaps for two to four months during the year. They cannot afford top management and provide sufficient services with such seasonal operations.

ECONOMIC INTEGRATION

It is often said that cooperatives attempt to eliminate the middlemen. A more nearly correct statement would be that cooperatives attempt to substitute for the middlemen usually through the process

FIGURE 12-11

Some cooperatives are multi-purpose, operating several lines of activity. This co-op exchange is part of a co-op federation. It sells farm supplies, mixes feeds, markets grain and performs other services for its members. (Courtesy, MFA, Columbia, Mo.)

of vertical integration. In other words, the cooperative attempts to become the coordinating agent for its members, wholesaling supplies or produce and, in some cases, retailing besides doing other functions. But before a cooperative can succeed at vertical integration, it must first succeed in some measure at horizontal integration. That is, it must aggregate a sufficient number of independent firms so that sufficient volume can be mustered to effect economies in whatever it chooses to do.

The objective of vertical integration for cooperatives is a noble one in theory. In actual practice, however, these problems remain: (1) can adequate funds be assembled to capitalize the integrative process? (2) can adequate management be recruited to manage the integrated enterprise(s)? and (3) can adequate competition be furnished alongside profit-type corporations? Successful ventures in co-op integration are becoming more abundant.[2]

A cooperative also has to compete with at least two other types of integrators:

(1) Profit-type companies which use contracts with farmers and others and

(2) Profit-type companies which operate their own farms and other production and marketing facilities.

---

[2]Roy, E. P., *Contract Farming, U.S.A.*, The Interstate Printers & Publishers, Inc., Danville, Ill. 1963. Chapter 12.

CO-OP LIQUIDATIONS, MERGERS
AND CONSOLIDATIONS

Liquidation

An incorporated cooperative in most states may be dissolved by: (1) voluntary act of its members, (2) bankruptcy or (3) failure to renew its charter by the expiration date. The statute under which a cooperative is chartered usually specifies, in varying detail, the necessary steps to accomplish liquidation. The counsel of an attorney should be retained.

Cooperatives are permitted by the state, and the charter represents an agreement between the state and the incorporators. Because of the manner in which cooperatives are created, the state has control over dissolution. The right of a majority of the stockholders or members to force dissolution of a cooperative against the opposition of the minority is not so well established. Some authorities hold that the majority can force a dissolution whereas a contrary doctrine has been laid down. Of course, if there are statutory or charter provisions on the subject, they control. In some states, the directors of a cooperative at the time of its dissolution continue for some time thereafter to act as trustees with reference to the payment of obligations of the cooperative and the proper distribution of its assets. Some of the main reasons for dissolution of cooperatives are:

1. The assets are insufficient to pay all just demands for which the cooperative is liable; or

2. The objects of the cooperative have wholly failed or have entirely been abandoned, or their accomplishment is impracticable; or

3. The directors and the voting power are equally divided respecting the management of the corporate affairs; or,

4. The cooperative has been guilty of gross and persistent *ultra vires* acts.

Mergers and Consolidations

Technically, a *consolidation* is a union of two or more organizations which results in the creation of a new association and the termination of the original organizations involved in the consolidation. A *merger,* on the other hand, constitutes an absorption of one association by another with only the acquiring cooperative retaining its corporate identity.

In many states, especially in the Middle West, there is an increasing interest in merging and consolidating farmer cooperatives rather than organizing new ones. Due to improvements in highways and transportation, more people are linked closer together. The farmer and consumer cooperatives which served a small, local area effectively in the past often find that they can no longer compete effectively with larger firms which have come into the territory. Also, many cooperatives are operating along single-commodity lines with seasonal operations, while the economic trends dictate larger, multi-purpose cooperatives operating year-round.

A merger is likely to strengthen economic efficiency by reducing unit costs, by improving bargaining power and by helping to compete better with other firms. Eliminating overlapping memberships and making more effective management possible are examples of how mergers may improve cooperatives of all types.

Either consolidation or merger must comply with state law and the charters of the organizations involved. When an association plans to sell its assets, its directors and those of the buyer must agree upon the terms and conditions of sale. Generally there must be statutory authority for such a sale and agreement of the members of the selling cooperative. Also, the articles of incorporation and provisions in the bylaws must be considered in each case. Usually the purchasing organization requires neither statutory authority nor member authorization to acquire the assets of another association, only board approval.

Plans and agreements for a proposed *merger* are usually prepared and then resolutions approving the agreements affirmed by each board of directors involved. Members of each organization then vote on adoption of the agreements, which must be accepted by a proportion of the members ranging from a simple majority to a three-fourths majority. Statutory provisions covering rights of dissenting stockholders, if any, must also be studied carefully.[3]

There is no doubt that co-op mergers are on the increase. According to the Farmer Cooperative Service, the total mergers since 1958 stand at 271, or an average of 4.5 cooperatives a month involved in mergers and consolidations. Since these figures do not include mergers, consolidations and acquisitions involving both cooperatives and non-cooperatives, the data underestimate the merger trend.

---

[3]Mostow, E. and others, "Legal Problems Involved in Mergers," *News for Farmer Cooperatives*, USDA, Washington, D.C. May 1961.

The types of cooperative involved in these mergers were as follows:

Type of Cooperative	Number	Percent of Total
Dairy	130	48.0
Farm supplies	63	23.2
Other (grain, livestock, cotton, service)	38	14.0
Fruits, vegetables and nuts	23	8.5
Poultry	17	6.3
	271	100.0

In merger or consolidation proceedings, legal advice concerning antitrust laws should be retained. The Federal Trade Commission, among other regulatory agencies, is especially concerned with mergers in the dairy, food store and processing industries. Usually, mergers of small, local cooperatives are not questioned, but mergers between state- and regional-type cooperatives may be. Prior clearance from the Justice Department is advisable.

Hartenfeld suggests that the following steps be considered in a merger procedure:

1. A meeting of management of the two organizations.
2. Comparison of balance sheets and operating statements.
3. Definite procedure on methods to reduce costs upon merger.
4. Decision on filling key positions.
5. Opinions of attorneys, C.P.A.'s and banks.
6. Recommendations to board of directors on terms of procedure.
7. Agreement on contract regarding equities, distribution, representation and legal structure.
8. Vote of members of each organization.[4]

Coordination Among Cooperatives

Two or more cooperatives not involving merger or consolidation may jointly perform several types of operations such as: (1) engage in mutual product differentiation or branding, (2) conduct quality control tests, (3) sponsor research and development projects and (4) pool their products for marketing.

Converting a Profit-type
Corporation into a Cooperative

Frequently it is desired to reorganize a profit-type corporation so that it will be a cooperative in organization and operation. Generally,

---

[4]Hartenfeld, L. J., *Survival of a Small Cooperative*, Hayward Poultry Producers Association, Hayward, Calif. 1963. p. 28.

such a re-organization involves restriction of voting rights to producers, restriction of the returns on capital to not more than 8 percent per annum, provision for the payment of patronage dividends and elimination of the voting rights of nonproducers. It may also be deemed advisable to limit the number of shares which any stockholder may own.

If the nonproducer members are willing to accept nonvoting preferred stock, revolving-fund certificates or some other form of certificate that does not carry a vote, then little difficulty should be encountered. On the other hand, if some or all of the nonproducer voting members are unwilling to make such an exchange, an association is confronted with the problem of how such persons may be eliminated from the organization. Generally speaking, if neither the statute under which an organization is incorporated nor its charter, bylaws or stock certificates provide for doing so, then an amendment to the articles of incorporation or bylaws may not be adopted to accomplish this purpose, which is binding on the nonproducer members who do not consent thereto.

In many instances, however, it will be found possible to form a cooperative and effect a sale to it of all the assets of the old organization. This must be done on a basis which is fair and just. Ordinarily, in such a situation the members of the old organization who are desirous of becoming members of the new one take stock certificates, or certificates of some other character, equal in amount to their interest in the old organization. Only producers who are to patronize the new association are given certificates carrying voting rights; the certificates given to others do not carry a vote. This would mean, in the last analysis, that the only persons who would receive cash for their interests in the old organization would be those persons who were unwilling to accept some form of certificate or obligation of the new organization.[5]

Competent legal and tax counsel should be retained in converting a profit-type corporation into a cooperative.

Converting a Cooperative into a Profit-type Corporation

In some cases, cooperatives are converted into profit-type corporations. Co-op members may lose interest in their organization and permit the board to operate as it will. The cooperative may be con-

---

[5]Hulbert, L. S. and R. Mischler, *Legal Phases of Farmer Cooperatives*, FCS Bul. 10, USDA, Washington, D.C. Jan. 1958. pp. 62-63.

verted or dissolved with all or a part of the co-op membership reorganized into a profit-type corporation.

Competent legal and tax counsel should be retained in converting a cooperative into a profit-type corporation.

A Cooperative Purchasing an Existing Profit-type Business

In some instances, profit-type businesses are available for sale. A cooperative is often organized to effect purchase of a profit-type corporation, such as a gin, grocery store, processing plant, etc. This is often a good move, especially when the regular corporation has good sales outlets or a brand name already established. Caution should be exercised, however, in making such purchases unless the cooperative is assured of enough business volume and has adequate capital and management.

A Cooperative with Subsidiaries

A cooperative may choose to organize and operate subsidiary corporations for some specific reason, such as: (1) to handle nonmember business, (2) to provide capital or financing of certain risky ventures, (3) to purchase or to market certain goods, (4) to qualify for business in another state or (5) to conduct export trade.

The parent cooperative controls the subsidiaries through the common voting stock and possibly by service contracts.

A subsidiary may be operated as a nonprofit corporation similar to its parent, or it may choose to operate on a profit basis, paying taxes as a regular corporation. The choice will depend upon the circumstances surrounding the formation of the subsidiary.

Use of Contract Agents

There are at least three types of agency relationships which a cooperative might use. Feed cooperatives often employ such agents, for example.

In the first type, a county or community cooperative is formed, but puts up no money, owns nothing and contracts with an agent to handle the feed. This agent must keep patronage records, usually on feed only. His other farm supplies he handles strictly on his own and takes all the profit. In this kind of contract there is usually specified the feed markup permitted. The dividends are paid to the secretary of the cooperative, who pays them all out to the patrons on the basis of the records turned over to him by the agent or agents. The dividends encourage the people to trade more with the agent.

The second type occurs when a going local cooperative sets up a private dealer in another town, maybe 10 or 100 miles away. The dealer keeps patronage records. If the serving cooperative makes money and pays dividends, these go equally to the dealer's patrons. Under this set-up the dealer handles his feed on a narrow margin, making his money on volume. He may pay $1 per ton to the local cooperative over the cooperative's cost, plus delivery cost when the feed is delivered to him.

The third type involves the merchant who buys from the local cooperative at the actual feed cost to the cooperative. He sells the feed at whatever price he wishes. He does not keep patronage records and gets no dividends. The cooperative makes nothing on the cash sale to this dealer, but it retains the eventual dividends. This is strictly nonmember business. These merchants are mostly crossroads stores or stores in villages. They rarely move a large volume individually, but together they move a big volume. Such a merchant sets his own margin since he has bought the feed.

One weakness in using contract agents is that co-op patrons come to regard the agents as profit-type merchants, and they may lose any incentive for subsequent co-op developments.

In the next chapter, the sources of equity capital are discussed.

TOPICS FOR DISCUSSION

1. Discuss each of the eight events which usually transpire in the organization of a cooperative.
2. Distinguish between articles of incorporation and bylaws.
3. What is the procedure for obtaining legal status for cooperatives in your state, province or nation?
4. Compare strictly local but independent cooperatives with federated and centralized structures.
5. Distinguish between mergers and consolidations. Why are mergers and consolidations increasing in importance?

SELECTED REFERENCES

1. Alston, Clifford, *Agricultural Cooperatives*, Ark. Agr. Ext. Serv. Cir. 447, Little Rock, Ark. July 1947.

2. Hensel, Eugene, "Converting a Profit Corporation into a Co-op," *American Cooperation*, Washington, D.C. 1946. pp. 494-503.
3. Hoad, W. M., *Questions for a Prospective Manufacturer*, SBA Rept. 2, Washington, D.C. Mar. 1954.
4. Hulbert, L. S., "Important Legal Considerations of Co-op Organization and Operation," *American Cooperation*, Washington, D.C. 1935. pp. 149-172.
5. Manuel, Milton, *The Case for Merging Co-ops*, Kans. Agr. Exp. Sta. Cir. 375, Manhattan, Kans. Apr. 1960.
6. Mueller, W. F., *The Role of Mergers*, Calif. Agr. Exp. Sta. Bul. 777, Berkeley, Calif. Feb. 1961.
7. Salter, L. C., *Organizing and Incorporating Fishery Marketing Associations*, Fishery and Wildlife Leaflet 277, Dept. of Interior, Washington, D.C. 1948.
8. Staff, *Checklist for Going into Business*, SBA, Leaflet 71, Washington, D.C. Sept. 1961.
9. Staff, *Forming Farmer Cooperatives*, FCS, Educ. Cir. 10, USDA, Washington, D.C. Apr. 1956.
10. Staff, *Organization and Management of Consumers Cooperatives*, BLS, Bul. 598, Washington, D.C. 1934.
11. Staff, "Special Co-op Merger Issue," *News for Farmer Cooperatives*, Washington, D.C. Apr. 1961.
12. Staff, *What Is a Co-op?* FCS, Bul. Reprint 6, USDA, Washington, D.C.

CHAPTER 13 –

Cooperatives and
Equity Capital

Between the great sums of money that we cannot raise, and the small sums that we will not raise, the danger is that we shall raise none.
—*Anonymous*

All the perplexities, confusion and distress in America arise, not from defects in our Constitution or federation, not from want of honor or virtue, so much as from downright ignorance of the nature of coin, credit and circulation.
—*John Adams*

THE PURPOSE of this chapter is to discuss the extent, nature and sources of membership or *equity* capital. In Chapter 14, the sources of borrowed or *creditor* capital are discussed. The *extension* of credit by cooperatives to patrons and other selected financial topics are considered in Chapter 15.

INVESTMENTS IN FARMER COOPERATIVES

The proportion of farmers' investments in cooperatives to their total assets is shown in Table 13-1.

In more recent years, about 2 percent of the farmers' investments have been in cooperatives. This appears too small in relation to the jobs that need to be done in purchasing, marketing and servicing.

Fox cites the fact that the return the farmers in the United States receive on capital invested in their farming operations is about 7 percent, before anything is taken out for family labor. If the farmers who sell products in excess of $2,500 a year work for nothing, they can make 6 or 7 percent on their capital.

In contrast, the earnings of Consumers Cooperative Association and its member associations, for example, amount to 16 percent on net worth. This is an average figure for the last few years. In other words,

TABLE 13-1
Investment by Farmers in Farmer Cooperatives,
by Years, U.S.A.

Year	Value of All Farm Assets ($)	Total Co-op Investments ($)	Percent Co-op Investment of All Assets
		(000,000)	
1940	$ 52,900	$ 800	1.5
1950	131,600	2,100	1.6
1952	167,200	2,500	1.5
1954	161,500	2,900	1.8
1956	170,100	3,300	1.9
1958	186,700	3,700	2.0
1960	202,900	4,100	2.0
1961	200,000	4,300	2.2
1962	207,300	4,500	2.2
1963	216,500	4,800	2.2

Source: *Balance Sheet of Agriculture*, USDA, Washington, D.C. Annual issues.

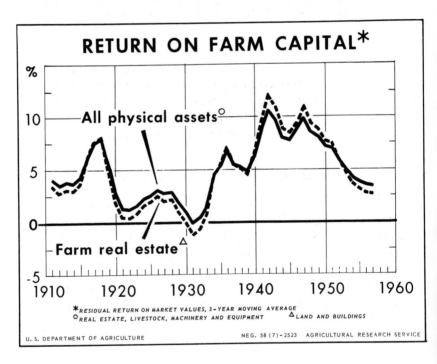

FIGURE 13-1

Some economists believe that investments in cooperatives will return much more per dollar than equivalent investments on the farm itself. (Courtesy, USDA, Washington, D.C.)

the farmers' capital invested in that cooperative makes more than twice the return of their capital invested on the farm. Fox concludes that the wisest business move the farmers of this country could make would be to double, triple and even quadruple their investments in cooperatives.[1]

There are many reasons why farmers and others do not invest more in cooperatives: (1) The individual's own business always requires capital. (2) The farm home and farm family compete for funds. (3) The individual is not always aware of the alternative returns on capital available for investment. (4) The individual in a cooperative may concentrate on the rate of interest paid on capital rather than on the rate of return on patronage. The latter rate is apt to be much higher than the former. (5) The individual's expectation of return in a cooperative varies greatly. Some are optimistic about cooperatives and will invest more, while others are dubious and have relatively more confidence in the investments made in their own businesses.

Cooperatives do differ in their rate of growth as expressed in net worth changes (Table 13-2). The rural electric cooperatives show the largest percentage increase in net worth, followed by PCA's and farm supply cooperatives. For the cooperatives shown, the percentage increase in net worth has averaged 10 percent per year over the last 13 years.

INVESTMENTS IN OTHER COOPERATIVES

While complete data concerning investments in nonfarm cooperatives are not readily available, some measurements are possible.

The investments, for example, of mutual savings banks, mutual savings and loan associations and credit unions total about as follows:[2]

	Billion Dollars
Mutual savings and loan associations	80.8
Mutual savings banks	41.3
Credit unions	5.7
Total	127.8

[1] Fox, Glenn, "Financing Farmer Co-ops," N.C.F.C. Meeting, New Orleans, La. Jan. 11, 1961.

[2] *Savings and Loan Fact Book*, U.S. Savings and Loan League, Chicago, Ill. 1962.

TABLE 13-2
Net Worth of Selected Types of Cooperatives, U.S.A.

Type of Cooperative	1940	1950	1960	1963	1950-63
		— — — — Million Dollars — — — —			Percent Change
Marketing associations	256	779	1,365	1,518	94.9
Purchasing associations	74	369	748	862	133.6
Rural electric	3	92	580	835	807.6
Federal land banks	203	298	501	583	95.6
Farmers' mutual irrigation	197	264	370	415	57.2
Production credit associations	31	122	276	367	200.8
Farmers' mutual fire insurance	42	108	207	219	102.8
Farmers' mutual telephone	23	23	23	23	0.0
Total	829	2,055	4,070	4,822	134.6

Source: USDA Agr. Info. Bul. 281, Washington, D.C. Sept. 1963.

PRINCIPLES FOR FINANCING

Certain principles have evolved over time which are considered basic to co-op financing:

1. Control of the cooperative should be vested in the common stock or membership fee either on a one man, one vote basis and/or in proportion to patronage but not on a one stock share, one vote basis.

2. Capital should be subscribed in relation to patronage, which is consistent with apportioning gains pro rata.

3. Additions to original capital should be on a pro rata basis of patronage.

4. Ownership and control should always be vested with active patrons. This necessitates a kind of revolving fund plan whereby the oldest equities are retired and replaced by current ones.

5. There is no adequate substitute for equity capital. A member's patronage will likely remain where his money is invested.

6. If capital is subscribed in proportion to patronage, there will be less need to pay interest on capital. Patronage refunds will be larger in such cases.

DETERMINING CAPITAL NEEDS

In the process of organization, a determination has to be made of the capital needed to capitalize the cooperative. Basically, this capital is divided into: (1) long-term or fixed capital and (2) short-term or operating capital. In addition, there is need for (3) organizational funds.

Long-term capital is for land, buildings, equipment and vehicles needed by the cooperative. In addition, it includes stock investments made in other cooperatives or corporations, such as membership in a federated buying or selling cooperative.

Short-term capital is for making crop and/or livestock advances, inventories, supplies and other items of current expenditure. If the cooperative extends credit, financing of accounts receivables is needed also. The cooperative may need large amounts of operating capital if it engages in contracting and vertical integration.

Organizational funds are those for legal and recording fees, business permits, incorporation fees, promotional supplies and expenses incurred in organizing the cooperative.

The exact amount of capital necessary depends upon: (1) the type of cooperative to be organized, (2) the extent of ownership or rental of fixed facilities, (3) the pledges of business volume, (4) the availability of borrowed funds and the ability of members to subscribe capital and (5) the type and extent of services to be provided, such as whether credit will be extended, among others.

Following is a discussion of the expected capital requirements for various types of cooperatives.

Agricultural Cooperatives

How do farmers who plan to organize cooperatively determine how much money they will need to start their organization on a sound basis? The answer to that question may best be provided through a hypothetical illustration of a group of growers in a fruit-producing area who form a cooperative.

When these growers have definitely agreed upon the economic need for a cooperative, they must determine whether or not an adequate volume of fruit will be marketed through the new association to assure efficient operation. For the purpose of this illustration, it may be assumed that enough producers will join the cooperative to guarantee a volume of 50,000 boxes of fruit the first season.

On each box of fruit the cooperative expects to have a margin between the proceeds of sale and the returns it will make to members sufficient to pay operating expenses and build reserves. For example the difference between the sale price and a grower's return may be 50 cents a box, of which 40 cents is earmarked for operating costs, leaving 10 cents for reserves and possible patronage refunds.

The expected volume of 50,000 boxes (pledged through marketing agreements), on which operating expenses are 40 cents a box, indicates the need of $20,000 for operating capital. The land, buildings and equipment necessary to conduct operations are valued at $25,000. The total, $45,000, is the amount of money which must be raised to conduct operations.

Rough estimates of the fixed and operating capital which may be needed by various types of farm cooperatives are shown in Tables 13-3 and 13-4.

Consumer-type Cooperatives

There is a wide variety of retail consumer cooperatives, from a small grocery store in a rural area to a large shopping center in a metropolitan area. The amount of capital required will differ according to the nature and needs of the business to be undertaken.

For a consumer store, the amount of capital needed will depend upon the number of members, the expected patronage and the expected turn-over of merchandise, as well as upon the location of the store (whether rural or urban) and the lines of goods handled. The savings made by the association are dependent on the rapidity with which the inventory is sold as well as the efficiency of the administration. No association, however small, should run a grocery business on a turn-over of less than 12 times a year, but a store carrying a more general line of merchandise may have a turn-over of fewer than 8 times per year.

TABLE 13-3
Estimate of Fixed Capital Required for Various Types of Farmer Cooperatives (Minimum Optimum Scale)[1]

Type of Cooperative	Fixed Capital ($)	
	Range	Average
	(000)	
Auction barn	$ 40- 80	$ 60
Broiler processing	300-1,000	650
Canning plant	100- 750	250
Cattle feedlot	75- 275	125
Container factory	125- 375	250
Cotton gin	150- 350	250
Egg packing plant	25- 50	35
Farm equipment	50- 100	75
Farm supply	15- 75	25
Feed mill	25- 500	200
Grain elevator	50- 500	150
Milk bottling plant	250- 800	475
Milk mfg. plant	180- 850	420
Mixed fertilizer plant	200- 300	250
Nitrogen fertilizer plant	2,000-3,000	2,500
Oil mill	1,000-2,000	1,500
Produce packing shed	50- 100	75
Raw sugar cane mill	3,000-4,000	3,500
Rice dryer	150- 300	250
Seed cleaning	25- 60	50
Slaughter plant	250-1,000	500
Sugar refinery	3,500-4,000	3,750

[1]The author in no way guarantees that the type of cooperative cited can be capitalized for the amounts shown. Fixed capital requirements will vary with the size of plant, automation, location and with many other factors.

Source: New Orleans Bank for Farmer Cooperatives and trade sources.

FIGURE 13-2

Co-op oil refineries also require heavy fixed investments. The refineries need to be integrated with crude oil sources, pipelines, bulk transports and retail service stations. (Courtesy, Farmer Union Central Exchange, St. Paul, Minn.)

It should be emphasized that no hard and fast rules as to capital requirements can be laid down. Each group before starting will have to take into consideration the local conditions and any special

TABLE 13-4
Estimate of Operating Capital Required for Various Types of Farmer Cooperatives (Minimum Optimum Scale)[1]

Type of Cooperative	Operating Capital ($)		Average
	Range		
	- - - (000) - - -		
Auction barn	$ 15-	25	$ 20
Broiler processing	100-	200	150
Canning plant	50-	500	150
Cattle feedlot	50-	500	250
Container factory	25-	150	100
Cotton gin	10-	20	15
Egg packing plant	5-	20	15
Farm equipment	25-	75	50
Farm supply	20-	50	25
Feed mill	10-	25	20
Grain elevator	10-	250	50
Milk bottling plant	50-	100	75
Milk mfg. plant	40-	50	45
Mixed fertilizer plant	100-	150	125
Nitrogen fertilizer plant	300-1,000		500
Oil mill	200-	500	300
Produce packing shed	10-	50	15
Raw sugar cane mill	100-	250	125
Rice dryer	10-	25	20
Seed cleaning	5-	25	12
Slaughter plant	50-	500	375
Sugar refinery	300-	500	400

[1]The author in no way guarantees that the type of cooperative cited can be capitalized for the amounts shown. Operating capital requirements will depend on advances made to patrons, amount of credit extended, perishability and seasonality of the product, etc.

Source: New Orleans Bank for Farmer Cooperatives and trade sources.

circumstances that may be present. One guideline for an urban store is a minimum of 1,000 families investing $50 each, or $50,000 capitalization. Assuming an annual grocery expenditure of $600 per family, the store would obtain sales of $600,000 per year. A drug department and other lines would enhance sales considerably.

Another available guideline is for a grocery store containing 6,000 square feet, handling groceries, produce and meats[3] (as shown at the top of the next page).

If the annual purchases per family are $600, some 1,560 families are needed as members. If the purchases are $1,000 per family, some 936 member families are needed.

_____

[3]Bureau of Labor Statistics Bul. 1024, Washington, D.C. 1951. pp. 22-23.

Annual sales $936,000
Capital needed:
  Inventory $24,000
  Fixtures and
    equipment   36,000
  Working capital   10,000
                                        _____

                                        $70,000

Investment in a housing cooperative varies, of course, in different parts of the country. An example of investments required in one New York City co-op housing association are as follows:

Apartment Size	Member's Equity Investment	Monthly Carrying Charges[1]
Studio	$1500	$ 76 to $ 93
1 bedroom	$2100	$ 96 to $117
2 bedrooms	$2700	$118 to $141
2 bedrooms with balcony	$3000	$130 to $151
3 bedrooms	$3600	$148 to $164
3 bedrooms with balcony	$3900	$165 to $181

[1]Including utilities.

The proportion which can be borrowed under FHA approval as well as from other sources will range from 70 to 90 percent of the total cost of the co-op housing projects. The balance, or from 10 to 30 percent, is supplied by members on a per member or pro rata basis. The initial cost of joining a housing cooperative may range from as little as $5 to as high as $3,000 or more depnding upon the membership policy, members' share of the land price and cost of development and other policies.[4]

Mutual Insurances and Credit Cooperatives

Before organizing any credit, medical or insurance cooperative, the appropriate statutes under which chartering is contemplated should be studied.

Mutual insurance statutes usually stipulate a minimum capitalization before the Insurance Commissioner will issue a charter to operate.

---

[4]Staff, *Housing Co-ops*, BLS Bul. 1093, Dept. of Labor, Washington, D.C. 1951.

Usually, a credit union should not be capitalized with less than $1,000 paid-in shares. However, the potential membership of a credit union, rather than its initial paid-in capital, is important.

Capital needed to organize Blue Cross, Blue Shield, mutual insurances, savings and loan associations and other credit and insurance institutions is often prescribed by law. For example, the Louisiana law on savings and loan associations prescribes the following capital requirements in relation to the city, town or village where such organizations are located:

Population	Subscribed Capital ($)	Paid-in Cash ($)
Less than 10,000	25,000	5,000
10,000 - 49,999	50,000	25,000
50,000 - 99,999	100,000	50,000
100,000 or more	150,000	100,000

Business and Industrial Cooperatives

Retailer-owned grocery wholesales usually capitalize at from $30,000 to $100,000 or more. If common stock shares are at $500 each, a minimum of about 60 stores is required. If stock shares are at $1,000 each, about 30 stores are required. Besides the initial capital subscribed, "retains" are usually made on sales to member stores to increase equity capital from them.

Service Cooperatives

Mutual water companies, artificial breeding, mutual telephone, health and other service cooperatives require much heavier fixed capital than operating capital because permanent facilities of an expensive nature are constructed to provide services. These cooperatives seldom need large amounts of working capital. It is not uncommon for them to borrow to pay operating costs and repay the loans when collections are made or premiums paid. For example, a co-op group health clinic must rely on initial subscribers for at least 50 to 75 percent of the fixed facility costs, which may range from $100,000 to $500,000. The monthly premiums paid will provide the working capital. Assuming a $100,000 subscription, 2,000 members could initially provide $50 each. Health cooperatives not operating facilities can sustain themselves on fees or premiums alone.

RELATIONSHIP OF CAPITAL REQUIREMENTS
TO EXPECTED PATRONAGE

A basic guideline in organizing any cooperative is one which attempts to correlate capital subscription with expected patronage. Since refunds are based on patronage, capital subscription should likewise be on patronage. If this is not followed, the large patron may get a much higher return on his investment than the small patron.

In the event that it is impossible to raise capital in proportion to patronage, the device of paying interest on capital may be employed to rectify the inequalities.

Numerous schemes may be used in raising capital proportional to patronage. Assessments based on number of trees, cows, acres, chickens or on volume of business, etc., may be employed.

RELATIONSHIP OF MEMBER AGREEMENTS
TO FINANCING

The prime purpose of a marketing, service or purchasing agreement between a cooperative and its member-patrons is to assure financial soundness. Without such assurances, the co-op management cannot very well organize, plan and conduct the business, and furthermore, its borrowing ability is more limited.

Marketing Agreements

A marketing contract is a written statement of the rights and duties of the members and of the association relating to the marketing of the products of the producers through the association. In some cases, it is referred to as a membership agreement.

What is the *purpose* of a marketing contract?

1. A contract is used to assure the association the continuous support of its members.

2. A contract is also used to lower the cost of assembling members' products by insuring their delivery.

3. A contract assures the association a certain volume of business upon which to plan future operations.

4. A contract is valuable in materially assisting the association in its financing operations.

5. It enhances the prestige of the association.

6. It enables the association to guarantee delivery of quality products on a definite schedule.

The *legal importance* of a contract is as follows:

1. It prevents minority groups from deserting an association and violating an agreement.

2. It has proved invaluable in numerous instances to restrain outside interference with the delivery of the members' products to the association.

3. It is a means of obtaining damages from the non-cooperating members.

4. A contract is a matter of record.

There are basically two *types* of marketing contracts: (1) purchase-and-sale and (2) agency. The purchase-and-sale contract provides that title to the goods in question be passed from the cooperative to the member (purchasing co-op) or from the member to the cooperative (marketing co-op). The agency contract provides that title not pass but that one party act as agent for the other.

In the case of *retains*, the members should authorize the cooperative to deduct not only operating and maintenance costs and expenses but also a reasonable amount for furnishing the association with capital to pay for fixed assets and for operating purposes. Likewise, in the case of a purchasing cooperative, the cooperative should have the assurance that it will have such a volume of business at going market prices as will enable it to take margins that will permit the association to meet its operating and maintenance costs and expenses and its capital requirements. Much of the overhead of an association is of a fixed character, and frequently this overhead is not affected by an increase in the volume of business. Ordinarily, as the volume of business increases, the overhead per unit of commodity handled decreases.

The *duration* of a contract is an important consideration for both the producer and the association. Contracts may be divided into (1) terminating contracts or (2) self-renewing contracts. The terminating contract contains a clause specifically stating the expiration date. The self-renewing contract runs for a definite period mentioned in the agreement, but in addition, as the name suggests, includes a renewing clause. There appear to be two important factors which influence the length of a marketing contract: (1) the market characteristics of the commodity and (2) the amount and the nature of the capital investment. Commodities which require storage, curing or preserving (as tobacco) and those which are produced seasonally but marketed over a period of years naturally affect the business of associations in an entirely different manner from those commodities which are sold in a relatively short period of time. The size of the investments in physical facilities, such as warehouses, drying plants and packing establishments, requires the assurance of a certain volume of business for a sufficient number of years in which these capital investments may be paid off.

The *enforcement* of contracts is no easy matter, particularly for the management of local associations. Large-scale associations which have legal departments find it less embarrassing. The breach of contract results in two types of damages: (1) economic damages and (2) the adverse psychological effect which the defection has on other producers. The remedies which are ordinarily open to an association are of three kinds: (1) liquidated damage, (2) injunction and (3) specific performance.

Liquidated damage is a payment for the estimate of the harm done following defection of a contract and is agreed upon by both parties in advance. A liquidated damage is a suitable, reasonable compensation for economic loss. Liquidated damage may be based on: (1) a percentage of sale value or (2) a flat sum per unit of product.

The *injunction* is a negative method of enforcement by restraining (through the courts) the producer from marketing his crops through anyone other than the association. A court injunction may be of two kinds: (1) It may enjoin the member from selling outside the association, or (2) it may enjoin outsiders or third parties from inducing members to violate their contracts. The use of injunction is especially significant for those associations that have made commitments to deliver the products anticipated from their members. Enjoining outsiders is important for another reason; namely, it has a psychic effect upon the association membership.

A decree of *specific performance* is a definite statement of the court directing the producer to deliver his crop to the association as he has contracted. However, a decree of specific performance does not force a producer to grow a crop under his contract nor even to harvest a crop which has been planted, but it does force him to sell the crop to the association if it is sold.

The literature on marketing contracts is both voluminous and technical. There are several good sources, however.[5,6] For a sample copy of a marketing agreement see Farmer Cooperative Service Bulletin 10.

Purchase Agreements

Although purchase agreements are not widely used in the United States, they are valuable for supply cooperatives when borrowing funds. The lending agencies recognize that sound purchase agreements between cooperatives that sell supplies and members who purchase them bolster the loan application. This is especially true for cooperatives just getting started in business.

Without purchase agreements, supply cooperatives often find that some patrons forsake their own cooperative for a small saving elsewhere which yields patrons only a temporary benefit. Purchase agreements help co-op management to better plan, purchase, promote and conduct its supply business.

A retailer-owned wholesale often uses purchase agreements because it desires to guarantee manufacturers that a certain volume of goods will be bought by the co-op wholesale. In turn, the co-op wholesale is assured that its retailer-members will buy the volume the wholesale has contracted for.

SOURCES OF EQUITY CAPITAL

Capital of any business may be classified as equity or creditor. Equity is that supplied by owners as the basic investment to make the endeavor possible. It may be referred to as ownership or risk capital, since the supplier of this capital is a part owner of the corporation in a real sense and shares the risk of sustaining a loss or stands to share gains realized. Upon liquidation some of this capital may be used to settle claims against the corporation, or residual equities may accrue to it, depending upon the solvency of the association and bylaw provisions.

Creditor capital is that made available on other than an ownership basis. Creditor capital is loaned money. It must be repaid. Because

---

[5]Mueller, W. F. and J. M. Tinley, *Membership Marketing Contracts,* Calif. Agri. Exp. Sta. Bul. 760, Davis, Calif. Mar. 1958.
[6]Staff, *Organizing a Farmer Cooperative,* FCS Cir. 18, USDA, Washington, D.C. Nov. 1956. pp. 15-18.

of the different methods used to evidence members' capital contributions in cooperatives, it is necessary that equity and creditor capital
be clearly differentiated. Enough equity capital must be provided on
a permanent basis to insure that the cooperative will be sufficiently
free from creditors' claims to perform the needed services. To require
$2.00 of equity for $1.00 of creditor capital is a sound rule of financing.
A net worth of 60 percent of total assets is a desirable goal for most
cooperatives.

A study conducted by the Farmer Cooperative Service revealed
the following sources of equity capital in farmer cooperatives:

Kind of Equity Capital	Percentage of Total Equity
Allocated patronage credits without maturity dates	42.6
Preferred stock	23.9
Common stock	20.9
Unallocated reserves	11.0
Miscellaneous equity and current margins	1.3
Membership certificates	.3
Total	100.0

Stock equities totaled 44.8 percent; nonstock equities, 42.9 percent;
unallocated reserves, 11 percent; and others, 1.3 percent.

STOCK COOPERATIVES

The organization of stock cooperatives involves the subscription of
common and preferred stock. About 78 percent of the farmer cooperatives in the United States are organized on a stock basis; 22 percent
are organized on a nonstock basis.

Common Stock

Most cooperatives on a stock basis use common stock as the voting
stock. In small cooperatives it is desirable to fix the par value of
this stock low—for example, from $1 to $25 a share. Some cooperatives pay interest on common stock; others do not. Most such stock
is non-assessable—that is, after the holder has paid its par value he
cannot be required as a stockholder to pay any more to the support

of the association. How the stock may be voted (one member, one vote no matter how many shares are held; in accordance with usual cooperative procedure; or on the basis of business volume furnished if desired and if state law permits) should be covered in the organization papers. The bylaws should provide for retirement or transfer of common stock if the member dies, moves out of the area or violates any of the bylaws or rules and regulations of the association.

Business cooperatives usually stipulate larger par values for their common stock, such as from $500 to $1,000 per share.

Common stock and preferred stock may also be divided into various classes, such as Class A, Class B and Class C. Each class of stock may have different par value, interest rate and/or voting rights.

Common stock is usually insufficient to provide all the capital required.

Preferred Stock

Preferred stock represents another type of invested capital used by cooperatives organized with capital stock. It draws a fixed annual rate. This interest rate may not exceed the current maximum legal interest rate, which is ordinarily 8 percent. Preferred stock usually does not have a maturity date; it is repaid by direction of the board of directors if redemption is permitted. Preferred stock usually carries no vote and may be held by non-members as well as members.

This stock usually is nonassessable, nonvoting and preferred on liquidation—that is, paid off before the common stock if the association goes out of business. There should be few restrictions on its transfer so it may freely circulate. Some cooperatives issue this stock in lieu of cash patronage refunds.

Preferred stock so issued may be either cumulative or noncumulative. Cumulative stock means that dividends missed one year are paid subsequently. Noncumulative stock means that dividends missed one year are not subject for payment in subsequent years. Cooperatives should, as a general rule, refrain from issuing cumulative preferred stock because of the obligation created to pay the interest. However, noncumulative stock is less attractive from an investment standpoint.

If net earnings in a stock cooperative are deferred, they are usually issued as preferred stock, perhaps of various classes, such as A, B and C.

Provisions might be made whereby the preferred stock held by

FIGURE 13-3

A common stock certificate issued by a farmer cooperative. (Courtesy, Vermilion Farmers Cooperative Association, Inc., Abbeville, La.)

nonmembers and/or nonproducers is to be retired by funding a portion of each year's net savings for that purpose.

NONSTOCK COOPERATIVES

Nonstock cooperatives usually utilize two types of capital subscription: membership certificates and capital certificates.

Membership Certificates

When associations are organized on a nonstock basis, the members are given certificates of membership upon payment of membership fees. The sale of certificates of membership may either supply all the capital which is needed or it may fall short. The latter is usually the case, for in many associations the collection of membership fees is considered merely an incidental means of financing. Since no interest

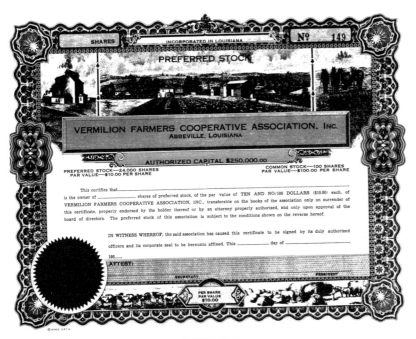

FIGURE 13-4

A preferred stock certificate issued by a farmer cooperative. (Courtesy, Vermilion Farmers Cooperative Association, Inc., Abbeville, La.)

is paid on membership fees, the manner of financing is insignificant from the cost standpoint.

Capital Certificates

Capital certificates are used in nonstock cooperatives and are equivalent to preferred stock certificates. They may be sold in larger denominations ($25, $50, $100, $500), may bear interest and may have due dates but usually do not. They usually have no voting rights.

These certificates are an efficient way of raising money in that they may be allocated to a member's account along with his membership fee and patronage credits. Non-members may also purchase capital certificates, which have no voting power. If capital certificates have no due date, the problem of retiring them arises. Some cooperatives provide a reserve fund consisting of ½ of 1 percent of the certificates outstanding each month to be used for cashing certificates for those investors desiring to liquidate.

If net earnings in nonstock cooperatives are deferred, they may be issued as capital certificates preferably without a due date. In this way, they are the equivalent of preferred stock.

Reserves

There are at least two kinds of reserves: (1) valuation reserves for depreciation and bad debts and (2) capital reserves, either allocated or unallocated.

Reserves for *depreciation* and for *bad debts* are the principal valuation reserves found in co-op financial statements.

There is considerable misunderstanding of the nature and reasons for *depreciation* reserves. In other words, a charge is made to opera-

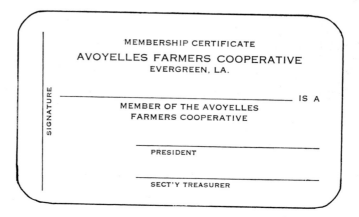

FIGURE 13-5

A membership certificate issued by a nonstock farmer cooperative to evidence the payment of a membership fee. (Courtesy, Avoyelles Farmers Cooperative, Evergreen, La.)

tions for the wear, tear and obsolescence of the principal assets, and the fixed asset account reduced accordingly. The funds accumulated from the depreciation charges are used to conduct the business, and total assets remain the same. No change occurs in the liability accounts. This is important to remember because some accountants erroneously show the fixed assets at cost and set up an account called "reserve for depreciation" among the liabilities.

Bad debt reserves are established by withholding from the proceeds of sale sufficient sums to provide a bridge between the occurrence of a loss and the period or periods responsible for the loss. They serve as a "pool" for losses from bad accounts. A charge is made against operations when they are established; however, no change is made in the accounts receivable until a loss is determined. Then the total accounts receivable is reduced and the reserve for bad debts charged accordingly. Many types of cooperatives are required by law to set up bad debt reserves. For example, production credit associations, to the extent their earnings in excess of other operating expenses permit, add to reserves for bad debts annually an amount equal to ½ of 1 percent of loans outstanding at the end of the fiscal year until such reserves equal or exceed 3½ percent of loans outstanding. Thereafter, further additions to such reserves may be made but are not required.

Reserves (other than depreciation reserves and reserves for bad debts) represent member (owner) claims against the assets. *Capital reserve* funds are increased by retaining net margins in the business, either on an allocated or unallocated basis.

Such reserve funds are needed and used: (1) to meet a definite obligation, such as the payment of a mortgage or note; (2) for increasing the operating capital of the association (improving the current assets-current liability ratio); (3) as insurance against possible future losses; or (4) for expansion of the business. There is no relationship between the amount of total reserves and cash on hand. For the reasons outlined, a cooperative may have a large reserve with only a small item of cash.

State laws for cooperatives usually specify both minimum and maximum levels for *unallocated reserves* or *earned surplus*. In some states, cooperatives are required to set aside at least 10 percent of net operating proceeds each year until the surplus reaches 30 percent of the total membership capital; no additions are made to surplus after it reaches 50 percent of the total membership capital. Federal credit unions, by law, must apply 20 percent of net earnings to reserve.

It is necessary to have reasonable unallocated capital reserves or surplus to make a cooperative financially secure. But if reserve and surplus are used as the primary method of financing the cooperative, they are objectionable because the individual member has no direct claim to his share of this capital unless the cooperative is dissolved. This practice is more sound for ordinary corporations, in which the amount of surplus is reflected in the market value of common stock.

The amount of reserves set aside for various purposes must also be justified if questioned by the Internal Revenue Service, else exemption from the payment of certain income taxes may not be obtained. The needs of an association should determine the size of the reserves.

Under income tax regulations, cooperatives are permitted to accumulate and maintain reasonable reserves for contingencies. However, they must pay federal income taxes on any amounts placed in reserve unless individual members are given notice of the amounts allocated or placed to their credit in these reserves in accord with income tax regulations. When notified, co-op patrons are required under present income tax regulations to take these amounts into account in preparing their own income tax returns when they affect the cost of their business operations.

Methods of Subscribing Equity Capital

There are various methods available for members to subscribe capital in their cooperative: (1) outright payment for the full value in cash, (2) giving a note and promising to pay a fixed amount on a certain date, (3) agreeing to let the cooperative make certain "deductions" from marketing receipts or add certain "charges" on goods bought, (4) applying patronage refunds on capital subscriptions or (5) borrowing the money from banks or production credit associations on a personal note and purchasing capital in the cooperative.

In some cooperatives, the co-op patron may agree that the cooperative shall make certain assessments per unit of product as contributions to capital. Over time, the patron-member accumulates and contributes to capital roughly in proportion to his patronage.

In credit unions, for instance, a member may agree to contribute a certain fixed sum each month as his contribution to capital stock or shares. In agricultural marketing cooperatives the association may retain 1 cent per dozen eggs, 5 cents per bushel of sweet potatoes or a percentage of gross sales to build up capital. Farm supply cooperatives may add 50 cents per ton of feed or 1 percent of the value of supplies furnished, for example.

Retained Earnings as a Capital Source

A study by the Farmer Cooperative Service of the disposition of net earnings of cooperatives showed that the largest amount, or 56 percent, went to allocated but retained earnings (Table 13-5).

These retained earnings are variously termed: deferred patronage refunds, certificates of equity, capital certificates, capital credits, certificates of indebtedness, advance funds, revolving funds, withholdings repayable, reserve funds, certificates of interest, capital retains, growers' equity, finance funds, book credits, among others. In addition, retained earnings may be distributed or allocated in stock, in which case they become part of the capital structure.

Legally, the classification of these retained earnings is very important for accounting and tax purposes. If the retained earnings are allocated to patrons without a specific due date, they become a liability under the *capital* or *net worth* section of the balance sheet.

TABLE 13-5
Distribution of Net Margins of Farmer Cooperatives, U.S.A.

Item	Distribution of Net Margins[1] (Percent)
Allocated retained earnings	55.6
Cash refunds	30.9
State and federal income taxes	4.2
Unallocated reserves	3.6
Dividends on preferred stock	2.8
Dividends on common stock	2.6
Interest on other equity capital	.3
Total	100.0

[1]Total net margins of $332 million for 9,793 associations.
Source: Staff, *How Farmers Finance Their Co-ops,* FCS, Cir. 145, USDA, Washington, D.C. Sept. 1957.

If the retained earnings are allotted and redeemable at a specific date, they ordinarily are a liability under the *liabilities* section of the balance sheet. If they are due in three years or longer, they would be classified under *fixed liabilities.* If due in less than three years, they would be classified under current liabilities as *current payables.*

One of the main distinctions between a patronage refund held as pure equity capital or held as a short-term or long-term liability is the *due date* specified in the instrument. The rate of interest paid on the instrument has less effect than does the name of the instrument itself. Any equity instrument without a due date and subject to the rights of creditors is comparable to the preferred stock of any corporation. Cooperatives vary in paying interest on retain certificates. Some pay up to 8 percent interest, while others pay no interest.

In a consumer cooperative, the amount to be returned on patronage may be paid back (1) in cash, (2) in credit toward patronage at the store, (3) in credit toward the purchase of additional shares or (4) as loan-capital certificates. The first and second methods are usual if the association already has sufficient capital for current needs, or methods (3) and (4) if more capital is needed. A common procedure is to pay nonmembers in credits toward shares and to notify members that their refunds are available in cash on request but, in the absence of such request, will be credited toward additional shares. The decision as to how the distribution of earnings is to be made should be that of the membership, or if the law allows otherwise, the directors may be empowered to make such a decision. The bylaws should specify that the association has a lien on the patronage refunds of members for any amounts owed to the cooperative, so that such refunds may be legally withheld in such cases.

One problem associated with allocation of retained earnings is the allocation procedure itself. When a cooperative markets several products, operates several departments or sells many different supply items, shall it allocate earnings based on overall performance or allocate by products or departments? If a supply cooperative operates feed, fertilizer, petroleum and hardware departments, net savings may vary greatly by departments. Fertilizer sales may net nothing, while petroleum sales may net a great deal. Patrons will not buy all supplies in the same proportion. A sound policy to follow in any case is to departmentalize refund allocations but not to the extent that bookkeeping and other costs exceed the benefits otherwise derived. For example, "feed" is a legitimate department; "fertilizer, seed and chemicals" are interrelated, as are "petroleum, oils and greases." These could constitute three departmental allocations.

REVOLVING THE RETAINED EARNINGS

A membership cooperative, and a stock cooperative as well, may provide for obtaining capital from patrons by adopting a revolving fund plan of financing. Under this plan, the patron contracts with the association that a flat rate per unit marketed, a percentage of the sales proceeds of all products marketed or a percentage of all net operating margins to which he may be entitled as patronage refunds is to be invested in or loaned to the cooperative for capital purposes.

Capital is accumulated in this manner until it reaches a level deemed adequate by the board of directors. The cooperative should never start revolving the funds unless it is financially sound. Thereafter,

FIGURE 13-6

Each member is obligated to support his cooperative. Usually, the voting shares are at a low par value and pay no interest. The nonvoting shares are at a higher par and bear interest. Each member should be required to enter into a stipulated program of capital subscription. (Courtesy, Consumers Cooperative of Berkeley, Inc., Berkeley, Calif.)

although additional investments are continued currently, excess cash funds are used to retire the earlier contributions in chronological order. Many consider this the most equitable plan of financing a cooperative, since it requires current patrons to furnish capital in proportion to their current patronage, and the capital furnished by the patrons of former years is returned to them after a reasonable interval.

Operation of Revolving Plan

The operation of a revolving capital structure is shown in Tables 13-6 and 13-7. In year 1, the cooperative began with facilities costing $25,000, a mortgage debt of $15,000, an original investment on the part of members of $15,000 and capital retains of $3,000 each year. The association will not revolve any portion of the membership capital until the mortgage debt is repaid. In order to simplify the illustration, it is assumed that there is no change in the association's total capital requirements over the seven-year period.

TABLE 13-6
Capital Statement of a Cooperative on Revolving Capital Basis

Year	Total Membership Investment at Beginning of Year	Mortgage Debt at Beginning of Year	Capital Added by 6-Cent-per-Unit Deduction	Capital Revolved	Total Membership Investment at End of Year	Total Capital
1	$15,000	$15,000	$3,000	—	$18,000	$33,000
2	18,000	12,000	3,000	—	21,000	33,000
3	21,000	9,000	3,000	—	24,000	33,000
4	24,000	6,000	3,000	—	27,000	33,000
5	27,000	3,000	3,000	—	30,000	33,000
6	30,000	—	3,000	$3,000	30,000	33,000
7[1]	30,000	—	3,000	3,000	30,000	33,000

[1]And so on, if operations are successful and no more funds are needed for capital.
Source: Nervick, O. and R. Gunderson, *Financing Co-ops*, S.D. Agr. Exp. Sta. Bul. 434, Brookings, S.D. Feb. 1954.

TABLE 13-7
A Member's Capital Equity Account in the Foregoing Association

Year	Investment at Beginning of Year	Capital Contributed by 6-Cent-per-Unit Investment on 1,000 Units a Year	Capital Revolved to Member	Investment at End of Year
1	$300	$60	—	$360
2	360	60	—	420
3	420	60	—	480
4	480	60	—	540
5	540	60	—	600
6	600	60	$60	600
7[1]	600	60	60	600

[1]And so on, if operations are successful and no more funds are needed by the association for capital.
Source: Same as Table 13-6.

Table 13-7 shows the revolution of capital belonging to a member who markets 1,000 boxes of fruit, for example, per year during the seven-year period shown. A capital retain of 6 cents per unit is deducted annually from sales. The member's original investment was $300.

The association revolves no portion of its capital until the mortgage debt is paid in full. Some associations do revolve a part of their capital prior to that time with funds obtained from other sources such as savings that are not distributed as patronage refunds. The principal considerations are the amount of funds available and the extent to which capital revolution can be made without jeopardizing the credit standing of the association.

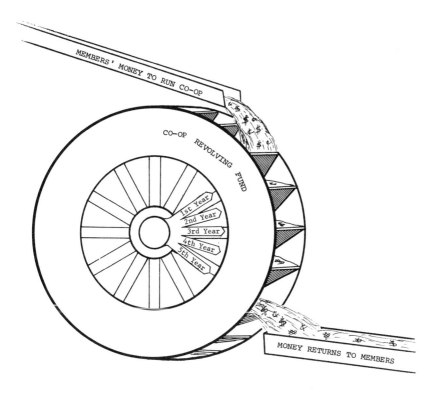

FIGURE 13-7

A co-op revolving fund is nothing more than a delayed refund settlement. In the above, the co-op member is getting his first cash refund in the 5th year. In the 6th year, he will get the refunds due him on the 2nd year's business, etc. (Courtesy, Farmer Cooperative Service, Washington, D.C.)

Legal Considerations

It is important for an association planning to build its capital structure on the revolving plan to provide authorization in the bylaws and/or marketing contract for deductions from the members' proceeds of sale for this purpose. If associations retain for capital purposes a part of each year's operating margins on a revolving fund basis, they should make proper bylaw provision therefor. At the same time, it is advisable to set forth in the bylaws and/or contracts other purposes for which deductions may be made, such as reserves and necessary operating expenses. The courts have held that no matter how advisable or essential the deductions other than those authorized may appear, they cannot properly be made.

It is also important to set forth in the bylaws that the membership capital is junior to the rights of creditors. At the same time, it is essential that the bylaws state the authority the directors may exercise in revolving capital funds. The tendency is to provide that the board of directors shall have broad authority as to the size of the capital fund, the time of revolving of capital and the amount of the deduction for capital purposes.

The principal advantages of a revolving capital plan are:

1. Members contribute capital to the cooperative in the same proportion that they use the cooperative and share its benefits.

2. Ownership is maintained in the hands of current member-patrons.

3. It permits members to acquire increased ownership in the cooperative. While this usually means gradual growth, it insures sound growth. The cooperative must make savings for its members; otherwise expansion financed by revolving capital cannot take place.

4. Once this plan is put into operation, a minimum of administrative cost is necessary for maintaining the capital required.

5. This plan reduces operating costs by avoiding the necessity of paying interest to attract invested capital.

6. The members can borrow from financial institutions on the basis of their revolving fund certificates, usually 90 percent of the face value.

Some disadvantages of a revolving capital plan are:

1. It does not take into account the differences in the ability of individual members to provide capital.

2. The period required for the fund to revolve cannot be main-

tained where continuous expansion takes place, unless some other method is used to obtain capital for expansion.

3. Members sometimes regard their equity in the revolving fund as a debt which their cooperative "owes" them rather than as their proportionate share of the capital requirements of the cooperative.

4. The plan may permit too rapid an expansion of the cooperative without the explicit approval of a majority of the members.

5. This plan may become unworkable and unacceptable to the members if the capital requirements of the cooperative make a long revolving period necessary.

6. Members have to pay income tax on patronage refunds when they are deferred. Since they have to make a cash payment for the income tax, they often feel that a corresponding amount should be paid out to them in cash. The Revenue Act of 1962 contains provisions

SOURCE OF POWER OF REVOLVING FUND CAPITAL

FIGURE 13-8

Small streams of capital from hundreds of farmer-members unite to form a powerful reservoir of capital to run the cooperative. By 1964 capital needs have been met, so 1960 revolving fund capital is being returned to the members who originally contributed it. (Courtesy, Farmer Cooperative Service, Washington, D.C.)

to accomplish this. However, any current dividend paid in cash has a tendency to prolong the length of the revolving fund.

The stock cooperatives may face problems when they attempt to adopt a revolving capital plan by revolving shares of stock instead of creating a separate revolving fund.[7]

Some associations organized with capital stock issue "certificates of stock" to evidence investments that increase the revolving fund. From a legal standpoint there appears to be no reason why an association formed with capital stock, as well as one formed on a nonstock basis, may not issue certificates other than certificates of stock. If an association revolves its capital stock, at least one share of voting stock should be held at all times by each producer who is to continue as a member of the association. If an association is formed with common and preferred stock, the preferred may be revolved while the common—usually issued on the basis of one share to each producer—would not be affected.[8]

Length of Revolving Funds

The average length of revolving periods for various farmer cooperatives is estimated as follows:

Type of Local Cooperative	Length of Revolving Period (Years)
Cotton gin	5
Milk marketing	9
Fruit and vegetable marketing	9
Grain elevator	10
Poultry and egg processing	10
Livestock marketing	11
Farm supply	11

Nonfarm cooperatives, especially wholesale grocery ones, also use revolving funds, but their revolving periods are usually much shorter, mostly from one to three years. Retailer-owned grocery wholesales in revolving retained earnings will usually use "merchandise credits" rather than cash. In this way, a member groceryman is obliged to purchase through his cooperative in order to consume his deferred patronage refund.

---

[7]Nieman, C. E., "Revolving Capital in Stock Co-ops," *Law and Contemporary Problems of Cooperatives*, Duke University, Durham, N.C. Summer 1948.
[8]Mischler and Hulbert, *op. cit.* p. 224.

Rural electric cooperatives also use the revolving fund plan. One of the most successful cooperatives in this respect is on a 10-year plan revolving this year the patronage allocation of 10 years ago. Consumer cooperatives likewise use revolving funds in a manner similar to farmer cooperatives.

As a financing device, the revolving fund plan is peculiarly well adapted to cooperatives. Its use is regarded by many as the most effective method of raising capital. The revolving fund plan of financing confines capital contributions to patrons, requires investment according to patronage and restricts equity financing to those currently patronizing the association.

Revolving Funds and the 1962 Revenue Act

The 1962 Revenue Act contains a provision whereby cooperatives have to pay at least 20 percent of their year's net margins in cash to patrons. This provision tends to upset previous revolving fund plans because at least 20 percent of the current net earnings are made in cash to current patrons. Correspondingly, there is less cash available to retire deferred equities of past years. This means that a 10-year revolving fund plan might become 20 percent longer, or 12 years.

Revolving Capital Retains

Many cooperatives are authorized by their members to make capital retains. These retains are actually deductions made on a per bushel, per ton, etc., basis as contributions to capital. These retains are not income to a cooperative but actual contributions to capital and may be revolved on a basis equivalent to the revolving of retained earnings. For income tax purposes, capital retains are not treated as income.

SUMMARY OF PRINCIPLES REGARDING
EQUITY CAPITAL

Some provisions which should be considered in connection with the equity capital of a cooperative are:

1. The right to acquire and to hold voting securities should be restricted to patrons of the cooperative. The objective of this provision is to keep the right to a voice in the control of the cooperative restricted to the persons who use its services.

2. There should be a workable and positive provision by which voting securities held by persons who cease to qualify as voting members of the cooperative are canceled and converted at par value or book value, whichever is less, into nonvoting securities.

3. The right to hold nonvoting securities need not be restricted either as to persons or as to the amounts which any one person may hold.

4. The board of directors should have authority to call and pay, at par value or book value, whichever is less, whenever in its judgment the cooperative has cash funds available for the purpose, nonvoting securities held by the estates of persons who have died, or held by firms adjudicated bankrupt, or by persons who have moved from or who no longer operate in the trading area served by the cooperative.

5. Capital permanently needed in the business should be represented or evidenced by permanent-type equities.

6. Operating capital may be evidenced by revolving-fund-types of equity securities or by revolving-type patrons' allocated equity reserves.

FIGURE 13-9

Co-op societies must depend on their own patrons and members for equity capital. (Courtesy, Co-operative Union, Manchester, England)

7. Patrons' allocated equity or capital reserves should be reducible for operating losses sustained by the cooperative.

8. Patrons should be notified of savings or losses distributed to them upon a patronage basis and credited or charged to their equity in the cooperative.

9. Equity reserves and revolving-fund-type equity securities should carry provisions by which they may be called for payment, by years, in the order in which they were accrued, the oldest outstanding to be called for payment before those subsequently accrued are called for payment.

10. Consideration should be given to payment of reasonable rates of interest or dividends upon equity securities before distribution of savings to patrons upon a patronage basis. This is not so imperative if capital is subscribed proportional to patronage.[9]

It should be noted that if patrons capitalize their cooperatives adequately from the beginning, the sooner the cooperatives will be able to afford to pay patronage refunds in cash.

In the next chapter, sources of borrowed funds for cooperatives are discussed.

TOPICS FOR DISCUSSION

1. How much do farmers in the United States have invested in their cooperatives?
2. Discuss the principles to follow in co-op financing.
3. Select one type of cooperative familiar to you and discuss its capital needs, both fixed and operating.
4. Why should capitalization of a cooperative be related to the patronage of its patrons?
5. Discuss a marketing agreement.
6. What are some sources of equity capital?
7. Contrast the stock and nonstock cooperatives.
8. Discuss the revolving fund plan of financing.
9. Discuss some of the principles regarding equity capitalization.
10. Develop a sound plan of equity financing for a cooperative of your choosing.

SELECTED REFERENCES

1. Antonides, R. J., *Financing Cooperatives with Revolving Funds,* S.D. Agr. Exp. Sta. Cir. 150, Brookings, S.D. Feb. 1954.

---

[9]Howland, A., *American Cooperation,* A.I.C., Washington, D.C. 1952. pp. 802-803.

2. Heitz, Glenn, *Will Farmers Invest Enough in Co-ops?* FCS Cir. A-31, Washington, D.C. Jan. 1961.

3. Henning, G. F. and M. Burkes, *Changes in the Financial Structure of Agricultural Business Organizations*, Ohio Agr. Exp. Sta. Bul. 952, Wooster, Ohio. Oct. 1963.

4. Hulbert, H. H. and others, *Revolving Fund Method of Financing Farmer Cooperatives*, FCS Gen. Rept. 41, USDA, Washington, D.C. Mar. 1958.

5. Manuel, M. L., *Financing Kansas Farmer Cooperatives*, Kans. Agr. Exp. Sta. Bul. 337, Manhattan, Kans. July 1956.

6. Miller, S. B.,"*How We Finance*," *American Cooperation*, A.I.C., Washington, D.C. 1955. pp. 159-166.

7. Staff, *Financing Farmer Cooperatives*, FCS Cir. 5, Washington, D.C. Sept. 1957.

8. Staff, "Special Financing Issue," *News For Farmer Cooperatives*, FCS, USDA, Washington, D.C. Apr. 1959.

9. Stokdyk, E. A., *Financial Structure and Policies of Cooperatives*, A.I.C. Washington, D.C. 1945.

10. Van Hemert, Purl, "Permanent Capital Financing for Co-ops," *American Cooperation*, A.I.C. Washington, D.C. 1956. pp. 352-355.

11. Zeddies, M. D., "Pay-as-You-Go Plan," Insurance-Finance Conference, Cooperative League, Chicago, Ill. 1963.

CHAPTER 14 –

Cooperatives and
Borrowed Capital

First you must give a little water to the pump. You may thereafter have all the water you want.

—*Benjamin Franklin*

FOR MOST types of cooperatives (excluding service cooperatives), a good guideline to use in capitalizing is as follows: (1) The membership should subscribe initially at least 50 percent of the fixed capital required. (2) The membership should provide all the operating capital needed by the cooperative at its lowest point in business volume.

With this guideline, the co-op management may approach financial institutions and other sources for borrowed funds.

SOURCES OF BORROWED CAPITAL

For farmer cooperatives, the Farmer Cooperative Service reports that the banks for farmer cooperatives supply 57.8 percent of their credit needs; certificates of indebtedness, 16.5 percent; commercial banks, 10.3 percent; insurance companies, 4.7 percent; individuals, 4.0 percent; co-op regionals, 2.8 percent; miscellaneous sources, 2.3 percent; and trade credit furnishes 1.6 percent.

Other types of cooperatives may use various government credit sources, banks, other financial institutions and trade sources.

The subsequent discussion of sources of borrowed capital is divided into three categories: (1) financial instrumentalities of the government, (2) cooperative, self-help programs and (3) general credit and capital agencies. In addition, ways and means of conserving capital are discussed.

FINANCIAL INSTRUMENTALITIES
OF GOVERNMENT

Banks for Farmer Cooperatives

There are 12 banks for farmer cooperatives in the United States and one central bank in Washington, D.C. The location of these banks and areas served correspond with the farm credit districts and are as follows:

1. Springfield Bank for Cooperatives
   Springfield, Massachusetts

   Maine, New Hampshire, Vermont, Massachusetts, Rhode Island, Connecticut, New York and New Jersey

2. Baltimore Bank for Cooperatives
   Baltimore, Maryland

   Pennsylvania, West Virginia, Virginia, Delaware, Maryland, the District of Columbia and Puerto Rico

3. Columbia Bank for Cooperatives
   Columbia, South Carolina

   North and South Carolina, Georgia and Florida

4. Louisville Bank for Cooperatives
   Louisville, Kentucky

   Tennessee, Kentucky, Indiana and Ohio

5. New Orleans Bank for Cooperatives
   New Orleans, Louisiana

   Louisiana, Mississippi and Alabama

6. St. Louis Bank for Cooperatives
   St. Louis, Missouri

   Illinois, Missouri and Arkansas

7. St. Paul Bank for Cooperatives
   St. Paul, Minnesota

   North Dakota, Minnesota, Wisconsin and Michigan

8. Omaha Bank for Cooperatives
   Omaha, Nebraska

   South Dakota, Wyoming, Nebraska and Iowa

9. Wichita Bank for Cooperatives
   Wichita, Kansas

   Kansas, Oklahoma, Colorado and New Mexico

10. Houston Bank for Cooperatives
     Houston, Texas

     Texas

11. Berkeley Bank for Cooperatives
     Berkeley, California

     California, Nevada, Utah, Arizona and Hawaii

12. Spokane Bank for Cooperatives
     Spokane, Washington

     Washington, Montana, Oregon, Idaho and Alaska

The banks were established in 1933 to provide a permanent source of credit, on a sound business basis, for farmers' co-op associations engaged in marketing farm products, purchasing farm supplies and furnishing farm business services. Funds loaned by the banks in addition to their capital come from several sources. The banks sell consolidated debentures—short-term bonds—to the investing public. They also borrow from commercial banks and the federal intermediate credit banks.

These banks are themselves true cooperatives. An association borrowing from a bank for cooperatives has an interest in the capital of

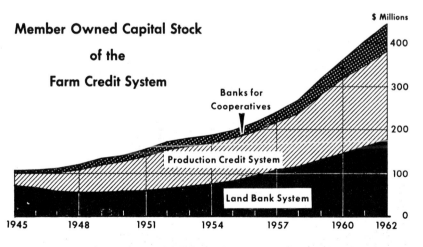

FIGURE 14-1

Cooperatives borrowing from the banks for farmer cooperatives are steadily buying-out the original government capital. (Courtesy, Farm Credit Administration, Washington, D.C.)

the bank. This interest is evidenced by ownership of capital stock or payments into the bank's guaranty fund.

Each borrowing cooperative must own at least one share of class C stock in the bank. In addition, the association is required to invest quarterly in class C stock in proportion to the amount of interest it owes the bank for the calendar quarter. The stock is paid for quarterly or on the interest payment date in the loan agreement. Any farmer cooperative or individual may also buy the bank's class B stock. Class B stock is an investment stock. Dividends are paid only on class B stock.

After paying dividends on class B stock and a franchise tax to the government, a bank shall pay patronage refunds in Class C stock. Patronage refunds are allocated to each cooperative in proportion to the interest it pays during the year.

The Farm Credit Act of 1933, amended in 1955, provides for eventual retirement of government capital and ultimate ownership of the bank by its borrowers.

After a bank has repaid all its government-owned stock (class A) and built sufficient capital to meet its needs, it may start repaying its oldest class B and C stock. It is estimated that by 1975, most of the cooperatives' bank stock will be owned by farmer cooperatives, and the federal government will have been retired from bank ownership.

The banks for cooperatives extend three types of loans.

Physical Facility.—These loans are made for the purpose of financing or refinancing the acquisition of land, buildings and plant equipment. The security generally consists of a first mortgage on the facilities, but it could be other collateral. Loans on such facilities may not exceed 60 percent of the bank's appraisal. Loans generally mature within 10 years or less, with annual or monthly repayments. The law does allow 20-year loans, however.

Operating Loans.—These loans are short- or medium-term loans. The short-term loans are repayable during an operating season and may be secured or unsecured depending upon the circumstances. Medium-term loans generally carry a three-year maturity and are usually secured. The amount loaned depends on the cooperative's financial condition, management and ability to repay.

Commodity Loans.—These loans are for a very short term. They are made on the security of staple commodities (cotton, sugar, rice, grain, etc.) usually over the normal marketing season. Each loan is secured by a first lien on commodities. A commodity loan cannot exceed 75 percent of the net value of unhedged commodities or 90 percent of the net value of hedged commodities.

Interest rates differ depending upon the type of loan. Commodity loans carry the lowest interest rate, operating capital loans the next highest rate and facility loans the highest rate.

Eligibility to Borrow.—To be eligible to borrow from a bank for cooperatives, a cooperative must be an association in which farmers act together in:

1. Processing, preparing for market, handling or marketing farm products.

2. Purchasing, testing, grading, processing, distributing or furnishing farm supplies.

3. Furnishing farm business services.

Associations performing a combination of two or more of these services are also eligible.

It is also necessary that an association be operated for the mutual benefit of its members and not do more business with nonmembers than with members. In an association eligible to borrow, no member may have more than one vote, or else dividends on its stock or membership capital must be limited to 8 percent a year. A further requirement is that at least 90 percent of the voting rights of a cooperative must be held by either farmer-members or by associations owned and controlled by farmers.

In the case of farmers' mutual fire insurance companies, at least 75 percent of the voting control must be held by their producer-members.

In summary, the banks for cooperatives consider these factors in granting a farmer co-op loan:

1. Evidence of the economic need for a cooperative.

2. Existence of sufficient volume to assure successful operation.

3. Quality of membership (stability, leadership, cohesion, etc.).

4. Market outlet or sources of supply.

5. Facilities needed, if any, and cost.

6. Capital requirements and source of capital, including amount contributed by members.

7. Determination that the cooperative is a legal cooperative and that its organization papers will permit the operation on a sound co-op basis.

8. Management capability.

9. Collateral offered as security for the loan.

FIGURE 14-2

The Bureau of Indian Affairs makes loans to cooperatives comprised of Indians, Eskimos or Aleuts. (Courtesy, Arizona Highways, Phoenix, Ariz.)

10. Financial strength of the cooperative.

11. Competitive and economic factors (both short- and long-range).

For more details concerning loans through the banks for cooperatives, contact the appropriate district bank.

Bureau of Fisheries

The Bureau of Fisheries in the Department of Interior is empowered to make loans to fishery marketing cooperatives engaged in marketing all catches of fish or shellfish by their members pursuant to contractual or other enforceable arrangements which grant the cooperatives the right to exercise full control over the conditions of sale of all such catches and to disburse the proceeds from all such sales.

The loans may be used for the operation, maintenance and repair of fishing gear and vessels. They carry a 5 percent rate of interest and cannot exceed a period of 10 years. All loan applications are processed through the Bureau of Fisheries in Washington, D.C.

FIGURE 14-3

The Bureau of Reclamation makes loans to certain co-op associations for irrigation and soil conserving purposes. (Courtesy, Bureau of Reclamation, Department of the Interior, Washington, D.C.)

Bureau of Indian Affairs

Indians, Eskimos and Aleuts, through their cooperatives, may borrow funds from the Bureau of Indian Affairs.

The reason for these loans is to encourage industry and income-producing enterprises and for the education of Indians needing funds for that purpose. Interest rates are 5 percent on loans to co-op associations.

Bureau of Reclamation

Loans and grants up to a maximum of $5 million are made by the Bureau of Reclamation to certain types of organizations for the development of small reclamation projects in the 17 western states. Such projects must be primarily for irrigation, including drainage, but may include as incidental purposes: commercial power, flood control and fish and wildlife conservation.

Loans are also made for certain purposes in connection with federal reclamation projects.

Farmers Home Administration

Water development and soil conservation loans are made to

eligible groups of farmers and rural residents to develop water supply systems for irrigation, household and livestock use; to drain farm land; to carry out soil conservation measures; and to shift land use to grazing, forestry and recreation. Each loan is scheduled for repayment in accordance with the borrower's ability to repay over a period not exceeding 40 years. The interest rate varies between 4½ and 5 percent depending on the type of loan. An association's total indebtedness cannot exceed $500,000 when the loan is made from appropriated funds and $1,000,000 when made from insured funds.

Watershed loans are made to local organizations to help finance projects that protect and develop land and water resources in small watersheds. Loans are made only under watershed plans approved by the Soil Conservation Service and, under certain conditions, by Congress. Eligible local organizations include soil conservation districts, irrigation districts, drainage districts, flood prevention and control districts, municipal corporations, nonprofit irrigation or reservoir companies, mutual water companies, water users' associations and similar organizations. Funds may be advanced to pay the applicant's share of the cost of flood control dams and reservoirs, water supply reservoirs, rural water supply distribution systems, diversion dams, irrigation canals, drainage facilities, easements and for similar purposes. Loans are repayable over periods up to 50 years. The interest rate is around 2.7 percent and is set at the beginning of each fiscal year and applies to all watershed loans made during the year. Once the interest rate is set on a loan, it will not change during the life of that loan.

Rural consumer cooperatives and other rural nonprofit associations may also borrow funds from the Farmers Home Administration to build rental housing for older people. This program is limited to rural areas and towns of up to 2,500 population. Insured loans may be made to individual farmers, groups of farmers and public or private nonprofit organizations to finance housing facilities for domestic farm labor.

Federal Home Loan Banks

Under the supervision of the Home Loan Bank Board, 11 district federal home loan banks fulfill the reserve credit needs of some 4,600 member savings and loan associations and co-op banks. The funds of these district banks come largely from their capital (which is owned by the member institutions), the sale of obligations in the market and deposits of excess cash of their members. The district banks lend only to their member institutions to meet the seasonal and emergency credit requirements of these institutions and to maintain an adequate flow of home loan funds in every state.

Long-term loans (up to 10 years) of member institutions of the Federal Home Loan Bank System are secured by either home mortgages or government bonds. Short-term loans for periods up to one year may be so secured or simply unsecured. Interest rates vary in the district banks.

Federal Housing Administration

The Federal Housing Administration operates the programs of insurance authorized by the National Housing Act. These programs provide against loss on specific types of loans made by private lending institutions for housing purposes. The premium charge for this insurance is about 0.6 percent annually on the unpaid balance. FHA does not lend money, and it does not plan or build housing. It does, however, approve the lending institutions which can make the various types of loans that it insures. Although the general term of a loan is a matter to be decided by the lending institution, FHA must approve specific items, such as the maximum interest rate permitted, amount of down-payment and amortization period, among others.

Co-op housing associations may qualify under Sections 207, 213 and 231 of the Housing Acts.

Rural Areas Development and
Area Redevelopment Administration

The Area Redevelopment Administration (ARA) was established by Public Law 87-27, signed on May 1, 1961. The ARA program provides financing, technical assistance and retraining to create jobs in rural and urban areas of greatest need. The ARA program is administered by the Department of Commerce.

The Office of Rural Areas Development (RAD), under the delegated authority of the Area Redevelopment Administration, is in the Department of Agriculture and has prime responsibility of reviewing and recommending to the Department of Commerce approval of overall economic development programs from designated rural areas, as well as reviewing and recommending approval of projects in rural areas for ARA assistance.

The work of the Office of Rural Areas Development is under the supervision of the Director of Agricultural Credit and is guided by a Department RAD board, made up of representatives from each Agriculture agency. The Director of RAD serves as Board Secretary. The actions of RAD are further guided by a 34-member public advisory committee on rural areas development, which meets periodically.

Farmer cooperatives needing assistance under ARA must apply under RAD starting at the local committee level, then proceeding to the state and then to the federal level.

Nonfarm and urban business cooperatives are likewise eligible for ARA assistance if the purpose of their loans conforms with an area's overall economic development plan. Congressional appropriations may vary from year to year, however.

Rural Electrification Administration

The REA offers loans for two purposes: (1) to finance the construction of electric power lines and other facilities to provide electric service to unserved people in rural areas and (2) to finance the improvement and extension of telephone lines and other facilities in rural areas. Loans are made for a maximum period of 35 years, at 2-percent interest. The long-term electric loans are available to non-profit cooperatives, to power districts and other public agencies and to electric companies. Telephone loans are available to telephone companies and to nonprofit cooperatives and mutual associations.

In limited cases, the REA may make loans to electric cooperatives to aid rural development.

Small Business Administration

The business loan program of the Small Business Administration is expressly designed to assist small enterprises—manufacturers, wholesalers, retailers, service establishments and other businesses—which are independently owned and operated and not dominant in their fields. SBA's business loans enable small business concerns to finance construction, conversion or expansion; to purchase equipment, facilities, machinery, supplies or materials; and to acquire working capital.

Generally, the SBA loan program is designed for small businesses that are unable to obtain from private sources the intermediate and long-term credit required for general purposes and normal growth. In addition to the fundamental requirements for government loans

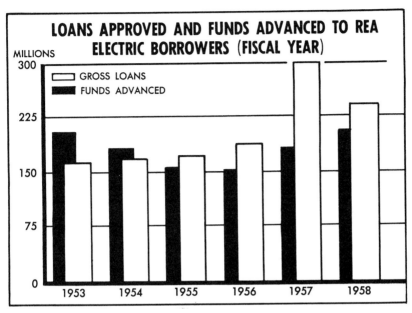

FIGURE 14-4
(Courtesy, USDA, Washington, D.C.)

previously outlined, an applicant for an SBA loan must also meet these other requisites:

1. The applicant must be of good character.

2. He must show evidence of ability to operate his business successfully.

3. He must have enough capital in the business so that with the SBA loan it will be possible to operate on a sound financial basis.

4. On a term loan—one repayable in installments over a period of several years—the past record and future prospects of the business must show sufficient probable future income to provide reasonable assurance of repayment. It is necessary that the loan be adequately secured by real estate, chattel mortgages or other suitable collateral.

The SBA makes several different types of loans:

1. *Bank Participation Loans.*—Through its bank participation plan, SBA cooperates with private lending institutions in meeting the credit needs of small firms. Often a bank is willing to make a loan to a small firm if SBA participates in it, i.e., purchases (immediate participation) or agrees to purchase on demand (deferred participation) a

share of it. SBA may participate in up to 90 percent of the amount of the loan. This participation may be immediate or deferred, as the bank may elect. The agency cannot enter into an immediate participation, however, if a deferred participation is available.

The maximum SBA share in a bank participation loan to any one borrower is $350,000. Exceptions to the $350,000 limitation are loans made to corporations formed by "pools" or groups of small business concerns (cooperatives) (a) to obtain raw materials, equipment, inventory or supplies for use by members of the group, or (b) to obtain the benefits of research and development for the members of the group, or (c) to establish facilities for such purposes. The maximum pool loan is $250,000 multiplied by the number of small firms which have formed and capitalized the pool corporation. (The interest rate on pool loans is 5 percent on the share which the SBA has provided.) Retailer-owned wholesale cooperatives have used this approach in obtaining short- to intermediate-term credit.

2. *Direct Loans.*—Where a private lending institution will not make the full loan and will not participate, SBA may make a direct loan. Terms for direct loans, including repayment, maturity, interest and amount, are the same as the bank participation terms. Similarly, applications for direct loans should be filed at the SBA's field offices.

3. *Disaster Loans.*—Various types of disaster loans are available to cooperatives and others that have suffered physical damage from floods, hurricanes, etc.

4. *Development Company Loans.*—The Small Business Investment Act, as amended, authorizes the SBA to make long-term loans to state and local development companies to help them assist small businesses in their areas. Twenty-year, 5-percent interest loans may be made to state development companies under Section 501 of the Act; 10-year, 5½-percent interest loans may be made to both state and local development companies under Section 502.

Farmer cooperatives which are not able to finance through the banks for cooperatives may apply for SBA loans. Other cooperatives are more eligible for SBA loans than are farmer cooperatives. Details on SBA loans are available from district field offices and from the SBA, Washington, D. C.

State Co-op Finance Agencies

Some states have loan programs designed to help agricultural marketing associations, especially in building and equipping processing and handling facilities. However, these loan agencies usually supplement funds otherwise loaned by the banks for cooperatives and other agencies.

TABLE 14-1
Government Instrumentalities Extending Credit to Cooperatives, by Types, U.S.A.

Instrumentality	Types of Cooperatives Served	Types of Loans
Banks for Farmer Cooperatives	Farm purchasing, marketing and service	Facility, commodity and operating
Bureau of Fisheries	Fishery	Operating
Bureau of Indian Affairs	American Indian primarily	Direct enterprise
Bureau of Reclamation	Irrigation	Irrigation primarily
Farmers Home Administration	(a) Farm, irrigation and soil conservation districts	(a) Water development, soil conservation and related purposes
	(b) Rural, nonfarm	(b) Housing for elderly and domestic farm labor
Federal Home Loan Banks	Savings and loan associations and co-op banks	Seasonal and emergency loans
Federal Housing Administration[1]	Housing[1]	Long-term housing[1]
Rural Areas Development[2] and Area Redevelopment Administration[3]	Farm and nonfarm business	Facility and equipment
Rural Electrification Administration	Rural electric and telephone	Facility primarily
Small Business Administration[4]	Farm and nonfarm business[5]	Vary with class of loan
Small Business Investment Companies	Nonfarm primarily	Equity and long-term
State Cooperative Finance Agencies	Farmer cooperatives primarily	Facility primarily.

[1]FHA does not loan funds; it guarantees from loss loans made by approved lenders.
[2]RAD is a coordinating office for ARA loans within the Department of Agriculture.
[3]ARA is the overall agency charged with making economic development loans and is located in the Department of Commerce.
[4]SBA regulations on loans to cooperatives are not precise. Each loan application is considered on the circumstances peculiar to the loan and the corporate structure of the party or parties to the loan.
[5]Consumer cooperatives ordinarily do not qualify for SBA loans.

COOPERATIVE, SELF-HELP PROGRAMS
Certificates of Indebtedness

Certificates of indebtedness represent a type of borrowed capital frequently used in cooperatives. They draw a fixed annual interest rate. They usually carry a due or repayment date ranging from 5 to 25 years from the date of issue. They may be held by nonmembers as well as members. When they have a due date, indebtedness certificates are a *liability* rather than part of the *net worth* structure. For nonexempt farmer cooperatives, interest paid on these certificates is tax deductible, while interest paid on permanent capital would be taxed to the cooperatives.

Certificates of Participation

These are actually certificates of indebtedness carrying with them preferred patronage rights to purchase fixed amounts of the products of the corporation. They differ from stock in every particular that certificates of indebtedness differ therefrom; the interest payable upon the certificates of participation is deductible as a part of the cost of doing business, and yet the certificates may carry with them preferred patronage rights to the same extent as stock. This means that holders of certificates of participation will have no vote in the business of the company but will be patrons on the same basis as stockholders, will have preferred patronage rights and will receive patronage refunds at the end of the fiscal accounting period. This carries with it the advantage to the investors of an agreed contractual payment of interest, with all the rights of stock ownership except voting, and carries the advantage to the corporation that the return in the form of interest paid upon these certificates is deductible as a cost of doing business.[1]

Co-op Credit Corporations

Some grocery wholesale and other cooperatives have formed financing subsidiaries to lend funds to member firms for short- and long-term purposes in building new stores or remodeling old ones and for fixtures and inventories. A subsidiary corporation is a corporation organized, owned and controlled, either directly or through trustees, by a parent corporation for the purpose of taking over certain duties and certain functions of the parent company. Although the subsidiary may appear as a department or branch or agency, it is a legal entity distinct from its parent.

There are a number of reasons for establishing subsidiary finance

---

[1]Satterfield, J. C., "The Co-op in Our Free Enterprise System," N.C.F.C. Meeting, New Orleans, La. Jan. 10, 1961.

corporations: (1) to provide a means of financing fixed capital investments, particularly in nonstock organizations; (2) to establish credit corporations for the sake of financing the production and marketing of growers' crops; (3) to limit the legal and financial liability of the cooperatives in certain marketing ventures.[2]

Co-op Mutual Funds

There exists a Co-op Mutual Fund organization which obtains its funds from sale of shares to member investors. The Fund invests part of its shareholders' money in profit-type corporations and part in cooperatives and federal government obligations. While local cooperatives are not ordinarily subjects of its investment, regional or statewide cooperatives are.[3]

Individuals

Cooperatives may borrow money from their own members and nonmembers by executing a promissory note payable with interest to the holder at some future date. In some cases, individuals will loan money to their cooperatives interest free, usually in small, local cooperatives.

Interco-op Loans

Local credit unions often borrow from other credit unions in the same trade area. For example, a credit union at a university may loan large sums to its faculty and staff in the summer and thereby exhaust its funds, while a trade union credit cooperative may have large sums on hand at that time of year. They borrow and lend funds to each other on a short-term basis.

Farmer cooperatives do not use interco-op loans so much because of the availability of funds from the banks for cooperatives.

Joint Ventures

Joint venture financing is becoming more important in cooperatives and other businesses. Where expensive facilities and high risk enterprises prevail, several cooperatives (and profit-type corporations) may come together and pool their risks and investments.

---

[2]Bakken, H. H. and M. A. Schaars, *Economics of Cooperative Marketing*, McGraw-Hill, New York, N.Y. 1937. p. 406.
[3]Fullerton, C. W., "Proposed Fifty States Mutual Fund," N.C.F.C. Meeting, New Orleans, La. Jan. 11, 1961.

In other cases, joint account dealings are prevalent. Wholesale produce houses, cotton oil mills and other similar business will advance funds to local cooperatives to purchase patrons' commodities. This lessens the cooperatives' need for operating capital.

In still other instances, processors and manufacturers may purchase and hold nonvoting preferred stock and capital certificates in a cooperative to obtain preference in procuring raw products.

Regional Cooperatives

Regional cooperatives may help finance their local retail affiliates. Such financing provides for inventories, expenses and, occasionally, facilities. Regional cooperatives are instrumental in providing funds which the local cooperatives use in extending credit to patrons. Under such an arrangement, the regional wholesale cooperative obtains funds on its own security from banks for cooperatives or commercial banks and uses these funds to advance operating capital to locals, with interest charged on the monthly balance outstanding. Operation of this financing service is usually performed by a department of the wholesale cooperative. The department must keep close check on operations of its borrowing locals, on their use of funds for inventory and open account credit and on the locals' potential loan security. In most cases, such locals are also under management or supervisory contracts with their regional cooperatives.

This type of arrangement is most adaptable to regionals where a uniform operating procedure is followed, where management of locals is regionally supervised and where audits of locals are made by the regionals.

Short-term Notes

Some cooperatives, especially those in wealthy areas, will issue 9-month notes bearing 4 percent interest in order to finance their seasonal operations. This gives patrons an opportunity to invest their surplus funds after the harvest season and until funds are needed by them for a new crop year.

Union and Bank Centrals

In some states, the credit unions set up a central credit union which receives deposits from some unions and lends to others. This type of operation strengthens all credit unions.

Mutual savings banks use somewhat the same approach. In the event that sufficient funds are not available locally to establish a mutual savings bank to fill the thrift and home financing needs of their town or city, citizens may apply for assistance from the Central Industry Fund, organized by the National Association of Mutual Savings Banks. One of the basic purposes of the Central Industry Fund is to extend the mutual savings bank system by aiding in the organization of new mutual savings banks. Depending on circumstances, the Central Industry Fund may lend to the new bank a part of the money required for the initial guaranty fund. This aid supplements the efforts of local residents. Technical assistance also is available.

There have been attempts in Congress to permit credit unions, especially, to develop a central banking system. So far, Congress has failed to act on such requests.

A third method of obtaining borrowed capital is for cooperatives to rely on general credit and capital fund agencies considered next.

GENERAL CREDIT AND CAPITAL AGENCIES

Bonds

Bonds are of three types: mortgage, income and debenture. A *mortgage bond* has definite security behind it, and a default on the interest can, generally speaking, permit the seizure of the security to satisfy the claim.

An *income bond* earns interest only if the company earnings are sufficient, and in case of interest default no legal action is forthcoming against the company.

A *debenture bond* has no mortgage security and merely constitutes a claim against the property and income of the corporation secondary to that of any outstanding mortgage bond. Its claim is, however, prior to that of preferred stock. The debenture is often regarded as identical with an income bond; but the distinguishing characteristic of the latter form of obligation is that in the event income is not earned, it does not carry over as an obligation to be met subsequently. For nonexempt farmer cooperatives, debentures are a good method of financing because the interest paid is tax deductible, while interest paid on equity capital is not.

Commercial Banks

Many cooperatives prefer to deal with commercial banks because of their flexibility in meeting credit needs. Local bankers usually know the co-op board of directors and are familiar with the local economic conditions. One obstacle in dealing with some commercial banks is their reluctance to distinguish a cooperative from a profit-type corporation.

In the case of new cooperatives with limited net worths, banks may require directors, and occasionally other members or the manager, to assign their personal signatures to notes and mortgages. Anyone signing such a note or mortgage, except as an authorized officer or agent of the association, is personally liable for the amount which the association might fail to pay when due, including unpaid interest. Personal indorsement of loans has been particularly frequent among newly organized local associations. It is not only an undesirable business practice, but if such a procedure is necessary even for a new association, it indicates unsound financing on the part of the cooperative.

A much better practice is for the directors of the association to authorize one or more of its officers, such as the president and secretary or treasurer, by a motion or resolution, to borrow money on behalf of the association for a specific purpose and not in excess of a stated amount. The designated officers should then negotiate for the loan on behalf of the association and sign only as officers of the association. In this way, no individual can be held personally liable for the payment of the loan.

Commercial bank financing constitutes a significant part of all co-op borrowings. Banks provide short-term to intermediate-term financing for receivables, inventories, equipment and other similar requirements.

Factoring

One source of cash that is sometimes overlooked is the "factor." The factor (a private individual or organization) buys accounts receivable (minus a flat commission charge) for cash rather than lending money against receivables used as security. As a rule, he takes on the responsibility of collecting from the customers under a nonrecourse agreement. Usually, but not always, customers are notified that such an arrangement has been entered into. Firms use factoring as a method of raising money when they are short of cash because customers have not yet paid their bills (due dates may be 30, 60, even 90 days in the future), but meanwhile there is a need to meet current bills, step up production or expand facilities. Incidentally, the factor often provides management and financial advice in addition to providing cash.

Some factors will go even further and finance inventories, payrolls, etc. In other words, they will furnish working capital for the client. There are two basic charges. One is the charge for services performed, such as credit checking, credit guaranty, collection work, etc. The other charge is the interest on the amount of money borrowed by the client. Here again, the needs of the particular enterprise will determine whether or not this type of financing is the logical one to be used.

Insurance Companies

Some insurance companies have provided long-term credit to cooperatives for land and fixed facilities. This has not been too widespread, however. Some mutual and co-op insurance companies are more interested in this type of program than are other insurance companies.

Security Markets

Cooperatives do not float stock on stock exchanges. This is because common stock or membership fees in cooperatives cannot be sold or transferred at will. The board of directors controls the issuance, transfer and retirement of co-op stock or membership fees. Also, co-op stock is not speculative and draws a fixed rate of interest. Patronage, rather than stock investment, is the key to co-op success.

However, there is a possibility that nonvoting preferred stock or other nonvoting securities of cooperatives could be publicly traded on a securities exchange. This is discussed further in the latter part of the next chapter.

Specialized Finance Companies

Many equipment manufacturers and others specializing in expensive machinery and installations have their own financing subsidiaries. Cooperatives often obtain financing with them, especially the nonfarm cooperatives.

Other types of specialized finance companies arrange loans on the existing plant facilities, inventories and, in some cases, on real estate. A line of credit repayable over a period of years may be arranged. Usually, minimum-sized loans are stipulated to reduce overhead costs of the lending company.

Trade Credit

Many types of cooperatives are extended credit by their suppliers and/or marketing agencies. Extension of trade credit is stimulated by the present-day business and social emphasis on production, the strong buyers' market and the necessity for an ever-increasing investment in equipment resulting from new technology. It has become necessary for trade suppliers to sell financing along with their products.

While most of the credit extended to small businesses by trade suppliers is short- or intermediate-term credit, the financing subsidiaries of certain manufacturers are providing their customers with much long-term credit.

The borrowing cooperatives may profit greatly from the supplier's technical and management assistance, and they may enjoy an elasticity of credit terms which is valuable when times become adverse. On the other hand, cooperatives may become more and more captive customers as credit extended is expanded and as the financing shifts from the short-term to the long-term. Under such circumstances, the real cost of the credit may become very high.

PREPARING TO BORROW MONEY

The following steps are necessary if the co-op management is preparing to borrow money:

1. Analyze the credit policy of the lender.
2. Prepare a list of accounts receivables on an aged-basis.
3. Have inventories verified and aged, and establish the turn-over rate.
4. Outline the wage, salary and employee training programs.
5. Outline the management training program.
6. Assemble minutes of board meetings and committee reports.
7. Provide an audited report of the previous fiscal year's operation as well as the current monthly operating statement and balance sheet.
8. Provide a summary of the cooperative's operation over the last few years, indicating trends in business volume, membership, etc.
9. Provide a biography of the board members and top management personnel.

10. Provide the lender with any additional documents or reports he may request.

METHODS OF CONSERVING CAPITAL

In addition to borrowings and equity capitalization, there are several techniques available which may conserve capital requirements, when properly managed.

BAWI Bond Programs

In many states, balance-agriculture-with-industry (BAWI) programs involve local counties which pass bond issues secured by property taxes to construct agribusiness-type plants, such as poultry processing, milk manufacturing, etc. A cooperative leases the facilities, and by rental payments it retires the bonds and may subsequently acquire the property, if the state law so permits. If it does not, the county continues to own the plant. Because such plants are owned by the county, no property taxes are assessed thereon.

Mississippi has used the BAWI program to excellent advantage. Over $95 million in land, factories and equipment has been floated since 1936 in that state. Many other states have similar programs.

Consignments

Some supply and retail cooperatives use consignments in order to conserve operating capital. Consignments consist of merchandise left by the supplier to be paid for as sold, with remaining stocks returned after a certain period of time.

Customer Pre-payments

Some cooperatives successfully engineer a policy of having their patron-customers prepay bills or accounts, sometimes up to several months in advance. The cooperatives pay interest on this money, and as the customer purchases goods his account is debited. There is a simultaneous advantage for the patrons (interest on surplus funds) and the cooperatives (lowered cost of borrowed capital).

Retailer-owned wholesale cooperatives may require member stores to deposit certain sums of money when joining. This helps a wholesale with its capital problem and encourages member stores to patronize the wholesale.

Lease-back Arrangements

An example of a co-op corporation engaged in lease-back arrangements is the M-C-M Corporation, a real estate holding and development corporation. The aim and purpose of the corporation is to develop, own and control real estate and to lease and sell this property to co-op organizations for their possession and use in their undertakings:

> "M-C-M Corporation" buys or builds facilities needed by local cooperatives. These facilities then are rented to the local associations.
>
> Sometimes M-C-M buys facilities the local association already owns and then leases these facilities back to the cooperative on a long-term basis or from 10 to 20 years. The local co-op may re-lease or buy them back when the lease expires. Rentals remain constant during the lease. Locals may be expected to provide about 25 percent of the facility capital. This arrangement provides the local cooperatives with needed facilities and at the same time releases some of their capital for current operations.
>
> A few of the more important benefits of the corporation are: (1) The local cooperative controls its property under a long-term lease; (2) the burden to the co-op of real estate investments is substantially eased; (3) it has more funds for working capital; (4) through their own and other insurance companies, cooperatives come closer to the money market that is anxious to make long-term loans on income-producing properties; (5) because both are liable on the same lease, the local and the regional become better integrated.[4]

Sometimes, profit-type corporations will build and then lease facilities to a cooperative on a straight rental basis or on a lease-purchase plan.

Members' Holding Company

In some areas, especially in the western United States, a group of farmers may form a holding company to construct and own the facilities used by a local cooperative. The local cooperative makes rental payments as part of its operating costs. Patrons, therefore, can enjoy the advantages of a co-op cotton gin, for example, with a minimum of capital investment on their part.

---

[4]Zeddies, M. D., "M-C-M Sell or Lease Plan," *News for Farmer Cooperatives*, FCS, USDA, Washington, D.C. Apr. 1959. pp. 5 and 17.

As mentioned previously, regional cooperatives, which sometimes can raise capital more easily than locals, often build facilities and lease them to locals. This permits the locals to use their limited funds for working capital.

Renting Facilities and Equipment

In some cases, cooperatives which are short of capital may consider renting certain types of equipment and vehicles. Generally, this is a short-term expedient. In the longer-run, the co-op management should probably endeavor to own equipment and vehicles.

Trade Acceptances

Trade acceptances can be used as a basis for loans when cooperatives need money due on accounts. By discounting trade acceptances at a bank or on the open money market before the due date, cooperatives can obtain liquidity in their accounts receivables, for example.

Trade Discounts

Managers can usually improve the economic position of their cooperatives by taking advantage of various trade discounts. These discounts are given by manufacturers and other suppliers to retail businesses and are expressed as a percentage reduction or a series of percentage reductions, such as 20, 10 and 5 percent from the list price. A special type of trade discount is the *quantity* discount which is used by sellers to encourage customers to buy in larger quantities. There is also the *cash* discount which is a premium given to buyers for settlement of accounts before they are due. The discounts normally offered by sellers are higher than the current rate of interest. Consequently, it is to the cooperative's advantage to pay the invoice even if it must borrow within the discount period to do so.

An example of several cash discounts and their equivalent rates of interest are:

1/10, net 30	18% per year
2/10, net 60	14% per year
2/10, net 30	36% per year
3/10, net 30	54% per year
3/30, net 60	36% per year
2/30, net 60	24% per year
2/15, net 30	48% per year
2/20, net 30	72% per year
2/20, net 60	18% per year

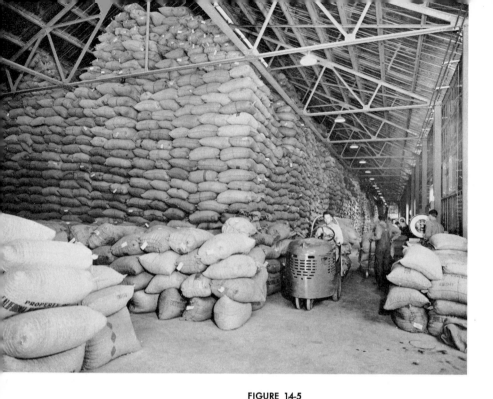

FIGURE 14-5

Warehouse receipts are one means of readily securing bank loans. (Courtesy, California Almond Growers Exchange, Sacramento, Calif.)

Assume that an invoice for $1,000 is dated April 2. It carries terms of 2/10, net 30, one of the common discounts in use today. If the invoice is paid by April 12, deduct 2 percent from the invoice and remit $980. If the invoice is not paid during the discount period, the full amount, $1,000, must be paid.

In effect, therefore, 2 percent can be saved (or $20) by paying 20 days before the due date.

Warehouse Receipts

The United States Warehouse Act authorizes the Secretary of Agriculture to issue a license to a warehouseman if his warehouse is suitable for the proper storage of the particular agricultural product or products for which a license is applied for, and if the warehouseman agrees to comply with the terms of the statute and the regulations thereunder. States also license warehouses.

A warehouse receipt gives all of the information and assurance which a prudent banker would consider in making a loan on the basis of the physical existence of the commodity. It, of course, says nothing regarding the market value of the product, but it becomes a negotiable paper acceptable at banks for a high proportion of the market value of the product stored.

In the grain, cotton and other similar commodity businesses, the commodity held in storage (in a properly bonded and licensed warehouse, etc.) can serve as collateral for loans. As the commodity is moved, the loan is repaid to the lending agency.

In farm supply or retail cooperatives, warehouse receipts are possible. The lending agency will lock and control the warehoused inventory, and as the merchandise is moved to the retail department, that much is paid against the loan by the week or month.

POOLING AND DELAYED SETTLEMENTS

Pooling is one of four methods used by cooperatives in settling for goods delivered to it. The other three are: (1) buying outright for cash, (2) buying on individual account and (3) commission sales. Each of these four methods has a definite effect on a cooperative's operating capital position.

Buying Outright for Cash

The cooperative pays cash and takes title to the products at time of delivery and then sells them in the market. If the association is successful in selling the products at prices above those which were paid for them and high enough to cover all expenses and reserves and still have a net earning, then the net earning may be described as a patronage payment at the end of the accounting period.

Individual Account

Instead of paying cash for products on delivery, some cooperatives, such as the livestock shipping associations, pay the farmers for the products after they have been sold in the market place. The expenses of the local association, transportation costs and terminal market expenses are deducted from the sales value, and the farmer is then given a check covering the remaining value. In this way, the local association does not take title to the products, does not need cash to buy the goods and does not have the financial risk inherent in ownership of the products.

Commission Sales

In the terminal livestock, fruit and vegetable markets, co-op terminal sales agencies handle products on a commission basis. Since there are no contracts between the local associations at country points and the terminal sales agencies, it is the practice for these agencies to handle products for members and nonmembers alike at the usual prevailing commission rates. A sales agency is ordinarily placed on the market by a federation of local associations and individual producers that regularly sell in the market.

Pooling

In selling goods through cooperatives, growers nearly always participate in some sort of pooling arrangement. This may include only a pooling of handling margins, as in the case of sales of cash grain to co-op elevators. Or a grower's lot may be pooled with the production

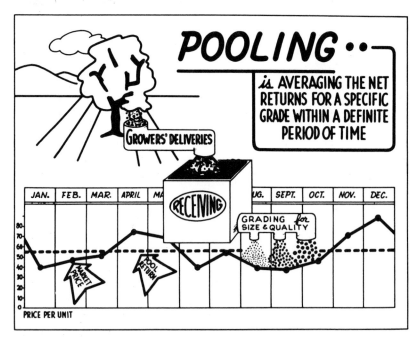

FIGURE 14-6

(Courtesy, Agricultural Council of California, Sacramento, Calif.)

of many other farmers, and at the time of delivery, the grower may receive an advance of a percentage of the basic price of the specific quality delivered. The final price is based on the proceeds of the entire quantity within the pool. In some cooperatives the grower may elect one of a number of different agreements.

Results may, and do, vary from one pool to another and from one season to the next. But the premise of pool marketing is that, on an average, the grower gets all there is between the selling price of the product and the cost of handling and marketing. After growers deliver products to the cooperative and they are pooled, the identity of the individuals' products is lost. Commingling allows the cooperative to operate, merchandise and sell at lower costs.

It is obvious that a "pooling" arrangement lessens the need for capital since the member or patron is advanced only a partial payment. At the end of the pooling period, the patron is paid the balance due him at a rate per unit determined by the success of the "pool."

Other advantages of pooling are: (1) The cooperative is provided increased bargaining power; (2) waste in marketing small, individual lots is eliminated; (3) market risks are spread out; and (4) better merchandising and market expansion is provided. The disadvantages of pooling are: (1) delays in settling with member-patrons; (2) complexity of pools; (3) commingling is sometimes disadvantageous to some patrons; and (4) the possibility of speculative operations.

The principal pooling feature is that of pooling the sales receipts and later distributing these minus the deductions for expenses, reserves and other purposes to the contributors to the pool. In doing this, any one of three distinct practices may be followed:

1. All products, ungraded, may be placed in one pool. The same net average price is paid all members.

2. All products may be graded, yet placed in only one pool. Poolers are paid prices for separate grades on a differential basis.

3. All products may be graded, and each grade, style, variety or class constitutes a separate pool.[5]

Most pooling associations use either (2) or (3). For an example of pooling computations see Table 14-2.

An equitable distribution of sales returns to growers involves at least three essential considerations: (1) pooling on the basis of quality,

---

[5]Bakken and Schaars, *op. cit.* p. 445.

TABLE 14-2
Method of Arriving At Average Pool Prices

Receipts From	Variety A			Variety B		
	Grade X	Grade Y	Grade Z	Fancies	Choice	Fair
	(Pounds)	(Pounds)	(Pounds)	(Pounds)	(Pounds)	(Pounds)
Farmer Jones	100	200	100	—	200	100
Farmer Smith	200	—	300	300	100	200
Farmer Henry	300	500	—	100	500	—
Total	600	700	400	400	800	300
Sales by cooperative....	300 lb. @ 10¢ 200 lb. @ 15¢ 100 lb. @ 20¢	200 lb. @ 8¢ 500 lb. @ 10¢	400 lb. @ 4¢	200 lb. @ 20¢ 100 lb. @ 22¢ 100 lb. @ 24¢	400 lb. @ 18¢ 400 lb. @ 19¢	300 lb. @ 15¢
Total sales	$80.00	$66.00	$16.00	$86.00	$148.00	$45.00
Operating costs— 2 percent of sales...	$ 1.60	$ 1.32	$ 0.32	$ 1.72	$ 2.96	$ 0.90
Net sales	$78.40	$64.68	$15.68	$84.28	$145.04	$44.10
Average price per lb..	13.06¢	9.24¢	3.92¢	21.07¢	18.13¢	14.70¢

Farmer Jones receives:

100 x 13.06¢ =	$13.06
200 x 9.24¢ =	18.48
100 x 3.92¢ =	3.92
200 x 18.13¢ =	36.26
600 lb.	$71.72

Farmer Smith receives:

200 x 13.06¢ =	$ 26.12
300 x 3.92¢ =	11.76
300 x 21.07¢ =	63.21
100 x 18.13¢ =	18.13
100 x 14.70¢ =	14.70
1,000 lb.	$133.92

Farmer Henry receives:

300 x 13.06¢ =	$ 39.18
500 x 9.24¢ =	46.20
100 x 21.07¢ =	21.07
500 x 18.13¢ =	90.65
200 x 14.70¢ =	29.40
1,600 lb.	$226.50

Total received	$441.00
Expenses 2 percent..............	8.82
Net	$432.18
Total paid out..............	$432.14
Difference	+.04

Source: Bakken and Schaars, *op. cit.* p. 448.

(2) pooling time or length of the pooling period and (3) pooling area or the territory to be included in the pool.

1. The aim of pooling by quality should be to reflect back to the individual grower the differentials in price which the market affords for the various grades of his product. The grower who, by better selection of his seed, better cultivation and better harvesting and handling, delivers a superior product for market should have the benefit of a higher market price.

2. The length of a pooling period depends upon the nature of the commodity, patron's needs for money, market institutions and practices, price variations over time, bookkeeping complexities and market demand. As a rule, the more perishable the product, the shorter the pool. The more durable the product, the longer the pool.

In the case of strawberries a daily "pool" may be used. Early berries return more than late berries; thus a short pool rewards growers who endeavor to market berries early. Eggs, fluid milk and potatoes may be on a weekly or semi-monthly pool. Grain, noncitrus fruits and some citrus fruits may be on a seasonal pool. Cotton, wool and tobacco may be on an annual pool.

3. The size of the pooling area will depend upon the homogeny of the product, seasonality of production and particular characteristics of the membership. A pooling area may be classified by individual, local associations, designated production districts or whole production areas. Much depends on the wisdom of the co-op management in allocating pooling areas.[6]

Bakken and Schaars conclude that:

> Generally considered, the pooling of products, expenses and receipts is valid in a cooperative provided the members have approved it in their bylaws or marketing contracts. The contracts usually state whether the products will be pooled and what options are open to the members. Unless an association is given the authority to pool its members' products, it cannot do so legally.[7]

In the next chapter, the matter of extending credit to co-op patrons and other selected financial topics are considered.

---

[6]Staff, *Cooperation*, Wisc. Agr. Exp. Sta., Cir. 420, Madison, Wisc. Chapter 16.
[7]Bakken and Schaars, *op. cit.* p. 460.

TOPICS FOR DISCUSSION

1. Discuss the various sources of borrowed capital available from instrumentalities of government.
2. Discuss the various ways cooperatives can, through self-help programs, obtain borrowed capital.
3. Discuss credit and capital availability from other financial institutions and trade sources.
4. Discuss the various ways cooperatives can conserve capital.
5. Discuss pooling. What are its advantages and disadvantages?

SELECTED REFERENCES

1. Christensen, Chris L., "The Place of Pooling in Cooperative Marketing," *American Cooperation*, A.I.C., Washington, D.C. 1928. pp. 122-134.
2. Dahncke, C. L., "FHA Makes Loan to Grazing Co-op," *News for Farmer Cooperatives*, FCS, USDA, Washington, D.C. Aug. 1963. pp. 13-14.
3. Gile, B. M. and Olin Quinn, *Farmers' Cooperative Credit Institutions*, La. Agr. Exp. Sta. Bul. 470, Baton Rouge, La. Nov. 1952.
4. Markeson, Clyde, *Pooling*, FCS Gen. Rept. 67, Washington, D.C. Dec. 1959.
5. Pursell, A., *Keys to Effective Rural Credit Unions*, FCS Cir. 19, Washington, D.C. Nov. 1961.
6. Smith, Harold T., *Equity and Loan Capital for Small Business*, Upjohn Institute, Kalamazoo, Mich. Nov. 1959.
7. Staff, *Banks for Cooperatives*, FCS, Cir. E-47, Washington, D.C. June 1960.
8. Staff, *Common Sale and Payment Terms*, SBA, Rept. 59, Washington, D.C. Aug. 1960.
9. Staff, *Loans to Farmers' Cooperatives*, FCS, Cir. 6, Washington, D.C. 1956.
10. Stevens, I. M. and J. T. Haas, *Feeder Cattle Pooling*, FCS, Rept. 565, Washington, D.C. Dec. 1962.
11. Stevens, I. M. and J. T. Haas, *Livestock Pooling*, FCS, Rept. 510, Washington, D.C. Dec. 1961.
12. USDA, *Rural Areas Development Handbook*, Agr. Handbook No. 245, Washington, D.C. June 1963.

CHAPTER 15 —

Cooperatives Extending
Credit to Patrons and
Other Financial Topics

If you would know the value of money, go and try to borrow some.
—Benjamin Franklin

*At this time when the chief complaint is that money is so scarce, it must be
an act of kindness to instruct the moneyless how they can reinforce their purses.
I will acquaint all with the true secret of money-catching, the certain way to fill
empty purses and how to keep them always full. Two simple rules well observed
will do the business. First, let honesty and labor be thy constant companions.
Second, spend one penny every day less than thy clear gains. Then shall thy
purses soon begin to thrive, thy creditors will never insult thee, nor want op-
press, nor hunger bite, nor nakedness freeze thee, the whole hemisphere will
shine brighter and pleasure spring up in every corner of thy heart.*
—Benjamin Franklin

EXTENDING CREDIT TO CUSTOMERS

CONSUMER, WHOLESALE, FARM SUPPLY
and other cooperatives are involved in extending credit to their members and, sometimes, to nonmembers. Although cash selling is a basic
Rochdale principle, many cooperatives have abandoned this principle
because credit selling has become such an established and wide-spread
practice in business. Demise of the cash selling principle, while sometimes necessary, is causing many difficulties for cooperatives.

The discussion which follows is based on these principles: (1) that
each cooperative should first attempt to operate on a cash basis, (2)
that each cooperative, if a cash basis is impossible, attempt to interest
existing credit agencies in extending credit and (3) that each cooperative, if (1) or (2) fails, extend credit cautiously and on the basis of
sound policies.

To Sell or Not to Sell on Credit?

Woodcock reports that it may cost cooperatives from 3.8 to 5.4 per-

FIGURE 15-1

Many cooperatives have had to extend credit because their competitors were engaged heavily in this practice. While credit extension by cooperatives is permissible, it should be carefully controlled. (Courtesy, Co-operative Union, Manchester, England)

cent of credit sales to extend credit. This cost averages out to an interest rate of 14 to 20 percent on the money involved.[1]

A major cost of accounts receivable is that they soak up scarce capital often badly needed in other phases of the business. A study by the Farmer Cooperative Service showed that the cost of credit totaled about 2.45 percent of credit sales in the cooperatives studied. The cost breakdown was:

Item	Cost as Percent of Credit Sales
Interest	1.10
Extension	.22
Bookkeeping	.66
Collection	.40
Bad debts	.07
Total	2.45

[1]Woodcock, L. A., *The ABC of Co-op Finance*, Cooperative League, Chicago, Ill. Not dated.

This illustration points out that a credit sale involves a great deal of cost other than just the interest on funds needed to finance the receivables. Even if there were no other costs involved, interest cost alone could slash away a substantial portion of any net margin realized on a credit sale.

To illustrate, let us assume that a $3 net margin (after $1 depreciation) is realized on a $100 credit sale. Assume the interest rate on funds to carry the receivables is 6 percent. The following schedule shows the amount of the $3 net margin which is left when the account is collected in full after different periods of time:

One month	$2.52
Two months	2.04
Three months	1.56
Six months	.12
Nine months	(1.32)
Twelve months	(2.76)

If, as the FCS study indicates, interest cost represents only about one-half of the total cost of extending credit, it is easy to see that money is often lost on a credit sale, even if the original amount of the sale is eventually collected in full. The principal factor which determines the amount of margin or loss is the length of time it takes to collect the account.[2]

Phillips concludes that:

> The total costs of making credit sales include all costs that would not be incurred if all sales were made for cash. They include the alternative opportunity costs of using the money, that is tied up in accounts and notes receivable, for some other purpose in the business. They include the added bookkeeping and administrative costs of credit sales. They include collection costs for such things as preparing and mailing notices, personal calls for collection and occasional legal proceedings. And they include the cost of bad debts that are actually written off.
>
> In order to determine how much credit he should extend, each co-op manager needs to estimate both the dollar benefits and the dollar costs of his credit sales. He can profitably extend credit so long as the total dollar benefits exceed the total dollar costs. But he cannot afford to extend credit to the point where the added costs are greater than the added benefits.[3]

---

[2]Tollefson, M. S., *Accounts Receivable—Their Cost and Control,* Bank for Cooperatives, St. Paul. Minn.
[3]Phillips, R., *Farm Store Merchandising,* Minneapolis, Minn. 1961 reprint.

SHIFTING CREDIT EXTENSION
TO CREDIT AGENCIES

Before cooperatives engage in extending credit to their customers, they should make a determined effort to shift credit extension to credit cooperatives and other agencies qualified to provide this credit. Even if a cooperative extended and made a sufficient charge to cover the costs of handling credit, this would not be the ideal situation because credit institutions can handle this service usually at a lower cost than the average cooperative.

Various co-op and other types of credit institutions are available to extend credit if proper working relations can be developed.

Co-op Credit Corporations

A type of credit organization used by cooperatives and others is the co-op credit corporation. Such corporations are usually organized as subsidiaries and supervised by regional marketing or farm supply cooperatives. Some of them were established by marketing associations before the formation of production credit associations. Most of them serve farmers directly, although some finance local cooperatives which in turn finance sales to patrons.

A credit corporation usually raises original capital through its parent cooperative, but it may also raise it by selling stock to farmers or cooperatives. Credit corporations that finance farmers directly may obtain funds by rediscounting farmers' notes with, or borrowing from, federal intermediate credit banks, or from other sources. Credit corporations that finance local cooperatives may obtain funds by borrowing from banks for cooperatives.

In both types of corporations an interest rate sufficient to cover the cost of borrowed funds plus operating expenses and required reserves is charged the borrower.

Co-op credit corporations operating either as subsidiaries of regional cooperatives or as independent cooperatives are in better position to spread their risks over a wider area and to raise or obtain capital more easily than local cooperatives.

Co-op credit corporations are not restricted to farmers. Feed dealers and other types of agribusiness extending credit to or financing farmers may organize credit corporations and discount farmers' notes through the federal intermediate credit banks. In this sense, co-op farm credit corporations operate similarly to the PCA's.

Credit bureaus organized to assemble credit information on customers in given localities are another type of agency which aids many businesses in reducing the costs of credit. However, these bureaus do not finance.

Production Credit Associations

The PCA's are organized to serve the short-term and intermediate-term credit needs of farmers. PCA's take crop liens and/or chattel mortgages as security for monies loaned, with repayments usually on a seasonal basis. A farmer is required to purchase $5 of stock for each $100 borrowed.

Most members use the associations' "budget" plans. Under these plans, members arrange for loans sufficient to cover financial needs during the entire season. They get the money as needed and repay the loans when they sell their farm products. Farmers do not pay interest on any part of a production credit association loan until the money is received. When a farmer repays any part of his loan, interest charges cease on the amount he repays. Thus, he pays interest on each dollar only for the number of days he uses it. This greatly reduces interest costs on such loans. Some PCA's provide approved credit cards which farmers use in buying supplies from supply stores.

Another service a PCA may render is helping the individual farmer buy capital securities in his cooperative. This helps the cooperative capitalize faster while it helps the PCA provide a full credit line to the farmer.

The manner in which a retail cooperative might tie up with a PCA to reduce accounts receivable held by the cooperative is roughly as follows:

> 1. Patrons secure special loan applications from their local member cooperative. These forms are completed and an estimate is made of the total farm supply purchases that a patron will need during the year. Application is made to the production credit association for a line of credit on behalf of the patron. A single note covering the patron's entire season's needs is executed. When the patron's application has been approved by the production credit association, his over-the-counter line of credit becomes available to him at the supply cooperative.
>
> 2. The cooperative must have and adhere to a definite credit policy; that is, limit its accounts receivable to convenience credit such as from 30 to 60 days.

3. The production credit association agrees to finance members of the cooperative beyond the convenience period if recommended by the farm supply cooperative.

4. The cooperative may guarantee repayment of the producer's loan to a certain extent; guarantee the accounts within certain agreed time limits and/or set up a specific reserve to pay any losses that occur.

5. The patron buys supplies from the cooperative as he needs them, and the cooperative submits the bills to the PCA and is reimbursed for them. The patron makes his payments direct to the PCA. Repayments are geared to the expected farm income of the patron. Simple interest is charged on the unpaid balance only for the number of days the loan is outstanding.

6. The plans provide for mutual exchange of credit information between the cooperative and the production credit association regarding the financial condition of the cooperative and the borrower.[4]

Implementation of these plans does not result in immediately freeing the capital a cooperative may already have invested in accounts receivable; but if properly administered, the plans can prevent the building-up of additional accounts receivable and free capital for other uses as the cooperative collects its outstanding accounts receivable.

Credit Unions

Some farm supply, marketing and consumer cooperatives use credit unions to assist their members with credit needs. A rural credit union can supplement its funds by rediscounting members' notes with the district federal intermediate credit bank. In many ways, a rural credit union operation is similar to a production credit association.

In urban areas, consumer cooperatives may work closely with urban credit unions in helping members finance appliances, repairs and other services. In some of the co-op housing centers, credit unions and consumer stores are located adjacent to or within the center for the convenience of members.

Interest rates vary from one credit union to another and sometimes within the credit union from one type of loan to another. In no case, however, do interest rates exceed 1 percent per month on the balance outstanding.

---

[4]Hulbert, H. H., "Credit Policy," Manager's Workshop, University of Florida, Gainesville, Fla. June 20, 1961.

Various supply and marketing cooperatives are instrumental in helping to organize and house credit unions. In turn, credit unions assist in accumulating savings, extending credit and providing other services. There is a mutuality of interests.

Commercial Banks

Some retail cooperatives work successfully with commercial banks in financing patrons of cooperatives. The critical points in this relationship usually are the willingness of both groups to work together, the interest rates charged by the bank and the character of the credit patron referred to the bank.

Some supply cooperatives and local banks have developed a program to meet more adequately the credit needs of the cooperatives' patrons. Under this arrangement, a farmer estimates his seasonal credit needs. His cooperative prepares a patron's note for a specific amount that is accepted by the bank for servicing and collecting.

The cooperative extends accommodation credit for 30 to 60 days, depending upon its financial strength and credit policy. At the discretion of the association, any balance on the account at the end of this period may be transferred to the bank to be charged against the patron's note. The bank charges interest only for the time the money is used by the patron.

When the cooperative forwards an account to the bank, the bank advances to the association the full amount of the patron's account up to the limit of the note. Such a bank carries notes at regular bank interest rates (around 6 percent), and these notes run from three to nine months.

Under this arrangement, the cooperative guarantees repayment of the note to the bank and so must be cautious in its selection of patrons eligible for notes. This practice has been working satisfactorily.

It is noted that the co-op and bank relationship is similar to the co-op and PCA relationship previously described.

Farmers Home Administration

This agency provides agricultural loans to deserving farm families who are unable to obtain needed credit from conventional private and co-op lenders. Loans are also available to residents in small rural communities to improve housing and to obtain water. Credit is furnished at reasonable rates and terms, and each loan is accompanied by technical farm and money management advice.

The Farmers Home Administration in its loan program usually works closely with farm supply cooperatives. Operating loans are made to eligible operators of farms not larger than family farms to assist them in making improved use of their land and labor resources and in making adjustments necessary for successful farming. Funds may be advanced to pay for equipment, livestock, feed, seed, fertilizer and for other farm and home operating needs and to refinance chattel debts. Each loan is scheduled for repayment in accordance with the borrower's ability to repay, over a period not exceeding seven years, with a possible additional renewal period of five years. The interest rate is 5 percent. A borrower's total principal indebtedness for operating loans may not exceed $35,000.

Farm supply cooperatives in selling supplies to Farmers Home Administration clients establish a close working relationship with the agency.

Nonfarm Credit Cooperatives

Small department stores, hardware and other retailers often have difficulty in handling credit accounts and accounts receivables. While credit bureaus are relied upon for screening credit applicants, the tying-up of much needed funds in accounts receivable poses a serious problem.

Some small- and medium-sized retail businesses have formed co-op credit corporations which discount customers' notes for the member stores, thus releasing much needed operating capital. Some have gone even further and established a centralized credit department for member stores, using electronic computers to handle the billing and computations required.

There are many examples of such operations. One company furnishes a central charge service to some 3,200 small merchants. Some chain stores are also included in its membership. Member-merchants sell their customer receivables to this central charge company at discounts ranging from 5½ to 7 percent, depending on volume. The company assumes the responsibility for collection and has no recourse on a member-merchant if a customer doesn't pay his bill.

Retailer-owned grocery wholesales often maintain a credit control department which supplies credit information and credit collections for member stores that extend credit. A centralized credit control department provides economies in checking on credit applicants and in collecting bad accounts. In other instances, subsidiary credit corporations are formed to handle credit needs of member stores.

Rural Electrification Administration

Besides loaning funds for rural electric co-op systems, there is another type of loan available under Section 5 of the REA Act:

> The Administrator is authorized and empowered to make loans for the purpose of financing the wiring of the premises of persons in rural areas and the acquisition and installation of electrical and plumbing appliances and equipment. Such loans may be made to any of the borrowers of funds loaned under the provisions of Section 4, or to any person, firm or corporation supplying or installing the said wiring, appliances or equipment.

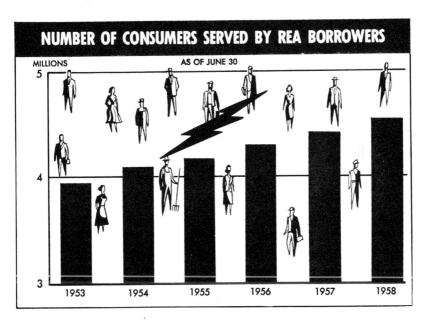

FIGURE 15-2
(Courtesy, USDA, Washington, D.C.)

Member-patrons may obtain these loan funds through their rural electric cooperative if the purpose of the loan qualifies under Section 5 and the cooperative qualifies for the funds from the REA.

RETAIL COOPERATIVES EXTENDING CREDIT

Some retail co-op managers believe that cooperatives should extend credit as a method of capturing the patrons' business. However, this is a superficial reason because, unlike persons involved in profit-type corporations, co-op patrons are both owners and customers. It seems illogical to assume that cooperatives need to capture their own stockholders through credit in order to foster patronage. A better reason for extending credit is because co-op members, generally, desire and need more credit services.

However, after all else has been tried and after the co-op management has proven through critical analysis that credit extension is necessary, a definite credit policy should emerge.

Many directors and managers have failed to come to grips with the problems of extending credit and collecting accounts. Their practices are determined by expediency and competitive conditions rather than by sound policies approved by the membership. As a result, practices often determine policies.

A credit policy developed by directors, understood and approved by member-patrons and supported by employees is a necessary beginning for sound credit operations. A policy is worthwhile to the extent that it accomplishes desired goals.

In formulating credit policy, co-op management should recognize at least three groups of credit customers.

The first group includes those for whom retail credit is a matter of convenience. They have adequate working capital and can (and usually do) pay their bills promptly. The second group of credit customers includes those who are short on working capital and need retail credit for a more profitable operation. For the customers in this class, credit is more than a convenience—it is a practical economic necessity. The third group of credit customers includes those who are short on working capital but are able to use only a limited amount of credit profitably in their operation. Retail credit above a limited amount is actually a disservice to this class of customers. Within these three classes, the credit needs of some customers will vary.

In any case, the essentials of a good credit policy are:

1. Establish a realistic credit policy by action of the board of directors.

(a) Adopt a formal, written credit policy.

(b) Obtain approval of the policy by the members at an annual meeting.

(c) Minimize exceptions to it.

(d) Hold manager responsible for enforcement rather than formulation of credit policy.

(e) Delegate the tasks of extending credit to a person who can become a specialist in this area.

2. Adopt specific procedures for extending credit.

(a) Select credit applicants carefully, using a formal application. A little time devoted to screening applicants will save a large amount of time later in collecting bad accounts.

(b) Maintain a list of patrons who are not eligible for credit (and those whose credit is limited).

(c) Discuss the policy and specific terms for mutual understanding between the cooperative and its members.

(d) Have employees sell the credit policy along with the commodities.

(e) Establish regular board review of credit practices and accounts. Age all accounts for monthly board review.

(f) Prohibit any employee and board member from buying on credit at the cooperative. This is to prevent conflicts of interest.

(g) To check on the credit reliability of a customer, use the services of a credit bureau, bank, salesman, other co-ops, other merchants and courthouse records.

(h) Limit the amount of credit extended to any one individual.

(i) Patrons who have demonstrated their credit reliability may be issued credit cards to facilitate transactions.

(j) Patrons who do not demonstrate their credit reliability should be dropped and removed from the cooperative by board action.

3. Establish sound collection practices.

(a) Send monthly statements to patrons with accounts.

(b) Be firm with account holders in enforcing policy. Make special efforts to obtain payment on due date.

(c) Check the ages of all accounts monthly and present to board.

(d) Protect the association by using notes on slow accounts.

(e) Use collection agencies and/or legal action as a last resort.

4. Recognize and allocate the costs of credit.

(a) Consider credit as a service and set a price on it.

FIGURE 15-3

Retail cooperatives which extend credit may belong to and use credit bureaus to obtain complete credit information on credit applicants. (Courtesy, Associated Credit Bureaus of America, St. Louis, Mo.)

(b) Allow a cash discount or make a charge for credit, but inform all patrons of the policy.

5. Encourage and assist farmers to use existing credit agencies.

(a) Establish close working relationships with PCA's, rural credit unions, local banks and other credit agencies.

(b) Recognize inefficiencies that result when both supply cooperatives and credit agencies provide the same type of credit services.

Aging Accounts Receivables

One of the key controls over credit extension is the aging of accounts receivables. As a credit account gets older, its collectible value decreases, as follows:

Age of Account	Percentage Collectible
Up to 30 days	100
Up to 60 days	90
Up to 180 days	67
Up to one year	45
Up to two years	23
Up to three years	15
Up to five years	1

A board of directors that looks at the accounts receivable list and aging classification at audit time only has neglected its duty and obligation to the membership. The membership of the cooperative should be given a report of the accounts receivable situation as a part of the annual report at each annual meeting.

Summary

Co-op management should recognize that unless all patrons are granted credit, those who pay cash subsidize those who buy on credit. Credit without a charge is costly, especially to the patron who pays cash. The cash patron must pay for the cost of handling the credit patron's account if no charge or too small a charge is made for this service. This is not in accordance with the co-op principle of treating all patrons equitably. A good policy to follow is to charge 1 percent per month on all outstanding balances after 30 days. This charge approximately covers the cost of extending credit. For example, one large mail-order house which makes over half its sales on credit charges 1½ percent per month on all accounts over 30 days. This charge has enabled the firm to make substantial profits on credit sales.

Some cooperatives differentiate between cash and credit customers by offering discounts for cash, adding a charge for credit or a combination of the two. Thus the credit customer pays the full cost of credit extension. Some customers may be lost, but others may be gained who look upon this type of credit policy as being business-like and equitable. Also, credit customers may shift to a cash basis under this policy.

SELECTED CO-OP FINANCE PROBLEMS

Cooperatives and Contract Farming

Contract farming and vertical integration are rapidly coming into the fore in American and world agriculture.[5]

Various proposals to help cooperatives finance these developments have been made. The key issue is whether cooperatives can obtain adequate capital from their members and/or finance institutions to manufacture, process, market or distribute supplies and extend credit to their patrons in competition with profit-type corporations.

---

[5]Roy, E. P., *Contract Farming, U.S.A.*, The Interstate Printers & Publishers, Inc., Danville, Ill. 1963. Chapter 12.

Some co-op leaders have proposed a new agency within the Farm Credit Administration to make the loans. These loans would enable cooperatives "to build or acquire facilities needed to round out the economic strength of their farmer-owners." The new agency would help farmers "develop as rapidly as possible effective vertical integration of agriculture through cooperatives, without invading the field of careful lending that banks for cooperatives carry on so well."

Other leaders believe that no new federal credit agencies for cooperatives should be created. They reason that, except for consumer cooperatives, credit is readily available to practically all other types of cooperatives.

Integration through a Cooperative

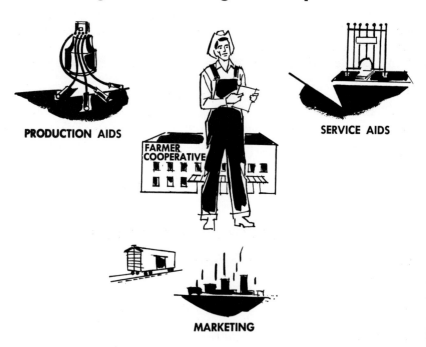

PRODUCTION AIDS

SERVICE AIDS

MARKETING

FIGURE 15-4

Cooperatives may integrate by furnishing production and service aids as well as marketing facilities and outlets. (Courtesy, USDA, Washington, D.C.)

The main points regarding cooperatives and their attempts at vertical integration are:

1. A cooperative may integrate horizontally and vertically just like a profit-type association, but it is more difficult for a cooperative to do.

2. The problem becomes more serious whenever a cooperative starts to contract with its members and/or nonmembers on a flat fee contract or other similar plan.

(A) If the co-op flat fee contracts make the contractees bona fide members of the cooperative, there is usually no serious problem.

(B) If, however, the flat fee contracts become too wide-spread and the cooperative suffers losses, the members not on contract may oppose the co-op management and insist that contracts be dropped. This has already happened in some co-op broiler contracting in the United States and Canada.

3. If the cooperative insists on using flat fee contracts, nonetheless, it may reduce its liability and protect its members not on contract by one or more plans, as follows:

(A) Organize its contract operations into a subsidiary corporation, either profit-type or cooperative.

(B) Issue contracts that contain profit-and-loss sharing clauses.

(C) Limit the extent of losses the cooperative may absorb under a particular contract.

(D) Pay federal income taxes on nonmember contract operations and distribute the remaining profits to the regular members.

4. A cooperative can develop contract services short of flat fee guarantees. That is, a cooperative can specify breed, variety, planting date, insect control, harvesting date, grades, sizes, delivery conditions and pricing methods. It would not attempt to guarantee a fixed return per unit of product produced. In this way, the farmer is contractually integrated, yet the profits or losses remain with him. If the farmer and the cooperative are both efficient, the losses will be minimized and, more likely, profits will accrue.

Co-op contract operations are dangerous to handle because not all members and patrons may be treated alike. As long as contract operations are profitable, no problem arises. But, when co-op contract operations start losing money, members not on contract start wondering as to who will pick up the loss. The cooperative, therefore, should outline its plan of handling losses to all members before embarking on contract operations. Each member and patron needs to be informed of this before the losses actually happen. There is no doubt that losses will occur in contract operations regardless of efforts made to insure against them. If co-op members understand what the cooperative is doing, they are more likely to support it in bad times as well as in good times.[6]

National Co-op Finance Agencies

The Cooperative League has proposed the creation of a general financing agency whose common stock would be owned by all kinds of cooperatives throughout the country and whose preferred shares would be objects of investment by many individuals, foundations and pension funds throughout the country. Such a financial institution is already in being in the Cooperative Finance Association. It could be made into an agency well enough capitalized to provide rediscounting services for cooperatives, to finance their growth and expansion and to develop a broad market for their securities.[7]

Do Cooperatives Need a Securities Exchange?

While voting stock in a cooperative cannot be traded publicly due to article and bylaw restrictions, other types of co-op securities can be traded. Henning and Laubis of The Ohio State University report on this possibility as follows:

> Another approach to the development of a market for cooperative securities would be for the state-wide associations or perhaps regional associations to act as a sponsoring agency in selling consolidated stock or debentures to the investing public. The average economic conditions at the time of issuance of consolidated stocks or debenture bonds would govern the security and interest rate necessary to sell a given issue. This security may be in the form of the facilities of the combined associations or the earning capacity of the combined associations. It is doubtful with the present limit upon earnings that cooperative securities will be exchanged for speculative motives but rather sold for long-term income investments.
>
> Another approach to the marketing of cooperative securities outside of the local community would be for the associations in a state to combine in a unified effort to establish a cooperative exchange facility which would function in much the same manner as any over-the-counter market. Such an exchange could operate on a bid and offer status on a state-wide basis. This procedure would permit holders of coopera-

[6]*Ibid.* pp. 397-399.
[7]Voorhis, Jerry, "New Sources of Capital," *Cooperative Digest*, Ithaca, N.Y. Nov. 1960.

tive securities to offer them for sale to other investors outside
of the local trade territory.[8]

Debenture bonds, preferred stock, revolving fund certificates and
other such securities could be traded over the whole United States if
a central co-op security market were established.

Compliance with the Securities and Exchange Act would have to
be studied. It is possible that Congress could legislate in this area to
provide a clearer atmosphere for a co-op securities market.

Public Financing

Many large cooperatives are already engaged in at least two types
of public financing: (1) preferred stock issues (nonvoting) and (2)
debenture bond sales. The former is really equity capital, while the
latter is borrowed capital. If a farmer cooperative is tax exempt, it is
wiser to use preferred stock (non-voting) since the interest payments
thereon are not taxable. On the other hand, for a nonexempt farmer
cooperative the debenture plan is wiser because the interest paid
thereon is an operating cost. If interest were paid on preferred stock,
it would be taxable.

Another aspect of public financing is the difficulty cooperatives
face with their "par" value securities and fixed interest rates. One large
cooperative has attempted to solve this problem by issuing a variable-
interest bond, with interest ranging from a minimum of 4.5 to a
maximum of 7.1 percent tied to the cost-of-living index of the Department of Labor. Capital stock issues likewise may be tied to the
cost-of-living index.

Any cooperative which attempts to tap public financing has to
recognize that public investors are interested in one or more of these
aspects: (1) safety of the security, (2) interest rate thereon, (3) its
marketability or liquidation and (4) growth or appreciation of the
security. Cooperatives can successfully meet (1) and (2) but have
difficulty in meeting (3) and (4). More research on these points is
needed.

Retiring Co-op Stock at Par Value

A critical problem in older cooperatives and those not revolving
capital is the question of retiring equities at par value.

---

[8]Henning, G. F. and R. E. Laubis, *Financial Structure of Agricultural Business Organizations*, Ohio Agr. Exp. Sta. Bul. 880, Wooster, Ohio. Apr. 1961. p. 39.

Phillips has well expressed the problem:

> This problem comes about largely because through custom
> and institutionalized practice (and often by charter and co-
> operative law) the value of securities and other evidence of
> the member's equity in his cooperative are held at par value.
> If a member's common and preferred stock (or membership
> and capital certificates) were originally acquired at a total
> of $300.00, they normally are retired for the same amount
> twenty years later when the member withdraws. Yet the co-
> operative may have doubled free surplus and may have
> enjoyed a 100 percent appreciation in the market value of
> assets over this period. The member's only opportunity to
> participate in this capital gain is to bring about a dissolution
> of the cooperative and a distribution of its assets. Otherwise,
> the new member who takes his place comes in at a real bar-
> gain, or would except for the fact that he too has no way to
> participate in the capital growth in the cooperative.
>   The solution may be to provide some way of determining
> the actual market value of the retiring member's equity in his
> cooperative and settle with him accordingly. This clearly
> would require amending articles of incorporation. In some
> states it would require amendment of cooperative enabling
> laws.[9]

The problem cited by Phillips also applies in reverse—actual market
value of co-op stock can depreciate as well as appreciate.

Retiring Equities of Inactive Members

A problem always arises in cooperatives regarding the equities of
deceased members, members who leave the community and members
who remain but stop patronizing the association.

Manuel recommends that this problem be handled as follows:

(a) Retire the control (voting right) of an inactive member as soon as possible after he stops using the services of
the association.

(b) Consider settling financial interests of inactive
members.

(c) Establish a priority for refunding financial interests,
since the redemption of financial interests of all inactive members upon demand may involve too heavy a burden on the
finances of the association. Give preference to cases where
circumstances are beyond the immediate control of the
member.

---

[9]Phillips, R., "A Modern Concept of the Co-op," *American Institute of Cooperation
Proceedings*, University of Illinois, Urbana, Ill. Aug. 7, 1959.

(d) Plan to retire all financial interests promptly upon the death of a member. This includes membership capital as well as allocations from local and regional revolving funds.

(e) As a minimum, members moving from the community should be refunded promptly the par value of their cost of membership.

(f) Inactive members remaining in the community should be handled like those moving from the community except they might convert their membership assets from a voting to a non-voting instrument when they become inactive.

(g) Bylaws should be amended to authorize retirement. Since drawing up and amending bylaws is a legal matter, it should be done only with the counsel of a competent attorney. The most desirable type of bylaw provision is believed to be one which defines the extent of a member's interest and authorizes the board to settle that interest but does not dictate that it shall be done nor state specifically how transactions will be handled.[10]

Getting Nonmembers to Become Members

If desirable, the cooperative should devise a plan whereby non-members are converted to members. This is important for tax purposes, for membership morale and for attainment of a true cooperative. Previously, mention was made that nonmembers in a cooperative do represent an element of profit-type operations to which some cooperatives might succumb. Three methods are available for conversion of nonmembers: (1) persuading them to purchase memberships, (2) withholding patronage refunds toward the purchase of memberships or (3) using retains on their sales or purchases to apply toward memberships.

Expulsion of Members

While most cooperatives desire to convert nonmembers into members, there are some instances where members need to be expelled from a cooperative. Those members which are poor credit risks or chronic agitators or those who refuse to abide by and support the cooperative should be promptly expelled. The articles and bylaws should control the expulsion procedures used.

---

[10]Manuel, Milton, *Retiring Control and Equities of Inactive Co-op Members,* Kans. Agr. Exp. Sta. Cir. 346, Manhattan, Kans. Mar. 1947. pp. 14-15.

What Is Adequate Capitalization?

All cooperatives should attempt to devise financial programs which will adequately fulfill their objectives, preserve their integrity and provide opportunity for their growth as continuing business institutions. While it is difficult to reduce this broad policy to a specific financial program, Hulbert has attempted it for a farmer cooperative, as follows:

> 1. Its seasonal borrowing is repaid once each year and it is free from such debt for at least 60 days.
>
> 2. Its unsecured seasonal borrowings outstanding at any one time do not exceed $1 of such debt for $1 of working capital.
>
> 3. Its seasonal borrowing that is secured by commodities does not exceed $4 of such debt for $1 of working capital.
>
> 4. Its term borrowing for fixed assets or facilities does not exceed 60 percent of the value of such assets.
>
> 5. Term loans used to acquire fixed assets or facilities will be paid within 50 percent of the time in which these fixed assets will become useless either from depreciation or from obsolescence.
>
> 6. It will have sufficient working capital to operate newly acquired facilities, realizing that it usually takes from $1 to $2 of current assets for each $1 invested in fixed assets.
>
> 7. It will not seriously deplete its working capital if new processing or merchandising programs are undertaken.
>
> 8. It will maintain adequate valuation, liability, contingent and capital reserves.[11]

In the next chapter, the management of cooperatives is discussed.

TOPICS FOR DISCUSSION

1. What does it cost for a store to sell on credit?
2. In what ways can cooperatives shift the responsibility of credit extension to other co-op finance institutions?
3. Discuss the credit tie-in between PCA's and retail farm supply cooperatives.
4. If retail cooperatives do decide to extend credit on their own, what should their credit policies include?
5. What role should cooperatives play in contract farming?

---

[11]Hulbert, L. S., "Sound Financial Program for Farmers' Co-ops," Co-op Association Clinic, University Park, Pa. June 3, 1948.

SELECTED REFERENCES

1. Abrahamsen, M., "Problems of Retail Credit and Accounts Receivables," Cooperative League Finance Conference, Chicago, Ill. May 23, 1957.
2. Bailey, J. M. and others, *Credit Control in Selected Retail Farm Supply Co-ops,* FCS Gen. Repts. 35, 36, 41, 43, 57 and 71, Washington, D.C.
3. Ecker, H., "What Is It Costing You to Extend Credit?" *Feedstuffs,* Minneapolis, Minn. Sept. 21, 1963.
4. Henning, G. F. and R. E. Laubis, *Practices Followed by Ohio Farm Supply Co-ops in Extending Credit,* Ohio Agr. Exp. Sta. Mimeo. Rept. 285, Wooster, Ohio. Not dated.
5. Hesser, L. F., *Scalogram Analysis of Farmers' Attitudes Toward Use of Credit,* Purdue University D.A.E. Paper 6105, Lafayette, Ind. Apr. 15, 1961.
6. Kniffin, Fred, *Retail Credit and Collections,* SBA Rept. 31, Washington, D.C. Apr. 1960.
7. Koller, E. F., "Vertical Integration of Agricultural Cooperatives," *Journal of Farm Economics,* Nov. 1950.
8. Phelps, C. W., *Building Sound Credit Policies for Small Stores,* SBA Rept. 6, Washington, D.C. Sept. 1955.
9. Phelps, C. W., *Credit and Collection Controls for Small Marketers,* SBA Rept. 33, Washington, D.C. May 1958.
10. Phelps, C. W., *Improving Collections from Credit Sales,* SBA Rept. 49, Washington, D.C. Oct. 1959.
11. Scanlan, J. J., *Vertical Integration in the Poultry Industry and Farmer Cooperatives,* FCS, USDA, Washington, D.C. 1961.
12. Staff, "Pointers on Credit and Collection Controls," *Farm Store Merchandising,* Minneapolis, Minn. Mar. 1963. pp. 54-56.

CHAPTER 16 —

Management of Cooperatives:
Members, Directors
and the Manager

Many an army has prospered under a bad commander, but no army has ever prospered under a debating society.
        —Lord Macaulay

There are two kinds of men who never amount to much: those who cannot do what they are told, and those who can do nothing else.
        —Cyrus H. K. Curtis

MANAGEMENT of cooperatives concerns three entities: (1) the members, (2) the board of directors and (3) the operating manager.

There is a reciprocal relationship between the members, the board and the manager. None of them can operate effectively without the others. The members need the board, and the board of directors requires a manager. The manager needs the board of directors, and the board exists only to meet the objectives of the members.

MEMBERSHIP IN COOPERATIVES

Co-op members are the legal owners of their business. It is not the board of directors or the manager who has the controlling authority over the cooperative, but the members. It is the members who usually plan and form a cooperative, and it is the members who receive the benefit from the cooperative. It is only through them, by their actions and authority, that the cooperative will be a profitable and sound business enterprise. Therefore, the key to any cooperative is its members. Realizing then that members are the key to a successful coopera-

FIGURE 16-1

Co-op members are the key to success or failure of any cooperative. How well they discharge their responsibilities and honor their obligations will decide the future of most cooperatives. (Courtesy, Consumers Cooperative of Berkeley, Inc., Berkeley, Calif.)

tive, it follows that they can likewise be responsible for an unsuccessful one.

Powers and Responsibilities

Members of a cooperative have specific "powers" under the law and as enumerated in the chartering documents. They also have "responsibilities," some moral and others legal, with regards to these powers.

Powers of the membership usually include:

1. To adopt the constitution, bylaws and agreements, as well as to amend them.

2. To elect and recall directors.

3. To vote upon appropriations of money for various purposes, to increase or decrease the capitalization, to decide upon pooling practices and contractual arrangements between members and the cooperative and to decide whether credit should be extended to patrons.

4. To require both directors and officers, as well as agents, to run the business legally and according to the constitution, bylaws and marketing contracts.

5. To hold directors and officers liable for any damage injurious to the members.

6. To elect a competent committee to examine the records and audit the books periodically.

7. To examine the annual reports.

8. To dissolve or merge the cooperative.

Regardless of the type of cooperative, members (those holding voting rights) have approximately the same set of responsibilities. These are:

1. Providing the necessary capital.
2. Controlling the organization through the board of directors as their elected representatives.
3. Patronizing their cooperative to the fullest extent possible.
4. Assuming the business risks.
5. Paying the costs of operation.
6. Keeping informed about the cooperative.
7. Maintaining the cooperative.

1. *Providing the Necessary Capital.*

Members as a group own the cooperative. The individual member should provide his proportionate share of the necessary capital. If all the capital cannot be raised in this way, the individual member must bear his proportionate share of the added cost resulting from paying interest on borrowed capital.

2. *Controlling the Cooperative.*

As owners of the cooperative, the members as a group are jointly responsible for its control and management. Every policy decision in the cooperative affects each member's operations. Therefore, only members or their elected directors are in a position to make sound policy decisions in the cooperative. Unless each member takes an active part in controlling his cooperative, he cannot be sure that it will operate for his benefit.

The members as a group may withdraw any decision-making authority which they have previously delegated to the board of directors. By majority vote the members may overrule decisions made by the board of directors or the manager. However, the members cannot rescind any contractual obligations made for the cooperative by the board of directors or the manager.

3. *Patronizing the Cooperative.*

Each member owes it to himself and other members to patronize his cooperative. This means he must use all services provided by his cooperative that fit his operations. Members join a cooperative for mutual benefit. Maximum mutual benefit can result only when each member provides maximum patronage.

4. *Assuming Business Risks.*

There are risks in the operation of any business. The cooperative

is no exception. The member-patrons as a group must bear these risks
in a cooperative. Each member bears his share of the risks in proportion to his equity and patronage. As a sound business practice, cooperatives generally establish reserves to absorb possible future losses.

5. *Paying Operating Costs.*

A member shares in the benefits of his cooperative in proportion
to the amount of business he does with the cooperative. The actual
costs of running the cooperative must be paid before anything is
available for patronage refunds. Therefore, each member shares in
the cost of operating the cooperative in direct proportion to his
patronage.

6. *Keeping Informed.*

Each member has a responsibility for keeping informed on the facts
about his cooperative in much the same way as he should be informed
about the operation of his own business.

In addition to this, members should understand the nature and
purpose, as well as the methods of organization and operation, of
cooperatives so that they can make effective use of cooperatives as a
business tool.

7. *Maintaining the Cooperative.*

Each member is obligated to maintain the cooperative by:

(A) Continuing to support his cooperative during temporary
adverse conditions, such as a price war.

(B) Bringing new members into the cooperative.

(C) Taking suggestions and criticisms to the board of directors or
to membership meetings, rather than airing them on the street corners.

(D) Abiding by majority rule concerning decisions affecting the
cooperative, even when personally in disagreement with majority
decisions.

(E) Serving conscientiously on the board of directors or committees when elected or called on to do so.

Qualifications for Membership

Membership in a cooperative is not automatic. It should be applied
for, reviewed by the board (or a committee of the board) and accepted
or rejected by a majority vote of the board. Most cooperatives make a
serious mistake by permitting memberships which are too open. Many
assume that a member's patronage is the only valid concern, forgetting
that, in a cooperative, the member is both patron and owner. While

most people have valid qualifications for being patrons, a much smaller number have valid qualifications for ownership. If membership in a cooperative is restricted and its qualifications are high, prospective members will place a higher premium on the value of the cooperative. A cooperative with loose membership qualifications is not apt to be respected.

FIGURE 16-2

Cooperatives which set high standards for membership are likely to be the most successful in the long-run. A member's voting right is his most precious possession in a cooperative. (Courtesy, Co-operative Union, Manchester, England)

Lazo lists nine qualifications for co-op members:
1. They are efficient in their own businesses.
2. They believe in cooperatives.
3. They are financially solvent and active in their own businesses.
4. They know the value of merchandise and are aware of buying and selling practices.
5. They are not looking for something for nothing.

6. They are self-reliant, able and resolute.

7. They understand business competition and do not expect to win each and every battle.

8. They are willing to forego immediate gains in trade for a better future.

9. They are interested in the cooperative, its affairs, its progress, its success.[1]

Another aspect of co-op membership is that all members should be thoroughly educated in co-op principles and practices before being admitted to membership. While this is a slow process, over the long-run both the members and the cooperative will be better off. The educational program can consist of a series of weekly meetings featuring lectures and discussion groups. Upon the termination of the study sessions, the cooperative can then be organized or the members admitted. This method has already been tested and proven by the St. Francis Xavier University's Adult Education Department in Nova Scotia, as well as by many other groups throughout the world.

Since cooperatives are controlled by the membership, there must be machinery for the members to exercise control. The annual meeting is a part of this machinery. It gives the members an opportunity to set policies for the board, to elect the board of directors and to hear and evaluate a report of the year's operations. The subject of annual meetings is discussed in the next chapter.

In addition to the annual meeting, special membership meetings may be called at any time by the board of directors. Official action can be taken at such meetings provided written notice is sent to all members in advance. By petition carrying a required number of members' signatures, the members can compel special membership meetings.

BOARD OF DIRECTORS

Within the broad policies laid down by the membership, the board of directors is the governing body in the cooperative. Acting as a group, the directors employ the manager, establish specific operating policies and supervise the management of the cooperative. The directors are the elected representatives of the members.

---

[1]Lazo, Hector, *Retailer Cooperatives,* Harper & Brothers, New York, N.Y. 1937. p. 34.

FIGURE 16-3

All the members cannot run the cooperative. They must select a board of directors which reflects the needs and aspirations of the membership. A good co-op board is the cornerstone of success. (Courtesy, Nationwide Insurance Co., Columbus, Ohio)

Powers and Responsibilities

Generally, directors have these powers:

1. To prescribe the form and maintenance of membership records and to approve memberships.

2. To prescribe the form, extent and nature of financial reports to members.

3. To make changes in the bylaws (when the power to do so is vested in the directors).

4. To adopt, use and alter the corporate seal.

5. To borrow money and issue such evidence of indebtedness as required.

6. To render services, furnish supplies and market products for members and patrons in accordance with the purposes of the association as spelled out in the organization papers.

7. To commingle funds of the association from all sources and to decide upon the investments in other cooperatives and/or other businesses.

8. To employ and dismiss the general manager and determine his responsibilities, duties and compensation.

9. To determine which employees are to be bonded, fix the amount of their bonds and provide for adequate insurance protection for all facilities, equipment and personnel.

10. To keep records of all meetings of the board.

11. To call special meetings of the board.

12. To elect officers of the board, remove them for cause and fill vacancies.

13. To provide for the installation of an accounting system.

14. To employ an auditor.

15. To establish rules and regulations regarding the transfer of memberships and other evidences of equity in the association.

16. To issue and sell stock or other evidences of equity.

17. To determine the manner, form and amount of patronage refunds.

18. To declare dividends on stock and patronage refunds on business volume.

19. To enter into contracts, sue and be sued.

20. To formulate and evaluate general and internal operating policies both for the short-run and the long-run.

The responsibilities of directors may be enumerated as follows:

1. They have both a moral and legal responsibility to serve the best interests of the members whom they represent rather than their own individual interests.

2. Their authority exists as a board in a duly called meeting and does not reside in them as individuals.

3. The board is responsible for hiring the best trained and most efficient manager that it can employ and creating the best possible working conditions for him that are compatible with the interest of the members and the success of the cooperative.

4. The board should not interfere in the day-to-day operation of the business but should determine, with the membership, the policies of operation and check to see that these policies are carried out.

5. The board must know and understand the financial operation of the association and satisfy itself that the records kept are accurate in every detail.

6. The board should keep the membership informed about the cooperative and insure that the entire organization is permeated with spirit of service to and respect for the membership.

7. The directors should maintain the cooperative as an efficient business institution worthy of the good will of the community and area it serves.

8. Remuneration to any director should be only for actual out-of-pocket costs when representing the cooperative. Records on such remunerations should be available for membership inspection and examination.

9. No member of a director's family, either by birth or marriage, should be employed by the cooperative. If there is an exception, approval should be given by members at a regular meeting.

10. Directors should receive no preferential treatment with respect to services of the association.

11. No director should have a financial interest in private facilities or businesses that provide supplies or services to the cooperative.

12. Credit should not be extended to directors.

13. Directors have a responsibility to further their knowledge of and training in management and to familiarize themselves with the co-op law of the state, the certificate of incorporation and bylaws of their cooperative. Every director should have a copy of each for his ready reference.

Size of Board

Most co-op boards have a tendency to be too large. The minimum number is, of course, set by the incorporation law. An extremely large board is cumbersome, slow and expensive. A small board is more vigorous, quick and effective. Also, it is generally true that smaller boards will have more frequent and effective meetings; larger boards will have less frequent and less effective meetings. Profit-type corporations have found over long experience that small boards are better than large ones. The members, nevertheless, set the size of the board above the required minimum.

Qualifications for Board Membership

In considering the election of a member to the board of directors, the membership might well ask the following questions:

1. What is his business record? Does he manage his own affairs well? Does he possess sound business judgment? What is his educational background?

2. Is he willing to work at the job of being a director, or is he more apt to be inactive? Has he shown a capacity for working with others, or is he an "individualist?" Does he think for himself?

3. Do his neighbors regard him as a leader? Does he enjoy their confidence for honesty and integrity? What capacity has he shown as a leader? Has he been active in community affairs?

4. Does he possess a high degree of loyalty to the association and to its principles? With regards to cooperative effort, does he possess a proper understanding of its limitations as well as what can be accomplished through it?

Officers of the Board

The officers of the board are usually elected from the board members, not the membership. The duties of the president are to preside at all meetings, carry out the will of the members and watch over all

FIGURE 16-4

Cooperatives which operate over wide territories usually elect board members by districts so that fair representation is assured for each district. (Courtesy, Southern States Cooperative, Richmond, Va.)

FIGURE 16-5

In electing a co-op board, care has to be exercised regarding nomination procedures, qualifications of nominees, fair balloting, honest vote counting and willingness of each member to abide by the majority.

affairs of the association. The vice president takes over the responsibilities of the president in the latter's absence. The secretary is sometimes also the treasurer. He serves as secretary both at the meetings of the directors and of the general membership. His duties are to keep the minutes and records and attend to correspondence. He should also be the official custodian of the seal, the stock book and the membership records. The treasurer keeps watch over the bookkeeping and accounts. He should take such steps as are necessary to assure himself that the accounts are being kept accurately and that the funds are being handled properly. He should also make periodic reports to the board and to the membership.

The officers and other board members usually meet once monthly to review the financial statements, receive the manager's report and decide on policy matters. The president issues the call and agenda for these meetings, while the secretary transmits the call and agenda to each board member. It is important that a detailed agenda be circulated to each board member ahead of any meeting.

Usage of public directors serving ex-officio is sometimes good. They bring a new insight into co-op affairs yet have no voting power.

Election Procedures

The procedures employed for nominating and electing board members may consist of nominations from the floor, use of nominating committees, members' caucuses, nomination petitions or mail ballots.

Nominating committees are recommended because careful and considered judgment can be exercised in making nominations. Guidelines for a nominating committee are as follows:

1. It should be set up previous to the regular annual business meeting and should prepare its slate before the meeting.

2. Directors, the manager or staff members should not be on the nominating committee.

3. Former directors should make good members for the nominating committee.

4. The nominating committee should be elected by the members to serve during the coming year for the next regular annual business meeting.

5. The nominating committee should consist of a minimum of three and a maximum of five members.

6. The nominating committee must be familiar with the qualifications for directors laid down in the law, the articles and the bylaws of the cooperative.

7. It is better for the nominating committee to bring in extra candidates or a double slate, so as to require an election.

8. Advance notice of the nominees should be provided the membership for their considered judgment.

9. There should always be plenty of opportunity for nominations from the floor.

10. Losing candidates may be made alternates in case board vacancies occur between annual meetings.

Secret ballots should always be employed in voting for directors. The reasons for this are obvious. Officers of the board whose terms have expired and who are nominees themselves should be very careful to exclude themselves from any part of the nominating and balloting procedures.

Proxy voting will depend on the cooperative's bylaws. If it is permitted, the rules should be clear and specific. As a general rule, proxy voting should be prohibited.

A cooperative that covers such a large territory that it is impractical for members to assemble in a central place to select directors must work out the voting procedures with great care to assure the individual members as much participation as possible. Where the territory can be divided into director districts, each district may hold a preliminary meeting. The district meeting may either nominate directors to be confirmed at the annual meeting or may actually elect the director who will take office at the annual meeting.

The problem of democratic procedure that will give the individual member a sense of personal participation in the election of directors becomes much more difficult for cooperatives covering whole states or several states. In this matter the federated type of organization probably has an advantage in that the individual member can have the feeling of genuine participation in the electing of directors of his local cooperative and be given the feeling that his cooperative is well represented on the board of directors of the federation.

The centralized type of organization has a real problem in reaching the distant individual member and in making him feel that he can have a real voice. This is often attempted through the holding of meetings of local groups which each elect a delegate to attend the annual meeting. The member's sense of participation in the selection of a director to represent him on the board can be heightened by setting up director districts and providing for nomination of candidates by nominating petition. A circular can then be prepared setting forth the qualifications of the various candidates in each district and sent to all members prior to the meeting of their local. The members in each local can then instruct their delegate to the annual meeting.

Board Tenure

The length of service of board members should be regulated in some way to avoid extremely long tenures. One recommendation might be to limit service to three 3-year terms. After an absence of one year or more, they could be subject to re-election.

Another plan, more unique, merits consideration. All directors are elected for one year. Subsequently, the existing board is renominated, but only the two-thirds of its members receiving the largest number of votes is retained. The other one-third of the board membership is chosen from a slate of new candidates.

This type of rotation plan accomplishes several things.

    1. It protects an association against turnover of the entire board at one time even though all directors are elected for one year and all terms expire simultaneously.

    2. It enables an association to get rid of a poor director in one year, rather than be stuck with him for three years, the usual length of a director's term, by enabling the membership to diplomatically rotate undesirable directors off the board promptly.

3. It enables an association to constantly upgrade its directors by retaining its strong board members indefinitely rather than rotating them off the board automatically at the end of some predetermined period.[2]

Board Policies

Upon taking office, some of the policies with which a co-op board is obliged to define are these:

1. "Finance" policy, which includes determinations of equity and creditor capital, revolving funds, rates of expansion or contraction, operating budgets, construction programs, etc.

2. "Service" policy, which includes the type and scope of services to be offered or provided the membership.

3. "Pricing" policy, which includes markup practices, quantity discounts, etc.

4. "Credit extension" policy, which includes the type and terms of credit extended, credit application procedures, collection methods, etc.

5. "Membership relations" policy, such as newsletters, member grievances, etc.

6. "Public relations" policy, such as joining trade groups and co-op councils, working with youth groups, releasing information, etc.

7. "Employee relations" policy, which includes salary and wage scales, incentive and training programs, promotions, fringe benefits, collective bargaining, etc.

8. "Internal operations" policy, which includes the status and organization of the business, operating and technical records, etc.

9. "Management development" policy, which includes a program of seminars, courses, workshops, etc., for the managerial staff and directors.

Making the Board Function

Suggestions as to how a board should function are as follows:

1. Have regular meetings, usually monthly.

2. Select a good president or chairman and expect him to take the time to plan each meeting in advance.

3. Insist on attendance. Pay the directors for meetings so their businesses do not suffer, but do not pay them for not attending.

---

[2]Hulbert, H. H., "Business Management Problems," Florida Co-op Workshop, Gainesville, Fla. June 20, 1961.

4. Insist on good minutes. It is not necessary to write down everything that is said. But understandable records of all actions are essential.

5. Do not waste time on minor details. A board that spends its time approving bills, etc., is lost. The time to control expenses is before they are incurred, not after the bills have arrived.

6. Insist on a regular report, including financial statements, from the management.

7. Use special committees to look into particular problems when the need arises. Use standing committees to keep abreast of certain ongoing areas, such as finance, membership, etc. The work of active committees saves the time of other board members.

8. Prepare an agenda in advance of every meeting. This, together with pertinent relevant facts, should be circulated to members prior to the meeting.

9. Allow for full discussion at all meetings. Invite specialists to advise on problems beyond the scope of knowledge of board members.

Board Committees

The use of board committees in formulating, executing and evaluating policy areas is a valuable tool.

An executive committee is employed by most boards consisting of the president and as many other board members as required. In some instances the executive committee has full authority to act for the board on emergency matters between regular board meetings, but such actions are generally reported back to the full board for confirmation. Most of the other board committees serve primarily as fact-finding, advisory or coordinating groups. Such committees are usually in the areas of financing, budgeting, membership and employee relations.[3]

Other types of board committees employed are: nominating, grievance, purchasing, education, inventory, salary and bonus, loan, auditing and supervisory, future plans, retirement, public relations, commodity, services and legislative, among others.

Membership on these committees need not be confined to board members. At least one member of the cooperative who is not a director should serve ex-officio on each committee. Retired board members often make good committeemen.

---

[3]Griffin, Nelda and others, *Director Committees of Farmer Co-ops*, FCS Gen. Rept. 85, Washington, D.C. Nov. 1960.

FIGURE 16-6

This cooperative has six committees to assist the board of directors in its work. (Courtesy, Cooperative League, Chicago, Ill.)

Board Training

Cooperatives have been slow to adopt methods for developing prospective members of boards of directors. Many members, who have splendid qualifications for membership on a board of directors, are often unaware of the duties and responsibilities of this position. They are not acquainted with board procedures and know little concerning legal and financial matters, financial statements or proper methods of conducting board meetings.

Volkin, in his study of 752 co-op directors, found that only 58 percent of those interviewed identified correctly the responsibilities that were theirs in the cooperative. In identifying the joint responsibilities of the board and manager, only 53 percent were correct. In identifying the manager's responsibility, only 60 percent were correct.[4]

The in-service training of co-op directors is usually meager. Only 26 percent of 4,083 cooperatives surveyed in one study reported any type of management training. Only 43 percent of these cooperatives reported any training program for their directors. Only 13 percent indicated their directors attended three or more training programs during the year. Those directors that did receive training obtained it principally in the areas of directors' responsibilities, co-op principles, financing, policy making and membership relations.[5]

There is little doubt that cooperatives will have to match, and even surpass, the progressiveness of profit-type corporations if members are to have strong business associations. In at least one respect, private business corporations have done a better job than cooperatives. This has been in the management training of their boards of directors.

When a member is first elected to the co-op board, a clear-cut training program should be provided so that details of the cooperative's business may be learned quickly and a better understanding gained.

How should a cooperative proceed to render this training? Much depends on how big the cooperative is and how complicated it has become, as well as how much it can reasonably afford for such training. Although directors attending meetings and schools is often thought of first, this is not necessarily what is needed.

---

[4]Volkin, David and others, *Directors of Regional Farmer Cooperatives*, FCS Gen. Rept. 83, Washington, D.C. Aug. 1960. pp. 1 and 10.
[5]Volkin, David and N. Griffin, *Management Training Among Farmer Co-ops*, FCS Gen. Rept. 65, Washington, D.C. June 1959.

Let us assume that the cooperative is rather small and has been only a few years in the business. It is one that cannot afford to spend too much money on board training. The following steps are suggestions that such a cooperative might consider.

The co-op manager should make available to each new board member a packet of materials, including a copy of the articles of incorporation, bylaws, marketing and purchasing agreements; the most recently audited annual financial statements; and as many of the monthly board minutes as are available. Additionally, the board member should be provided with a brief manual of basic questions and answers concerning the cooperative's operations. All this material, made available to the board member, will amount to about $10 for paper and reproduction costs. It will require some of the manager's time, but it will be time well spent.

After the board member has examined these materials, he should spend at least a few days with the manager to learn about office procedures, office routine and other details. This will give him some insight into the day-to-day operations and will help him at the board meetings.

After this step, the board member might attempt to specialize in board problems, depending on his special talents. The manager may have each member acting as a specialist for him to rely upon for sound advice.

Larger cooperatives usually have more formal procedures in training their board members. They may send their directors to various management institutes, workshops, seminars, etc. Internally, they can afford more sophisticated training programs. Regional cooperatives often assist member locals in training their board members.

Some cooperatives try to develop director training programs for members prior to their becoming directors. They use several approaches:

1. The board chooses several younger members and asks them to attend meetings in order to become better acquainted with the operations of the association.

2. An advisory board, elected annually by members at meetings in each community, serves for one year. This board is the committee that selects nominees for the board of directors. These local boards meet four or more times each year in an advisory capacity to consider the major problems confronting the directors.

3. The membership chooses three "associate" directors who attend all meetings and take part in discussions, but have no vote.

Compensating the Board

Directors should never prescribe their own salaries or compensations for mileage and per diem. This should be done by the membership at an annual meeting. Most co-op directors draw no salaries but are paid mileage and per diem of varying rates.

Liability of the Board

It is possible for board members to be sued for certain acts committed against the best interests of the members. To prevent such lawsuits, the board must act as a body, and the minutes should reveal the circumstances surrounding the board's decision in a given matter. Withholding information from members might serve as a basis for lawsuits as would preferential treatment for some board members.

THE CO-OP MANAGER

In many businesses, success or failure hinges on management competence. In a cooperative, the manager is commonly thought of as the spearhead of management. He has a dual challenge. He must (1) solve the technical business problems which include external operating policies, such as sales promotion, preparation of products for market, purchasing and all problems that relate to the physical distribution and pricing of commodities and services; and (2) manage the accounting, financing, personnel and other problems of internal operations. Furthermore, the board of directors must be a constant challenge to the manager if he is to work effectively with them.

The manager is selected by the board, and he is accountable to them.

Powers and Responsibilities

The powers of a manager are as follows:

1. To hire and fire his subordinates according to a general policy created by the board.

2. To make periodic reports to the board of directors together with his recommendations concerning the cooperative's operation.

3. To plan, organize, direct, coordinate, conduct and control all the administrative and financial operations of the cooperative.

4. To train or have trained employees of the cooperative for greater efficiency.

5. To supervise, conduct and direct all jobs and activities specifically delegated to him by the board of directors.

6. To represent the cooperative to the public as the board may decide.

It is not a wise policy to designate the manager as a member of the board and/or its secretary. The manager is an employee of the board and therefore should not be part of the board which hires him and sets his salary. However, the manager should be required to attend all board meetings and be an active, nonvoting participant.

The board may outline the manager's responsibilities as follows:

1. The manager shall supervise the detailed operations of the cooperative in accord with the policies agreed upon by the board of directors.

2. The manager shall maintain an adequate bookkeeping and accounting system; provide for its regular examination by competent outside auditors, which are selected by the board of directors; and present to the members at the regular annual meeting a statement of the financial condition of the cooperative.

3. The manager shall attend all board of directors' meetings and make available a business report and a monthly financial statement.

4. The manager shall devote full time to the affairs of the cooperative. No employee shall have a financial interest in any business concern with which the cooperative does business, or engage in sideline activities or business in competition with the cooperative.

5. The manager shall develop budgets of anticipated income and expected operating costs and present such budgets to the board as it may require.

6. The manager shall bring to the board's attention all matters requiring board consideration and action.

7. The manager shall confer with the board of directors on the development of new policies and appraise the effectiveness of policies already adopted.

8. The manager shall develop membership loyalty.[6]

Relationship of the Manager to the Board

All operating decisions, employment and supervision of personnel, election of methods by which the policies are implemented, planning of

---

[6]Staff, *Sample Guide for Better Management Policies*, Iowa Institute of Cooperation, Ames, Iowa. pp. 7-8.

day-to-day activities and organization and coordination of operations are clearly a part of the manager's responsibility. He and he alone is charged with these responsibilities.

The manager shares some responsibilities jointly with the board, such as long-range planning. Here is the area in which teamwork is most productive. Long-range planning is the most important function of the board of directors and a primary function of the manager.

The manager usually provides the initiative and then helps the board make intelligent decisions. The purpose, future direction, broad basic policies, aims and objectives of the cooperative are decided upon by this process. Note that the board members make the policy decisions and that the manager must be careful to confine his activities to helping them make these decisions.

The exact relationship of a co-op manager to his board and of the board to the manager may be gleaned from President Lincoln's letters to two of his generals (Exhibit 16-1). President Lincoln, as "Chairman of the Board," delegated command to his "Manager," first, to Hooker and later, to Grant. It is noted that Lincoln in no way attempted to tell his generals *how* to win but instead enunciated *why* they should win. Lincoln also outlined a policy for them and admonished Hooker about his shortcomings, although he praised Hooker's qualifications at the

EXHIBIT 16-1
Lincoln's Letter to Hooker[1]

Executive Mansion
Washington,
January 26, 1863

Major General Hooker:
General,
    I have placed you at the head of the Army of the Potomac. Of course, I have done this upon what appear to me to be sufficient reasons. And yet, I think it best for you to know that there are some things in regard to which, I am not quite satisfied with you. I believe you to be a brave and skillful soldier, which, of course, I like. I also believe you do not mix politics with your profession, in which you are right. You have confidence in yourself, which is a valuable, if not an indispensable quality. You are ambitious, which, within reasonable bounds, does good rather than harm. But I think that during Gen. Burnside's command of the Army, you have taken counsel of your ambition, and thwarted him as much as you could, in which you did a great wrong to the country, and to a most meritorious and honorable brother officer. I have heard, in such a way as to believe it, of your recently saying that both the Army and the Government needed a Dictator. Of course, it was not for this, but in spite of it, that I have given you the command.

Only those generals who gain successes, can set up dictators. What I now ask of you is military success, and I will risk the dictatorship. The government will support you to the utmost of its ability, which is neither more nor less than it has done and will do for all commanders. I much fear that the spirit which you have aided to infuse into the Army, of criticizing their Commander, and withholding confidence from him, will now turn upon you. I shall assist you as far as I can, to put it down. Neither you, nor Napoleon, if he were alive again, could get any good out of an army, while such a spirit prevails in it.

And now, beware of rashness. Beware of rashness, but with energy, and sleepless vigilance, go forward, and give us victories.

Yours very truly,
A. Lincoln

---

[1]The original letter is owned by Mr. Alfred Whital Stern, of Chicago, Ill. Now in Library of Congress, Washington, D.C.

Lincoln's Letter to Grant[2]

Executive Mansion
Washington,
April 30, 1864

Lieutenant General Grant,

Not expecting to see you again before the Spring campaign opens, I wish to express, in this way, my entire satisfaction with what you have done up to this time, so far as I understand it. The particulars of your plans I neither know or seek to know. You are vigilant and self-reliant; and, pleased with this, I wish not to obtrude any constraints or restraints upon you. While I am very anxious that any great disaster, or capture of our men in great numbers, shall be avoided, I know these points are less likely to escape your attention than they would be mine. If there is anything wanting which is within my power to give, do not fail to let me know it.

And now with a brave army, and a just cause, may God sustain you.

Yours very truly,
A. Lincoln

---

[2]The original letter is in the Henry E. Huntington Library and Art Gallery, San Marino, Calif.

same time. These two masterpieces of composition give a good insight of how a co-op board should relate itself to the manager who is in charge of the "field army." If the manager does not produce victories, then he, not the "troops," is replaced.

Qualifications of a Manager

A good co-op manager should possess all or most of these qualifications:

1. Intellectual ability, to think and think correctly and possess technical and administrative competence.

2. Creative ability, to be imaginative.

3. Visionary ability, to look ahead at the trends in his business.

4. Leadership ability, to have others to want to follow him.

5. Work ability, to carry forward the details in operating the business.

6. Decision ability, to be able to make good decisions rapidly.

7. Moral ability, to distinguish right from wrong and to hold high standards of conduct.

8. Judgment ability, to be flexible enough so that variations in people are recognized.

9. Public relations ability, to write and speak effectively in behalf of the cooperative.

10. Coordinating ability, to be able to bring together different viewpoints, analyze them and compromise these views in an effective manner.

Very few men can have perfect scores in all 10 abilities. Some of these abilities are native to the person; others can be learned through study and experience. Persons with high scores in all 10 abilities must be paid adequately since they are so rare.

Selecting a Manager

When a smaller cooperative is ready to locate a manager, its board of directors should do the following: (1) specify the nature of the job, qualifications sought and method of compensation, (2) advertise the vacancy in the community by word-of-mouth and, more importantly, in the local and area press, (3) prepare and distribute application blanks for prospective candidates and (4) interview the most likely prospects at a special board meeting. After the hiring is completed and depending on the person's qualifications, a short but intensive training period in another cooperative should take place. If that is not feasible, visits should be paid to other similar cooperatives. Other management assistance may be available from colleges, co-op councils, trade associations and other sources.

In a larger cooperative, selection of a manager is more formal. Assistant managers and department heads both in the cooperative and in other cooperatives are likely candidates. Very often, junior executives in other cooperatives, who have no room to move to the top, are a good source of personnel. Management staffs should never be too inbred. Cooperatives should periodically hire management from other cooperatives, other areas and, sometimes, from profit-type businesses.

There are no exact criteria for selecting a good manager. Perhaps the best overall criterion is for the board to know exactly what kind of a manager it is looking for. In cooperatives which are not too complex to manage, a certain kind of manager will best do the job. In cooperatives which are very complex and very exacting, another type of manager will have to be located.

Compensating the Manager

A cooperative, like other business institutions, must pay salaries high enough to attract and retain management sufficiently capable to attain the goals and objectives of the membership expressed through its board of directors.

Various compensation methods may be used, such as: (1) straight salary, (2) salary plus commission, (3) salary plus a percentage of net savings, (4) salary plus various fringe benefits (life insurance, health insurance, retirement plan), (5) salary plus bonus on net sales, (6) salary plus bonus based on percentage of annual salary, (7) straight commission and (8) combinations of the aforementioned. Each of these methods has advantages and disadvantages. It is likely that a straight salary plus a modest bonus of some type plus fringe benefits will yield the best results. For the more skilled management, a retirement plan in place of bonus scales might be better welcomed.

Stock or debenture options are another possibility for compensating a co-op manager and managerial personnel. Opportunity for employees to buy into the company is very common in profit-type businesses, primarily through stock options. The cooperative might consider paying half of the bonus in cash and half in nonvoting preferred stock or debenture bonds. Voting control, however, must always remain with the members.

Fringe benefits include paid vacations, sick leave, sabbatical leave, life insurance, hospital and medical insurance, discounts on merchandise and retirement plans. One or more of these have become firmly established in almost all personnel compensation plans.

Cooperatives, in order to attract and hold competent managerial personnel, might employ some kind of retirement plan, such as: (1) group annuity, (2) individual annuity contract, (3) self-administered trust and (4) group permanent plan, among others.[7]

Retirement plans also need to be coordinated with provisions of the Social Security Act.

Training the Manager

Of the cooperatives employing management training in one study, 86 percent indicated that the manager received training. The marketing associations gave their managers training primarily in co-op principles, financing, membership relations, management principles and public relations. The farm supply associations encouraged manager training primarily in selling and advertising, management principles, credit control, employee relations and co-op principles. The source of this training came mostly from regional cooperatives serving locals and from land-grant colleges and banks for cooperatives.[8]

As cooperatives become larger and as their organizational structures become more complex, more attention will have to be given to executive management. Top management will have to delegate some areas of managerial control to subordinates. In the larger operations, the cooperatives and their members will not be so close. Some of the common touch will be lost. Members will have to delegate more decisions to management; otherwise there will not be enough flexibility in decision-making. This does not mean that the principles of democratic representation will be lost, but it does imply that the practice of democratic control will be implemented in a manner quite different from that now practiced in small co-op associations.

Regardless of size, cooperatives need greater managerial flexibility. Managerial responsibility needs to be spread so as to develop a "management team," not just a manager. Young men should be trained and developed to fit into management teams with the depth of management and flexibility needed to steer cooperatives through the roughest of business competition and through any emergency that might arise.

---

[7]Hyre, French, *Retirement Plans of Farmer Cooperatives*, FCS Cir. 21, Washington, D.C. Sept. 1957. pp. 5-10.
[8]Volkin and Griffin, *op. cit.* pp. 12 and 16.

OUTLINES OF GOOD MANAGEMENT

Management is both the science and art of combining ideas, facilities, processes, materials and people to produce and market a worthy product or render service profitably. The foremost essential of good management is for the manager to be able to manage himself—organize his own work and thoughts, decide on a course of action, execute decisions and impartially analyze the results therefrom. He must also be his own best critic—not wait to hear criticism only from others. Unless he manages himself effectively, no amount of ability, skill, experience or knowledge will make him an effective executive.[9]

Good management is considerably more than being technically competent. Many technically competent people make inferior administrators. Many persons who are technically incompetent make productive administrators. Managers who are both technically and administratively competent are rare and therefore command premium salaries. This superior management is often the scarcest resource and very often the most limiting resource in a business. Land, equipment, capital and labor are usually not so scarce as good management. A superior manager can make a success of an otherwise poor business potential, while a poor manager will fail even with a great business potential.

On the whole, cooperatives require superior managerial ability because of the dual position of their customers, that of patrons and stockholders. Since most cooperatives are formed as a defensive weapon to correct some abuse in the economic system, co-op management is often pressed for quick and decisive results requiring strong leadership and fortitude during the many crises.

The board of directors, manager and his employee team are charged with the responsibility of planning (P), organizing (O), directing (D), coordinating (C) and controlling (C) the cooperative. These steps are often referred to as the PODCC of management.

Planning

Planning is the thoughtful determination and systematic arrangement of all the factors required to achieve the goals and objectives of

[9]Godfrey, Eleanor, Fred Fiedler and D. M. Hall, *Boards, Management and Company Success,* The Interstate Printers & Publishers, Inc., Danville, Ill. 1957. Chapters 6 and 8.

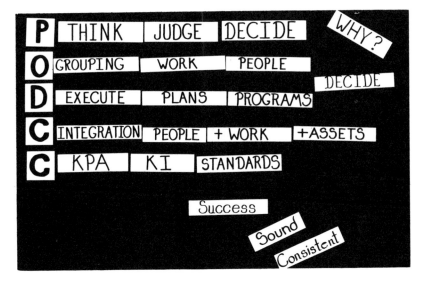

FIGURE 16-7

The PODCC of management refers to planning, organizing, directing, coordinating and controlling. (Courtesy, N.C. Agr. Ext. Serv., Raleigh, N.C.)

the business. It is getting ready to do the work, not the actual performance of the job. It is the function of predetermining what shall be done. It includes the preparation and research, development of policies and procedures, preparation and scheduling of work programs, determining needs for equipment and facilities, scheduling manpower requirements, forecasting results, preparing budgets, creating new ideas and improvements and any other activities which involve getting ready to do rather than doing. There is day-to-day planning, year-to-year planning and long-range planning. Planning should take place before "doing." There are vital steps in planning: (1) establishing objectives, (2) searching for alternatives, (3) selecting "the" alternative and (4) formulating derivative plans.

Organizing

Organizing is the grouping of activities and the fitting together of people in the best possible relationships to get the work done effectively and economically and to help achieve the objectives and goals of the cooperative. This involves responsibility for the organizational structure. It includes activities related to the personnel directly supervised, such as selection, assignment, training, appraisal, coaching and counseling and responsibilities for pay, morale and discipline.

Organization also involves two phases: (1) structure of administration and (2) coordination of individuals within that structure. In the former, each person must know "who does what." In the latter, someone must guide effectively so that the sum total of all individual efforts reaches an optimum point for that business.

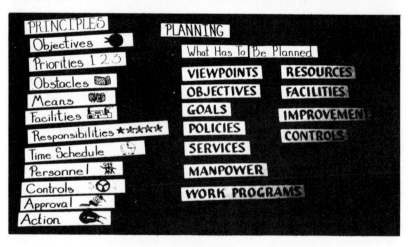

FIGURE 16-8

Planning is the first job of management. Time spent in planning the work to be done is not wasted time but yields considerable returns. (Courtesy, N.C. Agr. Ext. Serv. Raleigh, N.C.)

ORGANIZING IS

Grouping

Work

Objectives

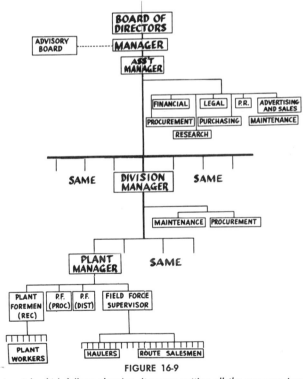

FIGURE 16-9

Organizing is a job which follows planning. It means getting all the resources together to get the work done. (Courtesy, N.C. Agr. Ext. Serv., Raleigh, N.C.)

The cardinal points in organization are as follows:

1. Specifically, there are four accepted types of organization today: (a) line, (b) line and staff, (c) functional and (d) committee. In the *line* type, authority and responsibility are direct from head to assistant to worker. In the *line and staff* type, the line command is dominant, but there are certain staff personnel who furnish specialized advice to the line managers. Larger and more complex enterprises use this technique. In the *functional* type, assignments are made according to the job to be done, such as transportation chief, inventory chief and warehouse supervisor, etc. The last type, or *committee*, consists of two or more persons acting jointly in their authority and respon-

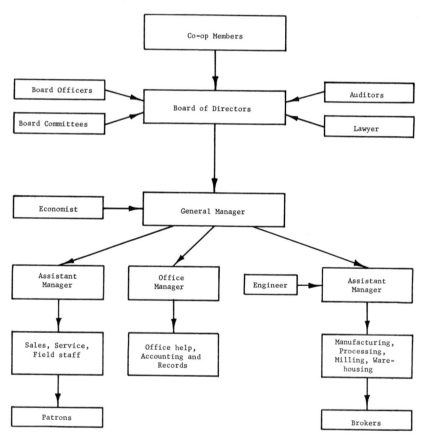

FIGURE 16-10

Simplified organizational chart for a typical farmer cooperative.

ORGANIZATIONAL CHART OF SOUTHERN STATES COOPERATIVE, INC.

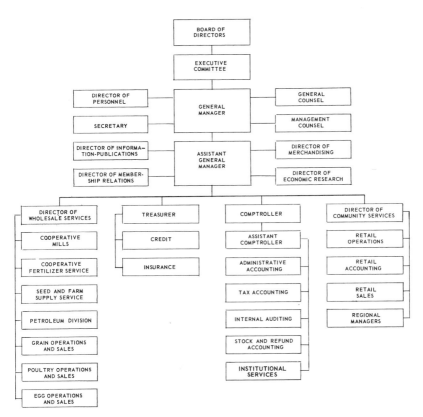

FIGURE 16-11
(Courtesy, Southern States Cooperative, Richmond, Va.)

sibility. This is used less as a dominant type than others, although it may be used widely as a supplementary management tool.

2. There should be a definite hierarchy with clean lines of authority running from the top to the bottom of the organization, and it should be understood by everyone.

3. A subordinate should not have to receive orders from more than one superior.

4. Unity of command, like functions, should be grouped together.

5. Responsibility should be coupled with commensurate authority.

6. Authority should be delegated as far down the line as possible.

7. Administrative efficiency increases with an increase in specialization.

8. Continuous in-service training is essential for staff members to be competent in performing their assignments.

9. Committees can be a useful adjunct to the organization, but they should be limited in number and have specific duties.

CONSUMERS CO-OPERATIVE OF BERKELEY   BOARD AND COMMITTEES

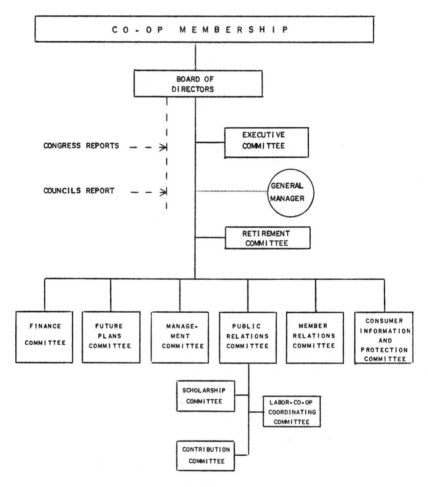

FIGURE 16-12

(Courtesy, Consumers Cooperative of Berkeley, Inc., Berkeley, Calif.)

10. No administrator should be required personally to supervise and account for more than 10 persons and should have fewer if the administration is complex.

Various organizational structures are shown in Figures 16-10 through 16-14.

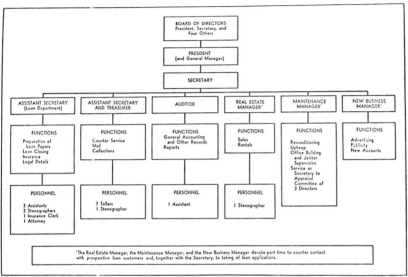

Organization Chart of a Savings and Loan Association with Assets of $15,000,000.

FIGURE 16-13

(Courtesy, College of Business Administration. Louisiana State University, Baton Rouge, La.)

Directing

Directing is getting the day-to-day execution of plans and projects accomplished. This includes the activities performed by others for which the incumbent is responsible and also those which he performs personally. Included are job delegations, specific assignments, instructions, communications, human relations and motivation. Among the items of personal performance are approvals, decisions, recommendations, conduct of and attendance at conferences, review or preparation of reports, interviews and negotiations. The managerial functions of planning and organizing must have been properly handled for the directing functions to be effectively performed.

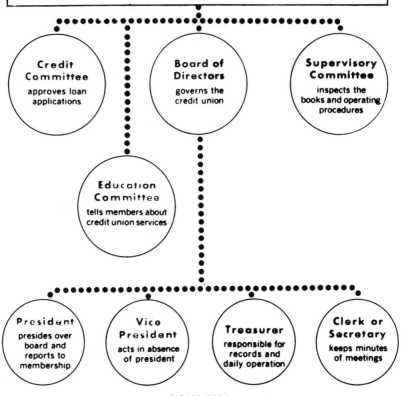

FIGURE 16-14

Above is the basic structure of the credit union. As the credit union grows, it may hire an office staff which is responsible to the treasurer. More committees may be added to improve service. Furthermore, some laws now permit appointment of a loan officer, or membership officer, to speed up procedure. (Courtesy, Credit Union National Association, Madison, Wisc.)

One of the most important factors in directing a business is the delegation of work and authority to subordinates. Too often a manager does not delegate authority. Since the manager is responsible for the whole business and its operations, he often tries to do all of the directing. Many managers wind up actually performing the jobs of employees. Such a situation does not leave time for the management to perform the actual functions of management—mainly, decision-making on the basis of a careful analysis of the best information available.

The essence of directing is the ability to command the work of others. In doing this, management should recognize ability in others. Authority goes hand in hand with responsibility. The responsibility must be delegated along with authority. It is of prime importance that a manager know what and when to delegate. A few simple rules are listed.

The manager should:

1. Delegate anything anyone else can do as well as or better than he can. Use specialists to do the jobs which they can handle and for which they were hired to handle.

2. Delegate things which he might do poorly because of a lack of time.

3. Delegate when a subordinate can do the job well enough for the cost or time involved. Often a subordinate cannot do the job so well as the manager could, but if the manager did the job, it would interfere with other more important jobs. It may take the manager less time to coach a subordinate than it would take to do the job himself.

4. Delegate when it costs too much for him to do the job.

5. Delegate the job as a means of developing subordinates if costs and time permit and if the job does not involve too much risk.

6. Always delegate when he has something more important to do.

7. Delegate if he finds he is spending too much time on operations and not enough time on managing. Delegate the work or develop someone to whom this work can be delegated.

8. Not delegate when he has the time and know-how to do the job.

Written Policy.—Policy must be written. Writing is concrete. A ruling is not a policy if it is made up in the person's mind at the spur of the moment.

The advantages of written policy are many. It is available. It can be seen and read by all employees. It is available when the boss is gone; written policy will enable the business to run without the manager being around. Writing is nonpersonal. It relieves "people" of telling someone what to do or gets them "out of a trap" and "off the spot."

A written policy might include these areas of business: (1) sales, (2) purchasing, (3) production, (4) finance, (5) office procedures and (6) personnel, among others.[10]

---

[10]Cochrun, I., *Do You Need a Written Policy?* Agricultural Industries Forum, Urbana, Ill. 1962.

FIGURE 16-15

*Directing is the job which follows organization. It means guiding the resources while they are
at work to accomplish the plans. (Courtesy, N.C. Agr. Ext. Serv., Raleigh, N.C.)*

After the policies have been formulated, meetings with employees and others concerned should be held to explain these policies. If necessary, policies can be revised in light of suggestions made by employees. They will feel that these are their policies as well.

Coordinating

Coordination is the function of management which results in the integration of the activities of people, of the use of facilities and materials and of the handling of the assets of an enterprise to accomplish a unified approach to a predetermined goal or objective. This involves the integration of relationships with other departments and applies specifically to activities for which the incumbent is responsible that involve others in sharing, checking, reviewing, appraising or controlling activities. It includes working-team relationships with the board of directors.

There are basically four major areas of coordination. These are:

1. Coordination in planning.

2. Coordination of individual assignments. Coordinated individual activities provide teamwork.

3. Coordination of the activities of the various departments or units. This is particularly necessary when the success of one department depends on another for services, materials, etc.

4. Coordination of internal activities of the business with the political, social and economic activities outside the business.

Controlling

Controlling is the function which involves seeing to it that the plan of action is followed according to specifications and taking remedial action when needed to prevent unsatisfactory results. This includes the responsibility of the incumbent to keep informed of progress within his organization; to interpret trends and results; and to know when, where and how to initiate timely remedial action. Some controls may be exercised over the work of others who do not report to the incumbent. These may be preventive or facilitative. Some necessary preventive controls are personal signatures, inspections and approvals. Facilitative controls, such as budgets, are very important. Controlling is not a restrictive measure. Rather it is an informative measure. It is likened to the gauges on the dashboard of an automobile. It indicates how the various parts are performing.

COORDINATING IS

KNOW FIVE PURPOSES

Diagnose →

Remember →

Inform →

Predict →

Prevent →

FIGURE 16-16

Coordinating is the fourth job of management. It consists of integrating the activities of people and things to accomplish a unified approach to the predetermined goals of the cooperative. (Courtesy, N.C. Agr., Ext. Serv., Raleigh, N.C.)

FIGURE 16-17

Controlling is the final job of management and involves the assessment of what is being done against what should have been done. (Courtesy, N.C. Agr. Ext. Serv., Raleigh, N.C.)

Main purposes of controls are: (1) to prevent unauthorized actions, (2) to keep people informed on progress, (3) to give predictions of trends and to forecast results, (4) to provide a maximum amount of information for remedial action and (5) to provide information useful in future planning.

Other aspects of managing cooperatives are discussed in the next chapter.

TOPICS FOR DISCUSSION

1. Name and discuss at least five powers and five responsibilities of co-op members.
2. Name and discuss at least five powers and five responsibilities of co-op board members.
3. What makes a good board member?
4. Discuss the powers and responsibilities of co-op managers.
5. Discuss the PODCC of management.

SELECTED REFERENCES

1. Abshier, George and Bob Dahle, *Management for Agricultural Marketing Firms*, N.C. Agr. Ext. Serv., Raleigh, N.C.
2. Alanne, V. S., *Manual for Cooperative Directors*, Co-op Publishing Association, Superior, Wisc. 1938.
3. Beall, Hayes and P. J. Dodge, *Signposts for Directors of Cooperatives*, Cooperative League, Chicago, Ill. 1962.
4. Bock, R. H. and others, *Long-Range Planning*, Purdue University Agr. Eco. Dept., Lafayette, Ind. Mar. 1960.
5. Drucker, Peter, "How to Be an Effective Executive," *Nation's Business*. Apr. 1961.
6. Gardner, K. B., *Managing Farmer Cooperatives*, FCS Circ. 17, Washington, D.C. Nov. 1963.
7. Garoian, Leon and A. Haseley, *The Board of Directors in Agricultural Marketing Businesses*, Oregon State University, Corvallis, Ore. 1963.
8. Hulbert, H. H. and others, *Bylaw Provisions for Selecting Directors*, FCS Gen. Rept. 78, Washington, D.C. July 1960. p. 15.
9. Jaynes, M. C., *Handbook for Directors of Farmer Co-ops*, Tex. Agr. Ext. Serv. Bul. 170, College Station, Tex. 1949.
10. Jones, J. B. and Ray Mischler, "Test Your Understanding of Directors' Responsibilities," *News for Farmer Cooperatives*, Washington, D.C. July 1962.
11. Kuehn, W. H., *The Pitfalls in Managing a Small Business*, Dun & Bradstreet, New York, N.Y. 1956.
12. Leith, Gordon, "CCA Puts a Local Under the Microscope," *News for Farmer Cooperatives*, Washington, D.C. Sept. 1960.

13. Ray, Oakley and C. B. Cox, *Selection and Responsibilities of Co-op Directors*, Ind. Agr. Exp. Sta. Bul. 666, Lafayette, Ind. Aug. 1958.
14. Smith, Eldon, and W. C. Binkley, *How Kentucky Farm Credit Cooperatives Are Controlled*, Ky. Agr. Exp. Sta. Circ. 567, Lexington, Ky. May 1960.
15. Staff, *Better Boards and Committees*, Adult Education Association, Chicago, Ill. 1960.
16. Staff, *Board Manual for Directors*, Midland Cooperatives, Minneapolis, Minn. Not dated.
17. Staff, *Cooperative Management and Administration*, I.L.O., Geneva, Switzerland. 1960. Chapters 2, 3, 4 and 6.
18. Staff, *Decision Making by Management*, Royal Bank of Canada, Montreal, Canada. Jan. 1963.
19. Staff, "Directors: Drivewheel of Co-ops," *News for Farmer Cooperatives*, Washington, D.C. Jan. 1958.
20. Staff, *Guide to Modern Management for Cooperatives*, Cooperative League, Chicago, Ill. Jan. 1962.
21. Staff, *Handbook for Federal Credit Unions*, FCU-543, Washington, D.C. 1961. Chapter 7.
22. Staff, *Manual of Excellent Managements*, American Institute of Management, New York, N.Y. 1959.
23. Staff, *Review of International Cooperation*, International Cooperative Alliance, London, England. Mar. 1963.
24. Staff, *Story of Sears-Roebuck*, Fairchild Publications, New York, N.Y. 1961.
25. Thach, W. T. and others, *Using Deferred Compensation in Small Business*, SBA Rept. 107, Washington, D.C. Sept. 1959.

CHAPTER 17 –

Management of Cooperatives:
Other Aspects

The United States of America would not amount to as much as it does if the young men of 50 years ago had been afraid that they might earn more than they were paid for.
—*Thomas A. Edison*

To put the affairs of the people in the hands of the people without first educating the people is a prelude to either a tragedy or a farce.
—*James Madison*

Wanting to work is so rare a merit that it should be encouraged.
—*A. Lincoln*

MANAGING THE EMPLOYEES

SOME OF THE ASPECTS of managing the employees have already been discussed in the previous chapter. Although the co-op manager must be a man of competence, he must realize that he is not an expert in all fields. He selects and trains capable employees and knows the art of delegating responsibility. This means that he realizes training does not cost money; what costs money is paying for the mistakes of untrained people. He creates conditions that encourage employees to maintain high productivity on their own accord, and advancements are made upon the basis of merit, performance and planned standards.

It must be remembered that co-op employees are the key link between executive management and the membership. If the employees do not perform adequately and efficiently while serving the cooperative's patrons, a large measure of the cooperative's membership relations program is damaged, often beyond repair.

Job Evaluation

Job evaluation involves three main steps: analyzing the job, writing up the job sheet and making the classification and pricing the job.

Properly done, these steps permit management to relate job pay to job requirements, to give the same pay for equal work, to use a consistent method in classifying new jobs and to obtain data for use in wage incentive plans.

In *analyzing the jobs*, the objective is to be able to describe them in specific and common terms. The main items to cover in such analyses are the kind of work performed, the skill needed, the responsibility required, the effort called for and the working conditions involved.

The comprehensive written statement of the analyzed facts about a job is often called a *"job sheet."* It is valuable in making certain that the elements of the job are clearly identified. It gives an established "road map" with which to proceed to the further classification and pricing of the job. Every job sheet has two parts: (1) the job description—the what, how and why of the job—and (2) the job specification—the degree to which the various elements are found.

A *job description* is a working tool. In a well-coordinated organization it is constantly referred to and is used to ensure smooth working relationships. When prepared carefully, in accordance with a sound and workable plan, position descriptions can be used in many ways to improve management efficiency. They serve as a basis for recruitment, selection, training and development of personnel; save time in interpreting responsibilities to newly appointed personnel; facilitate the proper assignment of functions to positions and the incorporation of changes in positions; and guide the planning, coordination and control of work. They also provide the basis for appraising the soundness of the organization's structure.

Job pricing is the last phase of job evaluation. It is the procedure by which a dollar rate of compensation is adopted for the jobs which have previously been analyzed. Two important problems are involved: (1) The pay for the various jobs must conform to the values of those jobs as established by the analysis within the cooperative. (2) The resulting pay plan must fit the going wage scale of the labor market in which the cooperative competes.

Selecting Employees

In the process of hiring employees, the co-op manager should observe these steps:

1. Have each applicant complete an application for employment.

2. A physical examination should be required, and, if possible, some type of aptitude tests given.

FIGURE 17-1

Employees working in a good environment, with adequate and sanitary facilities and efficient equipment will produce top results for the cooperative. (Courtesy, California Almond Growers Exchange, Sacramento, Calif.)

3. When hired, the employee should be given a probationary appointment.

4. The employee should be given a copy of the co-op articles, by-laws, membership agreements, job manuals and his job description. He should be quizzed on these sometime later.

5. As a matter of personnel administration, the manager or supervisor should:

(A) Make it clear at the beginning of the employment *what* the employee is supposed to do and *how much* of it he is expected to do during an hour, day or other time unit.

(B) Give proper training for the job.

(C) Observe and inspect the employee's work at regular intervals to make certain it is done right.

(D) Tell each subordinate how he is doing, what the weaknesses in his job are and how to overcome them. Help him if necessary.

(E) Create work happiness—giving the subordinate a sense of self-satisfaction on the job and the feeling that he is doing worthwhile, useful work. He must also understand his role in the overall co-op organization and possibilities for advancement.

Compensating Employees

Various types of compensation are used depending on the nature of the jobs involved. Obviously, the warehouse boy will necessitate a different compensation plan from those for salesmen. Straight salary alone, salary plus incentives, hourly wage, piece-rate pay, commissions and other methods are available.

In any case, incentive-type payments plus a straight salary are recommended whenever applicable. The competition for employees in an area, minimum wage laws, union wage scales and other factors must be considered.

Of the three basic methods for figuring how much money a salesman is to be paid—straight salary, straight commission or a combination plan —the first two have long been familiar. Most current variations derive from combination plans. These involve a balancing of some fixed income (salary) with various sorts of variable income (commissions, bonuses, profit sharing and the like).

Fringe benefits are important. Vacation with pay, sick leave, life and disability insurance, hospital and medical insurance, credit union, discounts on merchandise, funeral leave pay, jury duty leave pay, retirement plans, educational courses, among others, are involved.

An effective employee benefit plan should give the worker some protection against at least four major financial hazards:

1. Loss of future earnings because of premature death.

2. Loss of current earnings due to disability.

3. Excessive medical expenses arising from illness or accident.

4. Need for lifetime income following retirement from productive employment.

Effective coverage can be given in each of these areas through an employer's voluntary benefits plan working in conjunction with the governmental plans required by law, such as social security.

A study by the Farmer Cooperative Service showed that farmer cooperatives had a good record in providing fringe benefits to their personnel:

Benefit	Percent Having
Medical insurance	92.3
Life insurance	84.6
Retirement	75.0
Bonus, etc.	48.5

A well-defined promotion policy is important to employees. Employees will work harder and demonstrate more initiative if they are aware of the opportunities open to them in the cooperative. Often, capable assistant managers in cooperatives leave their jobs when their future opportunities are not discussed.

Merit-rating plans are sometimes employed as a tool for salary increases and promotion. While sound in theory, these plans do have pitfalls and must be administered carefully.[1]

Employee Morale

The strongest incentives management can use to develop employee morale include:

1. Recognition of individual abilities.
2. Opportunity to make optimum utilization of abilities and interests.
3. Pride in a job well done.
4. Rewards based on performance.

The attitude of employees towards the executives and supervisors of the cooperative for which they work is about the most important factor in determining their morale and efficiency.

Employee Training

The organization and operation of an employee training program is a basic necessity in the successful functioning of a cooperative. Trained employees are so vital to any cooperative that it is not necessary to elaborate on their importance.

While membership understanding and support of cooperatives are essential to success, it is also true that the success or failure of most cooperatives is tied directly to personnel. A cooperative cannot be successful unless it has well-trained, capable and aggressive personnel. Inefficient personnel are usually a major factor when cooperatives fail.

---

[1]Bentley, Robert, "Merit Rating," *American Cooperation*, A.I.C., Washington, D.C. 1948. pp. 205-210.

FIGURE 17-2

Co-op employees are interested in training for advancements in rank and pay. Top-notch employees who are well trained, well paid and who are aggressive are a cooperative's best chance for success. (Courtesy, Florists' Telegraph Delivery Association, Detroit, Mich.)

The average employee wants a program of information and training. It makes him feel important to the success of the cooperative. It gives him status, prestige and is good for his morale. It contributes to his job satisfaction and increases his productivity; he has a vested interest in the welfare of the cooperative. This is where he gets the paycheck that feeds, clothes and shelters his family. The more successful he can make the cooperative, the better chance he has for a promotion, either within or without the association.

Training of employees below the manager's level is probably a weak point in many cooperatives. There are at least two areas of training an employee which are necessary: (1) training in co-op principles so that the employee himself can educate and inform those whom he serves and (2) training in the technical phases of his employment (feed salesman, warehouseman, deliveryman, bookkeeper, etc.).

A study on the training of managers' assistants showed that 60 percent of the cooperatives giving management training enabled managers' assistants to receive this training. The primary areas of training received by those in marketing associations were bookkeeping, co-op

FIGURE 17-3

The cooperative's fieldmen are among the key personnel because they meet regularly the own-
ers and customers of the cooperative. They must be up-to-date in their knowledge, know how
to work with people and understand that their customers are also owners of the cooperative.
(Courtesy, Southern States Cooperative, Richmond, Va.)

principles, membership relations, selling and advertising and public relations. For farm supply associations, the primary areas were selling, principles, membership relations, credit control and public relations.[2]

The most important personnel to train, as far as meeting and serving the member-patrons, are the fieldmen or servicemen, sales clerks, salesmen and deliverymen.

There is much that can be done within a cooperative in training employees instead of sending them to formal workshops and seminars. An employee must be well versed on all phases of the cooperative itself, on co-op principles, on the history of their cooperative, and on characteristics of the membership. Training in the job itself should make use of manuals, booklets, books, etc. A modest library or information rack should occupy space in every cooperative. In addition, each year there should be a two-way evaluation program: (1) where the management

[2]Volkin, D. and N. Griffin, *Management Training Among Farmer Co-ops*, FCS Gen. Rept. 65, Washington, D.C. June 1959. pp. 2 and 15.

evaluates the employees and (2) where the employees evaluate the management. Such evaluations can cover working conditions, rates of pay, quality of work, quantity of work, dependability, cooperation, fringe benefits, morale and confidence in management, among other things.

In any event, the communication channels between workers and management must remain open so that both the good and bad information can find a proper channel. Cooperatives need to devise types of communication which will adequately serve their needs.

Unionized Employees

The whole labor problem, particularly as it affects the co-op organization, should be continuously observed and carefully studied. Heretofore, much difficulty has been experienced by sheer lack of understanding between labor and cooperatives. Labor should be given an opportunity to know the aims of the cooperative and of the management. Most of the unionized employees in cooperatives are working in plants or warehouses, or as truck drivers. Very few office employees are members of unions. The board or a committee of the board together with the general manager should represent the cooperative in all union negotiations.

Several cooperatives have experienced certain operating problems, particularly relating to seniority, which have arisen in connection with unions. Also cooperatives have had strikes to deal with, none of which, however, have been as serious as some labor difficulties experienced by other types of business organizations. Some co-op executives frankly admit that they would prefer not to deal with unions. On the other hand, some executives indicate that they prefer to deal with employees through unions, for, as one manager put it, "It provides a systematic means of talking things out. We feel that, as long as the union does not try to run the business, everything will be satisfactory."

MEMBERSHIP RELATIONS AND EDUCATION

Ideally, the membership should be educated concerning cooperatives before organization. The St. Francis Xavier University movement in Nova Scotia, Canada, pioneered this concept with much success. Before any cooperative is organized and chartered, the Extension Department of St. F. X. conducts educational classes in the community for a period of up to one year. This gives the instructors an idea of the leadership available, the need for a cooperative and the persistence of prospective cooperatives in attending classes regularly. This system of adult education and orientation is the best which can be devised.

In the United States, particularly, a basic weakness in co-op endeavors has been the too quick and too uninformed response to co-op organization. The net result has been the necessity for spending large amounts of time and money educating the membership after the cooperatives have been organized. In many cooperatives, the educational program has not yet begun, and in others, the program is lost in a maze of confusion and controversy. Relatively few cooperatives have successful membership education programs.

Many different studies conducted in the United States and throughout the world confirm most emphatically the viewpoint that relatively few members fully understand their cooperatives.

A Canadian survey of consumer co-op members revealed that 53 percent did not know of the one man, one vote principle; 43 percent had never attended an annual meeting; 65 percent never took their criticism to the directors; and 90 percent joined for reasons other than for ownership purposes.

Ohio sociologists found that three-fourths of the dairy co-op members surveyed did not know what happened to their milk check deductions. One-fourth understood little, if any, of their contract with the cooperative.[3]

Beal reports that in his study 43 percent of the respondents had never attended an annual meeting, 20 percent were getting no information from their cooperative and 31 percent stated they had no responsibility to their cooperative. He found a high correlation between the members' use of the cooperative and their knowledge of basic co-op principles.[4]

Brown and Price found in their study that co-op members were not very active in their milk cooperative, were poorly informed about their organization but were slightly satisfied with the results of their cooperative. They found that an active member is likely to be a well-informed member and a satisfied one at the same time. The most important channel of information was the co-op membership publication or house organ. Those members who went to meetings of the cooperative, read

[3]Andrews, W. H. and J. P. Clark, "Member Relationships in a Milk Co-op," *Ohio Research*, Columbus, Ohio. Nov.-Dec. 1961. p. 94.
[4]Beal, G. M., *News for Farmer Cooperatives*, FCS, Washington, D.C. Aug. 1955.

the printed material sent to them or were visited by one of the fieldmen or local officers were significantly more active, better informed and had more favorable attitudes toward the organization.[5]

FIGURE 17-4

This cooperative is trying to educate better its members as to the operations and services it provides. Many cooperatives neglect this phase of the membership program. (Courtesy, Greenbelt Consumer Services, Beltsville, Md.)

Gibson, in a Michigan study, found that one-third of the co-op members surveyed would desert their cooperative if prices for supplies ran a little higher at times. Forty percent would desert if marketing prices were a little lower than at other businesses. About 80 percent stated that no marketing contracts should be used and that members should drop out at any time they pleased. Twenty-one percent replied that members should vote according to shares of stock as in profit-type

[5]Brown, E. and H. Price, *News for Farmer Cooperatives*, FCS, Washington, D.C. Sept. 1956.

corporations. Twenty-four percent of the members felt that they were not part-owners of the business although they were members and had capital in the cooperative. Thirty-one percent felt they had no voice in the cooperative. About one-fourth had never attended their co-op meetings. Half did not know the tax status of cooperatives. Twenty percent thought consumer cooperatives were against the best interests of farmer cooperatives.[6]

Danner, in an Alabama study, reported that less than half of the patrons expressed the belief that the farmer cooperative was owned by farmers. Very few members had any knowledge as to their voting privileges or as to the number of votes to which they were entitled. Less than a third of the patrons received cash refunds, but most of them were apparently satisfied with the way the cooperative was handling savings. Few patrons indicated that they had any information about or evidence of any equity or share in the savings of the association from having done business with it. Less than half of the members and about a fifth of the nonmember-patrons knew one or more directors. Patrons who knew some board members felt that these directors were doing a satisfactory job. Only 10 percent of the patrons interviewed had attended the association's last annual meeting.[7]

In a North Carolina study, farmers had limited knowledge as to how prices for products marketed and supplies purchased at cooperatives compared with prices at other private business establishments. Farmers had given little consideration to the scope of business activity in which they desired their cooperatives to engage. This is indicated by the large number who were undecided when asked if they believed cooperatives should increase their electrical equipment business, establish service stations and add freezer-locker plants. About three-fourths of the farmers reporting attended no co-op meetings. Wide differences of opinion prevailed with respect to whether or not cooperatives are essentially different from other private businesses.[8]

Bell found in his study that 14 percent of the consumer co-op members had never shopped at their stores and almost two-thirds purchased less than 25 percent of their merchandise there. Yet, when asked for their reasons for joining, most replied that they believed in cooperation.

---

[6]Gibson, Duane, Co-ops as the Farmer Sees Them, Michigan State University Social Research Service, East Lansing, Mich. Oct. 1947.
[7]Danner, M. J., A Study of Patrons' Attitudes and Knowledge, Ala. Agr. Exp. Sta. Bul. 279, Auburn, Ala. Dec. 1950. p. 19.
[8]Abrahamsen, M. A. and C. L. Scroggs, What North Carolina People Think About Farmer Co-ops, N.C. Agr. Exp. Sta. Rept. 16, Raleigh, N.C. May 1948.

Thus, it can be concluded that, on the whole, most Americans probably believe in cooperatives as a good business philosophy, but they certainly are not willing to pay extra for this philosophy. It stands to reason that good business methods and efficiency will, in turn, enhance the spirit and philosophy of cooperatives. People usually come to believe in and admire business success rather than a mere philosophy of business.[9]

At least two points need to be explored: (1) how are cooperatives attempting to reach their memberships, and (2) what kind of program is needed to alleviate the lack of membership knowledge of cooperatives?

Sources of Co-op Information

Gibson found that the four most important sources of information for co-op members are: (1) the manager, (2) co-op publications, (3) meetings and (4) other members.[10]

Rust, in his study, found that co-op periodicals, personal contacts and annual meetings were the most important sources of information for co-op members. Other sources of information were circular letters, annual reports, educational exhibits, radio programs, newspapers and special pamphlets.[11]

Often the main drawback to these various practices is that they fail to deal with the fundamentals of cooperation. Superficial success stories and broad generalities are offered, while the basic co-op principles are ignored.

Who should carry the responsibility for the membership relations program? Lebeau found in his study that the manager takes the major responsibility for educational work in about half the associations reporting. In the remaining instances, this educational responsibility is generally assigned to one of the following: (1) an association official, (2) a public relations employee, (3) an educational or editorial employee or (4) a field worker.[12]

---

[9]Bell, Martin, "A Revised Concept of the Consumers' Cooperative," *Journal of Marketing*. Jan. 1961. pp. 37-41.
[10]Gibson, *op. cit.* p. 29.
[11]Rust, I. W., *Making Member Relations Succeed*, FCS Info. 32, Washington, D.C. Feb. 1963.
[12]Lebeau, O., *Educational Practices of Farmer Co-ops*, FCS Misc. Rept. 140, Washington, D.C. Jan. 1951.

Developing a Sound Program

In devising a sound membership relations program, a cooperative should endeavor to identify and classify its members and patrons into homogeneous groups. Some cooperatives have been known to send expensive brochures and materials to members who cannot read or write. Obviously, a different approach is needed here.

Henning and Poling suggest that the following group classification of patrons would help in planning a membership relations program:

1. Very well satisfied with the cooperative.
2. Intelligent and well informed.
3. Loyal and have a preference for the cooperative.
4. Easily influenced by others.
5. Not well informed.
6. Dissatisfied—had difficulty with the cooperative.
7. Retired—not engaged actively in business.
8. Those who have lost faith with the cooperative idea.[13]
9. Part-time farmers.
10. Income levels: low, middle and high.
11. Others: _____.

In order to obtain this kind of information on its patrons, each cooperative needs to make a thorough and critical survey of its members before it can efficiently design programs to educate or inform them.

The board of directors must take the initiative in a membership relations program since the board's existence comes from the members. An educational committee can meet this need. This is a special committee of members appointed by and responsible to the board of directors or elected by the membership. The educational committee plans a well-rounded educational program to be carried on by the local cooperative. In some instances it may direct its efforts to solving particular problems, such as excessive accounts receivable, the need for additional capital or a planned program of expansion. In some cases committeemen are selected from the various sections of the cooperative's trade territory so that each committee member has specific responsibility for the section he represents. Such a selection makes the committee more valuable to the board of directors in getting useful suggestions from members. Of course, the co-op manager should be on

---

[13]Henning, G. F. and E. B. Poling, *Attitudes of Farmers Toward Cooperative Marketing*, Ohio Agr. Exp. Sta. Bul. 606, Wooster, Ohio. Sept. 1939.

the educational committee, preferably as its secretary or advisor. Credit unions have utilized this type of educational committee with considerable success. Appointment of husband-wife teams on the educational committee has proved helpful also.

Advisory committees appointed by the board of directors can also be useful. Such a committee, comprising one board member and two other member-patrons, may advise on purchasing, marketing and/or servicing activities of the cooperative. These committees often serve as a testing ground for future board members.

Educational Content of the Program

Blair concludes that an educational program should deal with:

The *nature* of cooperatives, the *use* of cooperatives and the *potentials* of cooperatives.

Regarding the *nature* of a cooperative, members need to see it first as an *economic tool* or means to an end. Assuming that the desired end is increased net income, they need to become acquainted with the characteristics of a cooperative which make it useful as a tool for increasing net income. They need a clear explanation of the meaning of such terms as "service at cost," "nonprofit organization," "patronage dividends," "democratic control," "equal treatment of members versus fair treatment of members" and a host of other terms and concepts not normally used in reference to noncooperative types of businesses. They need to understand clearly the major differences and similarities of structure and operation between cooperatives and other types of business organizations operating in our economy.

With respect to the *use* of cooperatives, members need to be informed of the extent to which cooperatives of various types have been used in the past. They need to know what contributions cooperatives have made toward improving production and marketing efficiency. They need specific information as to how cooperatives were able to (and did) promote and encourage these more efficient production and marketing operations. They need to understand the personal responsibilities implied in co-op membership. They need to understand the social aspects of using a cooperative—the process by which decisions are wrought and implemented at the ground level. They need to understand the legal framework underlying co-op organization and be prepared to take advantage of such opportunities as may exist.

In dealing with the *potentials* of cooperatives, special care needs to be taken. In my opinion, we would do members a disservice by emphasizing the potentials of cooperatives without carefully setting forth their limitations also. This would amount to overselling cooperatives at a time when it is vitally important that members understand what cooperatives *cannot* accomplish as well as those things they *can* or *may* be able to accomplish. It seems to me imperative that the potentials of cooperation be evaluated in light of the structural changes in the market complex during recent years and the trends expected in the future.[14]

Specific steps which might be taken in implementing a membership relations program are:

1. Develop directors and employees into an educational staff.
2. Make each annual meeting a red letter day.
3. Hold additional membership meetings in local neighborhoods.
4. Prepare a good annual report, simply stated, with visual aids.
5. Issue a periodic membership publication of some type.
6. Prepare special leaflets for members' use.
7. Distribute selected educational materials through schools, etc.
8. Maintain an up-to-date mailing list.
9. Supply news regularly to local papers and magazines.
10. Use the local radio and television.
11. Foster the family approach to member relations involving wives and children.
12. Provide educational opportunities in cooperation for youth groups.
13. Maintain attractive headquarters and facilities and sponsor "open house" tours.
14. Cultivate community relations and clarify co-op principles.[15]
15. Have educational committee contact members who otherwise might not be reached through various media.
16. Provide each member with a copy of the articles, bylaws and agreements.
17. Employ an educational director or delegate the educational work to board members working with the manager.
18. Maintain a co-op library, with films and educational exhibits, where materials can be purchased or borrowed for use.

---

[14]Blair, Paul, Tri-State Co-op Committee Meeting, Auburn, Ala. Nov. 27, 1962.
[15]Lebeau, O. R., *Membership Practices of Local Co-ops*, FCS Gen. Rept. 81, Washington, D.C. July 1960.

FIGURE 17-5

Each cooperative should have a library containing books, pamphlets, circulars and magazines, on cooperation especially. This farmer cooperative in Mexico allows the members' children to use the library. (Courtesy, Food and Agriculture Organization, United Nations, N.Y.)

19. Provide scholarship funds for co-op members' children who demonstrate high academic achievements.

20. Develop co-op adult study groups.

Treatment of Large-Scale Versus Small-Scale Patrons

Considerable controversy has arisen over the question of how to treat small-scale and large-scale patrons of cooperatives. The North American cooperatives are especially plagued with this question.

As stated previously, there is a difference between equal and equitable treatment. Cooperatives are obligated to treat their members equitably, not equally. This means that it is legitimate and consistent with co-op principles to give quantity or volume discounts, for example. Equitable treatment can be related to cost data in the best interests of the members as a whole. Price and cost differentials need to be available to all members and published so the members will understand them.

The practice of giving unequal but equitable treatment is a long-standing one in cooperatives although frequently misunderstood. For example, the Rochdale Pioneers were known as the *Equitable Society*.

NONCOOPERATORS BENEFIT FROM COOPERATORS

Very often those who do not participate in a cooperative reap substantial benefits nevertheless. There have been many instances in which the price of a product has shown an immediate increase when farmers first formed a cooperative to market produce or in which the price of farm supplies has dropped when farmers started retailing or manufacturing their own through a cooperative, at times as much as 30 to 40 percent on some supplies in some areas. This is a contribution to all farmers in those communities, not just to members of the particular cooperative. In fact, noncooperators, without providing any capital or patronage, benefit from cooperatives. Cooperatives often serve as an "insurance policy" against economic catastrophe for their members and often for nonmembers.

THE ANNUAL MEETING

The annual meeting is the most important single activity of the cooperative. The prime purpose of an annual meeting is not recreation but information. This does not mean that the meeting should not be entertaining, but it should always be informing.

Bylaw specifications usually spell out the procedures to be employed in calling an annual meeting. However, the cooperative should not limit itself to legal notices only. Newspaper, radio, TV and other means and media may be employed to publicize the meeting, especially when the membership is large or scattered.

A good attendance depends upon a good program, adequate facilities, good planning and publicity. Every attempt possible should be made to encourage member participation at annual meetings. Food, guest speakers, prizes, entertainment programs, films, demonstrations, talent shows, style shows for wives and other devices may be employed for encouraging attendance. However, the main drawing card must

FIGURE 17-6

The annual meeting of the cooperative is the one most important activity of the year. While a co-op annual meeting should be entertaining, its primary function is to be informative. (Courtesy, MFA, Columbia, Mo.)

necessarily remain that of informing members about the past year's operation.

Scofield well expresses the problem of attendance at annual meetings:

> Any answer on how we get them to take part in meetings will be a definite answer on how we can motivate our members. One of the basic premises in getting members to take part in their meetings means setting up and agreeing upon at least these basic objectives, these being: that we really want them to take part in the meetings; that we really want our co-op run by the members, not just for the members; that we really want the facts, not just promotional material; that, first of all, the meetings must be run by the members and not just for publicity of the cooperative; that they do want democratic voting by ballot, not just railroading; and that they do want new people, new experiences and new ideas. That we do want factual figures that have meaning and not excuses; that they are members and stockholder-owners, not just patrons or customers; that they do participate in investing and are made conscious of this; and that they do receive their overcharges

and underpayments returned to them on a patronage basis; that the basic theme of the cooperative is for use and not for sale.[16]

One procedure often overlooked is to give more responsibility to the members themselves in planning and arranging for the annual meeting. Members should be invited to plan, publicize and arrange for the meeting so that they can honestly feel it is their meeting too.

FIGURE 17-7

Members should be given an opportunity to express themselves at a co-op annual meeting. Too often, nothing is ever heard from the members in the audience. (Courtesy, Cooperative League, Chicago, Ill.)

[16]Scofield, Alton, *Midwest Membership Relations Conference Proceedings*, Kansas City, Mo. Apr. 30, 1959.

The usual agenda for an annual meeting is as follows:
1. President's call to order.
2. Secretary's roll call of the membership and reading of minutes.
3. President's comments on the past year's progress.
4. Manager's report on the volume of business and operational results.
5. Treasurer's or auditor's report on the profit and loss statement and balance sheet.
6. Directors' reports and/or other business.
7. Election of board members.
8. Questions from the floor and/or panel discussions.
9. Educational and/or entertainment program.
10. Adjourn.
11. Dinner and/or entertainment.

Since the financial statements and the manager's report are the key documents at the annual meeting, these should be mimeographed or printed and a copy given to each member preferably 15 days in advance of the meeting.

An adequate presentation of the financial statements at the annual meeting is discussed in the following section.

ACCOUNTING TO THE BOARD AND MEMBERS

One of the most important features of a successful cooperative is a sound accounting system. Co-op accounting does not differ greatly from accounting for profit-type firms. The distinguishing features of co-op accounting are as follows:

1. An accurate record must be kept of each patron's purchases and sales through the cooperative. After deducting the cost of doing business, the net proceeds are the property of the member-patrons and must be allocated or paid to them in cash, exactly proportionate to the patronage of each. This cannot be done unless accurate patronage records are kept.

2. Accurate departmental cost accounts are usually required in cooperatives with more than one department. Operating costs and margins usually vary between different departments. Since individual members do not make equal use of all departments, departmental accounting is necessary to be fair to all members.

3. Capital in the business which originates from operating proceeds must be allocated to member-patrons in a cooperative. Each individual

member-patron has a definite equity in such capital. Unless it is definitely allocated and disclosed to him, he has no individual claim to his share of this capital.

4. Member and nonmember business must be separated in a cooperative. For state and federal income tax purposes, this separation is advisable.

5. Cooperatives are obliged to notify each member-patron of the amount of his patronage allocation after the close of the fiscal year. Such an allocation is the actual property of each individual member-patron. Unless this allocation is disclosed to him, he cannot report it in his individual income tax return.

6. A monthly balance sheet and operating statement are usually required in a cooperative. Statements should be sent to board members prior to the meeting to encourage study and reflection.

7. The amount by which the assets exceed liabilities is shown as member equity (member ownership) in a co-op balance sheet. In an ordinary business organization this amount would be called net worth. The cooperative itself has no net worth. The difference between assets and liabilities in a cooperative is the property of the member-patrons.

8. An audited annual statement should always be presented to the membership in a cooperative. Members, as owners and patrons of the cooperative, must have this information in order to understand and appraise the past year's operation.

The two basic types of financial reports are: (1) the operating statement (Table 17-1) and (2) the balance sheet (Table 17-2). The operating statement shows how the cooperative fared over a given period of time, while the balance sheet is a snapshot picture at a given point in time.

Accounting by Departments

A combined income and expense statement is not sufficient by itself. An operating statement of income and expense should be prepared for each major department. From such statements, the per unit operating cost for each department can be determined. Per unit costs are significant in indicating the efficiency of a business. Inefficiency and small "leaks" in some departments, if not discovered at an early state, may soon drain off all savings from efficient operations in other departments and cause real difficulty to the association (Table 17-3).

TABLE 17-1
Operating Statement
———————— Cooperative Marketing Association
January 1, 19___, to December 31, 19___

Returns from Products Handled:			$480,275.69
Cash advance to patrons.........................$412,534.20			
(1) Inventory, beginning of year.............	10,453.47	$422,987.67	
Less (2) inventory, end of year..............		6,974.20	416,013.47
Gross Margin			$ 64,262.22
Operating Expenses:			
Labor and wages.....................................		$ 22,800.00	
General supplies		5,321.40	
Fuel		3,867.07	
Light and power.....................................		3,311.40	
General repairs		1,390.23	
Other plant expenses..............................		713.19	
Depreciation: buildings ....$	833.57		
Depreciation: machinery and equipment	2,245.13		
Depreciation: delivery equipment.........	725.00	3,803.70	41,206.99
General and Administrative Expenses:			
Office salaries		$ 1,850.00	
Directors' fees		1,185.00	
Payroll taxes		928.00	
Local taxes		1,527.30	
Insurance		684.65	
Office supplies		723.00	
Advertising and printing.........................		504.60	
Telephone and telegraph........................		123.20	
Auditing		352.65	
Annual meeting expense.......................		359.05	
Depreciation: office equipment..............		61.62	
Bank service charges..............................		51.50	
Miscellaneous items		199,50	8,550.07
Total Expenses			$ 49,757.06
Balance Due Patrons—Net Margin..............			$ 14,505.16

Source: Dankers, W. H., *Know Your Cooperative Association*, Minn. Agr. Ext. Bul. 232, St. Paul, Minn. Jan. 1963.

Management needs to know which products and services have been most profitable and why some have not been so profitable as they might have been. The accounting by department should be sufficiently complete so that the figures needed to prepare operating statements for each department will be readily available. Not only is it necessary to have the gross profit for each principal product, but it is also necessary that the major expense items, such as salaries, depreciation, insurance, repair and taxes, be allocated among departments.

TABLE 17-2
Balance Sheet
December 31, 19___
_____ Cooperative Marketing Association

ASSETS (what the association has)

Current Assets:

Cash on hand............................		$ 408.20
Cash in bank..............................		5,250.00
Accounts receivable—patrons ....$ 1,466.10		
Accounts receivable—general 20,376.92	$ 21,843.02	
Less: allowance for bad accounts	856.85	20,986.17
Notes receivable		3,468.53
Inventory—merchandise		7,651.30
Inventory—supplies		7,303.85
Prepaid expense		1,193.72
Total current assets............		$ 46,261.77

Investments:

Stock and equities in other cooperatives		20,500.00

Fixed Assets:

Land		$ 2,516.68
Buildings	$108,343.32	
Less: allowance for depreciation	31,941.37	76,401.95
Machinery and equipment........	$ 47,451.12	
Less: allowance for depreciation	10,295.62	37,155.50
Office equipment	$ 3,116.22	
Less: allowance for depreciation	298.65	2,817.57
Trucks and delivery equipment	$ 2,900.00	
Less: allowance for depreciation	1,250.00	1,650.00
Total fixed assets................		120,541.70
Total assets		$187,303.47

LIABILITIES (what the association owes)

Current Liabilities:

Short-term notes payable............	$ 1,497.93	
Accounts payable—patrons	33,884.70	
Accounts payable—general	1,254.62	
Accrued taxes and interest payable	1,413.00	
Total current liabilities......		$ 38,050.25

(Continued)

TABLE 17-2 *(Continued)*

Long-term Liabilities:			
Mortgage or long-term notes payable			$ 48,875.00
Total Liabilities			$ 86,925.25

MEMBER AND PATRON EQUITIES
(what the association owns—the members' and patrons' share)

Capital stock—authorized	$ 37,500.00		
Less: unissued stock................	10,250.00		
Capital stock outstanding..........		$27,250.00	
Capital stock credits.................		1,025.50	
Patrons equity credits— prior years	$ 57,597.57		
Patrons equity credits— current year	14,505.15	72,102.72	
Total member and patron equities			100,378.22
Total liabilities and member and patron equities			$187,303.47

Source: Same as for Table 17-1.

Usable Financial Reports

If annual financial reports of cooperatives are to get through to the membership, they need to be made more readable, more understandable and more attractive.

The financial sections of most annual reports are usually the dullest, least understood parts of the reports. Yet they are the most important. And much of their importance can be entirely lost on the membership because unfamiliar words and terms are employed.

Most financial reports appear too formidable to the average member to read, study and understand. Few, if any, of the members are accountants or bookkeepers. They are thus handicapped in digging the facts out of the report. All too often, when left to their own devices, members interpret financial statements wrongly. This is just as damaging as furnishing no financial report at all.

All of this lends emphasis to the need for simplifying a cooperative's annual financial statement to the membership.

TABLE 17-3
Departmentalizing an Operating Statement

Elevator department:
Sales and other income from grain..$1,253,610
Less: Amounts paid patrons for grain.. 1,128,725

Gross margin on elevator operations...$ 124,885
Less: Expenses of operating the elevator................................... 78,490

Net margins and savings: elevator department......................... $46,395

Oil department:
Sales and other income from gas, oil and greases.......................$ 171,825
Less: Cost of gas, oil and greases sold.. 132,865

Gross margin in oil department...$ 38,960
Less: Expenses of operating the oil department......................... 23,770

Net margins and savings: oil department.................................. 15,190

Lumber department:
Sales and other income from lumber...$ 134,750
Less: Cost of lumber sold.. 105,385

Gross margin on lumber..$ 29,365
Less: Expenses of operating the lumber department................. 24,540

Net margins and savings: lumber department........................... 4,825

Farm store:
Sales and other income...$ 74,655
Less: Costs of goods sold.. 60,833

Gross margin in farm store...$ 13,822
Less: Expenses of operating the farm store............................... 10,157

Net margins and savings: farm store... 3,665

Total net margins and savings in all departments...................... $70,075

Percent savings of sales:
Elevator 3.7
Oil 8.8
Lumber 3.6
Farm store 4.9
All departments 4.3

Cooperatives should not shy away from making their financal reports elementary. They should not hesitate to use the ABC's of bookkeeping rather than some of the hard-to-understand, technical accounting terms. The plainer the reports can be made, the more people will grasp their meaning. Understanding should be the objective of any financial report. Often illustrations can be used to drive home important facts.

FIGURE 17-8

Complex accounting and auditing reports must be simplified when making oral presentations to co-op members at an annual meeting. The reports themselves are made available to each member for his examination preferably prior to the meeting. (Courtesy, Bank for Farmer Cooperatives, Columbia, S.C.)

Financial reports to a cooperative's membership should emphasize only salient facts. Details should be available to those interested enough to make inquiry. But including too many details in the annual financial report only tends to confuse the membership and should be avoided.[17]

In presenting a simplified statement of a cooperative's financial position to the membership, it is generally necessary to revamp or remodel the auditor's formal report (Table 17-4).

Interpreting the Financial Statements

Members have to exercise caution in appraising a co-op operating statement. Unlike that of a profit-type corporation, the operating statement of a cooperative is not an "end" in itself but a "means" to an "end." A co-op operating statement might indicate a loss for the year,

TABLE 17-4
Remodeling a Balance Sheet

Current Assets owned, including cash, accounts receivable, inventories and accrued charges, totaling	$500,000	
When converted to cash will pay— Current Liabilities owed, consisting of accrued expenses, accounts payable and annual payment on term liability	100,000	
And provide— Net Working Capital of—		$ 400,000
When added to— Fixed Assets, including land, building and equipment at book value after depreciation, totaling	900,000	
After allowing for— Term Liabilities owed to bank for cooperatives	400,000	
Give us an— Equity in our fixed facilities of—		500,000
Added to— Other Assets, investments in other cooperatives and prepaid costs		200,000
Adds up to— TOTAL NET ASSETS ABOVE LIABILITIES		$1,100,000

These net assets are represented by—
Investment of Members in—

Common Stock	$ 4,000	
Preferred Stock	700,000	
Allocated equities	396,000	
TOTAL INVESTMENT OF MEMBERS		$1,100,000

[17]Hulbert, H. H., "Clarifying the Financial Report," *News for Farmer Cooperatives*, Washington, D.C. Nov. 1959. p. 14.

yet in the aggregate the individual co-op member's operating statement might have profited at the expense of the co-op's operating statement. For example, assume a co-op manager has underestimated the operating costs and charged less than he should. At the end of the year, the cooperative shows a "loss," yet the members benefited all year long by paying less than cost; therefore, their operating statements are better than they should have been, and the co-op's statement is worse than it ought to have been. This indicates that in a cooperative there is no pure profit or loss—only "overcharges" or "undercharges." This point will be reconsidered in the next two chapters on taxation of cooperatives.

Audits

The task of appointing and retaining an auditor belongs to the board of directors, never to the manager. The job of an auditor is to determine the adequacy and accuracy of the manager's bookkeeping system; therefore, the manager should never be a party to hiring of an auditor. Whenever possible, an auditor experienced with cooperatives should be retained. An auditor who audits several cooperatives is to be preferred to one who works primarily with profit-type corporations. In many cases, cooperatives in an area, state or region set up their own auditing firms cooperatively, thereby having exclusive use and counsel of auditors who are thoroughly familiar with cooperatives.

There are at least two kinds of audits which may be rendered: (1) qualified and (2) unqualified. A "qualified" audit means that the auditor assumes no responsibility for the accuracy of certain information, such as inventories and accounts receivable. An "unqualified" audit means that the auditor states no significant reservations on his work. In most cooperatives, it is wise to request an "unqualified" audit, especially where inventories and accounts receivable are a significant part of the current assets.

For certain types of cooperatives, such as credit unions, an auditing or supervisory committee drawn from the membership performs certain auditing and control functions. In federal credit unions, this committee files quarterly reports with the Bureau of Federal Credit Unions. In addition, federal agencies empowered to charter cooperatives usually perform annual audits of them. State agents, such as the Bank Commissioner, may also perform annual audits of state credit unions.

Ratios

Financial ratios used in evaluating a cooperative's performance are valuable tools. A most valuable technique is to compare financial ratios of similar cooperatives, such as farm supply and rice dryer cooperatives, co-op grocery wholesales, credit unions, etc. Comparisons of co-op financial ratios with profit-type company ratios are not sound for obvious reasons.

A list of all financial ratios applicable to cooperatives would be too cumbersome, but a few selected ones can be mentioned:

1. Accounts receivable to current assets.
2. Current assets to current liabilities.
3. Current assets to total assets.
4. Fixed assets to total assets.
5. Fixed assets to fixed liabilities.
6. Member equity to fixed assets.
7. Member equity to total assets.
8. Member equity to total liabilities.
9. Merchandise to current assets.
10. Net sales to fixed assets.
11. Net sales to member equity.
12. Net sales to receivables.
13. Net sales to working capital.
14. Net savings to member equity.
15. Net savings to net sales.
16. Net savings to member equity.
17. Net savings to total assets.
18. Notes payable to accounts payable.
19. Plant and equipment to fixed liabilities.
20. Total cash, receivables and marketable securities to current liabilities.
21. Total liabilities to member equity.
22. Total liabilities to total assets.
23. Total units of business (pounds, tons, dollars, etc.) to fixed assets.
24. Year's sales to year-end inventories.
25. Year's sales to average inventory.

To determine the desirable ratios, it is recommended that comparisons be made with similar cooperatives in an area or state. In making comparisons of the operating ratios of an individual business with standard or common figures, care should be taken to insure that the firms included in the computation of the averages or medians used are similar to the individual business being analyzed. National averages with no breakdown for size or type of operation are of little use in this connection except as very rough guides. Variations between different size businesses or different types of operations within a single trade may be extreme. Even when a high degree of selectivity and classification has been used in combining the reports included in a computation of averages or medians, the range of performance of the firms included will be considerable. For these reasons, it would be expected that variations between the ratios of an individual firm and standard or common figures are to be expected and can be justified. Nevertheless, such variations provide an indication of places to look for improvements in operations and increased earnings.

In addition to ratios, another useful technique is to provide comparative results between this year, last year and five years ago. In this way, the trend in operating results and status of the balance sheet are more meaningful. In preparing an operating statement, the cost of goods sold, gross margin, expenses and net earnings should also be expressed as a percentage of sales.

Other Vital Records

There are certain other records vital to co-op operations. These are:

1. An up-to-date membership roll in a conveniently usable form. If any member is legally entitled to more than one vote, his number of votes must be shown on a record available for use at each business meeting.

2. Accurate and permanent records of stock ownership, revolving fund and other equities.

3. For computation of patronage dividends, accurate records of patronage must be kept each year. Sound custodianship requires that these records be preserved for at least five years. A so-called exempt cooperative should not destroy any records without approval by the Internal Revenue Service.

Use of Budgets

The use of budgets as vital records is also recommended. An operating budget accommodates the operating statements; a financial budget accommodates the balance sheet. Labor and other type budgets

FIGURE 17-9

Many cooperatives can profitably use electronic data processing in their patronage accounting and in many other ways. Shown here is a machine which receives punched cards (lower left), tallies the information and prints it on monthly statements. To do the same job with an adding machine, 112 rows of keys would be needed. (Courtesy, Midland Cooperator, Minneapolis, Minn.)

may also be used.[18] Budgets are helpful in forcing co-op management
to think through next year's operation. This thought process is likely to
yield beneficial results in itself.

Electronic Data Processing

Larger cooperatives have adopted the use of computers as an aid
in inventory control, statistical forecasting, general ledger accounting,
payroll accounting and all types of management reporting. In cases
where individual cooperatives are too small to justify electronic data
processing, either co-op computer centers or computer service organizations offer a possibility for pooling this expense over many more
units.

Cooperatives operating service stations at many locations, for example, are obliged to adopt some type of tape-card-computer system.[19]
More cooperatives in the future will require this type of accounting.

Some retailer-owned co-op wholesales report significant sales gains
obtained by comprehensive utilization of computer systems in sales
analysis, inventory control and in other ways.

The growing importance of electronic data processing cannot be
minimized. Cooperatives, due to their extensive patronage accounting,
cannot afford to overlook the possibilities offered by computers in solving this and other problems.

One of the most powerful and inevitable of the factors which will
force the independent store owner in self-defense to join a cooperative
is the tremendous growth in the application and use of electronic data
processing equipment. This promises to enable giant retailing to obtain
more of the competitive advantages, and it clearly means that the
independent, unless he can obtain such benefits, will find himself at a
greater disadvantage than ever before.

Handling Patronage Refunds

There appears to be a lack of understanding as to patronage refunds
and patrons' equity. Savings should be returned or credited to patrons
in relation to the amount of business that is done with the cooperative,
particularly if the eligible cooperative wishes to retain exemption from

---

[18]Kaiser, H. M., *Getting Results from Your Budget,* SBA Aid 128, Washington, D.C.
Sept. 1961.
[19]*Midland Cooperator,* Minneapolis, Minn. Nov. 26, 1962. p. 8.

the payment of corporate income taxes. If capital is needed, retaining savings is entirely proper. The amount retained, however, should be carefully allocated to each patron's account, and the patron should be given proper written notice of his share or equity in the association, both annually and cumulatively for previous years. Under the provisions of the 1962 Revenue Act, cooperatives have to pay at least 20 percent of their net earnings in cash to patrons in order for them to meet their tax obligations while reporting noncash patronage refunds.

Adequate Insurances

The assets of a cooperative should be adequately insured at all times. These assets include the land, buildings, equipment and inventories to be protected from fire, theft, windstorm and other hazards. Vehicles likewise need protection resulting from collisions and liability damage. Personnel of cooperatives need to be protected for unemployment, disability, injury, death and other liability. Injuries or death to third parties resulting from actions of the cooperative or its personnel need to be covered. Funds and the handling of funds in the cooperative need bonding. There are other hazards. A competent insurance agent or broker should be consulted.

Cooperatives should always investigate the possibility of mutual insurance where insurance is provided at cost.

Adequate Accounting, Legal and Economic Counsel

In the modern business world, few cooperatives can exist successfully without adequate and competent accounting, legal and economic counsel. The increasing complexities in tax matters, especially with the passage of the 1962 Revenue Act, are sufficient reason to retain competent accounting counsel. The increasing use of contracts, development of economic integration and merger proceedings require that competent legal counsel be retained. Complexities of business management often require also the use of economic counsel. All three types of counsel (accounting, legal, economic) can be made as staff appointments either on a full-time, part-time, retainer fee or consultant basis. The board of directors has to authorize such staff appointments, and the appointees are responsible to the board although they will probably work mostly with operating management.

PUBLIC RELATIONS

Public relations for cooperatives includes their relationship to and image held by those not associated with them by patronage and/or ownership.

The viewpoint that cooperatives suffer seriously in a public relations sense can be well documented.

An Indiana study of attitudes held by business and professional leaders toward retail farmer cooperatives shows real cause for concern (Table 17-5). Fewer than one-half (48 percent) of all business and professional men believed that retail farmer cooperatives operating in their communities were an asset to such communities. There was, however, great variation in attitudes among different professions and businesses. Thus, 90 percent of the ministers, 73 percent of the lawyers, 60 percent of the political leaders, 39 percent of the bankers and 23 percent of the business competitors thought retail farmer cooperatives in their communities were an asset. One-third (32 percent) of this com-

TABLE 17-5
Attitudes of Business and Professional Leaders
Toward Retail Farm Supply Cooperatives, Indiana

Item	Percent of Respondents Giving Affirmative Answers
Farm retail cooperatives are an asset to the community.	48
Net effect of farmer cooperatives is beneficial to:	
Members.	44
Community.	37
Farmer cooperatives stand for:	
Free enterprise.	29
Communism and socialism.	32
Farmer cooperatives should not be permitted to operate.	35
Cooperatives provide unfair competition.	55
Cooperatives have caused other retail firms to fail.	23
Farmer cooperatives fail to participate in community activities.	21
Know personally the farm co-op personnel.	94
Co-op managers should be accepted in local business associations.	66
Cooperatives are nonprofit organizations.	21
Co-op earnings distributed in cash should be taxed the same as corporate profits.	84
Cooperatives pay their fair share of:	
Local taxes.	39
State taxes.	29
Federal taxes.	14

Source: Sandage, C. H., *Survey of Opinion of Business and Professional Leaders,* Farm Research Institute, Urbana, Ill. Not dated. (Courtesy, Indiana Farm Bureau Cooperative Association, Indianapolis, Ind.)

bined group thought that farmer cooperatives stood for or promoted socialism, and only 38 percent thought they promoted honest competition. About three-fourths (79 percent) of the total indicated that cooperatives were not nonprofit organizations, and 86 percent believed that cooperatives did not pay their fair share of federal taxes.[20]

A public opinion poll in Arkansas showed that only half of those citizens surveyed knew that rural electric cooperatives were consumer-owned. Only 1 in 15 knew the status of REA as strictly a lending agency. The surveying experts observed that the better informed and the better educated the people questioned were, the more favorable they were to electric cooperatives. Two out of every three such persons thought the cooperatives were good for the economy and the country and were willing to accept them as permanent segments of the private enterprise business society. Thirty-one percent of those surveyed, however, had little knowledge of electric cooperatives.

Bohlen found that the business and professional people interviewed showed a lack of understanding of co-op organization and operations. Fifteen percent of the people interviewed thought that a cooperative was a group of farmers going into business to make profits as merchants, while 5 percent believed that cooperatives were a form of socialism and communism. Forty-five percent said there was no difference between patronage refunds and stock dividends, and 40 percent thought a revolving fund was "breaking faith" with members. Almost half had no idea how voting was done in cooperatives. On the tax issue, 43 percent said cooperatives pay no income taxes.[21]

In a North Carolina study, nonfarmers interviewed had only a limited knowledge of cooperatives in general and very little knowledge concerning the tax issue. As a general rule, however, nonfarmers believed that cooperatives were beneficial to the community. There was a tendency for them to associate cooperatives with a "foreign" nation, such as with Russia.[22]

Improving Public Relations

The public appears concerned with the following topics in relation to cooperatives: (1) How do cooperatives fit into the capitalistic eco-

---

[20]Sandage, C. H., "What Do Your People Think of You?" *American Cooperation,* A.I.C., Washington, D.C. 1959.
[21]Bohlen, Joe, *Iowa Farm Science,* Ames, Iowa. July 1955.
[22]Abrahamsen and Scroggs, *op. cit.*

nomic system? (2) Why are they called nonprofit corporations? (3) What is a patronage refund? (4) How are cooperatives taxed? (5) Do they eliminate small business? (6) Do they favor the federal government's price support programs? (7) How do members vote in cooperatives? (8) Are cooperatives monopolistic? (9) Do cooperatives give small entrepreneurs increased bargaining power? (10) Are cooperatives good for the community, state and nation?

If cooperatives will address their public efforts to answering one or more of these 10 questions, a great step toward better public understanding should result. The means taken to answer these questions are not so important as the end results. Any means taken are good if better public understanding results.

The public relations job is continuous. So, whether the association is large or small, the first step is to assign someone to the job of keeping the program going. Since members and employees are the real public relations messengers, the next step is to be sure that they have enough information about and pride in the association to tell a good story about it. Then the next step is to study the community, getting acquainted with the different groups, their attitudes toward and experiences with cooperatives.

Then, someone should be assigned to work with each major segment of the community. This involves getting acquainted, joining the organizations, attending their meetings, working on their committees and being a real factor in their activities.

Since public relations is a general obligation of all cooperatives, it appears that cooperation among cooperatives in financing, planning and executing a public relations program through magazines, newspapers, radio, television and other media should yield useful results.

Many false rumors may circulate about a cooperative in a community. The cooperative cannot answer each and every rumor. However, it can, by adopting a sound public relations program, avert rumors.

Relations with News Media

Since the public-at-large and even some co-op members do not fully understand cooperatives as an institution, time spent with news media is apt to be rewarding. Of course, not every item of co-op news can be handled as a news story—some news is actually advertisement. The cooperatives should be prepared to pay for advertisements. But, in the general area of what a cooperative is and what it does, news media will certainly welcome co-op management in telling its side of the story.

Cooperatives and the Community

Because it is community-owned, a cooperative has an extra responsibility to be an extra special good neighbor. Because it's also a membership organization, a cooperative should take leadership in setting the tone of a community—determining what a community needs and going ahead to get it. A business has a good image when the people in it are part of the community in their individual lives.

Too often cooperatives have not met fully their civic responsibilities. Civic clubs, chambers of commerce, charity drives and other community undertakings require cooperation from all segments for their success. Cooperatives have a serious responsibility in such endeavors.

Trade Relations

As a rule, cooperatives deal with many profit-type firms in buying, manufacturing, selling and financing. The day when cooperatives will deal strictly with other cooperatives is far in the future, if ever. Therefore, it is imperative that both cooperatives and profit-type firms recognize the legitimate aspirations of one another in the present business world. Co-op membership in appropriate trade associations is highly recommended.

Profit-type businesses often find that dealing with cooperatives is a blessing, not a curse. For example, in selling supplies, a wholesaler may find that through the farmer cooperative he can move a large volume of goods with a very low cost of distribution which helps his tonnage and improves his overall efficiency. At the same time, the wholesaler may find that it is more economical to deal with 100 farmers through one organization than to try to sell to each farmer individually.

Relations with Other Cooperatives

In some counties where there are several cooperatives, a county co-op council can be very effective in improving membership and public relations at a lower cost per cooperative. Since members may belong to several cooperatives, a coordinated educational program by a county co-op council is very worthwhile.[23]

Henning and Mann concluded that cooperatives in a given area can work together in several respects, such as:

1. Joint educational and advertising programs in a county or counties.
2. Exchange of membership lists.
3. Joint field service staffs.
4. Joint truck transportation and delivery services.
5. Joint offices and personnel at local points.[24]

FIGURE 17-10

Cooperatives work with youth groups and assist them in their programs. Here a farm credit bank official buys their lambs and then gives them back to the clubs. (Courtesy, Farm Credit Banks, New Orleans, La.)

---

[23]Dvoracek, D. C., *County Cooperative Councils*, Minn. Agr. Ext. Serv. Bul. 217, St. Paul, Minn. Jan. 1941.
[24]Henning, G. F. and L. B. Mann, *Relationships Between Cooperative Organizations Serving Farmers*, Ohio Agr. Exp. Sta. Bul. 660, Wooster, Ohio. Mar. 1946.

FIGURE 17-11

Youth groups come to learn about the building blocks of cooperatives: capital, business and dividends. (Courtesy, The Ohio State University, Columbus, Ohio, and A.I.C., Washington, D.C.)

There are probably many other activities which can be jointly conducted by cooperatives.

Relations with Youth Organizations

As good business citizens of the community, cooperatives have an obligation to work with youth organizations, such as the Boy and Girl Scouts, Future Farmers of America, 4-H Clubs, Future Homemakers of America and other such organizations. Cooperation with these organizations may involve many different activities: sponsorships at summer camps, public speaking contests, quiz contests or having a junior co-op board of directors drawn from a local FFA chapter, for example.[25] Many organizations, such as the American Institute of Cooperation, have fine youth programs in cooperation.

---

[25]Lebeau, O. R. and J. H. Heckman, *Cooperative Business Training for Farm Youth,* FCS Circ. 1, Washington, D.C. Jan. 1954. p. 28.

Cooperatives can develop future managerial personnel by cooperating with schools in offering on-the-job work and training programs for the youth.

Cooperatives can help some youths by providing college scholarships such as the land bank associations are doing, among others. Some colleges and universities have cooperative school-and-work programs whereby students spend one semester in college and one semester in the employ of the cooperatives. There are other such opportunities.

Cooperatives should be concerned about fostering school-related activities for several reasons. First, carefully selected activities can help to acquaint young citizens with the way that cooperatives serve. Second, they help to vitalize the instruction by including lessons from the work-a-day world. Third, they lay the groundwork for training future co-op members and leaders.

Cooperatives and Secondary Schools

A few specific suggestions on ways co-op associations may work closely with the schools are:

1. Every cooperative should invite schools to send their pupils to visit its facilities. When this is done, the manager or some member of the staff should be ready to answer questions and tell something about the principles of cooperation.

2. Facts and information about local, regional and national cooperatives should be readily available for educators. Co-op associations should prepare brochures or booklets on cooperation for school use and distribute them widely.

3. Develop a library of information on cooperatives that can be used by boys and girls if they come to the cooperative. Or have a lending library that can be used over a wide area.

4. Hold frequent conferences with key educators and teachers on problems of co-op education.

Relations with Institutions of Higher Learning

The agricultural experiment stations and extension services of the land-grant colleges can be of great help to cooperatives in researching for and extending new knowledge. Cooperatives, however, must support these institutions wherever possible and should communicate their needs to them at regular intervals. The colleges of business administration and various technical departments of research and teaching may also be helpful. Most large colleges have general extension or adult education departments which are useful in assisting cooperatives in their membership education programs and in holding conferences, workshops, etc.

Women and Cooperatives

While women have had a minor role in farmer cooperatives, their role in credit unions and consumer cooperatives is significant. They serve not only as managers of credit unions and other cooperatives but also on boards of directors. Since women are assuming an increasing responsibility in work outside the home, their part in the future will become more significant in cooperatives.

Cooperatives and Co-op Trade Associations

Various co-op trade associations need the active support of cooperatives in developing educational, legislative and technical training programs.

Relations with State Co-op Councils and Leagues

Each co-op group, such as farmers, consumers, credit unions, health plans, rural electric cooperatives, etc., has a respective council or league working in its behalf. These councils operate on dues subscribed by member cooperatives, and the executive staffs often work for modest salaries. Greater support by cooperatives of these nonprofit councils or leagues should help materially in rendering better services to member cooperatives as well as to others served by them.

The general farm organizations (Farm Bureau, Grange, Farmers Union) have considerable interest in cooperatives, and a liaison with them can be mutually beneficial.

Working with Churches

Protestant, Catholic and Jewish religious groups often are vigorous supporters of cooperatives. They feel cooperation is a way to develop grass-roots business democracy whereby the "little man" can control his economic destiny and hence perform better as a church member. Religious teachings emphasize mutual aid, the brotherhood of man and high ethical standards. Many people find in cooperatives ways to translate their religious beliefs into action. There is a long history of the relationships between religion and cooperatives.

CAUSES OF CO-OP FAILURES

Co-op failures are probably no more numerous than failures in other types of businesses. However, it is not so much whether cooperatives fail or not as it is a problem of their not doing so well as they should. What are some of the situations which cause cooperatives to either fail or not reach their full potential?

1. Poor selection of board members, especially directors who fail to support their own cooperatives.

2. Members who join but never use their cooperatives but bypass them for a small gain somewhere else.

3. Members who use cooperatives but fail to take responsibility. Each member has to stand ready to accept responsibility when called upon or as the need may arise. Any member has an opportunity to be president of his cooperative.

4. Members who never ask questions and who let a few persons run everything and say everything.

5. Failure of members to attend annual meetings and failure of directors to attend board meetings.

6. Lack of consistent membership education in the problems cooperatives are facing and the challenges they must meet.

7. Failure to support with enough money to get the job done.

8. Cheaply priced management is the most expensive item in cooperation. High-priced management is usually the least expensive.

9. A cooperative is a true republic. If it fails as a democratic institution, the people fail along with it.

10. Cliques and special interest groups ought to be closely watched and expelled whenever necessary.

11. All the facts about a cooperative, both good and bad, should be put above the table, not under the table.

12. The blame for failure of a cooperative usually rests with the members, not with anyone else. It is the members who elect the board, and it is the board who selects the manager. Therefore, members are the key to the failure.

Warbasse has diagnosed several specific areas which cause cooperatives to fail. These are:

1. Errors in *financial* policy such as in over-extension of credit, too little capital, poor accounting records, paying patronage returns too soon and underselling competing stores.

2. Errors in *educational and social* work such as beginning with a membership unfamiliar with cooperation, neglecting educational programs, failure to develop loyalty and development of factions in the association.

3. Errors in *management* such as an inadequate inventory, poor store location, improper equipment, neglecting store appearances, employee dishonesty, ineffective management of staff, incompetent directors, nepotism, poorly conducted meetings and admittance of disloyal and disruptive members.[26]

In the next chapter, the legal aspects of taxing cooperatives are considered.

TOPICS FOR DISCUSSION

1. Discuss the most important factors associated with employee management.
2. How can cooperatives improve their membership relations?
3. What are the ingredients of a good annual meeting?
4. What are the elements of a good accounting to co-op members?
5. How can cooperatives improve their public relations?
6. In what ways can cooperatives work with youth groups?
7. Discuss how co-op management might counteract false rumors about it in a community.
8. What are some causes of co-op failures?

SELECTED REFERENCES

1. Beal, George and others, *Farmers' Opinions and Community Relations*, Iowa Agr. Exp. Sta. Bul. 379, Ames, Iowa. Feb. 1951.
2. Beall, Hayes, *Member Education Manual*, Cooperative League, Chicago, Ill. Not dated.
3. Beers, R. G., *Personnel Management in Farmers' Cooperatives*, FCS Circ. C-123, Washington, D.C. May 1941.
4. Bielinski, W. V., *Personnel Administration in Regional Farmer Co-op Associations*, A.I.C. Washington, D.C. May 1951.

---

[26]Warbasse, J. P., *Problems of Cooperation*, Cooperative League, Chicago, Ill. 1942.

5. Burkes, M. R. and G. F. Henning, *Ratio Analysis Used to Measure Financial Strength of Agricultural Business Corporations,* Ohio Agr. Exp. Sta. Rept. 340, Wooster, Ohio. Nov. 1963.
6. Farmer Cooperative Service,
   (A) *Midwest Co-op Membership Relations Conference,* Kansas City, Mo. Apr. 30, 1959.
   (B) *North Central Membership Relations Conference,* Minneapolis, Minn. May 13, 1959.
   (C) *Pacific Coast Member Relations Conference,* San Francisco, Calif. Feb. 22, 1960.
   (D) *Second Midwest Membership Relations Conference,* Omaha, Nebr. May 4, 1960.
7. Griffin, Nelda, *Employee Incentive Plans,* FCS Gen. Rept. 104, Washington, D.C. Aug. 1962.
8. Kelley, J. D., *Research Findings on Knowledge and Attitudes Concerning Cooperatives,* Cooperative Research Center, Paris, France. 1959.
9. Larson, Adlowe, *Membership Relations in Farmers' Cooperatives,* Okla. Agr. Exp. Sta. Circ. 122, Stillwater, Okla. Apr. 1946.
10. Lindberg, H. V., *Farmer Cooperative Audits,* Spokane, Wash. 1941.
11. Malinovsky, Emil, "What Makes a Co-op Fail or Succeed?" *Cooperative Farmer,* Richmond, Va. Dec. 1960.
12. Mather, J. W., *Pay Plans for Co-op Tank Truck Salesmen,* FCS Gen. Rept. 46, Washington, D.C. June 1958.
13. Miller, R. W., and A. L. Jensen, "Failures of Farmers' Cooperatives," *Harvard Business Review,* Cambridge, Mass. Winter 1947.
14. Schmalz, Carl N., *Operating Results of Consumer Cooperatives in the United States,* Harvard University Bureau of Business Research Bul. 108, Boston, Mass. Mar. 1939.
15. Seligsohn, I. J., *Using Computer Services in Small Business,* SBA Rept. 109, Washington, D.C. Nov. 1959.
16. Smith, Eldon, *How Much Do Farmers Know About Their Cooperatives?* Ky. Agr. Exp. Sta. Rept. 127, Lexington, Ky. Feb. 1963.
17. Staff, *Farmer Cooperatives' Educational Program for Young Farmers,* Wisconsin Council of Agricultural Cooperatives, Madison, Wisc. June 1952.
18. Staff, *Operating Ratios,* Dun and Bradstreet, New York, N.Y. 1958.
19. Stark, D., "Techniques for Handling Annual Meetings," *News for Farmer Cooperatives,* Washington, D.C. Dec. 1961.
20. Stern, J. K., *Membership Problems in Farmers' Purchasing Associations,* Pa. Agr. Exp. Sta. Bul. 268, State College, Pa. July 1931.
21. Upchurch, F. M. and S. C. Tarbell, "Personalized Accounting Rates Employee Approval," *News for Farmer Cooperatives,* Washington, D.C. Aug. 1963.

CHAPTER 18 –

Taxation of Cooperatives:
Legal Aspects

Cooperative groups cannot live for themselves alone. They have public obligations and relationships to fulfill and sound attitudes to assume on those questions which promote social unrest before they can be sure of permanent foundation.

—Bernard Baruch

HISTORY OF FEDERAL CO-OP
TAX LEGISLATION

THE FIRST FEDERAL STATUTE to refer to farmer cooperatives was the War Revenue Act of 1898, which had a section providing for stamp taxes. It also provided for the exemption of farmers' purely local co-op companies and associations organized for mutual benefit and not for profit.

The next federal tax act to mention farmer and other cooperatives was the Corporation Tax Statute of 1909. This Act placed a tax on the net income of corporations and joint-stock associations, but provided for the exemption of labor, agricultural, horticultural and domestic building and loan associations operating on a mutual basis. Furthermore, the United States Supreme Court upheld the right of Congress, which it considered had the right to exempt certain types of business from the tax, to select the objects for excise taxation.

The third federal income tax act to affect agricultural and other types of cooperatives was the Income Tax Statute of 1913. This Act provided for the exemption of labor, agricultural or horticultural organizations and mutual savings banks not having capital stock represented by shares.

The next federal revenue act affecting cooperatives was the Revenue Act of 1916. This Act considerably broadened the scope of the tax exemptions for cooperatives and listed exemptions for 14 types of cooperatives. It listed as exempt from the tax:

Farmers', fruit growers', or like associations, organized and operated as sales agents for the purpose of marketing the products of members and turning back to them the proceeds of sales, less the necessary selling expenses, on the basis of the quantity of produce furnished by them.

The Revenue Act of 1918 repeated this provision, and the Revenue Act of 1921 enlarged it by adding, "or organized and operated as purchasing agents for the purpose of purchasing supplies and equipment for the use of the members and turning over such supplies and equipment to such members at actual cost, plus necessary expenses." The Revenue Act of 1924 continued the combined provisions.[1]

Section 231 of the Revenue Act of 1926 contained the following provision:

> Farmer's, fruit growers', or like associations organized and operated on a cooperative basis (a) for the purpose of marketing the products of members or other producers, and turning back to them the proceeds of sales, less the necessary marketing expenses, on the basis of either the quantity or the value of the products furnished by them, or (b) for the purpose of purchasing supplies and equipment for the use of members or other persons, and turning over such supplies and equipment to them at actual cost, plus necessary expenses. Exemption shall not be denied any such association because it has capital stock, if the dividend rate of such stock is fixed at not to exceed the legal rate of interest in the State of incorporation or 8 percent per annum, whichever is greater, on the value of the consideration for which the stock was issued, and if substantially all such stock (other than non-voting preferred stock, the owners of which are not entitled or permitted to participate, directly or indirectly, in the profits of the association, upon dissolution or otherwise, beyond the fixed dividends) is owned by producers who market their products or purchase their supplies and equipment through the association; nor shall exemption be denied any such association because there is accumulated and maintained by it a reserve required by State law or a reasonable reserve for any necessary purpose. Such an association may market the products of nonmembers in an amount the value of which does not exceed the value of the products marketed for members, and may purchase supplies and equipment for nonmembers in an amount the value of which does not exceed the value of the supplies and equipment purchased for members, provided the value of the purchases

---

[1]Patterson, R. T., *The Tax Exemption of Cooperatives*, University Publishers, New York, N.Y. 1961. pp. 53-58.

made for persons who are neither members nor producers does not exceed 15 percent of the value of all its purchases.

This same provision was included in the Revenue Act of 1928 and again in the Revenue Act of 1932.

The Revenue Act of 1934 provided that business done with the United States or any of its agencies was to be disregarded in determining the right to the exemption under the paragraph. These combined provisions appeared in the same form in the Revenue Acts of 1936, 1938 and 1939.

The next significant revenue act regarding farmer cooperatives, especially, was passed in 1951 and still another in 1962. Both of these acts are discussed in subsequent sections.

TAX EXEMPT ORGANIZATIONS

Three sections of the Internal Revenue Code are important to cooperatives: 501, 521 and 522. In addition, the 1962 Revenue Act contained amendments to these three sections.

Section 501

Under Section 501 of the 1954 Internal Revenue Code is contained a list of organizations[2] exempt from paying federal income taxes:

    1. Corporations organized under Act of Congress, if such corporations are instrumentalities of the United States and if, under such Act, as amended and supplemented, such corporations are exempt from Federal income taxes.

    2. Corporations organized for the exclusive purpose of holding title to property, collecting income therefrom and turning over the entire amount thereof, less expenses, to an organization which itself is exempt under this section.

    3. Corporations, and any community chest, fund or foundation, organized and operated exclusively for religious, charitable, scientific, testing for public safety, literary or educational purposes, or for the prevention of cruelty to children or animals, no part of the net earnings of which inures to the benefit of any private shareholder or individual, no substantial part of the activities of which is carrying on propaganda, or otherwise attempting to influence legislation, and which does not participate in, or intervene in (including the

---

[2]Not all the organizations specified in Section 501 are cooperatives. For general reference, all of Section 501 is shown here.

publishing or distributing of statements), any political campaign on behalf of any candidate for public office.

4. Civic leagues or organizations not organized for profit but operated exclusively for the promotion of social welfare, or local associations of employees, the membership of which is limited to the employees of a designated person or persons in a particular municipality and the net earnings of which are devoted exclusively to charitable, educational or recreational purposes.

5. Labor, agricultural or horticultural organizations. (Agricultural here refers to fairs, festivals, etc., and not farm business cooperatives.)

6. Business leagues, chambers of commerce, real estate boards or boards of trade, not organized for profit and no part of the net earnings of which inures to the benefit of any private shareholder or individual.

7. Clubs organized and operated exclusively for pleasure, recreation and other nonprofitable purposes, no part of the net earnings of which inures to the benefit of any private shareholder.

8. Fraternal beneficiary societies, orders or associations:

(A) operating under the lodge system or for the exclusive benefit of the members of a fraternity itself operating under the lodge system, and

(B) providing for the payment of life, sick, accident or other benefits to the members of such society, order or association or their dependents.

9. Voluntary employees' beneficiary associations providing for the payment of life, sick, accident or other benefits to the members of such association or their dependents, if —

(A) no part of their net earnings inures (other than through such payments) to the benefit of any private shareholder or individual, and

(B) 85 percent or more of the income consists of amounts collected from members and amounts contributed to the association by the employer of the members for the sole purpose of making such payments and meeting expenses.

10. Voluntary employees' beneficiary associations providing for the payment of life, sick, accident or other benefits to the members of such association or their dependents or their designated beneficiaries, if —

(A) admission to membership in such association is limited to individuals who are officers or employees of the United States Government, and

(B) no part of the net earnings of such association

inures (other than through such payments) to the benefit of any private shareholder or individual.

11. Teachers' retirement fund associations of a purely local character, if

(A) no part of their net earnings inures (other than through payment of retirement benefits) to the benefit of any private shareholder or individual, and

(B) the income consists solely of amounts received from public taxation, amounts received from assessments on the teaching salaries of members and income in respect of investments.

12. Benevolent life insurance associations of a purely local character, mutual ditch or irrigation companies, mutual or cooperative telephone companies, or like organizations; but only if 85 percent or more of the income consists of amounts collected from members for the sole purpose of meeting losses and expenses.

13. Cemetery companies owned and operated exclusively for the benefit of their members or which are not operated for profit; and any corporation chartered solely for burial purposes as a cemetery corporation and not permitted by its charter to engage in any business not necessarily incident to that purpose, no part of the net earnings of which inures to the benefit of any private shareholder or individual.

14. Credit unions without capital stock organized and operated for mutual purposes and without profit; and corporations or associations without capital stock organized before September 1, 1957, and operated for mutual purposes and without profit for the purpose of providing reserve funds for, and insurance of, shares or deposits in —

(A) domestic building and loan associations,

(B) co-op banks without capital stock organized and operated for mutual purposes and without profit, or

(C) mutual savings banks not having capital stock represented by shares.

15. Mutual insurance companies or associations other than life or marine (including interinsurers and reciprocal underwriters) if the gross amount received during the taxable year from the items described in Section 822 (b) (other than paragraph (1) (D) thereof) and premiums (including deposits or assessments) does not exceed $75,000 [raised to $150,000 under the 1962 Revenue Act].

16. Corporations organized by an association subject to part III of this subchapter, or members thereof, for the purpose of financing the ordinary crop operations of such members or other producers, and operated in conjunction with such association. Exemption shall not be denied any such

corporation because it has capital stock, if the dividend rate of
such stock is fixed at not to exceed the legal rate of interest
in the State of incorporation or 8 percent per annum, whichever is greater, on the value of the consideration for which
the stock was issued, and if substantially all such stock (other
than nonvoting preferred stock, the owners of which are not
entitled or permitted to participate, directly or indirectly, in
the profits of the corporation, on dissolution or otherwise,
beyond the fixed dividends) is owned by such association, or
members thereof; nor shall exemption be denied any such
corporation because there is accumulated and maintained by
it a reserve required by State law or a reasonable reserve for
any necessary purpose.

 17. Religious or apostolic associations or corporations, if
such associations or corporations have a common treasury or
community treasury, even if such associations or corporations
engage in business for the common benefit of the members,
but only if the members thereof include (at the time of filing
their returns) in their gross income their entire pro rata shares,
whether distributed or not, of the taxable income of the association or corporation for such year. Any amount so included in
the gross income of a member shall be treated as a dividend
received.

Section 521

 Under the provisions of the 1951 Revenue Act, the Internal Revenue
Code Section 521 was codified as follows:

> Sec. 521. Exemption of farmers' cooperatives from tax:
> (A) Exemption from tax.—A farmers' cooperative de-
> scribed in subsection (B) (1) shall be exempt from taxation
> under this subtitle except as otherwise provided in Section
> 522. Notwithstanding Section 522, such an organization shall
> be considered an organization exempt from income taxes for
> purposes of any law which refers to organizations exempt
> from income taxes.
> (B) Applicable rules.
> (1) Exempt farmers' cooperatives.—The farmers' co-
> operatives exempt from taxation to the extent provided
> in subsection (A) are farmers', fruit growers', or like
> associations organized and operated on a cooperative basis
> (a) for the purpose of marketing the products of members
> or other producers, and turning back to them the proceeds
> of sales, less the necessary marketing expenses, on the basis
> of either the quantity or the value of the products fur-
> nished by them, or (b) for the purpose of purchasing

supplies and equipment for the use of members or other persons, and turning over such supplies and equipment to them at actual cost, plus necessary expenses.

(2) Organizations having capital stock.—Exemption shall not be denied any such association because it has capital stock, if the dividend rate of such stock is fixed at not to exceed the legal rate of interest in the State of incorporation or 8 percent per annum, whichever is greater, on the value of the consideration for which the stock was issued, and if substantially all such stock (other than nonvoting preferred stock, the owners of which are not entitled or permitted to participate, directly or indirectly, in the profits of the association, upon dissolution or otherwise, beyond the fixed dividends) is owned by producers who market their products or purchase their supplies and equipment through the association.

(3) Organizations maintaining reserve.—Exemption shall not be denied any such association because there is accumulated and maintained by it a reserve required by State law or a reasonable reserve for any necessary purpose.

(4) Transactions with nonmembers.—Exemption shall not be denied any such association which markets the products of nonmembers in an amount the value of which does not exceed the value of the products marketed for members, or which purchases supplies and equipment for nonmembers in an amount the value of which does not exceed the value of the supplies and equipment purchased for members, provided the value of the purchases made for persons who are neither members nor producers does not exceed 15 percent of the value of all its purchases.

(5) Business for the United States.—Business done for the United States or any of its agencies shall be disregarded in determining the right to exemption under this section.

Section 522

Section 522 of the 1954 Internal Revenue Code was repealed and replaced by subchapter T of the 1962 Revenue Act. However, due to its long-standing legal and economic importance, Section 522 is shown, as follows:

Section 522. Taxation of farmers' cooperatives.

(A) Imposition of Tax.—An organization exempt from taxation under Section 521 shall be subject to the taxes imposed by Section 11 (corporation income tax) or Section 1201 (alternative tax treatment of capital gains).

(B) Computation of Taxable Income.

(1) General rule.—In computing the taxable income of such an organization there shall be allowed as deductions from gross income (in addition to other deductions allowable under this chapter)—

(a) amounts paid as dividends during the taxable year on its capital stock and (b) amounts allocated during the taxable year to patrons with respect to its income not derived from patronage (whether or not such income was derived during such taxable year) whether paid in cash, merchandise, capital stock, revolving fund certificates, retain certificates, certificates of indebtedness, letters of advice or in some other manner that discloses to each patron the dollar amount allocated to him. Allocations made after the close of the taxable year and on or before the 15th day of the 9th month following the close of such year shall be considered as made on the last day of such taxable year to the extent the allocations are attributable to income derived before the close of such year.

(2) Patronage dividends, etc.—Patronage dividends, refunds and rebates to patrons with repect to their patronage in the same or preceding years (whether paid in cash, merchandise, capital stock, revolving fund certificates, retain certificates, certificates of indebtedness, letters of advice or in some other manner that discloses to each patron the dollar amount of such dividend, refund or rebate) shall be taken into account in computing taxable income in the same manner as in the case of a cooperative not exempt under Section 521. Such dividends, refunds and rebates made after the close of the taxable year and on or before the 15th day of the 9th month following the close of such year shall be considered as made on the last day of such taxable year to the extent the dividends, refunds or rebates are attributable to patronage occurring before the close of such year.

Farmer cooperatives which comply with Sections 521 and 522, as amended, are known as "tax exempt." Those which do not are known as "nonexempt." About half of the farmers' purchasing and marketing cooperatives in the United States are "tax exempt" and half are "nonexempt." Most of the other cooperatives are "nonexempt."

One of the main reasons why Congress passed and the President approved the 1962 Revenue Act was to correct the deficiency in the tations challenging the concept that noncash patronage allocations were constructively received by the patron and constituted income therein. 1951 Revenue Act. This deficiency resulted from certain court interpre-

DEFICIENCY OF THE 1951 REVENUE ACT

Prior to 1951 a farmer cooperative which met the requirements of Section 101 of the Internal Revenue Code of 1939 (Section 101 later became Section 521 of the Internal Revenue Code of 1954) was exempt from the payment of a corporate income tax. Congress in 1951 adopted provisions intended to insure that all net margins, or earnings, resulting from the business operations of farmer cooperatives would be subjected to a single income tax, either at the cooperative or patron level. The provisions which were then adopted made clear the right of a cooperative to deduct or exclude from its gross income the patronage margins which it was under an obligation to return to the patrons on a patronage basis, even though under its legally adopted operating plan the cooperative was authorized to retain such amounts for the necessary financing of its operations. Congress, however, made no specific provision in the 1951 Act for the taxation to patrons of such retained amounts. Relying upon Treasury Rulings which had been in effect for many years, Congress thought that its single tax objective would be accomplished under existing law through the continued taxation of these noncash patronage refunds to the patrons at face amount.

In the period 1952 to 1957 two principal cases—*Carpenter* and *Long Poultry Farms*—were litigated, with decisions by Circuit Courts of Appeals holding in effect that the noncash patronage refunds of the farmer cooperatives were taxable to the patrons, not at their face amount, but only at their fair market value. Thereafter, in December 1959, the Treasury Department amended its regulations to follow the principle enunciated in the *Carpenter* and *Long Poultry Farms* cases. Thus, to the extent that the noncash patronage refunds of a cooperative were not required to be included in the taxable income of the cooperative or the patron recipient, the single tax objective of Congress had been frustrated. In fact, as a result of these two decisions and the subsequent Treasury action based upon them, noncash patronage refunds generally were excluded by the cooperative at face amount, whereas farmers were required to report them currently only at their fair market value. Under the criteria contained in the Treasury regulations, in many cases the noncash patronage refunds were held not to have any fair market value.

The effect of these decisions was to make it impossible for the Treasury to collect, in all situations, a single current tax either from the cooperative or its patrons. The clear holding of these decisions was that noncash allocations were not taxable in the year made either to a cash or an accrual basis taxpayer unless they had a fair market value and then only at that value. In effect, the decisions permitted a tax deferment in most cases until a patron received his refund in cash.

The basic issue then was how the noncash patronage refunds of cooperatives were to be treated tax-wise to accomplish a single tax on patronage earnings. Congress applied itself to this issue in the 1962 Revenue Act.

THE 1962 REVENUE ACT

On January 1, 1963, most cooperatives, especially farmers', became subject to the provisions of the Revenue Act of 1962, mainly Sections 1381, 1382, 1383, 1385, 1388, 6042, 6044 and 6049.[3]

All income of all cooperatives[4] must be included in gross income in determining taxable income. No income as such is exempt. The only net income of cooperatives which is not subject to tax is that which has been distributed to patrons in certain forms or in accordance with certain provisions of the law, which then may be deducted in determining taxable income. Except for these deductions, cooperatives are generally taxed the same as private corporations except for tax exempt farmer cooperatives.

Tax Treatment of Cooperatives

Farmer cooperatives, both exempt and nonexempt, and other cooperatives may reduce their gross income for federal tax purposes to the extent of patronage dividends or rebates paid:

1. In cash.
2. In property other than allocations described in (3).
3. In allocations of which at least 20 percent is paid in cash if:

(A) The patron has the option of redeeming the remainder of the allocation in cash during a period of at least 90 days after the date of issuance and receives written notice of this option at the time notice of the allocation is given; or

---

[3]Mischler, R. J. and D. Volkin, *How the Revenue Act of 1962 Affects Farmers' Cooperatives*, FCS Gen. Rept. 105, Washington, D.C. Oct. 1962.
[4]Cooperatives exempt from the 1962 Revenue Act are mutual ditch, irrigation, rural electric, telephone, mutual savings banks, building and loan associations, mutual insurance companies and like organizations.

(B) The patron consents in any one of the following three ways to treat the allocation as income received by him at its stated dollar amount:

(1) By individual written consent. This written consent must be given the cooperative before the end of the fiscal year in which the patronage occurs and applies to that and subsequent years until revoked.

(2) By joining or continuing as a member of a cooperative having bylaws requiring its members to give this consent.

(3) If the patron has not given consent in either of the preceding methods, such consent may be given by endorsing and cashing a check representing at least 20 percent of the total patronage refund on or before a prescribed date provided the check has clearly imprinted on it a statement that endorsing and cashing it will constitute such consent. This type of check is designated as a qualified check.

Any such allocation mentioned is designated "qualified" by the act; and, since it is not taxable to the cooperative, it must be included in the income of the patron for tax purposes in the year received if the patronage refund arises from business activity of the patron.

Distributions made within 8½ months after the end of the tax year by either an exempt or nonexempt cooperative may be deducted.

Income tax returns of both exempt and nonexempt cooperatives need not be filed until 8½ months after the end of the tax year provided, that as to nonexempt cooperatives, this late filing privilege is given only to those cooperatives which are obligated to allocate or pay at least 50 percent of their net patronage earnings in patronage refunds, or which allocated or paid at least that percentage of their earnings in patronage refunds during the last year in which they had any such earnings.

Qualified Allocations

1. For any allocation to qualify, at least 20 percent thereof must be paid in cash (or by a so-called qualified check). A qualified allocation must be in the form of capital stock, revolving fund certificates, certificates of indebtedness or any written notice which shows to the recipient the dollar amount of the allocation.

2. The distribution must be made in a form which permits the patron to convert it into cash within a period beginning on the date of

the allocation and ending not earlier than 90 days after such date. Or,

3. The patron must have consented to take the distribution into his income for tax purposes. This consent may be given in any one of three ways, as follows:

(A) The patron may give his consent in a signed written statement given to the cooperative before the end of the tax year in which the patronage occurs. It remains in force until revoked in writing. A revocation is only effective beginning with the first day of the next ensuing year. (As to pooling arrangements, a revocation is effective only beginning with the next ensuing pool.) Written consent on sales tickets is considered valid if properly drawn. Written consent may also be incorporated in marketing agreements.

(B) As to members (as distinguished from nonmembers) the consent may be given by becoming a member or continuing as a member after the cooperative has adopted a bylaw provision providing that membership in the cooperative constitutes such consent. It must be observed in respect to this qualification:

(1) The bylaw provision must have been lawfully adopted after the tax bill became law and

(2) The member or prospective member must be furnished a written individual notice that the bylaws contain such a provision and must be furnished a copy of the provision. The consent cannot be revoked by the person while he is a member.

This consent is effective only as to patronage occurring after both (1) and (2) have been complied with. The Act became effective as to patronage occurring in a tax year beginning after December 31, 1962.

The bylaw consent applies only to members of the cooperative. Nonmember-patrons are not covered thereby. A nonmember-patron can give the required consent only in writing or by endorsing and cashing a qualified check. In cases in which the applicable state law and organization papers of the cooperative permit, a nonexempt cooperative may elect to pay the tax, if any, on income derived from nonmember patronage and be relieved of issuing qualified checks or qualified notices of allocation for such sums.

(C) The third form of consent is by giving a patron a so-called qualified check in payment of a portion of a refund and applies to both members and nonmembers. It cannot be used if any other form of consent has been obtained from a patron. A qualified check is a check or other instrument, redeemable in money, which has clearly printed on it a statement that its endorsement and cashing constitute consent of the patron to include the full stated dollar amount of the allocation mentioned on the check in his income to the extent provided by the federal tax laws. To qualify for the allocation of which the check is a part, the check must be cashed within 90 days after the filing date for the tax return of the cooperative. (The cooperative may, however, issue the check prior to that date and require that it be cashed within 90 days thereafter.) Nonmember patronage refunds can probably best be handled through the qualified check method.

Other Regulations

If a written notice of allocation does not qualify, it must be included in the income of the cooperative in the year issued. However, the cooperative is entitled to a deduction or refund of tax when the nonqualified written notice of allocation is finally redeemed in cash or merchandise.

A payment that is required by state law qualifies as a "valid enforceable written obligation" test for a distribution of patronage dividends.

Patronage refunds of less than $5 may be made by an "exempt" farmer cooperative solely in nonqualified written notices of allocation to the consenting patrons (for which, however the cooperative will get no current deduction) without jeopardizing its "exempt" status. The regulations permit the "exempt" cooperative making patronage allocations which are interest-bearing or are in the form of dividend-paying stock to make reasonable reduction in the amounts of the interest or dividends to the nonconsenting patrons to compensate for the fact that part of the funds are required to be paid as corporate tax on their allocations.

It is required that the 20 percent cash payment must actually be made *to the patron* to qualify the allocation for deduction and cannot be offset against amounts owed by the patron to the cooperative or against the purchase price of a share of stock or a membership in the cooperative.

Retains made by cooperatives from members' proceeds for *capital* purposes are not *income* to the cooperatives and therefore are not involved under the provisions of the Act.

In the case of a *new* member, the notification and copy of the bylaw consent provision must be given *before* he becomes a member and cannot be given simultaneously with his becoming a member.

Treatment of Tax Exempt Farmer Cooperatives

In addition to the deduction for qualifying patronage dividends paid to their patrons, exempt farmer cooperatives continue to have a deduction for amounts paid out as dividends on their capital stock. In addition, they are entitled to deductions for amounts paid to their patrons on a patronage basis where the earnings involved are derived from business done for or with the United States government or from sources other than patronage, such as investment income. The amounts must be paid, however, within 8½ months after the year in which the earnings were derived. Nonqualified allocations of less than $5 made by a tax exempt cooperative do not cause it to lose its exempt status.

Treatment of Patrons

The patrons must take into income their patronage refunds (including deductible distributions by exempt cooperatives of dividends and nonoperating income) which are paid in money, qualified allocations and other property. The amount they must take in is the stated face amount of qualified allocations and, in the case of property, its fair market value. They must also take into income nonqualified allocations which are redeemed. These must be included in the year received by the patrons (redemptions in the year of redemption).

Refunds with respect to purchases of personal, living or family items, or those which are attributable to depreciable property or capital assets, need not be included. The latter type of refund represents an adjustment in the price paid for the articles and, of course, results in a lower cost basis. For nonmember patrons, cooperatives may use either the written consent or qualified check methods.

Effective Dates

1. Generally, for cooperatives, the law applies to taxable years beginning after December 31, 1962.

2. For patrons, the law applies with respect to amounts paid to them on patronage during a tax year of the cooperative which is subject to the 1962 law.

3. Prior law applies with respect to patronage refunds paid before January 1, 1963, or after that date as to refunds paid with respect to patronage of a prior year. Prior law also applies with respect to redemptions made after December 31, 1962, if the scrip redeemed was actually issued with respect to an earlier period.

Reporting Patronage, Dividend and Interest Payments

All cooperatives which make deductible refund or stock dividend payments each of $10 or more to any person during a tax year are required to file annual returns with the Internal Revenue Service respecting such payments. A return must show the aggregate payments made to each such person with his name, address and identifying number, such as a social security number. The Secretary of the Treasury may require reporting of smaller amounts. If the payment to any person equals or exceeds $10 per year, a statement must be submitted to the recipient showing the amount of the payment and the name and address of the recipient as reported to the government. Penalties are provided for failure to comply with these provisions both on the cooperatives and the patrons as they may apply.

Consumer cooperatives can apply for exemption from the reporting requirement on the grounds that they are primarily engaged in selling goods at retail or services for personal, living or family use.[5]

Changes in Exemptions

Under the 1962 Revenue Act, the list of exempt organizations contained in Section 501 remained as is except for one minor amendment concerning mutual insurance companies.

Section 521 dealing with exempt farmer cooperatives remained unchanged.

Section 522 of the Code was repealed by the 1962 Revenue Act and replaced with the provisions just discussed or subchapter T.

Summary of the 1962 Revenue Act

Mischler has summarized the 1962 Revenue Act as follows:

> The 1962 Revenue Act preserves the principle of a single, current tax on income produced through cooperatives, provided they meet these conditions:

---

[5]Rumble, W. E., "The New Tax Law," *Co-op Grain Quarterly*, St. Paul, Minn. 1962. pp. 13-15.

1. Adhere to certain requirements as to the form in which they distribute patronage refunds.

2. Make the distributions within the prescribed time.

In the process of conforming with the law, however, a number of alternatives are available which must be evaluated and on which decisions must be made. Let us now throw the spotlight on these crossroads where choices are available.

Choice 1

The changes made by Section 17 do not repeal or modify in any way the requirements of Section 521 of the Internal Revenue Code of 1954 relating to qualification for a letter of exemption. Such a letter entitles an eligible farmer cooperative to two special deductions:

1. Amounts paid as dividends during the taxable year on capital stock (which has been construed to include any form of return on all genuine capital interests); and

2. Amounts of nonpatronage income (such as income on business with the United States, rents and interest) paid out on a patronage basis, if distributed within 8½ months after the year in which they were derived.

Thus the first alternative a farmer cooperative faces is whether to operate in compliance with the requirements of Section 521. Obviously, if the cooperative does operate under these requirements, it does not pay taxes on: (1) the part of its margins devoted to a return on capital interests and (2) the part arising from nonpatronage activities, including business done for or with the United States.

If the cooperative decides not to qualify under the requirements of Section 521, the cooperative will always pay taxes at regular corporate rates on a portion of its net margins.

Choice 2

The next choice the cooperative faces relates to the form and time in which it pays its patronage refunds. For, to emphasize, it is the form and timing of the refunds which determine their tax treatment under the law, at both the cooperative level and, in the main, at the patron level.

The law lays down precise rules on the circumstances under which cooperatives (both "exempt" and nonexempt) may use patronage refunds to reduce their gross income for tax purposes.

First—The refund must meet the definition of a "patronage dividend" set forth in the statute. This means that the refund must be —

1. Computed on the basis of quantity or value of business done with or for the patron;

2. Made pursuant to a pre-existing written obligation of the cooperative; and

3. Determined by reference to the net earnings of the organization from business done with or for patrons. (This excludes true "capital retains" from sales proceeds.)

Second—The refund must be paid in cash, property of a kind on which a current value can be placed, or in "qualified written notices of allocation."

Third—The refund must be "paid" within 8½ months following the close of the cooperative's fiscal year.

Choice 3

A third area of choice is in qualifying the "written notices of allocation." In all cases, these allocations to be "qualified" must meet the following requirements:

1. They must be in the form of a document that discloses the amount of the allocation and the portion thereof which is a patronage dividend (as compared to distributions of non-patronage income);

2. At least 20 percent of this patronage dividend must be paid in cash.

At this juncture, however, the cooperative can choose between issuing the paper (1) under circumstances in which it has a form of patron's consent, or (2) in a form redeemable in cash by the patron within a period of 90 days following the date of issuance.

Choice 4

If the cooperative elects to get a form of patron's consent, it again faces choices—three to be exact:

1. *Individual patron's written consent*

This form of consent must be given to the cooperative before the end of the year in which the patronage occurs. It applies to all patronage in that year. It also covers patronage in subsequent taxable years until a written revocation becomes effective.

A revocation is effective only on patronage occurring after the close of the cooperative's taxable year in which it is given.

2. *Consent by membership*

The patron may consent by obtaining or retaining membership in a cooperative having bylaws that require members, as a condition of membership, to take qualified written notices of allocation into account currently in computing their Federal income tax liability.

The bylaw must have been adopted after October 16, 1962, and it must clearly set forth this obligation. The consent under this method becomes effective only on patronage occurring after each patron receives a written notification of the adoption of the bylaw that explains its significance. A copy of the bylaw must accompany the notification.

Mailing this material by ordinary mail to the patron's last known address is permitted. New members must have this material before becoming members. Termination of membership terminates this form of consent.

3. *Consent by qualified check*

If neither of the first two methods is applicable, a patron may consent by endorsing and cashing a check or other instrument redeemable in money that represents at least 20 percent of the total patronage refund and has clearly imprinted on it that endorsing and cashing it will constitute such consent.

This endorsement and cashing must take place within 90 days following the end of the cooperative's payment period.

This latter method is a "one shot" deal, applying only to the patronage refund of which the check is a part.

Choice 5

Implicit in choice three, discussed above, is the alternative to pay some or all patronage refunds in the form of nonqualified written notices of allocation. A cooperative may deliberately elect to do this simply by failing to comply with one or all of the requirements as to *form* of the allocation. In this event, it incurs a current tax liability. A deduction is available, however, when the nonqualified allocation is redeemed in cash. If a deduction cannot be utilized, a refund of tax paid is available.

An exempt cooperative, without losing its exemption, has two further choices:

1. It may pay patronage refunds of less than $5 in nonqualified allocations even to consenting members; or

2. If it issues, to nonconsenting patrons, nonqualified patronage allocations which are interest bearing or in the form of dividend-paying stock, it may make deductions (reasonable in relation to the fact that it receives no tax benefit on such allocations until redemption) in the interest or dividends paid.[6]

TAX STATUS OF SELECTED COOPERATIVES

As mentioned earlier, there are two categories of agricultural business cooperatives with regards to federal income taxation: (1) exempt and (2) nonexempt.

---

[6]Mischler, R. J., *Handling Net Margins Under the New Tax Law*, Info. 39, FCS, USDA, Washington, D.C. June 1963.

Exempt Farmer Cooperatives

Those farmer cooperatives which qualify under Section 521 are known as exempt cooperatives.

Both exempt and nonexempt cooperatives pay corporate income tax on any reserves, including those required by state law, which are not allocated and disclosed to patrons. Neither must pay corporate income tax on amounts represented by qualified allocations to patrons. However, "exempt" cooperatives are not required to pay corporate income taxes on the following: (1) dividends paid on stock in the year accrued and (2) income from non-operational sources or incidental income when allocated and disclosed to patrons. Nonexempt cooperatives must pay corporate income tax on such income (Table 18-1).

The procedures for obtaining tax "exemption" are very involved. Section 521 spells out what farmer cooperatives must do to gain "exemption." Over the years, experience has shown that exemption is not denied under these conditions:

1. Exemption is not denied an association because it has capital stock if "substantially all" of such stock is owned by producers who market their products or purchase their supplies and equipment through the association. What constitutes "substantially all" of the capital stock of a cooperative depends upon the circumstances surrounding each particular case—it cannot be assumed that a certain percentage of producer-owned stock is satisfactory.

(A) An association is required to show that ownership of its capital stock has been restricted as far as possible to actual producers who market their products or purchase their supplies and equipment through the association.

(B) If an association is unable to purchase or retire the stock of nonproducers, owing to reasons beyond the control of the association, and if under such circumstances, a small amount of the outstanding capital stock is held by nonproducers, it will not destroy the association's exemption.

(C) If by statutory requirement the officers of an association must be shareholders, the ownership of a share of stock by a nonproducer to qualify him as an officer will not destroy the association's exemption.

(D) If a substantial part of the stock was voluntarily sold to nonproducers or is allowed to accumulate with them, exemption from federal income tax is denied the association.

TABLE 18-1
Comparison of Tax Exempt and Nonexempt Farmer Cooperatives

Tax Exempt Farmer Cooperative	Nonexempt Farmer Cooperative
1. Must apply for and obtain a letter of exemption.	1. Letter of exemption does not apply.
2. Final payments or refunds on patronage are not subject to a corporation income tax: (A) If provisions of the 1962 Revenue Act permitting "patronage dividends" not to be taken into account in computing "gross income" are complied with.[1]	2. Final payments or refunds on patronage are not subject to a corporation income tax: (A) If provisions of the 1962 Revenue Act permitting "patronage dividends" not to taken into account in computing "gross income" are complied with.[1]
3. Dividends paid on capital shares are not subject to tax if the dividend rate on capital shares does not exceed the legal rate of interest in the state of incorporation, or 8 percent a year, whichever is the greater, based upon the value of the consideration for which the capital shares were issued. Dividends on capital are deductible if provisions of the 1962 Revenue Act are complied with.[1]	3. Net earnings used to pay dividends on capital shares or available for this purpose up to the maximum rate authorized in the cooperative's bylaws are subject to income tax.
4. Not subject to a capital stock tax.	4. Must pay a capital stock tax.
5. Not subject to a stamp tax.	5. Must pay a stamp tax on the issuance or transfer of capital stock or bonds of indebtedness and on conveyances of real estate.
6. Reserves not subject to tax if properly allocated.	6. Reserves not subject to tax if properly allocated.
7. Income from non-operational sources or incidental income not subject to tax if properly allocated.	7. Income from such sources is taxable.
8. Income from business done with or for government agencies not taxable if properly allocated.	8. Income from business done with or for government agencies is taxable.

[1]The Revenue Act of 1962 provides for an applicable subchapter T in the Internal Revenue Code of 1954.

2. Exemption is not denied an association because it has issued preferred stock or bonds or other evidence of indebtedness for the purpose of providing necessary working capital or acquiring property which is necessary for the conduct of the association's business—

(A) If the holders of such securities are not permitted to participate, directly or indirectly, in the earnings (balances) of the association upon dissolution or otherwise beyond the regular fixed dividend or interest payments not to exceed 8 percent.

(B) If the voting control of the association is retained by shareholders who are actual producers, marketing or purchasing through the association.

3. Exemption is not denied an association because there is accumulated and maintained by it a reserve required by state law or a reasonable reserve for any necessary purpose. However, reserves required by state law must be distinguished from those merely allowed.

(A) The necessity for the existence of reserves other than those required by state law must be shown.

(B) A "reasonable reserve" has been construed to include reserves accumulated or maintained to meet capital expenditures of such an association.

4. Exemption is not denied an association because it engages both in marketing farm products and in purchasing farm supplies and equipment—

(A) If the exemption requirements are met as to each of its functions and,

(B) If records are separately kept for each function.

5. Exemption is not denied an association because it does business for nonmembers—

(A) If the business done for nonmembers does not exceed the business done for members.

(B) If the business done by a co-op purchasing association for nonmember-nonproducers does not exceed 15 percent of the total business.

6. When business is done with nonmember-patrons, such patrons must be treated the same as member-(stockholder-)patrons.

7. The income tax exemption status of each association is determined by its form of organization and its actual operations for a given year.

(A) If the articles of incorporation or bylaws provide for payment of patronage refunds to members (stockholders) only, the association is not suitably organized to come within the exemption provisions. To make payment to member- and nonmember-patrons alike would not remedy the situation because such action would be in opposition to the provisions of the articles of incorporation and bylaws.

(B) An association cannot qualify for tax exemption in earlier years by amending its articles of incorporation or bylaws to provide for the payment of patronage refunds to nonmember-patrons on the same basis of member-patrons and by allocating to them or paying nonmember-patrons the amount of patronage refunds due them for such earlier years.

Under the 1962 Revenue Act, if the cooperative is an exempt cooperative under Section 521, it can only retain its exempt status by allocating all earnings to members and nonmembers alike, whether or not consent is obtained from the patrons. The failure to obtain consent for all nonmembers will not be cause for denying exemption, however. According to the regulations, the cooperative is subject to tax on amounts for which consent has not been obtained.

8. Exemption from federal income tax is not automatic under the federal law—the burden of proof rests with the farmers' association.

(A) A formal application for exemption must be made to the Collector of Internal Revenue. Exemption may or may not be granted, depending upon the organization and operation of the association.

(B) Even though exemption has been granted, an association is subject to examination by the Internal Revenue Service at any time. If it is found that the original application for exemption did not correctly state the facts or that, since the exemption was granted, the manner of operation of the association has changed, the exemption status may be canceled and tax assessments made from the date of the changed conditions.

(C) It is provided in the Internal Revenue Code that when an organization changes its manner of operation, it must notify the Internal Revenue Service so that a ruling may be obtained regarding tax exemption under the new conditions.

9. Steps necessary for a farmer cooperative to secure exemption from federal income tax:

(A) Obtain necessary exemption application form (Form 1028) from the District Collector of Internal Revenue.

(B) Submit a copy of the articles of incorporation, the bylaws, the latest balance sheet and operating statement to the District Collector of Internal Revenue.

10. Cooperatives that have an exemption must file annual tax returns:

(A) Obtain necessary form (Form 990-C) from the District Collector of Internal Revenue.

(B) File with the Collector of Internal Revenue on or before 8½ months following the close of the taxable year.

Nonexempt Farmer Cooperatives

There is no difference tax-wise between a nonexempt farmer cooperative and an ordinary corporation except that nonexempt cooperatives more often make obligatory patronage refunds. Both are subject to double taxation[7] on any income distributed as dividends to stockholders; both are subject to single taxation on unallocated income retained in the business; neither must pay corporate income tax on earnings distributed to patrons where a prior contractual obligation exists to make such distributions, and provided that compliance with the 1962 Revenue Act is made. Because of their nature, cooperatives use patronage refunds much more extensively than ordinary corporations.

The majority of the nonexempt cooperatives do not pay patronage refunds to nonmembers, but they pay income tax on the income that results from the nonmember business.

Any cooperative, or other business, can reduce its taxable income and minimize its tax by making patronage refunds. However, the following must be kept in mind:

1. The contract between the company and the patron must be in existence before the tax year begins.

2. The contract must be such that the declaration of refunds is not left to the discretion of the board of directors.

3. It must be such that the patron can collect from the cooperative by court action if the cooperative does not get around to pay.

4. Only the earnings made on the respective patron's business can be so refunded to him. In other words, a cooperative cannot refund the income from nonmember business to the members by this arrangement and escape taxation.

5. It cannot refund non-operating income, such as interest and rent income, in this manner and escape taxation.

6. It must comply with all of the relevant provisions of the 1962 Revenue Act.

Nonexempt cooperatives can and do minimize their federal income taxes. However, they must pay taxes on non-operating income, on income used for dividends on stock, on income retained in the corporation and on patronage refunds not made under contract.

Co-op Capital Different from Other Capital?—It is necessary, at this point, to question whether co-op capital is different from corporate

---

[7]Double taxation refers to taxing income at the corporate level and then again after the recipient has received corporate dividends.

capital. Traditionally, everyone assumes that capital subscribed in a cooperative is similar to capital subscribed in other types of businesses. If we accept Emelianoff's thesis that co-op capital is nonentrepreneurial and is merely "loan" capital, then it does not earn "dividends" but rather "interest." As such, any interest or so-called dividends paid on co-op capital should be a business operating expense, not paid out of income. Under present tax laws, the tax exempt farmer cooperatives are treated in a manner consistent with Emelianoff's theory, but nonexempt farmer cooperatives are not.

Interest on share capital of a cooperative should be deductible as an expense of the cooperative and not treated as part of its profit or gain which is subject to tax in the hands of the cooperative before being paid to the members.

Cooperatives' share capital is unlike the share capital of ordinary companies and really is akin to the debt obligations of ordinary companies.

TAX STATUS OF OTHER COOPERATIVES

Banks for Farmer Cooperatives

These banks pay a franchise tax as long as government capital exists therein or as its Class A stock. When all the government capital is retired, the banks will be subject to income taxes. Interest refunds made by the banks to co-op borrowers are excluded from taxable income of the banks. Member co-op borrowers of the banks include patronage refunds as a reduction in their interest costs.

Consumer Retail Cooperatives

Cooperatives of this type pay taxes as regular corporations except for contractual liabilities to refund net savings to patrons. Consumer cooperatives pay tax on capital stock dividends, unallocated reserves, employees' trust funds, etc.

Consumers receiving refunds from cooperatives do not include such refunds in their income tax returns because these represent a reduction in household operating costs and not income. They pay tax on dividends received on capital stock.

Patronage refunds are similar to trading stamps given by profit-type stores. Both are tax-deductible refunds, and the patrons, in either case, pay no income taxes on these refunds since they reduce household expenses.

Credit Corporations

Section 501 of the Internal Revenue Code provides for exemption from federal income tax of certain corporations set up for the purpose of financing crop operations in conjunction with organizations which qualify under Section 521.

Credit Unions

The Federal Credit Union Act, as amended, provides that:

> The Federal credit unions organized hereunder, their property, their franchise, capital, reserves, surpluses and other funds, and their income, shall be exempt from all taxation now or hereafter imposed by the United States, or by any State, Territorial or local taxing authority. . . .

Federal credit unions can be considered instrumentalities of the United States since the Secretary of the Treasury is authorized by Section 17 of the Federal Credit Union Act to designate them as such.

All credit unions, federal and state, are now exempted under Section 501. The federal law exempts credit unions from taxation by state or local taxing authority except for real and tangible property which, it states, is to be subject to taxation " to the same extent as other similar property is taxed."

Interest received by shareholders in a credit union is subject to personal income tax rates. Interest or patronage refunds on money borrowed from a credit union reduce interest costs to the borrower and therefore reduce the interest deduction when filing personal income tax returns.

Federal Land Bank Associations

The Federal Farm Loan Act of 1916 exempts national farm loan associations (now federal land bank associations) from the payment of federal income taxes in Section 26, which reads as follows:

> . . . every national farm loan association, including the capital and reserve or surplus therein and the income derived therefrom, shall be exempt from Federal, State, municipal and local taxation, except taxes upon real estate held, purchased, or taken by said association under the provisions of section eleven of this Act.

That national farm loan associations are considered instrumentalities of the United States follows from the other language of Section 26 of the Act.

Housing Cooperatives

Housing cooperatives are not tax exempt under Section 501. They must pay income tax on any profits they make, just like other housing ventures. Each cooperative, of course, tries to operate at cost, without making a profit.

Housing cooperatives generally pay the same real estate taxes as levied on other homes and apartments. Sometimes a housing cooperative built on land where slums formerly stood will have the advantage of tax abatement.

A co-op member has the same tax benefits as an individual homeowner. He may deduct from his taxable income his share of the cooperative's interest payments and real estate taxes.

It is important to remember that a housing cooperative must derive at least 80 percent of its gross income from tenant-stockholders, which means that no more than 20 percent may come from the rental of commercial space. If this provision of the Internal Revenue Code is not observed, the tenant-stockholders will not be permitted to deduct their shares of the real estate taxes and mortgage interest.

In addition, Regulation 1034 (f) of the Internal Revenue Code provides, in effect, that if a taxpayer sells his co-op apartment and then buys a new one (being in each case the taxpayer's principal residence) within one year before or after the sale of the old one, any gain on the sale is not then subject to income tax, except to the extent that the sales price of the old residence exceeds the purchase price of the new.

Irrigation Cooperatives

"Mutual ditch or irrigation companies" are exempt from the federal income tax, "but only if 85 percent or more of the income consists of amounts collected from members for the sole purpose of meeting losses and expenses." The exemption is not affected by making assessments in advance, provided the balance of the assessments remaining on hand at the end of the year is retained to meet losses and expenses or is returned to members. Early revenue laws had granted exemption only where all income was derived from amounts thus collected from members, but the present requirement of 85 percent gives some leeway to a company which may be entirely mutual as to irrigation water service yet have certain additional income, such as from oil-producing lands, power plants or subsidiary domestic water companies.

Joint Ventures

Corporations may engage in a joint enterprise, taxable as a partnership, without being common law partners. Income received by, or accrued to, the venture is taxable to its members.

Mutual Fire and Casualty Insurance Companies

Mutual fire and casualty insurance companies are now taxed at ordinary corporation income tax rates on their total income, consisting of both investment and underwriting income, less amounts temporarily set aside in a protection against loss account. Under prior provisions, underwriting income or loss was not taken into account in computing the tax of mutual fire and casualty insurance companies. Instead, they were taxed under whichever of the following two formulas resulted in a higher tax: (1) a tax at ordinary corporation tax rates on net investment income or (2) a 1 percent tax on investment income and premiums less dividends to policyholders. The mutual fire and casualty insurance companies are now taxed on substantially the same basis as stock fire and casualty insurance companies.

Farmer mutual insurance companies or associations meeting the provisions set forth in Section 501 of the Internal Revenue Code may qualify for tax exemption. This paragraph (15) reads as follows:

> Mutual insurance companies or associations other than life or marine (including interinsurers and reciprocal underwriters) if the gross amount received during the taxable year from interest, dividends, rents and premiums (including deposits and assessments) does not exceed $150,000.

Mutual Funds

A regulated investment company which meets certain diversification of assets and source of income requirements (prescribed by the Internal Revenue Code) is accorded conduit or "pass through" treatment if it distributes to its shareholders at least 90 percent of its taxable income (exclusive of net long-term capital gain); i.e., it will be taxed only on the portion of such income which is retained. A shareholder receiving a distribution of such income from a regulated investment company treats it as a receipt of ordinary income in the computation of his gross income, and such shareholder is eligible to include it in computing the dividend received exclusion and the dividend received credit, as it may apply.

As to capital gains distributions, to the extent that a regulated investment company distributes the excess of net long-term capital gain over its net short-term capital loss, such capital gain is not taxable to the company but is taxable to the shareholder as a long-term capital gain. Shareholders receiving such capital gains distributions are not eligible to use them for the computation of the dividend received exclusion or the dividend received credit.

Mutual Life Insurance Companies

The nation's tax laws treat all life insurance companies the same, whether they are mutual companies or stock companies. None of the companies, of course, pay income tax on money they refund to their policyholder customers.

From 1921 to 1959, life insurance companies had been taxed upon their investment income from interest, dividends, rents and royalties (but not on premium income), less deductions on that income for policyholder obligations, less deductions for taxes, expenses and depreciation incidental to their investments and investment income.

With the enactment of the 1959 Life Insurance Company Income Tax Act, they are taxed partly on investment earnings and partly on general operations.

Mutual Financial Organizations

Since 1952, domestic savings and loan associations, domestic building and loan associations and certain co-op banks could deduct, as an addition to a bad debt reserve, any amount they felt was adequate, subject to two limitations: (1) Such amount could not exceed taxable income before the deduction, and (2) the total reserves and surplus could not exceed 12 percent of deposits or withdrawable accounts.

The Revenue Act of 1962 amended Section 593 to provide different limitations on the deduction for the bad debt reserve addition. These limitations are more restrictive and reduce this deduction, thus appreciably increasing the taxes paid by such organizations.

Mutual Savings Banks

Mutual savings banks are subject to taxes which may be imposed by the states in which they operate, and they pay local taxes to cities and towns. In addition, they are subject to the federal corporate income tax. In arriving at their taxable income, they are permitted, as are other corporate taxpayers, to deduct necessary operating expenses and the interest they pay their depositors. They are also permitted to deduct a portion of their earnings for additions to reserves that are used solely to protect depositors against any possible losses. This deduction for an individual savings bank may represent an amount that will bring the reserve for real property loans up to 3 percent of such loans held by the bank, or 60 percent of its otherwise taxable income, or an amount justified by the institution's experience if a need for larger deductions is demonstrated.

Mutual savings banks pay out the bulk of their earnings as interest to depositors. These earnings are regularly credited to depositors' accounts in the form of interest and are subject to the federal personal income tax payable by depositors.

Production Credit Associations

Section 63 of the Farm Credit Act of 1933 extends exemption from federal income taxes to production credit associations as long as the federal government owns any capital stock therein. This section reads in part as follows:

> The Central Bank for Cooperatives, and the Production Credit Corporations, Production Credit Associations and Banks for Cooperatives, . . . their property, their franchises, capital, reserves, surplus and other funds, and their income, shall be exempt from all taxation now or hereafter imposed by the United States or by any State, Territorial, or local taxing authority. . . . The exemption provided herein shall not apply with respect to any Production Credit Association or its property or income after the stock held in it by the Production Credit Corporation has been retired. . . .

Once all the government capital is retired, the production credit associations lose their tax exemption and become subject to taxes as regular corporations, except for prior contractual liabilities in refunding savings to their patrons. PCA's are included in the 1962 Revenue Act whenever patronage refunds are made in noncash form.

All production credit associations pay state and local taxes on any real or tangible personal property owned, as well as manufacturers' excise taxes on items purchased.

Retailer-owned Wholesales

Cooperatives of this type are nonexempt. They pay income taxes as regular corporations except that prior contractual obligations permit them to exclude patronage refunds from taxable income. They must pay out 20 percent of their annual net margins to qualify their allocations to patrons under the 1962 Revenue Act.

Rural Electric and Telephone Cooperatives

Rural electric cooperatives have no specific exemption under the tax laws, but Section 501 of the Internal Revenue Code provides exemption for:

> Benevolent life insurance associations of a purely local character, mutual ditch and irrigation companies, mutual or cooperative telephone companies, or like organizations, but only if 85 percent or more of the income consists of amounts collected from members for the sole purpose of meeting losses and expenses.

This section of the Code was written before the organization of rural electric cooperatives. By administrative interpretation they have been considered exempt under this section, however, provided they meet rigid qualifications.

To get this exemption, a rural electric cooperative must show the Internal Revenue Service (1) that it is like a mutual telephone company in character, (2) that it gets nearly all (85 percent) of its income from its members and (3) that it uses this income solely to meet losses and expenses.

Refunds received by consumer-patrons are not taxable because they represent a reduction in household electric bills. Farmers and businessmen are liable for tax on electric co-op refunds if applicable to their farms or businesses.

Some states exempt rural electric cooperatives from ad valorem property taxes and excise taxes on gross revenues.

Usually, rural electric cooperatives will issue capital credits in lieu of cash refunds and later revolve these credits on a 10-year plan, for example.

The struggle between rural electric cooperatives and investor-owned utilities is an interesting one. Refunds made by a public utility are in effect made on a patronage basis. This obligation to refund all amounts over and above expenses and a fair return on capital (usually 6 percent) is analogous in principle to co-op patronage refunds. The public utility obligation is created by law; the co-op obligation is created by contract.[8]

APPLICABLE TAX FORMS

The tax forms which are applicable to cooperatives are as follows:

Form 990 —Return of organizations exempt from income tax under Section 501 (except exempt farmer cooperatives). Information returns on Form 990 by organizations exempt under Section 501 are required to be filed annually by the 15th day of the 5th full calendar month following the close of the organizations' annual accounting period.

Form 990-C—Return of exempt farmer cooperatives under Section 521, to be filed by the 15th day of the 8th month following the close of the taxable year.

Form 1023 —Application for tax exemption for religious, charitable, scientific, literary and educational organizations.

Form 1028 —Application for federal income tax letter of exemption under Section 521, to be applied for after the first year's operation.

Form 1096 —Information return by cooperatives as to kind and amount (transmittal of interest, dividends and patronage refunds paid ($10 or form) and more). Any such corporation is required to file annual Form 1099 information returns on Internal Revenue Forms 1096 and (individual 1099. This requirement applies to all kinds of farmer record form) associations, except rural electrification cooperatives and mutual insurance companies under Section 501. In addition, the account numbers of taxpayers must be included on the form (Form 1099).

Form 1120 —Regular corporation income tax return for all cooperatives not otherwise exempt from Sections 501 and 521.

Form 3227 —Application request for account number for co-op patrons not having social security numbers.

---

[8]Hulbert, L. S., "Taxable Income," *American Cooperation*, A.I.C., Washington, D.C. 1950. p. 363.

Form 3435 —Account number of patron to be filed with the cooperative.

Form 3491 —Application by consumer cooperatives to obtain exemption from the patronage refund reporting requirements.

Other aspects of taxing cooperatives are considered in the next
chapter.

TOPICS FOR DISCUSSION

1. Trace briefly the history of co-op income tax legislation.
2. Name some organizations that are tax exempt under Section 501.
3. Discuss the provisions of Sections 521 and 522 relating to farmer
   cooperatives.
4. In what way was the 1951 Revenue Act deficient?
5. How did the 1962 Revenue Act correct the deficiency in the 1951 Act?
6. Discuss the present tax status of various types of cooperatives.

SELECTED REFERENCES

1. Griffin, George L., *The Taxation of Farmer Cooperatives,* Louisiana
   State University, M. S. Thesis, Baton Rouge, La. June 1962.
2. Harmanson, L. J., Jr., "The New Tax Treatment of Co-ops and Their
   Patrons," American Rice Growers Co-op Conference, Beaumont, Tex.
   Mar. 7, 1963.
3. House of Representatives, *Hearings Before the Committee on Ways and
   Means, Eightieth Congress, Part 4, Tax-Exempt Organizations.* 1947.
4. Newton, R. W., "Corporation Income Taxes as Applied to Co-ops,"
   National Tax Conference, Washington, D.C. 1945.
5. O'Meara, Joseph, Jr., "Federal Income Tax in Relation to Consumer
   Co-ops," *Illinois Law Review.* May 1941.
6. Parker, Florence, "Taxation of Consumers' Co-ops," *Monthly Labor
   Review.* Apr. 1942.
7. Pfann, Geo., "Problems in Changing from Tax-Exempt to Nonexempt
   Status," *American Cooperation,* A.I.C., Washington, D.C. 1949.
8. Small Business Committee, *Competition of Cooperatives with Other
   Forms of Business Enterprise,* House Rept. 1888. 1946.
9. Staff, *Revenue Act of 1962,* Commerce Clearing House, Chicago, Ill.
   Oct. 1962.
10. Staff, *Taxes—Cooperatives Have Them Too,* Cooperative League, Chi-
    cago, Ill. 1963.
11. Volkin, D. and Paul Mohn, *The 1962 Revenue Act—Its Relevancy to
    Farmer Cooperatives,* Federal Extension Service, USDA, Washington,
    D.C. Feb. 1963.

12. Weithorn, S. S., *Tax Manual for Nonprofit Organizations*, Social Legislation Info. Serv., Washington, D.C. 1960.
13. Wisdom, Earl, "The Law on Rural Electric Co-ops," *American Cooperation*, A.I.C., Washington, D.C. 1950. pp. 413-421.
14. Woodin, Martin D. and others, "Tax Status of Farmers' Co-ops," *Louisiana Rural Economist*, Baton Rouge, La. Aug. 1946.

CHAPTER 19 –

Taxation of Cooperatives:
Other Aspects

To tax and to please, no more than to love and to be wise, is not given to men.
—Edmund Burke

He that wrestles with us strengthens our nerves and sharpens our skill. Our antagonist is our helper.
—Edmund Burke

TAXABILITY THEORY OF PATRONAGE REFUNDS

THERE ARE at least three theories regarding the exclusion of patronage refunds from the taxable income of cooperatives. These are: (1) partnership, (2) agency and (3) price-adjustment theory.

The partnership theory holds that co-op patrons are partners in a business undertaking and are taxed as if they were partners. The defect in this theory is that a cooperative is not a partnership but a corporation affording limited liability to each investor. However, under present tax laws some small corporations under a 1958 Act are taxed as partnerships.

The agency theory holds that a cooperative is an agent or trustee for its patrons. A defect in this theory is that some cooperatives go beyond the agency relationship by actually taking title to patrons' commodities or the inventories sold to them.

The price-adjustment theory is perhaps the strongest of the three offered. It states that patronage refunds, either positive or negative, represent correspondingly overcharges or undercharges. These residuals belong to the patrons, not to the cooperative.

It is evident that the price-adjustment theory is more compatible with Emelianoff's definition of cooperatives, for example, and is more likely to withstand attacks upon patronage refund schemes.

The 1962 Revenue Act, while it recognized the price-adjustment theory, provided definite legal substance to the manner in which over-charges or undercharges are to be allocated and paid or distributed to patrons by the cooperatives. Consult the preceding chapter for a discussion of this Act.

LEGALITY OF PATRONAGE REFUNDS

The legality of excluding patronage refunds from the taxable income of cooperatives has been well established.[1,2]

The United States Treasury Department rulings on deductibility of patronage refunds have a long history.

In 1937, a Treasury ruling was promulgated which set forth the attitude of the Treasury Department:

> So-called patronage dividends have long been recognized by the Bureau to be rebates on purchases made in the case of a co-op purchasing organization, or an additional cost of goods sold in case of a co-op marketing organization, when paid with respect to purchases made by, or sales made on account of the distributees. For purposes of administration of the Federal income tax laws, such distributions have been treated as deductions in determining the taxable net income of the distributing cooperative. Such distributions, however, when made pursuant to a prior agreement between the co-operative and its patrons are more properly to be treated as exclusions from gross income of the cooperative. It follows, therefore, that such patronage dividends, rebates or refunds due patrons of a co-op organization are not profits of the cooperative notwithstanding the amount due such patrons cannot be determined until after the closing of the books of the cooperative for a particular taxable period.

The 1962 Revenue Act, especially, added legislative substance to these prior Treasury rulings regarding the exclusion of patronage refunds from taxable income. In effect, the Act requires certain types of contractual obligations between the cooperatives and their patrons regarding distribution of refunds, as explained in the previous chapter.

Error in Attacking Patronage Refunds

A common error made is to assert that a profit-type corporation cannot exclude patronage refunds from its taxable income unless it organ-

---

[1]Mischler, Ray and L. S. Hulbert, *Legal Phases of Cooperation*, FCS Bul. 10, Washington, D.C. 1958. p. 210.
[2]Satterfield, John, *The Co-op in Our Free Enterprise System*, National Council of Farmer Cooperatives, Washington, D.C. Jan. 10, 1961.

izes as a cooperative. This is incorrect. Any profit-type corporation can legally exclude patronage refunds from its taxable income provided it has a prior *contractual* liability to do so.

Commercial history is replete with instances in which refunds have been made to patrons and such allowances excluded from the gross income of the tax paying corporation. For example, in the past, many private enterprises have been subject to re-negotiation or re-pricing under war contracts. Re-negotiation is a first-class illustration of the operation of the co-op method. In this instance, the government is the patron. It determines that the contractor has charged an excessive amount for goods or services, and it requires an adjustment or refund of the excess realized by the taxpayer over cost, plus a reasonable profit. The Internal Revenue Code clearly recognizes that the amounts paid back to the government as a result of re-negotiations are not income to the taxpayer but are, rather, a reduction of gross income or an exclusion therefrom. In fact, the common practice of re-negotiating boards and of the Commissioner of Internal Revenue's office is to reduce both the sales and the profits by the amount of the recovery.

Any decision to construe patronage dividends as income to cooperatives while price adjustments by private corporations are recognized as costs of operations would result in confusion of existing practices.[3]

For example, many profit-type stores sell goods below the "list" price. If they had followed their "list" prices, their profits would be considerably higher. By reducing their prices, they reduce their profits and reduce their taxable income. In other words, they price-out some of their profits to customers and pay less tax to the government. Cooperatives follow the same methods except that the refunds passed to patrons are contractual obligations, not a business whim from day-to-day. Cooperatives could price-out all profits from day-to-day and end up their fiscal year with a balance of zero. This is what some cooperatives would do if patronage refunds were ever taxed to the cooperatives. A credit union, for example, could reduce its interest rate and end up its fiscal year with zero earnings and not be subject to any income tax.

Size of Cooperatives Not a Factor

The fact that a cooperative is large and may be engaged in manufacturing, mining, etc., does not alter the basic principles of patronage

---

[3]Staff, *Tax Liability of Co-ops*, Commerce and Industry Association, New York, N.Y. 1947. p. 19.

refunds. The size of a cooperative has nothing to do with its income tax liabilities as long as it operates with a prior contractual liability to return any net savings or losses to its patrons. Also, the fact that these patrons re-invest their patronage refunds in the cooperative does not change the principles of co-op operation.

Under the laws and regulations, either an exempt or nonexempt cooperative may, if the members so elect, provide for retaining a portion of patronage margins in the cooperative for capital purposes, if it pays taxes on the sum retained. Conversely, patronage margins properly "allocated" may be taken as an exclusion from net savings. This means that they may be excluded even though not refunded wholly in cash, provided the patrons have agreed in advance to have the amount of the refund re-invested with the cooperative for capital or in debt form and provided that the provisions of the 1962 Revenue Act have been complied with.

OTHER ASPECTS OF CO-OP TAXATION

Taxation Related to Vertical Integration

If patronage refunds were taxed to cooperatives, it would be equivalent to saying that regular business firms would have to separate their buying, production and selling departments so that each could be taxed separately rather than through a joint return.

Corporations owned by a common parent corporation may, subject to the provisions of the Federal Revenue Code, file a consolidated income tax return upon the payment of certain penalties, for example. This permits corporations under common ownership to minimize, if not avoid, the pyramiding of taxes, particularly in the case of integrated corporations engaged in the production of the same product or products.

Profit-type corporations integrate vertically and horizontally by mergers, consolidations and internal expansions yet are taxed as one firm. Farmers, and others too, integrate vertically and horizontally through their cooperatives, yet opponents would have them split up their integrated enterprises into various fragments so that they could be taxed several times at several places.

Therefore, to deny farmers and others the right to exclude patronage refunds from gross income would, in reality, discriminate against them by denying to them the right granted other forms of business to integrate procurement, production and selling functions into a unified operation. To attempt to tax patronage refunds owed to patrons pursuant to contract at the cooperative would be to attempt to tax as income that which is not income to the cooperative, assuming the same concept and definition of income as is applied to all other forms of corporate business.[4]

Since the cooperative represents an integral part of the total business of each of its members, the co-op activity itself is not an independent income-making unit. It can only add to the net income of the businesses of which it is a part, in the same sense that a tractor can only add to the net income of the individual farm business of which it is a part. Although both the tractor and the cooperative may produce income for the owners, the income they produce cannot be taxed logically or accurately, except as a part of the total income of the farm business.[5]

Cooperatives could counter their opponents by launching a movement designed to split up giant corporations into several companies and in turn have each company fragment itself into corporate departments. Then, the co-op versus corporate tax question might be resolved more equitably. It would then be a case of fragment versus fragment (Figure 19-1).

Patronage Refunds from Regional Cooperatives

When patronage refunds are deferred by regional associations, they are allocated to each local cooperative according to patronage. The local associations in turn have at least three alternatives for handling these refunds. They may combine the deferred patronage refunds from the regional associations with their own deferred patronage refunds and make allocations to their patrons from this total. An alternative is to allocate the deferred patronage refunds from the regional associations separately from the savings on their own operations. The third alternative is to pay income tax on the deferred patronage refunds from the regional associations and put them in surpluses without allocating them to members.[6]

---

[4]Davis, John H., *An Economic Analysis of the Tax Status of Farmer Co-ops*, A.I.C., Washington, D.C. 1950. p. 106.
[5]Phillips, R. and others, *Do You Know Your Cooperative?*, Iowa Institute of Cooperation, Ames, Iowa. 1957. p. 26.
[6]Merrick, O. and R. Gunderson, *Financing Co-ops*, S.D. Agr. Exp. Sta. Bul. 434, Brookings, S.D. Feb. 1954. p 27.

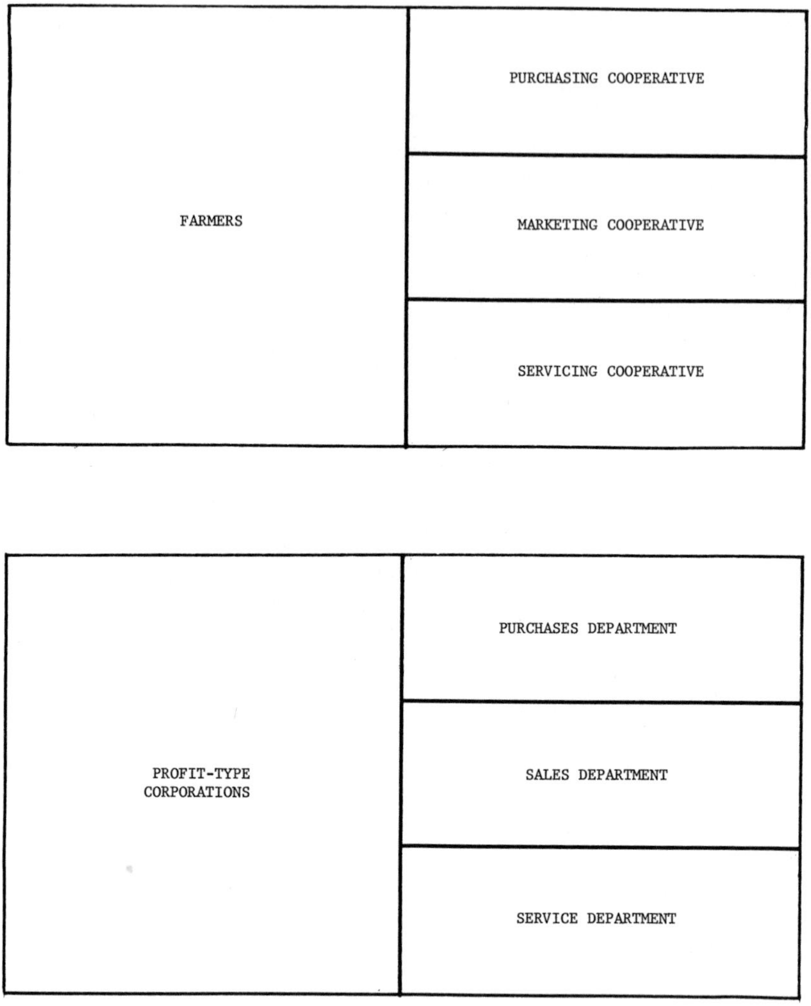

	PURCHASING COOPERATIVE
FARMERS	MARKETING COOPERATIVE
	SERVICING COOPERATIVE

	PURCHASES DEPARTMENT
PROFIT-TYPE CORPORATIONS	SALES DEPARTMENT
	SERVICE DEPARTMENT

FIGURE 19-1

Top—Farmers, by cooperating with other farmers, integrate purchasing, marketing and servicing functions through cooperatives which they control. These are all integral parts of the farmers' operations.

Bottom—Profit-type corporations are usually large enough entities in themselves to integrate purchases, sales and service functions within one firm. These are all integral parts of the profit-type corporations' operations.

Cooperatives and Economic Losses

The Internal Revenue Code provides that cooperatives shall have the same treatment of the items of operating income and expense as would any corporation. At times a cooperative may have a situation in which the operating expenses exceed the operating income, which results in a net operating loss. A cooperative is entitled to a net operating loss deduction just as any other corporation, provided certain conditions exist. In order to recover its loss the cooperative must have the authority to charge off the losses ratably against its patrons, i.e., to reduce its allocations in another year to the extent of the loss or to assess and recover from the patrons in the current or future years. The cooperative would be required to have specific authority by statute, by law or by contractual agreement with the patrons to charge the operating loss to the patrons. The loss may be recovered by the cooperative from its patrons by retaining from future years' allocations either in the cooperatives' discretion at some fixed percentage, or the entire loss may first be recovered before future margins are allocated. Losses cannot be allocated to patrons in such a manner as to create a tax deduction for the patrons, except in the form of a direct assessment. However, the patrons do receive an indirect benefit from the operating loss in that their future allocations will be reduced by the loss.

TAXING THE CO-OP PATRON

The tax liability of the co-op patron for his patronage refunds has been well established. This tax liability is incurred by all patrons except consumers who obtain refunds as a reduction in household or living expenses.

Refunds to Nonmembers

Farmer cooperatives which are tax exempt have to refund earnings to nonmembers in the same manner as to members.

Cooperatives which are nonexempt have a choice of either allocating refunds to nonmembers or paying federal income taxes on that amount.

Under the 1962 Revenue Act, treatment of nonmembers is complicated and requires considerable overhead expense. It is likely that many cooperatives find it easier to pay federal income taxes on non-

	Profit-type Corpora-tion	Partner-ship	Indi-vidual Proprie-torship	Non-farm Consumer Coopera-tive	Farmer Cooperative Exempt	Farmer Cooperative Non-Exempt
FEDERAL TAXES						
General corporation taxes:						
Capital stock tax	Yes	(1)	(1)	Yes	No	Yes
Income taxes	Yes^a	(1)	(1)	Yes^b	Yes^c	Yes^b
Individual income taxes (in the hands of the recipient):						
A. Cash distributed:						
(1) Patronage dividends	(1)^d	(1)^d	(1)^d	(2)	Yes	Yes
(2) Dividends on capital stock	Yes^e	(1)	(1)	Yes	Yes^f	Yes
(3) Cash with-drawals	(1)	Yes	Yes	(1)	(1)	(1)
B. Undistributed earnings:						
(1) Patron's divi-dends in non-cash form	(1)^d	(1)^d	(1)^d	(2)	Yes^g	Yes^g
(2) Allocation to surplus	No	Yes	Yes	No	No	No
Social security taxes:						
Old-age insurance	Yes	Yes	Yes	Yes	Yes	Yes
Unemployment com-pensation	Yes	Yes	Yes	Yes	Yes	Yes
Stamp taxes	Yes	Yes	Yes	Yes	No	Yes

(Continued)

member business and place the remaining balance into "surplus," or "unallocated reserves." Exempt cooperatives will, of course, lose their exemption in such cases.

SUGGESTED TAX REFORMS

Reduction of the burden of income taxes, greater equity, greater simplicity and ease of compliance are not the only criteria for income tax reform, but they are probably of the most immediate concern to most citizens and taxpayers. The overall operation of the free enterprise economy and the use of tax measures for specific economic effects are other important criteria for income tax reform which more thoughtful taxpayers and citizens must share with government. Questions of the need for revenues, alternatives to the income tax as a source of federal revenues, the balance between income and other types of taxes in the federal tax system and the allocation of tax fields between the several levels of government are also important. All must be considered in any program of basic income tax reform.[7]

---

[7]French, R. W., *Tax Review*, New York, N.Y. Sept. 1962. p. 38.

TABLE 19-1 (Continued)

	Profit-type Corpora-tion	Partner-ship	Indi-vidual Proprie-torship	Non-farm Consumer Coopera-tive	Farmer Cooperative Exempt	Non-Exempt
STATE TAXES³						
General corporation taxes:						
Capital stock taxes	Yes	(1)	(1)	Yes	No	Varies
Income taxes	Yes	(1)	(1)	Yes	No^h	Yes
Occupational and other licenses	Yes	Yes	Yes	Yes	Yes	Yes
Unemployment taxes	Yes	Yes	Yes	Yes	Yes	Yes
Property taxes	Yes	Yes	Yes	Yes	Yes	Yes
Retail sales taxes⁴	Yes	Yes	Yes	Yes	Yes	Yes
CITY AND COUNTY TAXES						
Occupational licenses	Yes	Yes	Yes	Yes	Yes	Yes
Property taxes	Yes	Yes	Yes	Yes	Yes	Yes

¹Not applicable.
²Usually, no.
³These items vary with state or local regulations. Applicability shown is the general position.
⁴Certain types of agricultural items are sometimes exempt from retail sales taxes in all forms of business enterprise, including cooperatives.
ªUnless, as a small business corporation, it is elected to qualify under subchapter S of the Internal Revenue Code of 1954.
ʰBut as provided in subchapter T of the Internal Revenue Code of 1954.
ᶜSubject to two special deductions and other provisions of subchapter T of the Internal Revenue Code of 1954.
ᵈCould be applicable if contracts with customers so provided.
ᵉNot subject to specified deductions and exclusions.
ᶠNot subject to deductions and exclusions in (e).
ᵍIf distributed to patrons as "qualified written notice of allocation" and otherwise in compliance with subchapter T of the 1954 Code.
ʰOr on basis similar to federal law.

Taxation by Types of Business

In Table 19-1 is presented a tax comparison for various forms of business enterprises.

In Tables 19-2 and 19-3 are illustrations of how four types of businesses would fare tax-wise under hypothetical conditions. Under other assumed conditions, the results might be different.

Heart of Tax Controversy

The heart of the tax problem is the amounts generally referred to as "patronage refunds" that the cooperative is obligated to return to the patrons on a patronage basis after the year's operations, pursuant

TABLE 19-2
Federal Income Taxes by Type of Business
(Illustration Only)

Item	John Doe Individual Single	Brown & Smith Partnership	John Mfg. Co. Corporation	Farmer Cooperative
	Proprietorship	4 Partners	10 Stockholders	100 Members
Sales	$1,000,000	$1,000,000	$1,000,000	$1,000,000
Expenses	900,000	900,000	900,000	900,000
Net margin	$ 100,000	$ 100,000	$ 100,000	$ 100,000
Federal income taxes paid:				
Single Proprietorship				
By the business	$ 000,000			
By the owner	45,180			
Partnership				
By the business		$ 000,000		
By the 4 partners		24,080		
Corporation				
By the corporation			$ 41,500	
By the 10 stockhold-ers on dividends received			3,500	
Cooperative				
By the cooperative				$ 000,000
By the 100 members on patronage re-funds received				14,000
Total federal income taxes paid	$ 45,180	$ 24,080	$ 45,000	$ 14,000
Percent of net margins paid in federal income taxes	45	24	45	14[1]

[1]This rate applies only to the lowest bracket of taxable income. In most cases, farmer-members of a cooperative are in higher income tax brackets.
Source: Adapted from Hulbert, H. H., *American Cooperation*, A.I.C., Washington, D.C. 1957. p. 115.

to provisions of the articles of incorporation, bylaws, individual agreements and methods specified in the 1962 Revenue Act.

Some business groups want the aggregate of these patronage refunds subjected to a corporate tax on the grounds that regardless of the nature of any contractual agreements between the individual patrons and the cooperatives, these patronage refunds are corporate profits. The cooperatives' position is that where there are bona fide legally enforceable agreements in effect between the patrons and the cooperatives, the cooperatives are obligated to distribute in cash the net earnings to the patrons on a patronage basis. The net earnings are so distributed, except for valid authorizations by the patrons themselves before the transactions take place, for a cooperative to retain the

TABLE 19-3
Federal Income Taxes by Type of
Business (Illustration Only)

	Ordinary Corpora-tion A	Individual Proprietor-ship B	Partner-ship C	Coopera-tive D
Volume of business	$400,000	$400,000	$400,000	$ 400,000
Expenses	40,000	40,000	40,000	40,000
Gross income	6,000	6,000	6,000	6,000
Qualified rebates and patronage refunds	1,000	1,000	1,000	5,000
Net income	5,000	5,000	5,000	1,000[1]
Taxable income to business	5,000	——	——	1,000
Taxable income to owners	3,900[2]	5,000	5,000	5,780

[1]We assume that the cooperative is operating under the general corporation law and that $1,000 of its net margins was realized from business done with customers with whom no patronage refunds were in effect.
[2]After paying 22 percent federal income tax and assuming net earnings after taxes are declared as dividends (state taxes disregarded, since same principles would apply).
Source: Adapted from Beall, Earl, "Cooperatives vs. Corporations," *Broiler Industry,* Sea Isle City, N.J. July 1963, p. 19.

patronage refunds, or parts of them, and the amounts represented thereby are in fact taxable income to the patrons. It is assumed here that the cooperative has complied with the provisions of the 1962 Revenue Act.

If the co-op method of doing business yielded such great tax advantages, it would be expected that profit-type corporations would all convert to the co-op method in order to enjoy these tax advantages. So far, there has been no rush to do so. There would be no tax exemption which would accrue to them unless they became in fact nonprofit institutions, returning their net savings to their customers.

Therefore, opponents of cooperatives may be using the tax question as a camouflage to thwart co-op competition. However, it is recognized that certain further tax reforms are needed for both cooperatives and profit-type corporations, and these are dealt with in the next section.

Eliminating the Double Tax on
Profit-type Corporations

The first federal income tax, introduced in 1913, used the corporate income tax chiefly as a withholding levy. The rate of tax on corporate income was the same as the normal rate of the personal income tax. Dividends were exempted from the normal personal tax. Thus double taxation was avoided. This policy continued through World War I, although both the normal and the corporate rates were raised to 12 percent during this period. In the early twenties, the relationship between the two taxes was broken when the corporate rate was raised to 12½ percent and later to still higher figures, while the normal personal tax was reduced to 8 percent and subsequently to still lower levels. In 1936, when dividends were made subject to the normal tax, the divorce between the two tax levies was completed. What had once been a withholding levy was thus converted into a full-fledged business tax. Both before and during World War II, the trend in federal tax policy was to rely heavily on the taxation of business as such.

The ordinary profit-type corporation pays 22 percent tax, first, on net income of $25,000 or less and 50 percent on amounts above $25,000 (in 1964) and 48 percent (in 1965 and thereafter). In turn, the dividends paid out to stockholders are taxed again on a personal income basis.

Since the 1964 federal income tax law, an individual pays no tax on the first $100 in dividends he receives on his investments. He may further deduct 2 percent of any additional dividend income he has from his tax bill (in 1964), but no such credit is allowed in the years thereafter. This discriminatory burden on the taxpayer is lightened only to a very minor extent by the flat exemption and the credit allowance on dividends. But the corporation (unless very small) has already paid a tax and surtax on the earnings from which the dividends were distributed. The result of this double levy is that a corporation, in order to give a stockholder in the highest income bracket an annual after-tax yield on his investment equal to the 3½ percent obtainable from a tax exempt bond, would have to earn before tax at a yearly per-share rate of more than 50 percent of the market value of its stock, even in the unlikely event that it paid out all its earnings in dividends. For a stockholder in the 50 percent tax bracket, the corporation would have to earn 13½ percent of the per-share price. This double taxation is unfair and injurious to free enterprise.

What is the solution? One solution is to exempt the stockholder from paying a tax on what he gets from his corporation, since it has already paid a tax. In that way, the corporation would pay a tax, but the stockholder would not. In a cooperative, it would pay no tax, but the patron would. This plan of taxation would be fair because a regular corporation would pay the tax where it earns it, while the co-op member would pay the tax where he earns it.

If this plan were followed, more money would be invested in businesses, more risks taken, unemployment reduced and federal spending reduced. Relief to corporation stockholders, who now perhaps carry more than their fair share of the tax burden, would be provided. Both cooperatives and regular corporations would become more competitive. As matters now stand, there is a strong incentive to retain earnings within a corporation in order that the individual taxpayer won't have to pay income tax on his portion.

This condition is undesirable from the standpoint of corporate investors and for the country as a whole because it means that investment is stimulated artificially in those industries which require large capital investments and which can be financed only by means of the corporate form of organization.

Opponents of cooperatives argue that cooperatives themselves should be double taxed, namely, on net savings and again when refunds are given to patrons. This argument is basically that two wrongs at two different places make a "right." The logical answer is to eliminate the double tax on profit-type corporations and convert it to a single tax comparable to the single tax principle on cooperatives.

Rumble has well expressed the matter at controversy:

> Practically all arguments against the present method of taxing cooperatives stem from the present double tax imposed upon the profits of ordinary business corporations. Most critics, lawyers, businessmen and farmers agree that this double taxation is wrong, but if patronage refunds were taxed to the cooperative there would be even more vicious double taxation and extension of the wrong.[8]

Many co-op leaders and scholars have endorsed the single tax concept for profit-type corporations levied at the corporate level and a single tax on cooperatives levied at the patron level. At least one co-op organization has endorsed this plan[9] in principle. Davis dealt with some aspects of this problem and made some recommendations thereto.[10]

Another plan suggests that elimination of the double tax on profit-type corporations take the form of shifting all the tax to the stock-

[8]Rumble, W. E., "Cooperatives and Income Taxes," *Legal and Contemporary Problems*, Duke University, Durham, N.C. 1948. p. 544.
[9]National Council of Farmer Cooperatives. 1960 Annual Meeting resolution.
[10]Davis, *op. cit.* pp. 111-118.

holders on a personal income basis. The corporation would merely withhold such a tax and forward it to the government. This would be similar to the tax policy in Great Britain.

Under such a plan, corporate net income would be allocated appropriately to each share of stock, both common and preferred. Then a withholding levy equal to the lowest rate applicable to individual income (16 percent in 1964, 14 percent beginning in 1965) would be assessed against each stockholder's equity in the net earnings of the corporation. The corporation would transmit to the Treasury an amount equal to all taxes withheld. Upon receipt of dividends in cash, the stockholder would pay on the surtax, the normal tax already having been paid for him by the corporation. Should an individual stockholder, in any year, not have sufficient personal income as to require him to pay an income tax, then he would be eligible for a refund from the Treasury equal to the amount of the withholding tax on the stock which he owned.

Actually, the withholding tax is not a tax against the corporation but a tax on personal income, collected in advance. Applied to corporate earnings, it is analogous to the payroll withholding tax now in use with respect to salaried employees.

That such a plan is administratively feasible is indicated by the experience of Great Britain as well as our own experience with the payroll withholding tax.[11]

President Franklin D. Roosevelt in 1936 seemed to have something like this in mind when he suggested that "the aim, as a matter of fundamental equity, should be to seek equality of tax burden on all corporate income whether distributed or withheld from the beneficial owners." The simplest approach to this objective might be to make dividends deductible on the corporate income tax form just as interest is at present. Thus profits distributed as dividends would be taxed solely under the personal income tax structure, and the undistributed profits would be taxed at an undistributed profits tax rate.

Some Corporations Taxed Like Partnerships

In 1958, Congress passed a law permitting small corporations (having 10 or fewer stockholders) to elect to pass all their profits directly to the individual stockholders at the end of every year. In effect, Congress extended to these pseudo-corporations all the advantages of

---

[11]*Ibid.*, p. 115.

corporations plus an advantage in being taxed as partnerships. Congress thus recognized in this instance the unfair burden of double taxation on corporations.

Repealing Section 521?

In the wording of the tax code, this exemption is limited to "farmers', fruit growers' or like associations." The regulations provide that co-op associations dissimilar from these are not exempt. The effect of such provisions is to grant the exemption solely to associations composed of producers of agricultural products, and not to associations formed by producers of nonagricultural products or services, or to consumer cooperatives.

Since Section 521 provides relatively little benefit to farmer cooperatives but does create much public and private controversy, it is possible that Section 521 is not worth retaining. About half of the farmer cooperatives in the United States are already outside of Section 521. For the dollars that this exemption has provided, it has cost all cooperatives perhaps a much larger sum in bad public relations, community ill-will and a host of other costs impossible to quantify.

Brooks has expressed his position as follows:

> Your Board and management felt that as long as there was any tax exemption of any kind on any of the funds of a farmers cooperative, they were subject to violent and malicious attacks. Consequently, at many farm co-op meetings, I made the statement that the Board of Cotton Producers Association felt farm cooperatives should give up this so-called tax advantage, as it was not worth the cost of the attacks being made against farm cooperatives.[12]

Davis has cited the lack of economic justification for such an exemption.[13]

The Cooperative League does not believe that Section 521 is of much value:

> These restrictions, extra bookkeeping and added effort have proved so onerous that this partial tax exemption is of doubtful value to most farmers' marketing and purchasing cooperatives. Half of these cooperatives do not even bother to apply for this partial exemption. They pay income tax on exactly the same basis as any other corporation.[14]

---

[12]Brooks, D. W., "Co-op Taxes," *Dixie Co-op News*, Atlanta, Ga. Feb. 1962. p. 3.
[13]Davis, *op. cit.* p. 102.
[14]Staff, *Cooperatives and Taxation*, Cooperative League, Chicago, Ill. 1960. p. 12.

How much tax burden would be created on exempt farmer co-operatives if Section 521 were repealed?

One Treasury Department official has stated that, although it was difficult to determine the exact figures, the Treasury would estimate that repeal of the exemption might increase federal revenue by $10 to $20 million a year.[15]

According to another report, some 5,141 farmer cooperatives reported as tax exempt associations for 1953. Aside from patronage refund exclusions, these tax exempt cooperatives were allowed to deduct $9.5 million for dividends or interest paid on capital stock and $5.7 million for nonpatronage income allocated to patrons, or a total of $15.2 million in deductions from taxable income. On a per co-op basis, this averaged $2,957 which, if taxable at a 30 percent rate, would have taxed each cooperative an average of $887.[16]

If Section 521 were repealed, cooperatives could still minimize their tax burden by eliminating stock interest payments and, instead, increasing patronage refunds which are tax deductible.

Those who are for the retention of Section 521 argue as follows: (1) The exemption is not a special privilege since many other groups also have exemption. (2) It provides a close check on farmer co-operatives and forces them to maintain truly co-op operations. (3) The revenue loss to the federal government is very small. (4) Congress has always believed that this exemption is in the public interest. (5) It would be unfair to farmers as a group unless all other tax privileges were likewise repealed.

Repealing Section 501?

Some argue that Section 501 should be repealed. If such a repeal were attempted, however, almost every religious, charity, civic, com-munity, tax exempt foundation, trade group, Chamber of Commerce, etc., in the United States would be involved. It would then be a matter for each group to try to protect its exemption status. Congress has the power and responsibility to repeal if it so desires. It is not likely to do so because it probably feels that the public interest is being served by Section 501. It should, however, review this section

---

[15]*Hearings Before the Committee on Ways and Means on Proposed Revisions of the Internal Revenue Code*, 80th Congress. First Session. 1947.
[16]Staff, *Farmers' Co-ops Income Tax Returns*, IRS Rept. 386, Washington, D.C. 1953. p. 8.

from time to time to see whether all the groups so exempted are truly serving the public interest or serving only themselves.

Congressman Wright Patman has brought to light some gross inequities under Section 501, especially concerning tax exempt foundations. Large and small corporations and the families owning them may manipulate such tax exempt foundations for purposes other than the public trust or the public good.[17]

Tax Reform Should Not Be Confined to Cooperatives

Some persons like to stress the so-called tax privileges of cooperatives, while in reality, tax privileges are afforded to many groups. The point is that any tax reform legislation has to encompass a multitude of privileges, including those for tax exempt foundations, the oil depletion allowance, other special depreciation allowances, tariffs, quotas, price maintenance, subsidies, etc.

In addition, there are tax advantages given to churches and religious groups which own considerable property, to say nothing of wealthy individuals who profit by translating ordinary nonfarm income into capital gains which are then taxed at a lower rate.

Only about half of the personal income in the United States is now taxable. The present approximate loss of $45 billion in revenue is accounted for as follows:

Type of Exemption	Revenue Loss to the Federal Government ($) (Billions)
1. Personal exemption	23.0
2. Interest, charity, etc., deductions	8.0
3. Income-splitting	3.5
4. Pension and security exemptions	2.5
5. Fast write-offs (business)	2.1
6. Capital gain favoritism	2.0
7. Nonprofit or co-op exemptions	1.0
8. Depletion allowances	1.0
9. Relief for handicapped	0.9
10. Municipal bond exemptions	0.6
11. Dividend income rules	0.4
12. Family partnerships	0.1
Total	45.1

[17]Staff, *Tax Exempt Foundations*, Small Business Committee of the House of Representatives, Washington, D.C. 1962.

Co-op exemptions rank 7th in revenue loss to the federal government.

In 1959, a Treasury Department official stated that of the dividends paid by corporations in 1956, $1.5 billion were not reported on individual tax returns and that more than $3 billion of interest paid to individuals were not reported on their individual tax returns for that year. The total unreported dividend and interest income ($4.464 billion) substantially exceeded the net worth of all types of farmer cooperatives on January 1, 1957 ($3.468 billion), and was almost 20 times the total patronage refunds of all farmer cooperatives in 1954.

Taxing of Patronage Refunds to the Cooperatives

Under no conditions should any cooperative accept the thesis that patronage refunds should be taxed at the co-op level. There is nothing to compromise on this point. If cooperatives and others should ever accept this thesis, then the cooperative as a business organization is violated. In fact, there is nothing left to the co-op institution as such except to price-out all margins so that a zero balance remains at the end of the year. This would have to be the cooperatives' last line of defense. This co-op practice in itself could wreck many profit-type corporations because nothing would be left to their investors as an incentive to capitalize their own corporations. Again the warning must be sounded—that any undue attack on the co-op patronage refund at the co-op level could result in a large-scale demise of the very corporations which seek to impose such a tax on the cooperatives. It is good economic policy to leave the co-op patronage refund alone at the co-op level. Instead, the refund is and should be taxed at its source—the patron of the cooperative. The 1962 Revenue Act fully implements this principle of taxation.

What Would Cooperatives Do If Earnings Were Taxed?

If cooperatives were to be subjected to a federal income tax on net earnings, most of them would probably adopt a "price-out" policy. Such a policy would, in effect, cut retail prices or advance patrons more for their produce so that there would be left no earnings to tax. Opponents of cooperatives readily fear this "price-out" method because it could mean a radical price-cutting effort which could seri-

FIGURE 19-2

"Divi day" brings happy faces to the table of a consumer cooperative in Great Britain. In nearly all countries of the world, bona fide patronage refunds made to co-op members are not taxed to the cooperative. (Courtesy, Co-operative Union, Manchester, England)

ously threaten profit-type corporations and other businesses in many areas of the United States. Take the example of a co-op fertilizer manufacturer which has been selling fertilizer at the going market price but refunding anywhere from $10 to $20 per ton on high-analysis fertilizer to its patrons. Profit-type corporations are not now openly affected because the price structure is not disturbed under this method. If this cooperative were to be taxed on its net earnings, it could then cut fertilizer prices from $10 to $20 per ton and adversely affect profit-type manufacturers while the cooperative itself would no doubt gain in sales, reduce unit costs and cut prices still further.

The "price-out" method is a powerful tool in the cooperative's arsenal which best be left alone by profit-type corporations and other businesses. Cooperatives will only use this "price-out" method as a last resort if and when co-op savings become subjected to federal income taxes at the co-op level. The "price-out" method, however, beautifully demonstrates the real nature of a cooperative—that savings or profits belong to its patrons, not its investors.

The United States Treasury Department has recognized the pitfalls in attempting to tax refunds at the co-op level:

It appears, therefore, that there are substantial grounds for questioning the appropriateness of patronage dividends as a base for taxing the income earned by cooperatives. In many situations, a statute requiring the inclusion of patronage dividends in the gross income of cooperatives would operate most inequitably. It would result in overtaxation of cooperatives in cases where patronage dividends overstate the economic income earned by the cooperatives. It would result in unfair discrimination among different types of cooperatives in cases where patronage dividends understate the economic income earned by the cooperatives, or where patronage dividends are not used at all. It would not be an effective means of equalizing taxes on cooperative and other forms of business organizations.

Moreover, if patronage dividends were included in the gross income of cooperatives, the result might merely be to reduce those associations which now report substantial patronage dividends to change their methods of doing business so as to have little or no net proceeds to distribute at the close of the year. In the case of an ordinary corporation it is always in the interest of the firm to maximize its net income, regardless of the fact that the income is subject to the corporation income tax. But the situation with respect to the cooperative is quite different. The primary objective of a cooperative is not to maximize the income shown on its own accounting statements but to maximize the income of its members. Success in achieving this objective is not dependent on the size of patronage dividends.[18]

Who Is Going to Pay Taxes?

Some persons maintain that if net earnings are not to be taxed at the co-op level then the federal and state governments are losing much needed revenue and that other types of businesses and taxpayers must make up this loss. However, the overlooked fact is that any income not taxed at the co-op level is taxable at the patron level.

In the highly unlikely event that all business and corporation profits were returned on a wide-spread basis to customer members, there would be a corresponding increase in the ability of taxpayers to provide their own services.

This, however, is only part of the answer. These earnings would, in any event, begin flowing into the economy, there to be subjected to the numerous other taxes which governments at all levels have seen fit to impose.

---

[18]*Taxation of Farmers' Cooperative Associations*, U.S. Treasury Department, Washington, D.C. Oct. 1947.

We cannot be sure of how much the governments are losing until we know how these patronage refunds generate business and prosperity in the hands of patrons. It could well be that governments gain, rather than lose, when the ultimate effects are appraised.

If the poorer segments of the economy get a major share of the patronage refunds, they in turn spend all they get and sometimes more (by borrowing). The local drugstore, department store, bakery, dentist, doctor, etc., have higher sales and net incomes corresponding to the patronage refunds spent. Thus, these businesses pay taxes on these increased revenues, and the net loss of tax revenues to the government may be nil. It is difficult to prove the case either way.

Congress has the power and authority to enact tax legislation which, first, must attempt to cover federal expenditures and, second achieve some goal or aim which Congress considers in the best interests of society. Such goals do undergo change over time and with each new Congress. Thus far, Congress has felt that cooperatives serve some useful purpose in providing increased bargaining power for some groups. If cooperatives were not able to provide this help, Congress itself might have to legislate in this area with a concomitant increase in federal expenditures.

The obvious answer is that the ability of a country to pay taxes depends upon total productivity and resulting national income and not upon how much of that may be deemed to have been earned by corporations and how much by individuals. This being true, then a given quantity of revenue to be raised by income taxation, when related to a given total national income, is no greater in the aggregate whether paid partly by corporations and partly by individuals, or whether paid wholly by individuals. Actually, the final incident of all corporate income taxes rests upon individuals and not corporations as entities. Therefore, the income tax paying ability of a country does not depend upon whether part is paid or collected indirectly through corporations or whether all is collected directly through a personal tax.[19]

Cooperatives Destroying Competition?

Cooperatives have expanded appreciably in the past. However, the records do not show that co-op business in the aggregate has grown

---

[19]Davis, *op. cit.* p. 117.

more rapidly than other business in the fields in which cooperatives are prominent.

While the stronger cooperatives have improved their position, so have the stronger noncooperatives.

There has been no marked tendency in recent years for co-op marketing associations to take over a larger share of the total marketing business at the farm level, although there has been a material growth in the business done by farmer purchasing cooperatives.

During the period 1950-1957, farmer marketing cooperatives handled less than 24 percent of the total farm production, and during the same period, farmer purchasing or supply cooperatives handled substantially less than one-sixth of the total supplies and equipment sold to farmers.

Cooperatives still do only a small part of the total business of the United States, and their share of that business is not likely to increase greatly in the future; their earnings are relatively small, and even if all patronage distributions were taxed at regular corporate rates, the revenue gain would not be significantly large, not nearly large enough to justify the harm which would be done to farmers and others by such action. As stated by the Treasury Department: "Considerations of revenue and equity must be weighed against the advantages to the economy as a whole which result from this particular form of encouragement to the flow of capital and effort into cooperatives."[20]

STATE INCOME TAXATION

While income tax laws vary from state to state in their application to cooperatives, they are basically similar to the federal law and Internal Revenue regulations. Patronage refunds are excludable from taxable income in most, if not all, cases if a prior obligation exists. There are certain variations from state to state regarding the exclusion of interest paid on equity capital, non-operating income, etc.

In some states, cooperatives are subjected to franchise taxes computed on the basis of a percentage of net income, the same as profit-type corporations. Excise taxes computed as a percentage of all net income are used in some states in lieu of all other taxes except those on real estate.

---

[20]Rumble, W. E., "Cooperatives and Federal Income Taxes," Co-op Grain Quarterly, St. Paul, Minn. Winter 1961. pp. 26-27.

Some states, like Wisconsin, have in their revenue codes an exemption which permits certain qualified cooperatives full exemption from the state income tax and from the necessity of filing an annual income tax return. Those cooperatives which do not qualify are still permitted to exclude bona fide patronage refunds from taxable income. For an excellent summary of state income tax exemptions for cooperatives, see Davis.[21]

Many state income laws are patterned after or conform with federal income tax laws; many vary tremendously. For the next few years there will be much need for advising state legislators so that their concepts of depreciation, taxable income, patronage refunds and the like will be in harmony with those embodied in federal statutes and court decisions.

Since most states are facing increased financial burdens, it is likely that the taxation of cooperatives will be adversely affected in the future. Federal guidelines on co-op taxation will, of course, be very important to the states when they are reviewing the tax status of cooperatives domiciled therein.

TAXATION OF COOPERATIVES IN OTHER COUNTRIES

The best sources available on taxation of cooperatives in various nations of the world are by Tracey[22] and Davidovic.[23]

The future of cooperation is considered in the next chapter.

TOPICS FOR DISCUSSION

1. Discuss the three theories of patronage refunds exclusion. How does the 1962 Revenue Act affect the price-adjustment theory?
2. Discuss the need for tax reform.
3. Should the double tax on profit-type corporations be eliminated?
4. Should Section 521 be repealed?
5. Should Section 501 be repealed?
6. What might cooperatives do if patronage refunds were ever taxed to the cooperatives before these refunds were distributed to their patrons?

---

[21]Davis, *op. cit.* pp. 78-79.
[22]Tracey, Joan, "The Taxation of Co-ops," *Yearbook of Agricultural Cooperation,* Plunkett Foundation, London, England. 1950. pp. 30-56.
[23]Davidovic, George, *The Tax Position of Cooperatives in Various Countries,* Co-operative Union of Canada, Ottawa, Canada. 1963.

SELECTED REFERENCES

1. Adcock, A. W., "Patronage Dividends: Income Distribution or Price Adjustment," *Law and Contemporary Problems*, Duke University, Durham, N.C. Summer 1948.
2. Anderson, Tom, "Co-ops Should Be Taxed," *American Mercury*. Aug. 1958. pp. 110-112.
3. Bradley, W. L., "Taxation of Co-ops," *Harvard Business Review*, Cambridge, Mass. 1947.
4. Casselman, P. H., *Cooperatives and Taxation, Social Centre,* University of Ottawa, Canada. Feb. 1945.
5. Ford, T. K., *Taxation of Co-ops,* Editorial Research Reports, Washington, D.C. Jan. 11, 1946.
6. Gardner, K. B., *What Are Patronage Refunds?* FCS Info. 34, Washington, D.C. Feb. 1963.
7. Groves, Harold, "State Taxation of Wisconsin Cooperatives," *Wisconsin Law Review*. No. 4, 1954. p. 617.
8. Guthmann, Harry, "Tax Favoritism to Co-ops," *Harvard Business Review,* Cambridge, Mass. Nov.-Dec. 1960. pp. 116-125.
9. Lasser, J. K., *Farmers' Tax Handbook,* Prentice-Hall, New York, N.Y. 1950.
10. Markin, Rom J., "The Rationale of Cooperative Taxation," *Montana Business Review*. May 1959. pp. 3-11.
11. Mason, Noah M., "Uncle Sam's Untapped Millions," *The American Magazine*. Feb. 1950.
12. Olmstead, F. R., "Relinquishing Federal Income Tax Exemption," *American Cooperation*, A.I.C., Washington, D.C. 1951.
13. Satterfield, John C., "The Cooperative in Our Free Enterprise System," N.C.F.C. Meeting, New Orleans, La. Jan. 10, 1961.
14. Staff, *Taxes and the Public Interest,* Conference on Economic Progress, Washington, D.C. June 1963.

CHAPTER 20 —

Cooperatives and the Future:
Reflections and Projections

The world turns aside to let any man pass who knows where he is going.
—David Starr Jordan

It is vain to be always looking toward the future and never acting toward it.
—Boyes

With cooperative organization, it's possible to start from the smallest unit of production and consumption and build extremely powerful industrial, commercial and banking organizations. Linked with co-ops, public organizations become more effective.
—Dag Hammarskjold

COOPERATIVES AND CAPITALISM

IF IT IS TRUE that cooperatives are a competitive yardstick within the capitalistic system, it stands to reason that cooperatives should provide more and better yardsticks. The real, tough economic issues have, in many cases, been sidestepped. This sidestepping of issues has been rationalized on many grounds too numerous to enumerate here.

If the basic industries in capitalism have been oligopolized, such as rubber, steel, oil, metals, fertilizers, paper, autos, chemicals, glass, farm machinery, etc., should not cooperatives then rise to the challenge and provide more competitive yardsticks? Without doubt this is a challenge for co-op leaders in the years ahead. The challenge is not directed solely at farmer cooperatives but at all other cooperatives as well.

COOPERATIVES NOT BIG ENOUGH

Perhaps the greatest obstacle to cooperatives in the future is the thought of many co-op leaders and others that cooperatives are already big enough. A few figures ought to dispel this thought quickly. For example, all the dairy cooperatives in the United States taken together sell about $3 billion of milk and milk products. But, the Borden Company alone sells over $1 billion, and the National Dairy Products Corporation alone sells over $1.8 billion.

Of the 500 largest corporations in the United States (excluding retail businesses), only five are co-op corporations:[1]

Co-op Corporation	Sales ($) (000)	National Rank in Sales (1962)
Land O'Lakes Creameries	232,258	227
Consumers Cooperative Association	203,191	249
Grange League Federation	196,291	257
Southern States Cooperative	130,582	350
Eastern States Farmers' Exchange	97,643	450

In 1958, the Great Atlantic & Pacific Tea Company sales were $5.1 billion, or more than 30 times the sales of all urban consumer co-operatives; its net earnings after taxes in 1958 were $54 million as compared with $1.7 million for the 26 leading urban store cooperatives.

In 1958, the sales of International Harvester Company exceeded by more than 10 times the farm machinery and equipment sales of all farm supply cooperatives and were only slightly less than one-half as much as the total sales of all farm supply cooperatives.

The total gross business of all the cooperatives in the United States in petroleum is less than the net profit after taxes of just one of the major oil companies.[2]

General Motors, the largest corporation in the United States, is bigger than all farm marketing and purchasing cooperatives combined. GM has sales of around $15 billion and assets of over $8.5 billion. Farmers in the United States have only about $5 billion invested in all their cooperatives.

Cooperatives are in no danger of getting too big. While it is true that some of them have grown rapidly during the last decade, it is likewise true that some have not. It is also true that profit-type businesses are growing too.

Another approach reveals that farmer cooperatives account for about 3 percent of the gross national product, and all other cooperatives account for another 3 percent for a total of 6 percent. Some economists

---

[1] *Mergers and Superconcentration*, Small Business Committee, Washington, D.C. 1962. pp. 46-53. And trade sources data.
[2] Wysor, W. G., *The Southern States Story*, Richmond, Va. 1959. p. 164.

FIGURE 20-1

Although many large-size cooperatives exist, the percentage of total business done by cooperatives is still quite small. (Courtesy, Eastern States Farmers' Exchange, West Springfield, Mass., and Cooperative League, Chicago, Ill.)

maintain that cooperatives would have to do about 20 percent of the total business to be effective competitors and provide the economic yardsticks that are needed in combatting monopoly.

It is estimated that cooperatives make and distribute about 20 to 25 percent of all the fertilizer sold today. Because of the cooperative yardstick of quality and price, the fertilizer industry is far different today from what it was in the past. Abuses have been reduced to a minimum, and generally speaking, private fertilizer manufacturers put out a good product at a reasonable price.

COOPERATIVES AND THE FEDERAL GOVERNMENT

The long-range danger for cooperatives in relying on the federal government is the latter's increasing tendency to paternalize. For farmer cooperatives, the situation is especially precarious since non-farm groups are gaining political power in relation to farm groups. For consumer cooperatives there is no assurance that government interests will not yield to nonconsumer groups. While short-run gains may be possible from government help, the long-run effects could be adverse.

There is one hope, however. If any further federal government aid or program for cooperatives should be enacted, steps should be

FIGURE 20-2

President Dwight D. Eisenhower signed the Farm Credit Act of 1953 giving more representation and control to the farmer-members who own and use the farm credit system in the United States. In any piece of federal legislation relating to co-op financing or otherwise, control should be at the grass-roots. (Courtesy, Farm Credit Administration, Washington, D.C.)

incorporated in the legislation whereby government control is steadily withdrawn and replaced with control by the cooperatives themselves.

Aaron Sapiro, in 1926, warned of the danger of government aid to agriculture as a substitute for cooperative, self-help programs:

> Where you get the farmer inbued with the thought that he can hop down to Washington and work out some hand-made solution of his troubles through governmental aid, he is

going to let the Government do it instead of trying to do it himself. You can promise much more than you can possibly do by any achievement of cooperation. So I think the outstanding and obvious paralysis of the cooperative growth has been caused primarily by the deflection of the farmer's interest into political channels.[3]

HELPING COOPERATIVES WORLDWIDE

Without doubt, North American cooperatives will be asked to play an increasing role in economic development in some foreign nations. This role will involve men, money and techniques. If these efforts are properly coordinated with the recipient nation(s), much good can result. If, however, certain factions undermine the co-op program in either or both the "giving" and the "receiving" nation, then these co-op efforts will be useless.

In 1961, the Act for International Development proclaimed it to be the declared policy of the United States to encourage the development and use of cooperatives in its foreign aid programs.

Two additional steps appear creative in extending a helping-hand to cooperatives in other parts of the world: (1) the International Cooperative Training Center at The University of Wisconsin and (2) the International Cooperative Development Association headquartered in Chicago, Illinois.[4]

In other instances, cooperatives in many nations may form international cooperatives to engage in various lines of business.

COOPERATIVES AND UNDERDEVELOPED NATIONS

The use of the co-op method by governments of underdeveloped countries poses two risks: (1) loss of autonomy of the cooperatives and (2) loss of efficiency in the cooperatives. These risks come about whenever cooperatives are organized simply as arms of the state without due regard to their private role in the economic system.

Also, industries and/or enterprises may be preserved or initiated

---

[3]Sapiro, Aaron, *American Cooperation*, A.I.C., Washington, D.C. 1926. p. 34.
[4]"Co-ops Organize to Do Business Overseas," *Feedstuffs*, Minneapolis, Minn. June 29, 1963. p. 63.

FIGURE 20-3

The Western Co-operative College at Saskatoon, Saskatchewan, Canada, sponsored by cooperatives in western Canada offers education and training services for co-op officials and employees.

primarily to give employment, and though their form may be co-operative, they will in fact be in the nature of relief works if the test of economic viability is not applied. Cooperatives for the joint use of land may be established on social, ideological or other grounds, but if they do not in fact increase productivity, pay off investment and operational credits and offer their members an economic return for their labor and capital, they may be interesting experiments but still not qualify as efficient business enterprises in their own right.[5]

FOREIGN TRADE

Farmer cooperatives especially are concerned with foreign trade expansion. Rice, cotton, wheat, broilers and many other commodities have a large stake in foreign trade. Efforts on a co-op basis to expand trade in the future should prove rewarding.

At the same time, cooperative buying in foreign markets will be important. Many retailers, consumer stores and farm supply co-operatives will need to purchase foreign-made goods cooperatively in order to remain competitive here at home. Farm supply cooperatives, for example, have found that imported steel products are considerably cheaper than domestic steel products. Since it is their job to provide their farm customers with economical supplies, imported products are often used.

---

[5]I. L. O., *Co-op Management and Administration*, Geneva, Switzerland. 1960. p. 219.

FIGURE 20-4

*Many cooperatives operating country elevators own this huge water terminal in Duluth, Minn.
Cooperatives need to develop foreign trade to a greater extent. (Courtesy, Cooperative League,
Chicago, Ill.)*

FUTURE SCOPE OF COOPERATION
IN THE UNITED STATES

Farmer Cooperatives

With the trend to fewer but larger farms, higher capitalization and
more exacting market requirements, it is easy to see why cooperation
in agriculture will expand. Number-wise, farmer cooperatives may
not expand greatly, but volume-wise their gains should be significant.
Much, of course, will depend on the federal government's farm
policies. If a more centralized and paternalistic federal government

evolves, cooperation will be less in favor. If the federal government should lessen its involvement in agriculture, cooperation will take up much of the slack. The choice is up to the farmers themselves and the citizenry through their elected representatives.

The efforts of the National Farmers Organization (NFO) to bargain collectively for farmers are a symptom of the basic disease confronting much of agriculture, namely, its lack of bargaining strength. However, co-op bargaining alone, without a federal cover for such a bargaining activity, probably will not succeed. The labor unions preceding the Wagner Act (National Labor Relations Act) were likewise powerless to impose their demands. Farm bargaining groups are today in the same position labor unions were prior to the Wagner Act.

If a National Agricultural Labor Relations Act were to be enacted, giving farm groups the right to bargain collectively and, simultaneously,

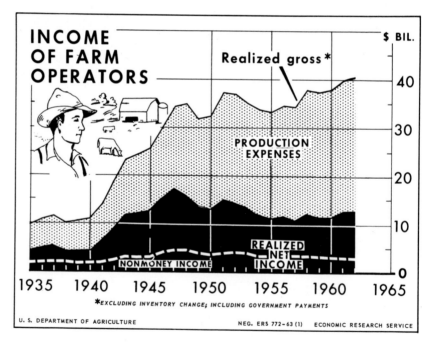

FIGURE 20-5

Although farmers' incomes have gone up, so have production expenses. Farmers are relying more on purchased inputs, thus the increasing importance of farm supply cooperatives. (Courtesy, USDA, Washington, D.C.)

requiring that processors and handlers bargain in good faith, an approximation to the Wagner Act would be realized for agriculture. An evaluation of such legislation as well as its long-range implications is beyond the scope of this book.

Even without a Wagner Act for agriculture, however, cooperatives can be useful in many bargaining situations, especially when they control a sufficient volume of outputs and/or inputs. Farmers and others can, without ownership of facilities, gain some benefits if they are willing to pool their produce (outputs) or their purchases (inputs) and negotiate terms with handlers and/or suppliers.[6]

There are many phases in agriculture which need additional co-op organizations, such as: (1) farm and home chemicals, (2) forestry, (3) machinery and equipment, (4) foreign trade, (5) farm product utilization and (6) rural recreational facilities, among others.

Workers' Cooperatives

Workers' productive cooperatives are not important presently because trade unionism is the goal of American labor rather than the actual ownership of industrial plants and businesses. In the future, no changes are expected although, in isolated instances, workers will operate plants cooperatively.

A more significant role for labor unions will likely be their encouragement of urban consumer cooperatives of all types. In some instances, labor unions will show increasing interest in farmers' bargaining associations.

Consumer Cooperatives

Leaders in the co-op consumer field often apologize for their rather modest display of cooperation. However, their accomplishments are more significant than commonly believed. This modesty arises because consumer cooperation is thought of as being only that portion covered by retail food stores. If one defines consumer cooperation this narrowly, the gains indeed have been modest. But, consumer cooperation is more than buying food. It involves housing, health, credit, savings, insurance, burial, education and many other fields

---

[6]Adams, K., "The Food Retailing Experience," *Michigan Farm Economics,* East Lansing, Mich. Sept. 1962.

(Table 20-1). In this sense, consumer cooperation has not been modest. But it could be much better. The future, however, holds great promise in this area. In years to come, families will have much larger incomes, be better educated, more analytical, more quality conscious and have more managerial talents. The organization, capitalization and management of various consumer cooperatives will be much easier than they have been. The future of consumer cooperation also depends on the efficiency of profit-type businesses, especially the role played by chains and discounters.

In addition, consumer service cooperatives will have a significant role in the future. Phases of consumer activity needing the cooperatives' attention are: (1) truth-in-lending or declaration of true interest charges, (2) consumer goods and consumer finance counseling, (3) proper labeling of foods, (4) consumer goods testing, research and education, and (5) consumer communications.

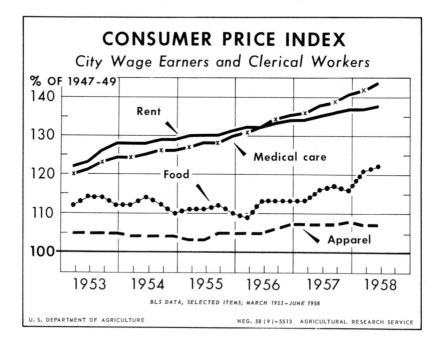

FIGURE 20-6

The consumers' price index keeps going up. Rent (housing) and medical care offer the best opportunities for co-op development. Food and apparel costs show less rise. Competition among profit-type corporations and others in these latter two items has been healthy. (Courtesy, USDA, Washington, D.C.)

TABLE 20-1
Consumer Expenditures, by Items, U.S.A.

Item	Percent of Disposable Income
Food	20.3
Household operations	13.0
Housing	12.0
Transportation	11.5
Clothing	9.8
Savings	6.9
Recreation	5.4
Liquor	2.8
Tobacco	2.0
All others	16.3
Total	100.0

Source: USDA, Washington, D.C.

Nonfarm Business Cooperatives

Industrial cooperatives, while having good prospects in theory, are not apt to expand considerably because of antitrust implications. In areas where firms are already few, any further combination, even cooperatively, may subject them to antitrust prosecution.

Business service and retailer-owned wholesale cooperatives have a brighter future. These businesses are in a very competitive era with far too many firms. In addition, management and capital problems will increase which small individual firms are not geared to meet adequately. The growth of profit-type chains and discount houses is an added pressure on them. Thousands of small retail and service businesses face extinction and bankruptcy if they do not form cooperatives.

Earl Lifshey of *Home Furnishings Daily* well expresses the situation confronting independent dealers:

> Is the future of the independent dealer in jeopardy because he can't survive competition—or because he just won't do what's necessary? I think the independent dealer is more in danger because he won't do the things he should be doing. Or at least he all too often isn't doing them well enough or intensively enough.
>
> More and more the concept of co-op group action holds increasing appeal—and with good reason.
>
> While the co-op group is far from perfect, it appears to be one of, if not the best, formula for the average independent dealer's survival. Certainly some of the existing groups have

been rolling up an impressive record, and it's my guess that we're on the threshold of an era which will see considerable growth of the co-op group movement. That this won't happen without a lot of noisy—and sometimes damaging—grinding of the gears in our distribution machinery already has been demonstrated. But it seems certain to happen—and if new gears or even a new type of machine is needed, so be it.[7]

Small businessmen can cooperate to survive by engaging in joint ownership of repair and service centers, joint transport and shipping facilities, mutual computer centers, joint purchasing of imports, joint export sales, common shopping centers, joint engineering and other technical staffs, co-op credit corporations, mutual insurance, central packaging and processing, joint building and equipment maintenance staffs, joint manufacturing and processing, mutual recruitment and training of personnel, mutual product differentiation and joint advertising and promotion, among others.

The future for cooperatives is closely linked with the future of independent farmers, workers, businessmen and consumers. If it is desirable to maintain some semblance of independent entrepreneurs and consumers in the economy, then cooperatives offer a solution for preservation of independence. Without cooperatives, the trend toward the elimination of the independents will accelerate.

EXPANSION OF FARMER COOPERATIVES IN THE UNITED STATES

The southern United States has more areas of low-income farmers than other geographic regions. This is certainly not conducive to co-op organization so far as capitalizing and managing cooperatives are concerned, although it may indicate a need for them. It is perhaps not a coincidence that in many low-income areas of the South, contract farming, rather than cooperation, has come to the fore. By using the capital and managerial assistance provided by profit-type agribusiness corporations, many low-income farmers have, through contracts, achieved a higher standard of living than they had before. Among the larger, commercial-type farmers in the South, cooperatives are more important and do have a good future.

---

[7]Reprinted by permission of *Home Furnishings Daily*, New York, N.Y. Copyright Nov. 9, 1962. p. 19.

In other regions of the country where low-income areas are far fewer than in the South, cooperatives are more significant and will continue to be important as family-farms get fewer but larger (Figure 20-7).

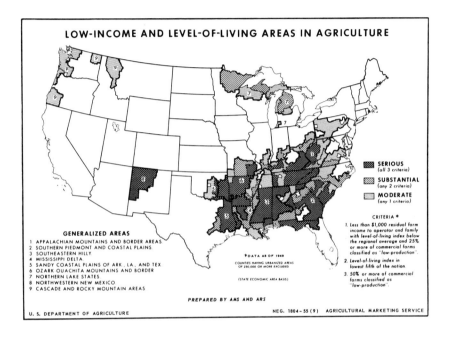

FIGURE 20-7

Farmer cooperatives are more likely to expand in areas with better incomes, greater capital resources and better sources of management talent. Contract farming is more likely to expand in areas having low incomes, less capital and more family labor. (Courtesy, USDA, Washington, D.C.)

THE GULF BETWEEN FARMER AND CONSUMER COOPERATIVES

Perhaps the biggest cleavage or gulf in the co-op field is the lack of cooperation between farmer and consumer cooperatives. The farmer cooperatives believe, as a rule, that consumer cooperatives are labor union oriented and that their main objective is to force down the prices paid to farmers. The consumer cooperatives often maintain that farmer cooperatives are concerned with their own narrow economic interests. There is not much economic validity to either argument.

If farmers and consumers together owned businesses to process, package and distribute food from farm to table, then:

1. When consumers paid higher prices, it would bolster farmers' incomes.

2. If farmers' prices fell, prices paid by consumers would go down. Consumers would buy more.

3. Marketing margins would not be so rigid as they are presently. Bowen illustrates the stickiness of marketing margins as follows:

> On one side of a river lived a farmer, on the other side a tailor. A bridge spanned the river, on which a trader set up his place of business. The farmer, wanting some clothes, brought two pigs to the trader. The tailor, wanting some pork, brought two suits of clothes to the trader. To the farmer the trader said, "I am sorry, but pigs have gone down in price while suits have gone up. The best I can do is to give you one suit of clothes for your two pigs." And the farmer said, "Well, if that is the best you can do, I'll take the suit and leave the pigs." To the tailor, the trader said, "I am sorry, but pigs have gone up in price while suits have gone down. The best I can do is to give you one pig for your two suits of clothes." And the tailor said, "Well, if that is the best you can do, I'll take the pig and leave the suits." The trader ended with a suit of clothes and a pig for making the exchange. The farmer and the tailor went home without meeting one another directly.[8]

A line of handlers and processors between the farmer's gate and the housewife's kitchen gets paid for a variety of services. Cooperatives —farmer-owned on one end and consumer-owned on the other, or even jointly owned by farmers *and* consumers—could wring out some of these handling costs and perhaps better distribute income to farm and city people alike.

ADEQUATE STATISTICS ON COOPERATIVES

Presently, data coordination concerning the number and extent of cooperatives is very inadequate. The exception is farmer cooperatives, due largely to the able work of the Farmer Cooperative Service. Perhaps a dozen or more agencies in the federal government are assembling data on cooperatives in the Departments of Labor; Commerce; Agriculture; Interior; and Health, Education and Welfare.

---

[8]Bowen, E. R., *American Cooperation*, A.I.C., Washington, D.C. 1937. p. 129.

Yet, none of these agencies coordinate their data to present a true overall picture of cooperatives. It is imperative that a single agency of government be authorized and directed to compile and maintain complete and accurate records and make periodic reports to Congress on the operation of all types of co-op enterprises and that this single agency be held responsible for supplying all other interested agencies

WHAT FARMER GETS
FOR COTTON
IN BUSINESS
SHIRT

Retail Price
$4²⁴

Farmer's Share
28¢

DATA BASED ON
1st 9 MONTHS OF 1962

U. S. DEPARTMENT OF AGRICULTURE   NEG. ERS 814-63 (1)   ECONOMIC RESEARCH SERVICE

FIGURE 20-8

The consumer pays $4.24 for a cotton shirt, but the cotton farmer gets only 28 cents of that. What goes on in-between the farmer and the consumer needs to be analyzed to see whether the farmer could get more and the consumer could pay less. (Courtesy, USDA, Washington, D.C.)

of the federal government and the public with information pertaining to cooperatives.

There may be a need also for a policy statement from the various government agencies concerning their relationships with cooperatives. The United States Department of Agriculture has issued such a policy statement as shown in Exhibit 20-1.

FIGURE 20-9

The consumer pays 21.2 cents for a loaf of bread. The wheat farmer gets 3.1 cents of that. The retailer, for allowing the bread on his shelves, gets more than the wheat farmer. (Courtesy, USDA, Washington, D.C.)

EXHIBIT 20-1

Secretary of Agriculture's Memorandum No. 1540

Policy Statement on Cooperatives

The Department of Agriculture, by the Act which created it in 1862, is directed to acquire and diffuse useful information on matters pertaining to agriculture, in the most general and comprehensive sense of that term. By numerous subsequent acts, the Department is also specifically directed to carry on research, educational and service work respecting agricultural cooperatives, and to cooperate with local and State agencies to that end, provide credit to rural electric and telephone cooperatives, utilize the cooperative pattern in carrying out a number of its action programs, and accord "recognition and encouragement" to agricultural cooperatives.

It is the policy of the USDA to carry out the full intent of these legislative mandates effectively in terms of today's conditions and needs and in the light of the economic problems confronting American agriculture today.

The trend toward greater concentration of economic power in the non-agricultural segments of our economy—and, particularly, in recent years, in those segments that sell an increasing number of necessities to farmers as well as those that buy from the farmer and process and market his products—makes it more essential than ever that the farmer's bargaining power be strengthened.

The factors that, in decades past, resulted in repeated action by the Congress and the state legislatures to encourage farmers to strengthen their position through cooperatives become more impelling and urgent as the concentration of non-farm economic power increases.

Cooperatives help farmers to improve their bargaining position. As farmers cooperate with each other to gain mutual advantage and protection through self-help, they strengthen the American family farm system, and enhance the benefits that it provides to the general public.

The USDA will therefore accept fully its responsibility to encourage the growth of cooperatives and through its various agencies provide research, educational and advisory services that will help to strengthen cooperatives in all appropriate activities in the interest of their members and the general welfare. To that end each of the agencies of the Department will give proper recognition to the basic nature of cooperative enterprise, and will exercise its functions and perform its activities in full accord with the concepts and responsibilities stated above.

The head of each agency in the USDA is expected to insure that full support to the policy herein stated is given through his agency. The Assistant Secretary for Rural Development and Conservation shall serve as liaison to insure coordination within the Department and shall be responsible for working with the National Advisory Committee on Cooperatives.

CO-OP CONCEPTS

Co-op concepts and principles are perhaps dominated too much by history and historical development. A revised concept of the cooperative as a special type of corporation adaptable to modern business conditions and flexible enough to meet people's needs is urgently needed.

For example, the principle of *open membership* will not be so valid in the future as in the past. The principle of *one man, one vote* will restrict cooperatives from serving the larger operator. Low interest rates on capital will be unrealistic as alternatives increase for this capital. Nonproducer business will increase as the rural areas become less farm and more urban.

ANTITRUST PROBLEMS

The Sherman and Clayton Acts have not worked too effectively in restricting monopolistic trends in nonfarm industries. To the extent that these Acts fail to provide competitive conditions, cooperatives are obliged to protect their members by integrating more vigorously, short of violating the Sherman and Clayton Acts. A more vigorous prosecution of monopoly under the antitrust laws would lessen the need for cooperatives, however. The role of cooperatives as a "balance wheel" is fundamental to the survival of the capitalistic system. It is also fundamental that cooperatives tend to make more people more capitalistic, thus spreading the capitalistic foundation and securing it more firmly. Cooperatives too have to recognize that, in some lines, they might tend to create either monopolies or imperfectly competitive conditions. If they do so, they should likewise be prosecuted.

Expansion of Federal Charters

One group of cooperatives which has no option of a federal charter is the mutual savings banks. Since credit unions and savings and loan associations do have such an option and the results have been good, there is considerable merit in considering a federal charter option for mutual savings banks.

COOPERATIVES AND ECONOMIC NEED

The principal economic objectives of cooperatives consist of: (1) getting economies to scale in buying, selling, processing and servicing; (2) preserving the small entrepreneurs in agriculture, business and industry; and (3) aiding the consumers in getting the most mileage out of their dollars.

Many persons mistake the economic motives of cooperatives. The main mission of cooperatives is to enable rather small-scale production, retailing and consumption entities to exist while providing such entities the economies of large-scale buying (of inputs) and selling (of outputs) at cost and providing services at cost.

Blair of Mississippi State University suggests that the economic need for a cooperative be recast as follows:

Historically, in talking about the economic need for a cooperative we have left the impression that such need does not exist unless one, or a combination, of several conditions exists—namely high margins being extracted by private firms, poor service or poor quality.

Let us assume that a cooperative is established due to the existence of the conditions just mentioned. Suppose, further, that the cooperative operates at a high level of efficiency and forces its private competitors into line. Suppose now that the cooperative and its private competitors continue to improve their operations over a time period of several years and reach a very high level of efficiency where there are no significant differences in prices, service or quality. This has happened in the past and will, I believe, happen more frequently in the future. When this stage is reached, many farmers reason that there is no further economic need for a cooperative. They have been told that there is no need for the cooperative unless it can do a better job in terms of prices, services or quality of supplies. This is not necessarily true.

It is true that the cooperative must be able to do as good a job as its competitors, but it does not have to do a better job in terms of such visible factors as price, service or quality of supplies. It is at this point that the farmer's thinking about cooperation must make a sort of transition. He must now add to the observable factors such as price, quality and service availability at least one other factor which is not so readily apparent. He needs now to shift his attention from what formerly constituted the *visible economic need* for the cooperative and make allowance for the *invisible economic need* which still exists. I use the word "invisible" in the sense that the economic need becomes less apparent or much more difficult to quantify. The real question then becomes—would the noncooperative firms do as good a job as they are doing if the cooperative were dissolved? If the answer is no, then there is definitely an economic need for the cooperative even if there is no difference in price, service or quality of supplies between it and its competitors. To the extent that the cooperative is able to influence noncooperative firms to remain competitive and efficient, it serves an economic need just as surely as it does in forcing these firms to more competitive levels in the first place.

This point is often misunderstood or not taken into account at all in the farmer's thinking about cooperation and its role in agriculture.[9]

[9]Blair, Paul, Tri-State Co-op Committee Meeting, Auburn, Ala. Nov. 27, 1962.

COOPERATIVES AND CONSOLIDATION

There are far too many cooperatives in certain areas of the United States—as many as 10 or more per county. Consolidation of co-operatives, greater business volume and efficiency are the important factors, not the number of cooperatives. In most cases, co-op members do not resist mergers and consolidations. Rather, resistance comes from board members and operating management of the cooperatives to be involved.

One problem consists of frequent absences of cooperation among cooperatives themselves. Some co-op leaders recommend that others cooperate but exempt themselves from this recommendation.

This shortcoming is especially costly whenever joint efforts among several cooperatives could result in substantial savings to members in purchasing, servicing, marketing or manufacturing activities. Although some notable steps in this direction have occurred, they certainly could be more numerous.

An alliance between farmer cooperatives and retailer-owned wholesale cooperatives could make a substantial dent at the food retailing level and might promote more marketing efficiency, for example.

Also, in the future, more multi-purpose cooperatives will no doubt evolve. The reasons for this are simple. It is both cumbersome and uneconomical to split up various economic processes into separate cooperatives. With better finances and better management, multi-purpose cooperatives can perform effectively, and their patrons will benefit increasingly.

Some lessons can be learned from the diversified management structures of profit-type corporations. There are no valid reasons why co-op management cannot be structured along these lines with the same or even better results.

COOPERATIVES AND CAPITAL

Capital has been, is and always will be a major problem for cooperatives as well as for other businesses. Since cooperatives are more inflexible in their capital structures, they will continue to bear frustrations in matters of par stock, lack of security trading, inactive stockholders and in other ways. The situation is not hopeless, however. Economic research can provide breakthroughs in this area by studying closely matters of corporation finance and adapting these findings to cooperatives. Efforts in this area of research could pay off handsomely.

Despite all financial pressures incumbent on co-op members, they are the ones who must continue to bear the major responsibility to furnish capital. This does not preclude obtaining equity and borrowed capital on a sound basis from nonfarm and nonmember sources, however.

FEDERAL CREDIT

Some co-op leaders and others in the United States have argued for more federal co-op credit agencies, especially for: (1) farmers, to integrate vertically; (2) for consumers, to organize stores and health cooperatives; and (3) for credit unions, to develop a co-op banking system. Consumer retail cooperatives are about the only co-op group which have no access to federal credit agencies.

These adventures, while they appear to be needed, contain several limitations: (1) They would increase the cooperatives' dependence on the federal government. (2) They might create much antagonism against all cooperatives. (3) They might entail lending of funds at extremely low interest rates.

While these cited needs are real, credit avenues other than through the federal government should be explored first. If government credit is needed, the farm credit co-op system might be used as a model by which federal money would gradually be replaced by cooperators' money. There is always a danger for some cooperatives, and other types of businesses, to rely continuously on federal credit as a permanent source of borrowed capital. A wiser course dictates that government credit be replaced with cooperative, self-help financing programs as quickly as possible.

COOPERATIVES AND CONTRACT FARMING

Perhaps the most perplexing problem to face cooperatives in the years ahead is one of contract farming and vertical integration. Cooperatives, unlike profit-type corporations, cannot effectively use the technique of piece-rate, contractor-contractee type of integration.[10]

---

[10]Roy, E. P., *Contract Farming, U.S.A.*, The Interstate Printers & Publishers, Inc., Danville, Ill. 1963. Ch. 12.

However, they can and no doubt will compete effectively in pure vertical integration where the co-op members integrate several stages through their ownership and risk-bearing efforts. The cooperatives' greater inflexibility in these matters is a definite handicap, especially when some of them are trying to maintain a tax exemption status.

During the next few years, the issue as to who will control the integration of agriculture will no doubt be tested vigorously. National leaders should consider support of integration by cooperatives of the profitable part of the food and fiber business along with agricultural production, which is on the whole less profitable.

This would give cooperatives some control over primary sources of supply. It would also give them some control over processing, packaging and distribution of food and fiber from farm to ultimate user.

Consumers everywhere may ask why farmer control of economic integration is superior to nonfarmer, corporate control of economic integration. Economic history and economic fact bear out the propo-

FIGURE 20-10

Cooperatives can be successful at vertical integration and contract farming. This cooperative has integrated an egg program horizontally, vertically and circularly. (Courtesy, Mississippi Federated Cooperatives, Jackson, Miss.)

sition that farmer cooperatives in control of economic integration would plow-back earnings from this integration into more and better productive facilities on their own farms. They would be less inclined to gain market power and fix prices just for the sake of economic power and market domination.

Unionization and corporate control of agriculture are likely unless farmers gain control of their own businesses. Society may ultimately gain more by a farmer cooperative-organized and integrated agriculture than it will by a combination of corporation management and contract growers that may be unionized.

COOPERATIVES AND THE FAMILY FARM

Some believe that the family farm will be gradually replaced by corporate and contract farming.

Knapp of the Farmer Cooperative Service states that:

> Many people have a great concern for the future of our family farm system of farming. While I do not believe that we are going to lose the family farm, which is supported by good economic and farm management logic—yet it seems clear that the family farm must adapt itself to the times and become a much stronger operating unit than it has been in the past. We now have many very efficient family farms, and I do not anticipate seeing all of them rapidly swept away by the process of integration. What I would like to see is more strong family farms that would give a better basis for *integration through cooperatives.* Integration through cooperatives can help build stronger family farms, and stronger family farms can help build stronger, better integrated cooperatives. In this connection our concept of what constitutes a family farm may need to be revised. Mechanization, combined with greater specialization, may require a much larger and more efficient type of family farm.[11]

MANAGEMENT

Managing cooperatives is more difficult than managing profit-type corporations of the same magnitude, and very often it pays less. Therein lie two problems: (1) training and (2) paying for co-op management.

---

[11]Knapp, J. G., "Cooperatives and Integrated Agriculture," *Georgia Co-op Short-course Proceedings*, Athens, Ga. June 23, 1958. p. 11.

In the years ahead, both of these have to be corrected if cooperatives are to survive as a business institution. Few areas could have higher priority than the area of co-op management. In some cases, if a co-op board feels unable to recruit individual management, it could hire a professional management-team to operate the cooperative. This and other methods will have to be tried in order to improve management performance in cooperatives.

Smaller cooperatives, unable to train their management and employees on their own resources, could use the co-op technique to operate joint management and employee training centers.

MEMBER EDUCATION

Perhaps the biggest defect in co-op management is its lack of member education. Very often, the thinking of co-op management resembles that of profit-type corporate management; namely, affairs of the corporation are the province of the manager and the board alone. Unless cooperatives are willing and able to devise structures whereby their patron-owners are kept fully informed, co-op growth will be slowed and distrust created. Members have to be given a full accounting of the affairs of their cooperatives, and, in turn, members' desires and wishes need to be heard and taken seriously.

CITIZENSHIP

There are several ways in which cooperatives can help to develop better citizens, especially among their members. The fact that the individual is part-owner of a successful co-op business organization causes him to develop a certain pride of ownership. He becomes more interested in the affairs of his community, his state and his nation. He is more interested in the way in which new legislation and government policy will affect him and his organization. If the local group wishes to be heard in connection with pending legislation, it may be more effective to be represented as an organization rather than as individuals. Also being part-owner of local industry gives the citizen a greater feeling of civic responsibility.

PUBLIC RELATIONS

The public relations job facing cooperatives is largely related to the income tax issue. If the income tax issue were fully resolved, there would remain few public relations problems. The 1962 Revenue Act is a forward piece of legislation in this regard. In another way, cooperatives could conduct some very good public relations work by opposing more vigorously the double tax on profit-type corporations.

In conducting public relations, cooperatives should consider working together to reduce costs in terms of time and funds.

THE COMPUTER AGE

The era of electronic data processing has arrived together with the implications this holds for more sophisticated management and for other uses. It seems especially appropriate that computer adaptations be handled cooperatively. Many farmer, retailer and consumer associations individually cannot afford these installations. But, on a city, county, state, regional or national basis, these computer facilities could be afforded and the benefits jointly shared. An additional benefit would be the centralization in these computer centers of auditing, marketing, research, tax work and other services which could then be employed more effectively by member cooperatives.

Larger cooperatives with thousands of members will find computers especially helpful in maintaining individual patronage records and accounting to the members the results of their patronage.

CO-OP RESEARCH AND EDUCATIONAL CENTERS

Shew suggests that cooperatives should consider the establishment of a national research center supported by them to research effectively the problems unique to cooperation. A small cooperative could, for a nominal sum, obtain research counsel quickly and efficiently from a large, competent staff. Profit-type corporations have been utilizing these methods, and they appear effective.[12]

Some Canadian and European cooperatives likewise have established co-op educational centers where instruction unique to cooperatives is offered. Such a co-op center in the United States might prove useful. Research and teaching centers could complement the existing excellent co-op work being done by the Farmer Cooperative Service, the land-grant colleges and others.

---

[12]Shew, Randall, "A Co-op Market Research Center?" *Cooperative Digest,* Ithaca, N.Y. Nov. 1960. p. 6.

FIGURE 20-11

The computer age is now coming into its own. As shown above, automation with push button control is a feature of many co-op feed mills. An electronically controlled panel, operated by one man, permits automatic weighing, batch mixing and blending of formula feeds. (Courtesy, FS Services, Inc., Bloomington, Ill.)

Many more cooperatives could research jointly by constructing and operating "pilot plants" where new processes, plant designs and layouts and new machinery, etc., could be tested. Basic research and development laboratories could also be a part of these "pilot plants."

TALENT POOLS

Another example of a needed co-op effort is a national or regional overhead agency to provide engineering, architectural, management, tax, accounting, legal and other services for all cooperatives. Some profit-type corporations in various trade lines already employ this technique. The possible adaptations of this method are numerous. For example, cooperatives in one state needing the talents of a co-op feed mill engineer could acquire this talent from the pool. Experts in various lines could move freely and readily to help strengthen cooperatives in every part of the country and the world on a fee basis.

COOPERATIVES AND THE COLLEGES

Cooperatives have come to depend on colleges for various educational and research assistance. Colleges, however, are often restrained in the assistance that can be rendered for various reasons. For the colleges, a basic guideline to follow in assisting cooperatives in research is one which stresses information on features unique to cooperatives. The remainder of co-op practices can be covered under research which is applicable to any type of business.

In the future, cooperatives may have to develop more research programs of their own to get more useful and quicker answers for their situations.[13]

YOUTH AND COOPERATIVES

The co-op struggles of earlier years are well remembered by the leaders of today, but the youth has no conception of this background. Co-op history can serve a useful purpose in at least this regard. However, history is not enough. Youth has to be challenged—young people like boldness and a different order of things which stir their imagination. Cooperatives can, in many cases, offer such a challenge, not by reviewing the past only, but by indicating to the young people what tremendous tasks lie ahead in cooperation and how they can accomplish these tasks in their generation. There are enough undone tasks in cooperation to keep several generations busy. Too often, however, youth is told that the co-op tasks were completed in the 1920's and 1930's and there is nothing left to do.

TAXATION

The most pressing public and membership relations problem for cooperatives is the income tax issue.

Unfortunately, cooperatives have made some mistakes on this issue —the main one being the mistake of defensiveness and, in addition, their inability to explain adequately their position when on the offensive. Yet, this timidity is not necessary because the co-op tax position is clear

---

[13]*Cooperatives and the Future,* National Conference on Cooperatives Proceedings, Washington, D.C. Apr. 28-30, 1963.

FIGURE 20-12

The future of cooperation belongs to the youth of today. (Courtesy, The Ohio State University, Columbus, Ohio, and A.I.C., Washington, D.C.)

and justifiable. It needs no apology but does need explaining to the citizenry.

Periodically, Congress should re-examine the exemption status granted to certain types of cooperatives and nonprofit organizations as well as to other groups. This is necessary because times change and economic conditions vary. It may well be that in future years some cooperatives may lose their tax exemption status. Some cooperatives themselves may no longer feel tax exemption necessary, or Congress may decide that such exemption is no longer in the public interest. However, the principle of taxing the co-op patron on his patronage rather than taxing the cooperative's savings should never be compromised.

FINAL SUMMARY

The *cooperative* is an old and time-honored institution. In years past, it had basically a social and religious orientation. Presently, it has more of a business orientation.

The *cooperative* offers at least two general advantages which no other business institution can fully match: (1) It offers an opportunity for all people, rich and poor, in all walks of life, to help themselves by cooperating with others; and (2) it develops and strengthens the individual citizen in acquiring and controlling private property, yet it preserves individual freedom, dignity and responsibility.

These and other advantages are not automatic and painless. To achieve them through the auspices of a *cooperative* requires much hard work, thought, determination and perseverance. Above all, a successful *cooperative* requires good people with a good spirit, who are unselfish and dedicated and who have the desire to improve themselves, their fellowmen and their community.

> *I know of no safe depository for the ultimate powers of society but the people; and if we think them not informed enough to exercise their power with discretion, the remedy is not to take it from them but to inform them by education.*
>
> —Thomas Jefferson

INDICES

SUBJECT INDEX—

A

Accounting procedures, for co-ops, 462-65

Accounts receivables, aging of, 390-91

Act of International Development, 549

Advertising and sales associations, 173-74

Africa, co-ops in, 14, 103-04

Agency contract, by co-ops, 327

Agricultural Adjustment Act, 226

Agricultural bargaining co-ops, 112, 126-27, 272, 274, 552

Agricultural credit co-ops, 127-32, 255, 256-58, 259, 272

Agricultural experiment stations and co-ops, 235, 482

Agricultural extension services and co-ops, 235-36, 284, 482

Agricultural Marketing Act of 1929, 62, 225-26, 234

Agricultural Marketing Agreements Act of 1937, 63-64, 228-29

Agricultural marketing co-ops, 59, 80, 83, 112, 113-16, 132-34, 272, 318, 335, 360-61, 425, 448-49, 459, 542

Agricultural marketing legislation, 223-29

Agricultural producer co-ops, 112-17, 123, 125-40, 234, 255, 256-58, 315-18, 320, 321, 323, 330, 337, 344, 349, 350-54, 356, 361, 374-75, 476, 479, 487, 488, 492-93, 494, 495, 496, 497, 500, 501, 502, 505-08, 509-10, 517, 535, 551-53, 556-57, 558, 560-61 (See also, Farmer co-ops)

Agricultural purchasing co-ops, 318 (See also, Farm supply co-ops)

Agricultural service co-ops, 112, 134-36, 137

Alabama, 253, 256, 261, 262, 270, 350, 453

Alaska, 160, 256, 261, 264, 270, 351

Algeria, 103

American Automobile Association, 147

American Farm Bureau Federation, 62, 126, 483

American Hospital Association, 192

American Institute of Cooperation, 62, 80, 481

American Society for Equity, 59

American Stock Exchange, 175, 176

American Travel Association, 146

Annual meeting of co-ops, 459-62

Annual reports, filing of, 273

Antigonish Movement, 81

Antitrust laws and co-ops, 214, 275, 562

Appliance co-ops, 121, 183 (See also, Retailer-owned co-ops)

Aquatic Products Marketing Act, 227-28, 261

Area Redevelopment Administration, 357-58, 361

Argentina, 89

Arizona, 256, 259, 262, 268, 269, 272, 351

Arkansas, 256, 262, 264, 270, 350, 477

Articles of incorporation for co-ops, 293-94

Artificial breeding co-ops, 64, 112, 134-35, 272, 325

Associated Press, 171, 218

Australia, 107-08

Austria, 87, 98

Automotive store co-ops, 121

B

Babylonia, co-ops in, 42, 43

Bad debt reserves in co-ops, 334-35

Bakery co-ops, 183

Balance-agriculture-with-industry programs for co-ops, 369

Bank centrals, 364-65

Banks, commercial, and co-ops, 349, 366, 385

Banks for farmer co-ops, 112, 130-31, 222, 272, 349, 350-54, 361, 425, 510

Barbaric Age and co-ops, 47-49

AUTHOR INDEX—